hidden lives / secret gardens

the florentine villas gamberaia, la pietra and i tatti

R. Terry Schnadelbach

iUniverse, Inc.
New York Bloomington

hidden lives / secret gardens
the florentine villas gamberaia, la pietra and i tatti

Copyright © 2009 R. Terry Schnadelbach

All rights reserved. No part of this book may be used or reproduced by any means, graphic, electronic, or mechanical, including photocopying, recording, taping or by any information storage retrieval system without the written permission of the publisher except in the case of brief quotations embodied in critical articles and reviews.

LAUDpress is an international publisher of manuscripts and journals on landscape architecture and urban design publishing historical and prospective articles and manuscripts on aspects of the creation of the physical environment. iUniverse books may be ordered through booksellers or by contacting:

iUniverse
1663 Liberty Drive
Bloomington, IN 47403
www.iuniverse.com
1-800-Authors (1-800-288-4677)

Because of the dynamic nature of the Internet, any Web addresses or links contained in this book may have changed since publication and may no longer be valid. The views expressed in this work are solely those of the author and do not necessarily reflect the views of the publisher, and the publisher hereby disclaims any responsibility for them.

ISBN: 978-1-4401-3115-8 (pbk)
ISBN: 978-1-4401-3116-5 (ebk)

Printed in the United States of America

iUniverse rev. date: 12/17/2009

The book is dedicated to
Maxine Schnadelbach,
My reviewer, advisor, editor and critic
Accompanying me through life

Contents

Acknowledgments ix

Overture 1

Chapter 1 / Waltz 13
    Villa Gamberaia

Chapter 2 / Largo 81
    Villa La Pietra

Chapter 3 / Fugue 161
    Villa I Tatti

Continuo 245

Appendix 265

Photograph Credits: 266

Chronology 268

End Notes 279

Index 331

Acknowledgments

I HAVE ALWAYS THOUGHT the Villa Gamberaia in Settignano was one of the the most beautiful and at the same time, most unusual Villa gardens. I first discovered it when I was a Fellow in Landscape Architecture at the American Academy in Rome in the early 60s. Maybe it was the asymmetry in plan that drew my attention. Or maybe it was the Lawson drawings hanging on the Academy wall, ranked among the most beautiful of the Beaux Arts Villa renderings I had seen. Or maybe it was the illogical composition ofl its garden and house elements that only added to the allure.

From this first impression, my interest in the garden has never waned and has only grown stronger. The lifestyles of the garden's creators – hidden and secretive- intrigued and added to the mystery. Over time tidbits of historical trivia compounded my interest and filled in empty spaces in its history.

Later in my career, a friend loaned me a book on Bernard Berenson stating that he was the absentee caretaker of the Villa Gamberaia. Through research, I found that Berenson was more than that, he was part of an international expatriate colony living on the foothills surrounding Florence. Delving into Berenson's history and the creation of his Villa I Tatti from scratch revealed landscape architects who were forging a Moderne revival of the Renaissance gardens. They employed a new language and set the stage for the Modernist Italian landscape.

And there were others in this colony. I soon realized that the "restoration" of Florence's outlying villas was a movement. And, for the first time the social history of that movement could be pieced together from numerous sources. Here then was my book, *Hidden Gardens, Secret Lives*: which exposed the interconnectedness of three of Florence's major villas, Gamberaia, La Pietra and I Tatti.

Many have assisted in so many ways with this work and I would like to acknowledge and thank them for their help. First and foremost is my wife and architect, Maxine Schnadelbach, who has followed me on endless library searches and garden visits. Then she has also been my strongest critic of the book's subject matter and has edited numerous revisions of the final manuscript. Finally, she has endured the absence of her husband on weekends and week nights while he has written this work.

Nina Liebman, a friend of long-standing, has provided me with the Berenson connection. Patricia Osmand, the Gamberaia's historian has pointed me to numerous scholars and library sources. Fiorella Surpbi of the I Tatti Archives, provided access to Berenson's letters, and photographs and the Collection of Letters given by Barbara Halpern, the historian Amenda Lily has been a help on the general *villa* phenomena of 1900s Florence, the Canadian photographer Scott Gilchrist, graciously provided many of Villa Gamberaia's photographs.

Pauline Matarasso of Oxford, England provided details of Princess Ghyka's personal life and to publish photographs from their family collection. Anne Brooks of Owing Mills, Maryland provided detail of Miss Florence Blood's personal life and to publish photographs from their family collection. The architectural historian, Henry Hope Reed of New York provided insights into the life of Diego Suarez.

The author is especially grateful to the American Academy in Rome which, on two occasions provided studio and living accommodation where much of this work was produced. The Academy has given access to the Georgina Masson and the Edward Lawson Archives and permissions to publish their photographs.

Carlos Rappacini of New York University, Associate Director personally gave me a tour of the Villa La Pietra and was helpful with its recent history. The Kim Wilke, the landscape architect of La Pietra's remodeling, provided me with a detailed report of the garden and its landscape spaces. "Nick" Nicholas Danking-Elliot, the project horticulturalist supervising the reconstruction work was helpful with historic material of the personal relationships between Arthur Acton and Guy Mitchell, Arthur and Diego Suarez and Arthur and James Deering.

And finally, I would like to acknowledge the University of Florida's Architectural Library which has been a source throughout the writing of this work.

The first book to develop the theme of Italian Villas as pleasure gardens.

Overture

> "The upper class (humanist) Florentine played out a good part of their lives amidst gardens - in the small oasis of green and quiet which were the gardens of their city palaces, in semi-rural retreats in the suburbs or in the more expansive grounds of country villas. When a Florentine went indoors, he or she was quite likely to enter a room decorated with frescoes or panels of garden scenes, usually depicting the theme of the Garden of Love where the nature of love was conceived as a pleasant garden sheltering people in love." [1]
>
> — F. W. Kent, Professor of Art History

ITALIAN GARDENS ARE HISTORICALLY renowned for their sexcapades - sex or lovemaking in lovely landscaped spaces, designed for just that purpose. Historians of the Renaissance period give accounts of fun-loving parties, of roly-poly cardinals taking delight in surprising beautifully dressed young *signorinas* with jets of water up their underskirts. Perhaps, a suggestion would follow: "Oh, my dears, just drop behind this wall of greenery and dry yourselves," after which the cardinal would sneak into the gardener's space between hedges to play peak-a-boo, spying the nude girls drying their clothes on the lawn of an enclosed, sun-filled space - this at Villa Lante. Or tales of male royalty, voyeurs all, inviting young ladies to swim in the cool and refreshing cavernous pool, the nymphaea; the ladies frolicking naked amidst similarly unclad stone nymphs[2], and other mythical creatures of the sea; or the not-so-nobleman appearing from deep within the grotto, similarly unclad - this at Villa Caparola; or accounts of the infamous, lascivious aristocrat who staged seduction and lunch in his casino at the far end of his gardens; the casino equipped with a table, a sumptuous spread of exotic foods, and a bed. Musicians would play from the parterres up front, and then scatter into the *boschi* or woods at the aristocrat's signal, the dropping of the baroque drapes - this, again, at Villa Lante.

The English termed Italian gardens of the classical period "pleasure gardens," while the enticing landscapes surrounding their country seats were called "pleasances." The pleasure gardens were designed in crisp geometric spaces and were structured as extensions of the interiors of the country residence, where spaces flowed freely from interior to exterior. Contained within their geometry, diverse and often secret spaces, *giardino segretti*, were designed for the hidden lives of the nobility. These pleasure gardens were imbued with many human pleasures - food, theater, music, fireworks and, as we know, lovemaking. The latter term, "pleasance," referred only to a pleasing visual passage or informal, non-structured landscape space wrapping around a manor house, devoid of any architectural relationship to the surrounding site. In the English garden, the landscape was meant for viewing, and especially for viewing back to the manor house. If it had any function, it was predominantly for the mental reflection of the sublime. It is therefore plausible that books on Italian gardens, written largely by Anglo-Saxons, would describe the "pleasure gardens" in terms of the totally visual pleasance, rather than in humanist terms, as places of pleasure, love and sexual adventure.

What of the modern gardens of pleasures? Were they still created for sexual escapades, or rather were they the result of sexual liberation? Did sex still occur in them and what was the nature of the new erotic ethos? Three Florentine gardens, those found in the villas Gamberaia, La Pietra and I Tatti, were created at the turn of the twentieth century by foreigners seeking to return the Italian garden to its formal Renaissance root and re-introduce the subject of sex into the design of the gardens. All three newly arrived proprietors sought sexual liberty in what they believed to be the tolerant society found in Florence, Italy. The gardens of each of the three were unique responses to individual personal needs and sexual practices, and each reflected a changed world where standard sexual labels were fading, or non-existent, and where gardens were symbolic, coded places of intimacy.

The art of Renaissance Florence was termed humanistic art. Its values were based on the human experience and individual expression in art. Likewise, historic Italian villas were personal statements, secret retreats that revealed the hidden personality and personal history of each successive owner. We can easily read that owner number one built a farm house; that owner two expanded it into a country seat; and that owner three added important *salas*, gardens or other physical spaces - all with numbing discussions on the accuracy of dates, etc. Wouldn't it be fun to discover the owners' real passions and hidden motives for creating such secret villa gardens?

Lunette of Villa Pratolino, by Giusto Utens, Museo Frienza

The families of Renaissance

Florence, the Medici and Capponi, for example, owned many villas, if only for the income derived from crop production. It is unlikely that each was also the suburban retreat that served as counterpoint to the family's urban *palazzo*. One or two of the villas may have had special landscapes that were developed for specific social functions, such as hunting, equestrian sports or sexual pleasure, but what Medici or Capponi personal purpose was served in the separate and distinctly different villas?

In the Uten's lunettes[3] painted in the 1750s, now housed in Florence at the Palazzo Riccardi, we see how the Medicis used their numerous rural Villas. One lunette illustrates the Medici Palazzo Pogo at Cajano as a site of value for its fruit orchards; another lunette, the Villa Medici at Pratolino used for hunting; the Poggio Imperiale, with men on horses engaged in the practice of the competitive Florentine sport of jousting; and of the Villa Medici at Fiesole as a social retreat, a center for scholars and philosophers that became the Platonic academy of the Renaissance. We know that the Capponis, the Incontris and other prominent Florentine families had villas similar in number and uses.

Postcard of Villa Medici at Fisole

The turn-of-the-century owners of the still extant Florentine villas were the caretakers of the Renaissance tradition. Yet, the tale of a Moderne villa ownership was more fascinating than those of the historic initial owners, reflecting an even greater individualistic bent, one that included unique quirks and proclivities. At the turn of the twentieth century, the rural villas of the Renaissance became sought after by a contingent of foreign libertines seeking escape from the views of the restricted societies of Northern

Europe. The new owners adapted their newly acquired villas to impeccably suit their unique life style. The stories of the three Florentine villas presented here make for fascinating histories when read separately, but when read together they become even more interesting, as the owners and their landscape architects, friends and colleagues in the art community, were well known to each other, sometimes as friends or lovers, and were also famous or infamous to the outside world.

Superior in cultural accomplishment and deep with history, Europe became the preferred place for American and British artists to study abroad. Paris, with the Louvre Museum, the Sorbonne and the Ecole des Beaux-Arts promised superior instruction, and in Italy, Florence was considered to be the center of humanist studies. At the turn of the century,[4] art became a commercial commodity and dealing in art became a sometimes respected profession. The reason for this becomes clear when the financial and social context of the time is examined. Florence, in particular, became the center for a new breed of aesthete, a place where copies and fakes were turned out daily, where moneyed men and devoted aesthete alike led a new type of life hidden from the critics and press. It was the place of choice for the new breed that included such notables as Arthur Acton, Charles Loeser, Charles A. Strong, George Santayana and the high priest of attribution, Bernard Berenson, all proponents who left their mark on the city.

With the creation of several Modernist gardens based on neo-renaissance traditions, it was also the place where a renewed interest in Italian gardens emerged. The neo-renaissance garden tradition began in 1901 with the creation of a small, remodeled parterre garden, the water parterres of the Villa Gamberaia, then owned by Princess Jeanne (Giovanna, Italian) Ghyka of Serbia. The design principles used at Gamberaia spread throughout the group, surfacing again at Villa La Pietra, and again at I Tatti, defining a group of garden enthusiasts and landscape architects who are called here, the Second Renaissance Circle. It was the renaissance of the Renaissance garden which after a decade and a half, had codified a new landscape art form, the Moderne garden.

"Architecture is frozen music." [5]

Le Corbusier

This metaphor, by the noted French early Modernist architect, was meant to illustrate a larger point, i.e., architecture, as part of culture, is an art and that all art is related and because of this, art describes its cultural context. All the arts - music, architecture, painting and landscape architecture - are humanist arts and therefore can be described in rationale design terms. What is unusual in the metaphor is the intentional crossover between the visual and the performing arts. It suggests that music can be described in the same rationale terms as architecture, making the separation of the two irrelevant. Scale, rhythm, line, form, color and texture are but some of their common elements.[6] In his architectural manifesto, *Le Modulor: Essai sur une Mesure Harmonique a l'Echelle Humaine Applicable Universellement a l'Architecture et a La Mechanique,* Corbusier posited that architecture's facades, spaces and masses can be viewed as musical compositions, that they can be read in terms similar to those of a musical score; and therefore, music, art and architecture can be read and evaluated in similar rationale terms.

Certainly then, landscape architecture, which contains the same rationale language, can be described in similar musical terms. Gardens are meant to move through, they have a gait and tempo that are not too dis-similar to dance. The garden's music is the array of compositional elements that sweep the viewer through the composition at its various paces, its materials providing its mood, tambour and key. Color, scale are the same in both music and landscape. And repetition in the garden provides the rhythms and percussive elements of the composition. There are benefits to the use of such a metaphor. We are more familiar with classifying musical compositions than those of architecture or landscape architecture. These musical compositions have certain structural definitions that describe stylistic or historical precedents bases on time and movement. A waltz, with its three part measure and swirling tempo was the same terms of composition for Johann Strauss, the Younger, in the Baroque period as it was for the Romantic Modernist composer, Richard Strauss. A fugue was the same in terms of composition for Johann Sebastian Bach as for Maurice Ravel. So in describing formal gardens of different epochs, musical compositional comparisons can prove to be a valid device. Each of the Second Renaissance Circle garden will present its own musical metaphor.

Three gardens in outlying Florence, Italy - Villas Gamberaia, La Pietra and I Tatti - were Modernist compositions that were designed differently than their baroque or English garden predecessors. Since formal compositions in landscape architecture are not commonly classified into sub-categories - i.e., Villa D'Este's double cross-axis composition vs. Villa Lante's singular axial composition vs. the separated double axis parterre spaces of the Boboli gardens, etc. - it is more convenient and illustrative to relate these differences to known music compositional structures. Herein, Villas Gamberaia, La Pietra and I Tatti will be presented in their rationale and musical metaphorical terms and will be toured in movement, time and space.

As defined, a waltz is: "A kind of round dance performed to music in triple measure by dancers in couples, the partners going through a series of steps which cause them to whirl around and at the same time advance round the room,"[7] In the case of the Gambaraia, the room, or rooms, are to be found in the villa's garden.

Largo, here, refers to an expansive musical composition which is "very slow; stately, and broad in manner."[8] The largo also refers to a broad musical structure that builds and expands with multiple variations off common and often repeated themes. The cross axis structure of Villa La Pietra's garden expands into numerous sub-axes, often repeating the themes of the main axis. The overall repetition of theme produces an even consistency to the garden and a rather lethargic movement or pace throughout.

A fugue is "a polyphonic musical composition in which one or two themes are repeated or imitated by successively entering voices and contrapuntally developed in a continuous interweaving of the voice parts."[9] The voices here are those of Mary Berenson and Cecil Pinsent, and the full array of landscape elements, the polyphonic composition, are the repeated themes of the axial garden that emanates from the house and its main terrace. Further formally defined, the fugue is a composition of "contrapuntal rules, (where) the subject theme is first given by one voice part, which then proceeds with a counterpoint, while the subject, now called the answer, comes by or is repeated by another at intervals of a fifth or fourth and so on, until all the parts have answered one by one continuing their several melodies and interweaving them into one complex progressive whole in which the theme disappears or softens. The fugue has three general divisions; exposition, development and conclusion which are structured with symmetry."[10] The axial themes at I Tatti are first presented in one full length space, are halved and then divided into thirds with a further internal division into fourths. The architectural elements, in contrast to the garden elements, form the primary basis of counterpoint. There is even a counterpoint voice to be heard in the form of Bernard Berenson, himself, raging against "this folly" and answering the two primary design voices, those of his wife, Mary, and the architect, Cecil Pinsent.

But there are inherent differences between architecture and landscape architecture that must be discussed in the adoption of this useful metaphor. To appreciate any of the three Modernist villas presented here, there are three important landscape considerations to be kept in mind.

First, gardens are not static elements. In the metaphor, "architecture is frozen music," the implication is that architecture is in a state of stasis; architecture is frozen in time, lasting from generation to generation and often from era to era. If destroyed, it is possible to rebuild exactly as before, which is often the case. But the villa's landscape is musically different. The architectural term "frozen" cannot be applied to the villa's gardens, for the term does not account for the changes inherent in gardens. More similar to a performing art, gardens are an ever-changing caprice, each performance a differing artistic interpretation of the theme. The villa's landscape architecture changes with season end , and with each new owner as each brings to it differing design style and functional requirements.

As a living form, gardens change through natural maturation, usually every thirty to sixty years, depending on the vegetation used. Then, too, there are changes that reflect drought, and other life cycle conditions, and reflect the rate of adaptation to a site's micro-climate conditions. Gardens grow and need constant care. With differing gardener's skills and personal preferences, maintenance practices also produce landscape variety. Therefore, it is reasonable to expect the villa's house to remain unchanged for long periods of time while the villa's gardens constantly change with each change of *padrone* or *capo giardinere* (head gardener), its maturity, and the season when viewed. It is as if the conductor of a musical composition rendered a differing interpretation of the same composition.

Second, the compositional nature of the villa's garden must be considered in its entirety, as a total composition and not by its separate and distinct elements. The garden complex is the garden's design. The Villa Gamberaia is a composition that too easily allows one to focus on any one of its many magnificent spaces - the cypress allee and the water parterre garden, and less often mentioned, its *nymphaea*,[11] *lemonaia* or wooded *boscos* - each as separate elements. Too often these are described as separate stand-alone gardens, each assessed in individual design terms, such as cardinal orientation, proportion or scale. Rarely are plants mentioned and named and never are the parts discussed in unified terms. But describing Villa Gamberaia by its plantings alone would not adequately describe this garden's compositional nature. Walls, paths, sculptures and other built elements work in unison with planting to describe garden spaces and their design. Certainly, each element is an essential component in the design of each space, but even more critical to understanding the garden's beauty is to know how each garden space within works with any other part in the unified whole. Knowledge of the sum total of all its garden spaces combined is necessary to the understanding of the whole composition, both physically and aesthetically. Each of the three Modernist garden designs presented here are best comprehended primarily as a whole, and not by its individual parts.

The third consideration is to remember that the villa had a functional component - it did not exist solely as a residence. Throughout its modern history, each villa housed a prominent family that had social and economic agendas they wished to realize. Putting aside the fact that there were farmers and servants who had independent agendas for the site, there was also a coterie of friends whom the *padrone* wished to influence, or who were influenced by the villa and its owner. Each component of the social mix left its mark. No history or understanding of any Italian villa can be made without including most, if not all, of the functional and social components. At the beginning of the twentieth century, the Gamberaia, La Pietra and I Tatti each had a very unique functional and social agenda.

> "By the direct agency of mass and space, line and coherence upon physical consciousness, architecture communicates its value as art."[12]
> Geoffrey Scott

    The Moderne Florentine garden is a renaissance-revival garden, named here a second renaissance garden. The gardens of the Gamberaia, La Pietra and I Tatti show an amazing correlation of design elements, compositional principles and landscape palette. It is unlikely that one would miss their common root. The set of principles comprising the design philosophy and common development of vocabulary found in the gardens are the basis for identifying them as being of a common school of thought. Their designs, while based on the precepts of the earlier humanistic Renaissance, or classical Tuscan garden period, are yet different from the earlier realizations. The three villas examined here represent a new and distinct philosophy in landscape architecture.

    This book presents three descriptive art tours through the compositions of the Modernist Villas Gamberaia, La Pietra and I Tatti. Many of these gardens contain parts that have evolved over time and reflect several prevailing philosophies and periods of style. These are interconnected in support of uses and values reflective of the new era of the garden.

> "The (Tuscany) garden changed from a secret garden rich in flowers to an architectonic garden defined by evergreens."

    The "M" word is "Moderne." Who thinks of Florence as having Moderne gardens? We know of many gardens praised for their rehabilitation or their restoration to some former classic period, only to discover through veiled suggestion that these restorations were done in modern times in the modern philosophies of their thoroughly modern owners or designers.

These new and Moderne gardens were created not by Italians, but by foreigners who were trying to outdo the Italians, to out "Tuscan" the Tuscans. These gardens might even have had an underlying structure of a classical period, and one might have assumed that the imposed "restored" landscape matched that of a prior period, often existing only in the imagination of the later designer. A quick comparison, for example, of any twentieth century photograph of the famous Villa Medici, Fiesole, and its corresponding Uten's lunette will illustrate the point. The two appear to have the same building, terraces and garden structure, but the "rehabilitated or reconstructed" garden incorporates landscape features such as additional terraces, side gardens abutting main *salas*, trees planted in the center of parterres, etc., that are vastly different from its Renaissance model. They are latter-day garden iterations, Modernist garden implants. One can only puzzle at the purpose for these changes, what artistic thought they expressed and what personal conceits of owner and architect inspired their creation.

If walls could talk,
And gardens sing,
Ah! What duets they would bring.
Author

My interest in this problem began after I agreed to help a colleague assemble photographs of perhaps the most beautiful and famous of all Florentine gardens, Villa Gamberaia.[13] The mission was to illustrate the garden with historic photographs showing how the Renaissance garden grew and matured. The task was first thought easy enough, as there were books listing the garden's development spanning from the date of its very first day of "restoration" in 1901 to the present. Initially, guests visited the garden on a weekly basis, taking photographs as souvenirs. In modern times, hundreds of visitors would use the garden daily as a Kodak opportunity. Without doubt, the Gamberaia is one of the most photographed Italian gardens. In my research at the American Academy in Rome, I came across a beautiful classically rendered plan of the villa done in 1920. It was the work of Edward G. Lawson, the first Fellow in landscape architecture to be named to the Academy. He had measured and accurately recorded for the first time a classic Renaissance villa and its gardens. Understanding the significance of his work, and to better allow for comparison, Lawson included in the corner of the drawing a rendered copy of a plan of the Gambaraia done in 1770. The plans were entirely different. Comparing the photograph of 1901 to Lawson's Beaux Arts rendered plan of 1920, the rendered and photographic plans resembled each other, but subtle differences in aesthetics and function abounded.

R. Terry Schnadelbach

Lawson in his studio at the American Academy in Rome

Photography is a marvelous modern tool for the historian, and particularly so for the landscape architecture historian. In reality, gardens are perishable architecture and photography is the essential tool documenting landscape change. As powerful a tool as photography can be, inexplicably it is seldom used to document landscape architectural history, but in comparing over time the assembled Villa Gamberaia photographs, one to the other, those dated 1901, 1905, 1910 showed significant changes to the Gamberaia's water parterres. The 1770 plan of the parterre garden included by Lawson in his 1920 illustrative drawing, indicated nothing of the existing measured plan or any elements of the garden shown in the collected photographs.

My curiosity piqued, I began to delve into the piles of evidence to better understand the Gamberaia's historical context, especially that period of Moderne photographic record. It quickly became apparent that at the turn of the century, a new owner, Princess Giovanna Ghyka, created a new garden that was not a "reconstruction" of anything from a past era. It was a new garden that reflected not only her individual artistic training and beliefs, but the spirit and artistic tastes of turn-of-the-century Florence as well. The water parterre garden at the Gamberaia was thoroughly Moderne, and a large part of its design was attributable to her sexual orientation. The same was true in at least two other Florentine villas. The history of the period would support that having arrived at the beginning of a new century, a like-minded group of non-Italians had gathered in the foothills of Fiesole, outside of Florence, Italy, where they began a discussion on aesthetics that produced a new philosophy of art, and a new way of approaching landscape architectural design. That design philosophy re-immersed itself in the classics and in humanism, but idealized both in more abstract and more modern terms, devoid of the decorative and stylistics limits of any other humanist period.

There was another commonality among these expatriates. A new emerging art market was to produce art dealers, experts on attribution and overnight connoisseurs. It also produced experts who copied renowned works of art, reproduced and reformatted, that were circulated as part of the legitimate art world of the time. The humanist villa may have originally contained paintings, sculptures and works of art within the important *salas*, but religious art was to be found only in the churches of the Renaissance. Paintings of religious subject matter were normally considered holy, never to be bought or sold; it had no market or commercial value. That was all changed during the Moderne revival of humanism causing social, political, and most important, aesthetic changes in society. The new emerging art market at the beginning of the twentieth century now would include any subject, whether it be ecclesiastic or secular. In the Moderne art world, religious art was secularized, commoditized, and displayed next to secular subjects, and valued, on occasion, for the artist's name alone. It was now possible to find an ornate Renaissance crucifix by Sassetti irreverently hung over a sideboard in the dining *sala* at Villa I Tatti in Settignano.

Three villas, their owners and landscape architects emerged as being intertwined in their developments. They were the first of a wave of successive Moderne Florentine and northern Italian gardens that represented similar design philosophies. As the second coming of humanism in landscape architecture, I have named the period of their birth, the second renaissance.

Hidden Lives / Secret Gardens is a first attempt at defining the Moderne Florentine garden and its new garden art. It reflects on the personalities of the owners and landscape architects involved with three famous Florentine villas, and the art community and social milieu of Florence at the turn of the century. It aims to understand the common themes that drew the group together at that time, and to expose the social and cultural conditions that influenced and molded their philosophy of art. In short, this is a book on the development of second renaissance gardens in Florence at the beginning of the twentieth century.

Chapter Illustration for Villa Gamberaia by Maxfeld Pharrish, in the book Italian Villas and their Gardens by Edith Wharton

Chapter 1 / Waltz

Villa Gamberaia

> "The House of the Villa Gamberaia, now mellowed to a soft ivory color and perfectly embodying the Tuscan ideal of restraint and proportion, is the center of a garden that varies with every aspect: playful where the pools and box hedges and singing frogs lie basking in the sun; stately where the bowling alley sweeps into the dark grandeur of cypresses; and simple where the olive valley runs down to Florence. There is a place for every mood. Hamlet will find an answering chord in the twilight of the *bosco,* mysterious, elusive, fantastic with the shapes of ilex; the joker can go and joke among the water steps and grotto; and the two can agree to differ in the most delightful of lemon gardens. As one walks from place to place, there seems to be something about it more Italian than the Italians themselves." [14]
>
> Geoffrey A. Jellicoe, Landscape Architect

THE VILLA GAMBARAIA, SITUATED in the ancient agrarian town of Settignano, crowns the surrounding Tuscan hillside. Approached from the city of Florence and the valley floor below through tranquil orchards and poppy speckled fields of grain, the quaint town faces out to the messy eastern suburbs of Florence. To the side of its humble parish church is the piazza and fountain that serve as the town's center of village social life. From here, all development is left behind as one heads easterly along the slopes of Monte Ceceu on via Rossellino with its terraced olive orchards and uncut fields lined with cedars or abutting *bosci* of laurel oak. East of the town, via del Loretino is found, a straight ridge line road running north-south that provides direct access from the Villa Gamberaia to the valley floor, the Arno flood plain and the village of San Andrea below where the Villa Loretina is located. It is at the meeting of via Rossellino and via del Lorentino that the Villa Gamberaia stands, dominating an elongated flat section on the crest to the east of the Village of Settignano.

R. Terry Schnadelbach

    Above the dead air of the valley floor, the Gamberaia's perched terraces are positioned to receive even the most minuscule freshet. Here, the air is fresher; the sky is bluer; and the flowers more fragrant. Here, resides *natura viva* - rabbits, fox, boar and all the game animals that might be found on an Italian *tavola festa*. There are birds of every sort - song birds, falcons, and the favored nightingale (which seems only to inhabit villa gardens.) Here, too, one marvels at the view over the adjacent olive orchards, across ridge lines to neighboring villas and out across distant landscapes and the entire valley of the Arno River. The visual and romantic images of villa gardens are presented here in all their perfection.

    Set high upon the crest of the hill, the Gamberaia stands above the adjacent agrarian countryside. Its terraces are filled with simple but elegant architecture and ordered greenery. Entering through its gates, one is struck by its other-worldliness, the surreal character of the enclosed space. One cannot fail to see its beauty, to feel its grandeur, to marvel at its intimacy and to puzzle at the assemblage of separate garden spaces within. The siting and composition, a result of over four centuries of over-lapping interventions by its owners and their architects, is a simple yet subtle progression of garden design. Yet the villa is an integral part of the Tuscan landscape and its agreement with its surrounds clearly evident to the educated eye.

    Unlike the Italian urban *palazzo* residence, where building volumes predominated and open space was in the form of *cortiles* or secluded *parradi*, villas, historically, were small secondary homes set amid agrarian production landscapes. Villa architecture typically responded to its new role and opened up its building mass to the countryside, allowing the outdoors to penetrate the interiors, bringing into the interior, light, air and the country environment. Villas at their highest art form were therefore compositions responsive to their gardens, elements that integrated the house to the surrounding agrarian lands.

    Several transformations to the villa-type have taken place since the first villas were built during Roman times. To the Romans, the villa was a self-sufficient architectural complex, located in a scenic area having abundant water, such as thermal springs, the seashore, or remote wooded mountain areas. The complexes contained luxurious architectural spaces - libraries, baths, gymnasiums, cure facilities - and walled gardens of every sort; private atria, festive exterior reception areas, dining gardens and spaces for contemplation. When the Roman family and its entourage traveled to its villa, the party included servants, slaves, and related functionaries often numbering fifty or more. The villa, therefore, had to accommodate a sizable population, requiring it to be the size of a small village.

The Renaissance villa was very different in all but its name. It was not an architectural complex. In fact, its built component was a temporary residence and was of minimal size when compared to the family's city dwelling. The villa was not self-sufficient; it was an economic production unit with a revenue-producing agenda, often specializing in one type of agricultural production. It did not house a transient servant population; it housed, in separate clusters, permanent homes of peasant sharecroppers who, while inter-dependant on the *padrone* for its agriculture, lived totally independent of the owner. The villa's location and design did not depend on the scenic surrounds. As a working farm, its location was an agrarian setting. Today, we find these agrarian areas beautiful in their own right where they still exist. Many of these formerly agrarian settings have since been absorbed into the spreading suburban fabric.

The Villa Gamberaia belongs to yet another definition of the villa, the twentieth century villa. This villa-type was a rebuilt permanent rural residence, without any urban counterpart such as the urban *palazzo*. Its economic base was still useful, but only marginally, and often, when its owners were independently wealthy, its agricultural economic base was abandoned altogether. Where the production unit remained, its working population was day laborers who, together with servants required to support the resident owner, were required to live elsewhere, with the exception of the *capo giardiniere* and the *portiere* and their respective families. The twentieth century villa house and garden were considered things of beauty and were developed solely for the enjoyment, and at the whim, of its owner. With this proviso, the architecture of the building and design of the gardens were elevated to a level of fine art.

Since the turn-of-the-twentieth century, visiting writers and historians have lavished praise on the Villa Gamberaia. The American novelist Edith Wharton in her 1904 book, *Italian Villas and Their Gardens*,[15] detailed with rapture Gamberaia's charms. The villa was listed as a stellar site in every major guide book on Italian gardens since the first such guide was published by Aubrey Le Blond in 1926.[16] Since then, many guidebook authors and villa historians have described the gardens in general and in detail.[17] These writings and photographic records have become our eyes and ears, allowing us to witness the Moderne changes at the Gamberaia. The gardens we see today are reflective of the turn-of- the- century, when villa ownership and villa design fell into new hands. They are not reflective of the earlier grand epochs of Italian garden making - the Renaissance or the Baroque. Gamberaia represents Italy's first and best example of the Moderne style villa and typifies the cultural and aesthetic changes that occurred in the Florentine villas at that time. Gamberaia's success was the catalyst for the Moderne, second renaissance[18] gardens that followed.

R. Terry Schnadelbach

Princess Catarina Giovanna Ghyka-Comanesti,[19] the new proprietor of the Gamberaia at the turn-of-the-century, was one of Florence's great enigmas. Very little is recorded about her. From official records, we know only that she purchased the Villa Gamberaia on March 7, 1896.[20] The rest, we must construct from fragments of personal accounts, rumors and innuendoes of the day.[21]

" A narcissistic Rumanian lady who lived mysteriously, in love with herself perhaps, and certainly with her growing creation, the garden of Gamberaia."

"A mysterious being, almost as weird and invisible as Rider Haggard's She." [22]

Bernard Berenson, Owner of Villa I Tatti

Known as a ravishing beauty from birth, Jeanne Keshko was born in Nice, France, and was raised in the late 1860s in Florence, Italy. She was known to her family as "Bebe."[23] As a young adult, in the early 1880s, she went to Paris as an art student and circulated socially with the students of the male-only Ecole des Beaux-Arts. She was also reputed to be a courtesan among the Parisian nobilities; her signature feature was her collection of jeweled toe-rings. She mixed freely in these two circles and is even recorded as one of Gertrude Stein's friends attending her famous soirees.

Princess Jeanne Ghyka, circa 1897

In 1875, Jeanne Keshko's older sister Natalie, married Milan Obrenovic I, of Romaina, (Prince 1868-1882, King 1882-1889). Milan I's brother,[24] was named Prime Minister in his brother's Romanian government. Eugene was known to be very wealthy in his own right and had vowed not to marry so that his brother would inherit the family's fortune in its entirety. A noble in the Austro-Hungarian Empire, Eugene was a soldier of fortune and was widely acclaimed throughout Europe for having successfully fought at the side of General Ulysses Grant in the American Civil War.[25] The Prince[26] cut a dashing figure and was well known to the women of the international nobility in Paris and other European capitals.

Prince Eugene Ghyka-Comanesti

King Milan I, in an attempt to solidify his claims within the Austro Hungarian Alliance, and to subject a weaker Serbia, arranged a political marriage with Serbia's leading

hidden lives / secret gardens

family.[27] Milan I turned to his wife's part-Romanian family, the Keshkos, and proposed the hand of the yet un-married younger sister, Giovanna Jeanne Keshko as the perfect match for his brother. The couple was introduced and the marriage arranged in Paris.

The Eugene - Jeanne (Giovanna, Italian) marriage was ostensibly a political arrangement made to foster economic trade and reduce regional tensions between Serbia and Romania.[28] The wedding brought a commitment and monies from Vienna to both countries for a new railroad to be built through both Serbia and Romania, connecting Austria with Turkey, uniting by rail for the first time Europe and Asia.[29]

Unknown at the time to either of the families involved, Jeanne Ghyka's Paris love-life was bisexual to the external viewer and lesbian in her innerpersona. At this time, the practice of lesbianism was forbidden by law, or socially unacceptable to moral standards in most countries.[30] Its practice was concealed in almost all places except Paris. There, homosexuality in all its forms was open. Lesbians in England and the Teutonic nations on the continent had to be practice secretly and same-sex encounters were masked in order to protect social standing and reputation. This was usually accomplished by establishing heterosexual credentials through a formal marriage. Many socially prominent Sapphics married a bugger[31] maintaining the appearances of a heterosexual household. Under such guise, a gay man and a lesbian woman could attend social affairs as a couple while leading separate and homosexual private lives. Such was the case with Vita Sackville-West, the creator of the famous gardens at Sissinghurst, England.

Miss Florence Blood

Dorothy Wellesley and Virginia Woolf were both Vita lovers. Vita, however, was married to Sir Harold Nicholson who, not coincidently had numerous male amours - Victor Cunnard, Jean de Gaigneron, Raymond Mortimer, and Edward Molyneux. Harold called Vita "the second string to our bow."[32] They both openly stated that they never had sex together. Jeanne may have thought that her marriage to Eugene could provide a similar public cover.

Prncess Catherine
Jeanne Keshko Ghyka

"I hate the furtiveness and dissimulation, the petty hypocrisies and deceits, the carefully planned assignations, letters that must be 'given' not posted. It revolts and nauseates me."[33]

Violet Trefusis

As an art student in Paris, Jeanne Ghyka had known numerous gay artists and was free to lead a bohemian and un-orthodox life. Paris in the late 1800s was termed "Lesbian Heaven" and same-sex couples lived openly. Famous among the artistic and literary pairs were Natalie Rarney, English actress and American painter Romaine Brooks; Gertrude Stein, the American writer, and Alice B. Toklas; Rosa Bonheur, the noted French painter and the Greek painter, Natalie Micus; Alice Austin, the American photographer, and Gertrude Tate, the English dancer.[34] It was in Paris that Princess Ghyka first met Miss Florence Blood, an American who was to be her lifelong companion.

Late in the nineteenth century, scientific challenges to the long-established thinking regarding homosexuality came to the fore. German scientists published their case-studies on the subject around the same time that Freud's work was published.[35] In these technical writings, the word "homosexual" was used for the first time. The German studies were based on research into same sex relationships, defining the norm as opposite sex attraction and fulfillment, while defining same sex relationships as pathological and psycho-social aberrations. In Sigmund Freud's work, sex was identified as the motivator of all relationships and as the prime element defining the persona. No interpersonal relationship was innocent, Freud said, and body language communicated conscious as well as subconscious desires. Freud's work furthermore emphasized the deep hidden sexuality of the female, which he believed was revealed through dream interpretations. In this context of the sexually repressed Victorian age, Freud's work had the effect of liberating the female.

Jeanne Ghyka was a product of the attempt of women of her time to achieve equality and was, thus, considered one of the "New Women."[36] Entering the male-dominated art world of artists, critics and dealers, Ghyka was among the first women to attempt to study and paint in the milieu of the Ecole des Beaux-Arts. That she was not allowed entrance and did not achieve notoriety, the lack of recognition of her artistic talent was not surprising. Only a few women achieved entrance into the Ecole des Beaux-Arts; Rosa Bonheur was among only a handful of women who was to succeed in that man's world.

"Ghyka was rich, beautiful and hated men and mankind," [37]and......"was a notorious misanthrope." [38]

Ghyka's hatred of men could be little suppressed. The Eugene - Jeanne Catholic marriage, like the Romanian - Serbian political marriage, did not last long.[39] As divorce was not a possibility, they separated. The Prince made a settlement of money

hidden lives / secret gardens

to Jeanne in exchange for her permanent exile from both Paris and Bucharest. With the emotional support of her sister, Queen Natalie of Serbia, Jeanne returned in 1896 to the place of her youth, Florence. For Jeanne, it provided the best of all worlds then available to her. In its warm climate she would find herself sufficiently close to both her Balkan homeland and Parisian friends so that she could reasonably be in touch with both in their travels. But more importantly, Florence was the city of choice for lesbians, as all forms of homosexuality was practiced and tolerated there.[40] Florence possessed that strange mixture of conservative social structure and experimental artistic expression that attracted homosexuals of both genders. Although still against all Italian social strictures, the open practice of lesbos had not been deemed illegal in Florence as it had throughout England, and, with the exception of Paris, Europe.

Chateau "Les Ailes, Bidart, France

Queen Natalie's prime residence, the royal palace in the Serbian capital of Belgrade, was supplemented by other residences-of-state in Paris and London as well as a small seasonal villa in Biarritz. Called "the most callous and trivial of French watering places," the Biarritz villa was located just adjacent to the major chateau of King Edward VII of England.[41] Humiliated by the constant scandals caused by her husband's philandering, Natalie had separated from Milan I, in 1891.[42] With the support of King Edward VII, she was assisted at that time in buying a 40 hectare domain of forest just inside the Basque village of Bidart, a few kilometers south of Biarritz. There, she built," Les Ailes " an enormous chateau sited on a magnificent cliff overlooking the coast line.[43]

19

Princess Jeanne Ghyka spent many summer months there before her marriage, close to her sister, enjoying the beauty of the rough countryside.

When Jeanne separated from Eugene and established Florence as her new city of residence, Natalie joined her there by setting up a winter residence of her own. Florence, like Bidart, had a sizable community of Austro-Hungarian nobility, including many from Romania and Serbia. Natalie, without her scandalous husband, was still welcomed by many of the community. Through her Serbian connections, Natalie was able to rent a *villino,* or petite villa, on the estate of the Villa La Pietra[44] located just outside the walls of Florence. Located in the adjacent hillside community, the small but refined *palago and podere* owned by her sister Jeanne, was close enough for visits between the two when the Queen was in town and yet far enough to provide for separate personal lives. With their Florentine residences, the sisters settled into the life of the expatriate community that was increasingly populating the hills surrounding the city.

> "The multitude of villas dotting the Fiesole hills produces an embarrassment of choices. One can find any combination of house type, land orientation, woods, orchards, fields, etc. to satisfy the most difficult and demanding buyer."[45]
>
> Henry James, novelist

For Jeanne Ghyka to become the Gamberaia's new owner was revolutionary at that time. Married women, as Ghyka was still legally married, were unable to own property under Italian law. Following a similar change in British law, the Italian law was changed in the 1890s.[46] Prior to the revision, British women could not control the lands of their houses nor purchase cottages separately from their husbands, thereby limiting the control women had over the homestead. This, by necessity, relegated a woman's energies and interests in property to areas such as gardening, and was responsible for the surge of interest by women in the garden arts in the late nineteenth century. Although many middle class women did produce wondrous gardens, they were subjected to their husband's dictates and were held secondary to his economic judgment. Despite this, gardening in Britain became a respectable activity for middle-class women and was valued for its social, moral and physical improvements. When the repressed English woman moved to Florence, she sought out those properties which had garden possibilities. Gardening's importance to the "new woman's movement" was central, along with property ownership rights.

The villas of the Florentine hills became the focus of the newly emancipated women, and gardening was a part of her liberation, self-expression and social presentation.

hidden lives / secret gardens

The noted novelist and writer on Italian gardens, Janet Ross, who lived at the base of Settignano and had acquired her villa through her husband, put garden improvements above all others at their villa house. In so doing, Ross had the full support of her lesbian partner, Vernon Lee, the British essayist. In purchasing the Gamberaia and focusing her improvements on the gardens, Jeanne Ghyka was joining the new, liberated women's front.

Cabero map commissioned by Marchesi Capponi in 1717 of the Gamberaia Villa and its podere.
Of note: in the upper left side, the natural ravine of water from the sacred source to the north; the piped water system and its distribution to Villa and podere plots; the stables and their access from the left of the bowling green at the nypherium; the former entrance to the Villa house filled in by the grotto; and the configuration of the garden composed of a embroidery parterre and oval rabbit island..
Source; Photographic album, Villa Gamberaia, by Edward Lawson, Cornell University archives.

"(gardens functioned) as physical and spiritual arenas in which individual women strove to assert control, define their identity, struggle with sexual feelings or embrace the world."[47]
                                                            Sue Bennet, British writer on gardening

Engraving of the Villa Gamberaia by Giuseppe Zocchi in 1744.
Of Note: the columns of water seen above the flying arches and in the middle of the right cypress allee; the people standing on top of the flying arches; and the empty lower space where the current parterre garden is located.

In the move to Florence, Jeanne Ghyka wanted to fashion a peaceful and private retreat, a place in which to meditate and lead an aesthetic life. She had corresponded with Carlo Placci, a well-known Florentine who was well "connected" to almost every aspect of Florentine life.[48]. It was Placci who told her of the Gamberaia's availability and it was Placci that verified its conditions and negotiated the price for her while Jeanne was still in Paris. Ghyka's role was limited to pestering him for assurances of the *podere*'s viability and the villa's functioning state.[49]

Purchasing a *podere* was an economic necessity for Ghyka, a way for her to augment her limited monthly stipend. From others who bought and ran functioning *podere* at the same time, we know the yield above expenses were about five per-cent, plus a portion of the *podere*'s produce, i.e., fruit, wine, olives and olive oil.[50] As planned, the *podere* was to provide Ghyka a separate income and with it, the freedom from having to work as a courtesan.

Since the Renaissance period, villas clearly served two purposes, that of the summer residence for the *padrone* (or owner), and as local *poderes* (or cooperative farms). The prevalent local agrarian system was the *mezzadria* system of co-operative farming.[51] In almost all cases, the land would be utilized by many differing *contadino* (or farmers) who would plant and harvest a broad array of agricultural crops. At the time of harvesting, the produce was brought in, weighed, classified and accounted for by a *fattore* (or independent accountant). Usually, one half the harvests was paid to the *padrone,* or to his heirs for rent, taxes and land repairs while the *contadini* would retain the other half. The farmer would then reserve the percentage he wished to keep for his family's use, declaring the rest, along with the *padrone's* share, to be sold by the independent *fattore* on the commercial market. In this way the *contadini* was guaranteed the same price as the *padrone.*

Most owners were not directly involved in the labor and agrarian production, preferring instead to manage their land solely as a financial asset. The role of the *padrone* was to establish the *podere's* infrastructure, providing the best growing conditions for the farm. The provisions for boundary and roadway walls, terracing and water were his primary concerns, but among these infrastructure items, water was the most critical.

The villa was completed in the early seventeenth century by the Florentine nobel Zanobi Lappisi. He was recorded as having the rights to water from a spring just north of the property. He brought the villa's supply from this source. In the eighteenth century the property was sold to the Marchesi Capponi as one of his ten or more *poderes*. Water rights were then in dispute as the Capponis drained lands to the east and channeled water throughout the site. During the same period, in order to settle water rights claims with adjacent neighbors, the Marchesi Capponi had a *cabreo* or site survey of the entire *podere*. It showed the field plots, the buildings associated with the villa in plan and elevation and water channels for both farm and garden.

> "Certainly the minds of the Florentine family of Capponi were original and inventive. First, in 1570 they created the beautifully detailed asymmetrical garden at Arcetri overlooking Florence..... and in 1717 they finally synthesized and completed the slowly evolving complex of Villa Gamberaia at Settignano across the Arno valley whose concept of a domestic landscape is by general concent the most thoughtful the western world has known."
>
> Geoffrey Jellicoe

The Gamberaia was blessed with several natural sources of water and the original owners of the villa, the Lappis, in the 1700s, tapped these, diverting the various water sources into several aqueducts that served the villa and its *mezzadrias*. The 1744 engraving by Giuseppe Zocchi show tall massive columns of water in several parts of the garden.

> "There were several rills and springs of water forming a small lake or pond nearby where the country folk used to catch crayfish or *gamberi*, hence the name Gamberja - the abode of crayfish."[52]
> Edward Hutton

The *padrone* also granted land to the *contadini* to build their *case da lavatore* (or share-cropper dwellings) or their *case coloniche*, (farm houses). The latter was a more substantial building and usually contained separate units for the extended family - aging parents, young newly-weds or a dependant aunt or uncle. The Renaissance *podere* around Settignano all specialized in the production of olives, making them especially prosperous *mezzadria*.

The local agricultural system produced a unique *padrone villa*. The house was on a raised terrace and had a fully functioning basement within the foundation walls. Villa Gamberaia was just such a villa. The building's east side, meeting grade at the villa's ground floor level, was reserved for the *padrone*. The west side, meeting grade at one level below, in what appears as *terracemento* (a basement level), contained the spaces needed for operating the Gamberaia's *mezzadria*. Windowless and entered by just one barn door, this basement space securely stored farm equipment, animals, tools and produce when harvested and readied for the commercial market. This separation by level provided the villa's residents above, complete privacy from agrarian neighbors, out of sight below.

Typically, the *padrone*, with his *mezzadria*'s staff - the *facttore*, the *geometre* (or surveyor) - and the main *contadini*, inspected the property annually, usually in the fall after the crops were in and the year's productivity had been assessed. On their tour of the property, the needs of the *podere* were determined and the *padrone* would commit to having repaired whatever was that year's critical need. One can imagine the shock and skepticism surrounding the first meeting in 1896 between the gentlemen of the *mezzadria* and their new *padrone*, a woman, Princess Ghyka. With the change in Italian law allowing women ownership, Ghyka was among the first women to make this annual procession across the agrarian lands. It is possible to imagine Ghyka carrying herself regally, with complete self-confidence, as she marched through the landscape at a rapid pace, as was her norm, with the men following in tow.

A new owner's first year inspection was, typically, a predictable test of wills. Jeanne would have been presented with a long list of the *podere's* deficiencies, many being decades old. Typically, the new owner would try to decipher critical current problems while avoiding over-committing. The Gamberaia *podere's* main problem,

Beaux-Arts rendering of Edward Lawson's measured plans, and sections.

however, was inescapable, even to the new owner. The existing water system was in an unarguable state of disrepair, affecting the farmlands as well as the main villa. One of the first things that Ghyka would have had to undertake after purchasing the villa was to restore the water supply and return the *podere* to full production.[53] Her first two years were spent with laborers repairing the water works under the villa's long cypress-lined allee and converting some of the brick vaults to modern piping. An electric pump with control valves was installed between the allee and parterre garden. It was a startling scene at that time to see a woman, no less a princess, amid the Italian workers in the trenches, ankle-deep in mud.

The Villa Gamberaia of the Princess Ghyka era was a wonderfully small villa that the Princess endeavored to make only better. If architecture is frozen music, then the Gamberaia's gardens were composed like a waltz,[54] swirling from one space to the next. There are no straight line marches in experiencing this site. One constantly turns, moving smoothly through gardens that are connected one to other. One terrace wraps around the main villa only to meet another leading away in the opposite direction. The waltz ends in a grand, sweeping panoramic view or, in the opposite direction, in the oval hillside grotto. The waltz is danced through brilliant sunlight into the darkest shade, then back into light, in an ever-changing sequence. With direct connections, the eye, as well as the body, turns this way, then that; each space ending where the next begin – all in a continuous movement. The Gamberaia garden's musical tone throughout is a constant - either the green architectural walls of the planting or the yellow ochre walls of the villa buildings.

> "Color everywhere is a symphony of greens from deep cypress throughvarieties of box, yew, ilex and privet, to the light emerald of lemon-trees and grass."[55]
> J. C. Shepherd and G. A. Jellicoe, landscape architects

Our garden waltz begins at the entrance, *il portale,* which is found today, not at its original entry from the east along via Lorelina,[56] but from the north off via Rossellino, which originates in Settignano, to the west. The waltz begins outside the front gate, in a sunken semi-circular enclosed plaza where one suddenly arrives after a sweeping curve in the road. The first glimpse of the villa house, sited high on its terrace, is through olive orchards. The road dips and swirls into the walled enclosure, which is formed on one side of the entrance by towering ancient cypresses that line the top of a large embankment and on the other by boundary walls of yellow ochre. The road seems to end here, but a closer look reveals that it continues through a small opening - a tunnel through which only the smallest of autos could fit. It continues past a sharp, tight bend in the road and onward easterly through Gamberaia's olive orchards. (The small tunnel lies beneath a massive wall that is lined on top with majestic century-old cypresses that extend from the hillside over the entry road, to the villa's architectural complex.) From the sweep of the semi-circular entrance wall and its centered gate, one is offered a majestic view up a green allee of clipped laurels to the house. Buried within the clipped green walls are stone lions and other garden sculpture that were probably free-standing when originally placed but now, with the natural thickening of the hedge over time, have become engaged ornaments.

The walk up the drive from the entrance space brings the visitor to an open forespace, the *cortile,* and a view of the elegant light grayish-yellow facade of the house. Suddenly, one comes upon an architectonic landscape terrace that is part of the extended architecture of the villa house. A huge double-arched freestanding wall spans from the villa's chapel on the far left to the main villa residence on the right. The archway encloses the view on the left hinting of a space beyond. The opposite view to the right leads along the terrace that wraps around the building's west facade. It is designed to be a part of the facade as well as part of a landscape space, and thus, part of the garden. The irregular early Renaissance geometry of the terrace is hardly noticeable. The terrace houses a *cave,* for cold storage and its baseline walls are punctuated by only one small door. The terrace and house architecturally function as one. The view from the terrace, across the valley, extends to the crest of the distant ridge and the town of Settignano. Today, the corner of the terrace is marked by a singular large parasol pine, framing the view to Settignano - a theme that will be repeated elsewhere in the larger composition. The pine was planted in the late twenties by the Villa's successor owner. It is a late Moderne addition, but one that continues in the spirit of the waltz and the landscape of the earlier Moderne Gamberaia.

The Bowling Green Allee   To the left of the *cortile*, and through the arched openings in the wall spanning the chapel and villa house, we arrive close to the midpoint of the four hundred and fifty foot long allee that was originally lined on both sides for its full length in Italian cypresses. Today, only the northern third of the allee is still expressed in cypresses, and many of these majestic garden elders are twisted and gnarled with age. Originally, the allee's surface was paved in stabilized earth, or *terra battue*.[57] Sometime during the eighteenth century, when Anglicized gardens were fashionable in Italy, the allee was planted in grass and renamed the very un-Italian "bowling green."[58]

R. Terry Schnadelbach

> "A long grass allee...this is quite an unusual feature in Italian gardens; but nevertheless a very delightful one"
>
> Indigo Triggs, architect[59]

Beneath the allee's surface lie the Renaissance aqueducts that distributed water to the house and gardens, and possibly to the farmlands below. It connected springs, streams and farmlads north of via de Rossellino, at the nymphaea, and channeled them into the garden proper. In the northerly direction, the garden was made to not only conceal the aqueduct, but visually extend into the *podere* lands lying to the north side of the country road. The Princess, in making repairs to the *podere's* water supply, tore up most of the allee and, upon the completion of repairs, again resurfaced the allee's entire length with grass.[60] The sheer expanse of the grass surface was startling. In his 1926 garden guide, Aubrey Le Bonde stated: "The turf is kept as green as if it were in England."[61]

The cypress allee or "bowling green" is the main spine to the garden composition in its entirety. Sub-gardens project from both sides of this central organizing element. Unlike other Italian gardens, the house is part of the spatial definition of the allee. It forms part of the allee's edge, does not straddle its axis as is typical elsewhere, and is not the focal point of the axis. It is a composition that focuses solely on the landscape space while not relying on any aspect of the architecture as part of its compositional theme. One third of the allee is walled on both sides by golden-colored architectural elements - an unbroken tall, retaining wall on the eastern side, and the facades of the house, chapel and servant's apartments on the other.

The allee is a wonderfully proportioned space. In cross section, the space is formed by a width of eighteen-meters (sixty feet) and a height of ten meters (forty feet), the proportions of a golden rectangle as described in Renaissance art, and, in fact, the eighteen-meter width becomes the unified module for the composition of the entire garden. It is the width of the wrap around terrace and is multiplied to form the modules of the *lemonaia* and water parterre gardens.[62]

Turning into this long allee the waltz continues. A turn to the right brings one to the main entrance of the villa house. The main entrance at this location is a curiosity; however, the entrance is but a formality and little used. Another turn through the imposing entry door brings one into an colonnaded cortile.

View down the Portal / Corteli of clipped cypresses, circa 1957

*The Bowling Green allee showing the flying arches end-walls,
the villa house and the cypress allee to the nypherium*

The main entrance to the villa's house looking toward the Belvedere

The open views of the Bowling Green looking toward the Belvedere

The Grotto and its rocaille walls

South Bosco

Lemonaia and its summer garden

*View from the Villa house of the water parterre garden circa 1911
as designed by Cecil Pinsent and Geoffrey Scott*

View of water parterre garden from the exedra circa 1908 as designed by Princess Ghyka

A water parterre and the garden's original topiary, circa 1906

Water parterre circa 1957 as designed by Pietro Porcanaia

Exedra of trained cypress wall pierced by arches

Water parterre looking toward the central fountain and further to the exedra

Edward Lawson sitting on the wall of the new south parterre, sketching the garden

*Bernini-like columns with ivy swaggers
surrounding the central dinning ares*

hidden lives / secret gardens

If one had turned left on entering the entrance cypress allee one would enter a section of retaining walls and small architectural structures. As that allee continues past the architectural walls it, too, becomes lined in tall cypresses and with low, one-meter high walls, passing over via Rossellino, with its narrow tunnel below. The ancient cypresses, which were planted at two differing times, create the allee's strong architectonic definition. Together, the walls and cypresses cast deep shadows on the allee's green lawn, creating a shadowy setting for Neptune's nymphaea that terminates the allee's axis at the north. Here, Neptune and his underworld realm rule.

Nymphaeum   The nymphaea, an oval space in the front of the stage set fountain, houses a baroque statue of Neptune. With gushing water protecting the central figure, Neptune stands amid moss and lichen-laden, sea lions and musicians, resembling an imagined figure, perhaps from a Ravel waltz. The grotto's side retaining walls are faced in *rocaille* works - a mosaic of small colored stones and sea shells. The forespace is carpeted with a mixture of shade tolerant grass and wild ground orchids, natives of the Fiesole hills. In the spring, a carpet of grape hyacinths color the space, their deep purple hue made more intense by the presence of deep shade.

> "The shaded portions of the garden are the framework for the open spaces and join together on the bowling green. The planting of ilex and of cypress there has been varied in accordance with the desired perspective of heights."[63]
>
> L. Einstein, author

Like Orpheus descending into his underworld, music has always been associated with Neptune's watery environment. A dark and shady oval space carved into the hillside, the *rocaille* nymphaeum is surrounded by columnar cypresses as if they were pipes of the grand Gamberaia organ. The most aged and most massive of the cypresses surrounds Neptune as he rules the Gamberaia from his commanding fountain perch. As the cypresses were planted at two differing times and have been further graduated in size by sun and wind, their sizes range down from tallest, at axis terminus surrounding Neptune. Majestic and towering, these vertical elements were remarked upon by Gabriele d'Annunzio, the Italian playwright, Settignano resident and close Ghyka friend (1863-1938), after his first visit to the Gamberaia on April 27, 1898:

> Si vede pel vano dell'arcata sfondare l'aria del vespro, ove la selva di cipressi piu' a piu' s'infosca digradando come la canne d'uno smisurato organo di bronzo."[64]
>
> Gabriele d'Annunzio

R. Terry Schnadelbach

The cypress allee is remarkable in length and design environment. It is a space that begins in the darkest shadows of the nymphaeum, and progresses south through gradations of reflected ochre-tinged light in its mid section and continues into an open full-sun promenade ending in the brightest light at its opposite end, the allee's Belvedere. Here, in full sun, the light can seem glaring. To form one continuous architectural wall on the allee's western side, a matching pair of tall attenuated arches extend the house's façade, While the north façade's arches connects to the chapel, the southern arches fly out into free space unattached. Much speculation is made of this architectural feature. The arches have handrails atop its cornice that connected to the side façade's window. It is as if they were meant to be peopled. Perhaps, they were remnants from Gamberaia Renaissance past, and used when jousting matches or horse races were held on the allee in front of the villa's main façade. The arches would support banner-draped viewing stands for events below. It is quite possible that the allee was used on occasion for jousting; the allee would be divided along its length by a wooden barrier as jousting combatants on horseback would race toward each other in bloody combat to the cheers of spectators lining the iron rails of the archway above. Or it might have been used for small competitive horse races. Beginning at the open southern end, the race would proceed up to the oval space of the nyphaeum, where the competitors would turn around a central pole and race to the finish-line at the southern end of the house.

As jousting matches and horse racing were no longer fashionable, Princess Ghyka used the pair of south arches as her own special viewing perch to oversee her garden creations. She added to the farthest pier a small enclosed spiral staircase hidden in the pier of its end arch. The staircase is the only entrance from the house to the south garden.

Belvedere   The allee continues south, past the flying arches, and is lined on the eastern side by a one-meter high continuous hedge (similar to the one-meter high wall at the allee's northern end) and on the western side by closely planted one-meter high topiary "urns". The view ahead to the belvedere, (or overlook) is thus framed. The belvedere end of this treeless section of the allee is open to the sky and bathed in full sunlight. The huge, shaped laurel urns no longer exist. They pre-existed Ghyka's purchase and contributed to a much needed separation between the two.

The end of the cypress allee is a stone balustrade with a free-standing, towering sculpture of the huntress, Diana, set atop its rail at the center. Her archer's bow now but a fragment of the original and hangs like a rusting coat hanger, but to the right, and overhanging the balustrade, is a most magnificent mature parasol pine framing the view across the Arno valley. This is the garden's second pine, planted in the same exact relationship to its space's view as the previously mentioned parasol on the villa's entry terrace. These two pines are

hidden lives / secret gardens

diagonally opposite each other in the garden, with the house intervening, and give the visitor points of orientation on his initial trip through the garden composition. They also frame the only windows from the garden to the world outside. D'Annunzio described it as:

> *"Appare un giardino intercluso da siepi de cipresso e di bossolo donde si levano, a distanze eguali, densi alaterni tagliati a foggia di urne rotonde...a traverso un cancello, in fondo, si scorge il bosco selvaggio. Nel portico intorno si plinti delle colonne, sono adunati innumerevoli vasi di mughetti in fiori."*[65]

> "The long grass alley or bowling green, flanked... by high hedges...shows how well the beauty of a long stretch of greensward was understood...These bits of sward were always used near the house, where their full value could be enjoyed, and were set like jewels in clipped hedges or statue-crowned walls... (it) terminates in a balustrade.... For the main entrance, there is an opening in the wall that offers access to a side garden. allee, to the east and opposite the main house and on axis with its original Through a looks down on the Arno and across to the hills on the south."[66]
>
> Edith Wharton, author

The Grotto   At this point, if one feels turned about, it is only natural as the garden, as a waltz, swirls around each topiary urn along its southern course. They are part of the experience intended in its composition. But the waltz continues with yet other major turn, into a surprise entrance to a *rocaille*-mural room. If we were curious and particularly aware, we would have noticed that at midpoint on the wrought-iron gate bearing a lily motif, the symbol of Florence, one enters into the grotto garden, *camera rustico*, an enclosed room composed of side walls and terminus niche, both executed in exquisite *rocaille* incrustations. Every surface of this wondrous fountain, reminding us of spring, completes d"Annunzio's recollections. The Pan sculpture, perhaps tell the story that this rustic grotto garden is a perfect music room and the occasional concerts that were held therein attest to that fact. This form of grotto is uncommon to Italian Renaissance gardens in that it is a completely enclosed exterior room open to the sky. Rusticated walls with their ornamented tops allow wind to whistle by at venule induced speeds, making it the perfect spot for a brief, wind-induced concert and a moment's rest. As d'Annuzzio noted in his workbooks:

> I"*La musica del vento, degli insetti, degli uccelli, delle acque."*
>
> Gabreal d"Annunzzio

But Harold Acton saw this space differently (and perhaps knew stories of its other use): the room is rusticated, decorated with mosaic panels of ava, sea shells and *spunge*, a porous and highly irregular limestone. The walls are sculpted to create niches for statuary and plants. Many pockets are filled with trailing herbs, flowering rosemary and mop-headed pink to blue hydrangeas, softening the hard materials of the enclosing walls.

Stucchi, (sculpture type) in grey or red limestone, are found atop the grotto's walls and in the niches. The theme is the Four Seasons, attesting to provide the densest shade in the garden. The ground shrubs of azaleas, ivy, nature's gifts to this *podere.* Statues occupying the niches are the female representations of summer and spring, while autumn and winter are male figures. Around the top are twelve busts echoing the Four Seasons theme, perhaps representing the months of the year. Lacking arms or body parts to hold the season's fruit-of-the-land, the coiffure of each head instead contains appropriate seasonal bounty.[67] Several mythological characters, typical to a Baroque garden, are also found here. They, too, repeat the seasonal theme: A cavalier strumming on a mandolin represents summer's festivities; a bearded man, with long locks, holding a serpent to his breast is an allegory of death and winter; a statue of Pan, perched on the terrace over the water music of the central grotto.

"This grotto garden is one of the prettiest open-air boudoirs imaginable."[68]
Harold Acton

The South *Bosco* If the visitor climbed either of the grotto's end stairs they would enter a natural southern *selvatico* also called *sacro bosco* or wooded area. It is here that native holly oaks (*Quercus ilex*) myrtle and a unique wild Cyclamen fill the ground plane and delight the eye with variety. The *Cyclamen herderifolium* with its variegated leaves, flowers in late summer through the fall, its bloom a fluorescent shell pink. It is believed that in the Renaissance period, captured wild animals were penned in these *bosci* until readied for the *festa* meal.[69] The woods seemed to have remained an unused landscape area by Ghyka.

Lemonaia Ascending either of the grotto's end stairs again, the visitor would arrive in the *lemonaia* with its collection of citruses in movable clay pots. Defining the north side of the space, the large windowed *lemonaia,*(lemon house) is an efficient solar trap that protects the stored pots of citrus plants in winter. In the spring, summer and fall, the collection of large wooden boxes housing lemon, orange and grapefruit trees are placed outdoors in the garden where they provide lush green growth, punctuated with orange, yellow or green fruit as ornaments. The *lemonaia* garden is designed in rectangles of grass, bordered with showy beds of roses and peonies, originally all white in flower. With the addition of the summer blooming white flowered citruses, perhaps this garden was the inspiration for the white garden of Vita Sackville-West done at *Sissinghurst* in England. (Sackville-West was a Ghyka friend and Gambaraia visitor.) The garden in winter, when the citrus trees are kept behind the closed glass windows of the lemon house, dramatically marked the change of seasons at Gamberaia. In the bareness of winter in particular, it became especially apparent that the terrace of the *lemonaia* was exactly at the same level as the *piano nobile,* or second floor of the villa. Not an accident, this device allowed the *piano nobile* rooms direct view onto the garden. With handrails attesting to its use, Ghyka could exit along the top of the "flying arches" wall and inspect the *lemonaia* and its garden. This garden was never entered on center, the *lemonaia* and its formal four squares are accessed at its corners. Movement through it is non-axial and is yet but another turn in the variety of turns in Gamberaia's garden waltz.

The North *Bosco*   Exiting the *lemonaia* through its northern wall, or its far side, away from the rustic grotto, the visitor walks through the northern *selvatico* or *sacro bosco* (or wood.)   A north-facing copse of holly oak (*Quercus ilex*), evergreens such as rhodendrons and other mixed species native to Fiesole's north-facing slopes, filled this shaded garden. its floor is covered with ferns and azaleas, arum lilies, aspidistras, craniums and gardenias combine with the trees and groundcover to give the character of a native wood. Paths running through it lead down to the oval at the end of the long, grassed allee.

> "Probably the most perfect example of the art of producing a great effect on a small scale ... Aesthetic impressions were considered, and the effect of passing from the sunny fruit- garden (lemonaia) to the dense grove (bosco), hence to the wide-reaching view, and again to the sheltered privacy of the pleached walk (the bowling green) or the mossy coolness of the grotto - all this was taken into account by a race of artists who studied the contrast of aesthetic emotions as keenly as they did the juxtaposition of dark cypress and pale lemon-tree, of deep shade and level sunlight."[70]
>
> Edith Wharton

The Water Parterre Garden   The waltz of the Gamberaia, as the American writer on gardens Ethne Clark commented: "moves from one perfect garden picture to the next, stimulated and enchanted."[71]   The last garden, the south garden, is the grand finale, the triumphal finish to the Gamberaia's waltz composition. It is a cadenza based on a classical parterre theme demonstrating the virtuosity of its original creator, Princess Ghyka, and has had several variations since - cadenzas developed by other architects and *capo giardinere*.

The water parterre garden can be approached directly from the wrap-around terrace on the west, or it can be approached at any point from the cypress allee on the west. It can also be secretively approached from the internal circular stairway of the flying arches. But mysteriously it cannot be entered directly from the villa's south facade. Like the *lemonaia*, the water parterre garden is entered at its corners, and in the waltz that is the Gamberaia, requires the visitor who enters from any approach to turn again in yet another variation in the richly choreographed Gamberaia waltz. The villa's main garden fills in a space stretched-out and slightly sunken, along the western side of the allee. It is the formal *giardino acquatico*, the water parterre garden. The garden centers on the south facade of the house, but the architecture of this facade does not receive well the garden's main axis. There are no doors on the façade; the windows do not align with the garden's axis, and the corner positioned second floor loggia is aligned with the western side paths of the parterre garden. Even stranger is the separation of cypress allee and the parterre garden by the previously described "flying arch" wall with its concealed spiral staircase.

It is here in the south garden, that Princess Ghyka "restored the beautiful old-fashioned garden to its pristine splendor with infinite patience and taste."[72] Ghyka had found this area of the previous garden to be problematic. She rejected its existing plan[73] and in doing so, rejected any historic garden precedent for the garden. She embarked on designing her new garden, using parts of the existing garden structure to fashion her own composition, a cadenza based only on the structure of a parterre garden.

The Princess would choose to retain only parts of the garden useful in her new, original interpretation of a renaissance-like garden. It was Ghyka's intention that the south garden area be reflective of her new aesthete life. Hence, her goal in the design of the space was for a garden art piece. The Princess removed any existing vegetation in the oval and left in place only the central fountain and the center path system. Having just fixed the villa's water supply, she visualized a new parterre garden made up of water basins edged in plant and sculptural elements, perhaps reflective in sprit to those found in the famous Renaissance gardens at Villas Lante and d'Este. Ghyka's new *giardino acquatico* has four water parterres, each centered on an existing fountain. The parterre garden would be a totally enclosed space with the south end closed by an *exedra*, a new hedge wall formed as an apsidal end. In the *exedra*, arches would be incised to form an arcade as a backdrop to a semi-circular pool, a final pond that would be used for aquatics. When one thinks of the change from bedded areas to water areas, one can understand Princess Ghyka's logic.[74] In the summer, the parterre garden must have been stifling with full solar radiation and little breeze. Water, with its evaporation would have a cooling, soothing effect, both physically and psychologically.

The gardens were brought alive by the addition of water. Water, a mercurial material, offered so many differing characteristics. It could be still as glass or rough and animated, with movement and sound. At the garden's central circular pool, the jets from a dolphin provide the first of the garden's water music. Each of the four parterres provide for other jets forming a circle, as if the central fountain rippled out and captured each of the surrounding four parterres. This integration of forms is again Moderne and has no Renaissance precursor. The combination of jets from one to seven provides a cacophony of water sounds. The semi-circular pool at the garden's far end is without movement, a still life painting of water lilies and reeds. If none of the jets are operating in the central area, sounds of chirping, emanating from the small frogs inhabiting this contrasting still semi-circular pool can be heard.

The Princess's parterres were revolutionary in their treatment. Each water parterre was outlined by plantings, a perimeter hedge and an inside narrow border of flowering shrubs.[75] The design was an ingenious and original idea, as the typical Renaissance water parterre would have begun at the path edge and balustrade. Water would have filled the entire parterre area, as in those at Villa Lante, Villa d'Este and in the Pratolino at the Boboli gardens.

Furthermore, its edges would have been defined by "hard" architectonic elements - balustrades, sculpture, urns or clay pots. Ghyka's invention set Villa Gamberaia apart from all other historic-based gardens. The new parterres were reflective of new design concepts that would utilize plant materials in a new and freer way. The water parterres, built in green architectural hedges as contrasted to stone, would thus reflect the twentieth century Moderne design concepts of simplicity that were being discussed among artists in the art salons of Paris and other European capitals at that time.

Sir Harold Acton described the water parterres as "horizontal mirrors,"[76] as they reflected all planting, and through reflection brought the sky to the earth. The effect was to create a greater intensity of planting and the surreal illusion whereby paths seem to float in mid air. For the first time, water parterres were incorporated into the natural phenomena of the garden as poetry. The metaphorical garden was conceived as a sky garden, as fully bathed in sunlight as in moonlight, mirroring the clouds drifting by or the arcs of stars at night, its reflective picture framed by the deep evergreen borders of trimmed hedges.

> "The pools reflect such a feast of shimmering color that the eye is dazzled. It is a hall of horizontal mirrors terminating in a theatrical arcade of clipped cypresses. The liquid and the solid nowhere else in my recollection have been composed with such elegant refinement of taste on so human a scale. ...The whole conception of a garden to live with and in on intimate terms, responsive to loving care and constant culture, has been realized and expanded. It leaves an enduring impression of serenity, dignity and cheerful repose."[77]

The creation of water parterres that presented so many opportunities for mirrored reflections, certainly lent itself to the highest form of narcissism. Ghyka's daily visits to any one of the five pools in the nude, provided her gratification at every turn, but especially so at.the pool in the apsidal end. Here, she would narcissistically bathe in reflections of self, the ultimate centerpiece of the garden.

The original Ghyka design had an enclosed treatment for a dining table area amidst the water parterres. The edge of the second series of the water parterres contained thin Bernini-like spiral columns, on which clematis vines grew, forming a trellis. These, with the other new elements of the Ghyka design – posted rose standards planted along the perimeter edge, or bands of irises paralleling the hedges - added to the garden's musical rhythms. It was these Moderne innovations in design that defined the new, formal rules of landscape architectural composition and that began the second renaissance in garden design - a highly individualistic, and therefore as in the original Renaissance period, humanistic art form.

Exedra From the spiral columned dining area, the far southern pool edge was framed in raised seat walls for viewing performances in the new *exedra* terminus. Like so many other elements of the garden, it is interesting to speculate on the origin of the *exedra*. While its semi-circular plan, arch-penetrated exedra of clipped hedges existed in several Baroque theater gardens, none were of the proportions of the Ghyka creation. The Ghyka arches were exaggerated vertically; the to these proportions in order to complement the size and height of the western enclosing hedge, visually tying the two forms together and creating one enclosed space. It is through this unifying, yet asymmetrical space-defining relationship that the *exedra* is made Moderne and non-derivative of its Baroque antecedents. The creation of *exedra* as a new element in the garden correlated exactly with the development of another *exedra* at Villa La Pietra. Arthur Acton, friend and noted art dealer, had bought Villa La Pietra in 1903 and began its rehabilitation[78] just a few years after Princess Ghyka bought Villa Gamberaia. Princess Ghyka's sister, Queen Natalie, was in residence at La Pietra in one of the outlying *villinos* during this period, and as noted by Sir Harold Acton, Arthur's son,[79] Arthur and Ghyka had many opportunities to exchange ideas on garden design. Gamberaia's and La Pietra's *exedras* are both elliptical in shape and are the termini to their parterre garden's central axis. A symbiotic and collaborative relationship is apparent in this simultaneous garden development found at both villa gardens.

The 1904-05 Ghyka water parterre garden was a boldly fresh garden formed by hedges, furnished with flowering plants and rhythmically punctuated with oleander shrubs at the corners, spiral columns at the dinning space an posted roses throughout.

"One of the finest villas in Italy, Water garden designed by Princess Ghyka 1902.[80]

Richard K. Webel, Landscape Architect

"(Ghyka and Blood) cultivated their garden as Voltaire proposes in Candide, without heeding the outer world."[81]

Sir Harold Acton

When Florentines depicted a garden in frescoes it was as a Garden of Love - "the nature of love was presented in art by nature itself. Conceived as a pleasant bower sheltering people in love,"[82] it was the perfect place for the time spent at their villas, *villegiatura* or leisure time. *Villeggiatura,* coming from the combined root, *villa* and *leggare,* to read, meant all the things that were non-work that could be done in the gardens. Indeed, it covered, in addition to reading and writing, story telling, conversation, meditation, and lovemaking.[83]

At the Gamberaia, Princess Ghyka dazzled several social circles. Called a ravishing beauty by many, she had Slavic features, a strong pointed nose, high arched eyebrows, and chiseled facial features. She was tall, thin, and carried herself erect. From 1896 to around 1914, Ghyka hosted parties at Gambaraia that were the rage of society. At the turn of the century, the elaborate soirees and dress balls for international nobility were known as "the cult of the Gamberaia"[84] and were acclaimed worldwide. The villa's salons were nondescript spaces, adequate but not the showpieces of the Gambaraia. It was the Princess's beauty rather than architecture, her jewels and wardrobe for which the soirees were noted.[85] From several accounts, we learn that a broad roster of nobility and aristocrats attended these functions between 1896 and 1902: Countess Marie-Stani Cambaceres Stanislas de Montebello,[86] Prince of Turin and the Princess of Taxis, the self-effacing" Countess Serristori, and Lady Sasoon of Umbria.[87]

Carlo Placci, the writer and notorious Florentine-Parisian playboy, attended almost all of these social functions and was probably their real host.[88] As the Princess was on a fixed stipend, Placci's offer to sponsor many of the Gamberaia's soirees was mutually beneficial. Placci could hardly have found a more beautiful setting for his social events, and in exchange for the favor, the Princess enjoyed entree into the world of the social elite. Placci would spice up the party by including as guests a few of the expatriate *intelligenia* and *artisti*. Bernard Berenson, the noted American art historian, first met the Princess on one such occasion.[89] Commenting on their busy social schedule in the summer of 1896, Mary, his wife, noted that: "Still, time was found for moonlight walks, for rounds of visits to Princess Ghyka at the Villa Gamberaia."[90]

The aristocratic parties were elegant affairs, utilizing the garden's grotto, the cypress allee and the garden's showpiece, the water parterre garden. A crowd of bejeweled ladies in long colorful gowns, accompanied by gentlemen in long coats and brightly colored cravats, arrived either by horse drawn carriages or by the new motor coach. The latter, being so noisy, caused much commotion and had to be kept away from the horse drawn carriages. Guests were delivered to the "flying arches," where they were greeted and offered a garden version of the *passagata,* or stroll. A typical end-of-the-day Italian "meet-and-greet," the *passagata* would normally take place on one of the city's main urban streets. At the Gamberaia, the *passagata* took place along the cypress allee, animating this "green street." The tour would include a stop in the grotto where an elegant food and beverage table offered refreshments and where musical concerts were often held, the sounds reverberating off the *rocaille* walls. The tour would continue to the water parterre garden. Musicians, on occasion, would fill the arches of the *exedra* at the far end, the sounds of their playing drifting over the flower-lined water parterres. Finally, guests would inevitably gather on the wrap-around terrace for animated conversation while watching the sun set in the distance. After, in the mauve glow of the last light of day, all would retreat through the western front door to the *sala* for dinner and dancing. The garden, the featured space of the social gathering, was therefore, an important element in establishing the social status of its owner, and was known for its perfection in maintenance and its aesthetic composition. Princess Ghyka's renown was due in large part to her outstanding garden.

Ghyka's two other prominent social circles were those of artists and lesbians. As an artist of dubious skill and commitment, Ghyka was a part of the Fiesole hillside artistic community. We know little specifically of her paintings or sculptures. Except for a baptism font, her sculptures are reported to all have been stolen. A few paintings may exist in a Ghyka archive thought to be somewhere in Paris, or at another in England. (Both are in the control of distant relatives.) Her known works include a pencil sketch profile portrait of her sister, Queen Natalie, executed in the late 1890s, and a full-body sitting portrait of the Queen in her full royal dress. This latter work was executed in monochromatic hues in the style of the French artist Puvis de Chavanne. Other art works are reported to have been executed in-situ at the summer resort of Bidart. In 1902,

Queen Natalie converted to Catholicism. A large public ceremony marked the occasion, for which Queen Natalie commissioned her sister to design a new baptismal font for a side-chapel[91] within the town's *eglise*, Notre Dame.[92]

Also in Bidart, Ghyka painted a religious mural at the chapel of the Center Helio-Marin.[93] Painted at the end of World War I, the mural was behind the main alter and was reported to be light pastels or *grisaille.* Stylistically, it resembled the work of the French Modernist, Puvis de Chavanne under whom Ghyka had studied while in Paris. The chapel was remodeled after the Second World War, at which time the entry was redirected to the east side and the interiors were redone with mosaics and stain glass works by a contemporary artist-in-residence.

That Ghyka's artistic effort was in the Puvis vein is not so improbable. While she was an art student in Paris, Puvis was highly influential in establishing Modernist principles in art.[94] Many of his commissions were murals, the most famous of which was the diorama that filled the walls of the Grand Amphitheater of the Sorbonne in Paris, 1888.[95] Undoubtedly well known by all students, and certainly to the young student artist, Jeanne Keshko, it could not have escaped her critical eye. That her style of painting, her dress, her stated philosophy all mirrored this great artist of her day can not go without notice.

Pierre Puvis de Chavanne was "the" painter of his day in Paris and was considered a Modernist at that time. His work would better fit our terminology of "humanist" since it reverted stylistically to classic Greco - Roman artistic principles. His work was figurative and he painted and advocated the reduction of human form to classical simplicity. Employing the human figure in simple naked shapes - no muscle, fat, or anatomical detail - he dressed both his male and female figures in simple dress-like robes. Scant attention was paid to material folds or ornamentation of any kind. He placed these figures in a languid posture, as if in deep thought, at peace, usually staring at a distant, undefined point. The simplicity of the nude was meant as transcendence to the material state and was intended to represent universal beauty.

Puvis's paintings almost always contained landscape passages. These depicted generalized meadowlands surrounded by shading trees. The landscapes were always soft, elegiac, and never threatening. All were Eden-like Arcadian paradises, where every detail was perfect. It was in this setting that he placed his figures and wove a rich allegorical story. But Puvis's landscapes included hedges and other elements of the hand of man. In this way paradise was of human creation and as such reflected the human condition In his landscape painting, *Champs et Bois* (1879), the landscape was both soft and dreamy, but its simple areas of color and rhythmic linear patterns spoke to the emerging Moderne movement in painting, even as they reflected a renewed interest in both the Greco-Roman and Renaissance.

Puvis had several important philosophies that were innovative in the 1880s. He was deeply religious and influenced by the teachings of Saint Thomas Acquainus. As a Thomist, he advocated the return to Aristotlean logic and thought. His painting of the scourged and beaten Christ (1859), shown from the waist up, is a figure of immense dignity. It is remarkable for its title; *Ecce Homo, (Here is Man)*, reflecting Christ the human, and not the divine.

The second philosophical distinction to Puvis de Chavanne's later works was a deep interest in human desire and psyche. His works depicted dreams and fantasies in Elysian Fields and idealized Arcadian settings. In this vein, he painted *Jeunes Filles au Bord la Mer*, 1879, a work that depicted three young women at water's edge. One figure, facing forward, stares peacefully down at the ground. A second, dressed in robes, is standing with her back to the viewer, apparently staring off at the far horizon, where, in the painting's landscape, the ocean meets the sky. The third figure is seen in profile, kneeling and half clothed. This figure, too, stares tranquilly off the painting in yet a different direction. All three, in their pensive state, attempt to unleash the viewer's sub-conscious feelings and desires. On seeing the painting, the art historian, Bernard Berenson, sat consumed for more than a half hour, musing on Puvis's uncanny ability to paint sea, humans and the inner human psyche, "as no one else had ever seen it before. Puvis de Charvannes seemed as brilliant as a comet."[96] This painting was termed "the painting of the day." Another aspect of Puvis's psychological themes was narcissism. It played a role in a number of his works, including one of his most famous paintings, *Narcissus's Dreams*. In this work, the figures are languid, as if in a peaceful, contemplative state, not unlike the desired lifestyle of the Princess at Gamberaia. The image of a kneeling figure at water's edge is a well noted icon of narcissium, and the mirror quality of the still water pools in the garden is perhaps more than subliminal. As an admirer of all things Puvis, perhaps Ghyka did not consider narcissism a fault, but instead, a virtue.

Settignano was considered to be a *colonie di artisti* at the time and the circle of artists were regulars at soirees held at the Gamberaia. Mary and Bernard Berenson became close and "most regular" friends with Miss Blood and, along with Carlo Placci, would hold many conversations on art and the philosophy of aesthetics at dinners at their villa, I Tatti, where, with regard for intellectual sustenance, the colony was referred to as "those we count on every day."[97] Miss Blood liked Mary only, and

hidden lives / secret gardens

not Bernard, although Bernard liked her and would have liked their friendship to have been closer.[98] The Princess was mainly accepted by the Berensons as Blood's companion and Ghyka was never known to take part in their intellectual exchange or to visit I Tatti. Occasionally, and with declining frequency, similar affairs were held at the Gamberaia. Berenson remarked after one, that "it is a great treat to hear the brilliant French woman talk in a language unrivaled - of politics and men."[99]

On these occasions, a different pattern of entertaining was employed in the Gamberaia's garden. For discussions on art and life, the water parterre garden was used. Food and drink were laid out on the table inside the space defined by the fluted, Bernini-like spiral columns. On occasions when guests would read poetry or excerpts from their novels, the garden's *exedra* stage came into play; or music would be performed in the grotto, with its brilliant acoustics. The grotto's *rocaille* walls and enclosed space would brighten the cultured operatic voice, the reed and keyboard instruments, especially the harpsichord. And the oval of the *nymphaeum* - was it not a stage-in-the-waiting for a dance or a tableau? These performances were typical to the art scene of the time and certainly were the delight of the Florence community. Carlo Placci was a celebrated monologist and is described by Bernard Berenson as spontaneously performing with Ghyka's friend, Serge Wolkonski,[100] an actor, "Did you ever see him act? He does it well. The other night, at Gamberaia, he and Placci acted some charades, and in one, the great Miss Paget (Vernon Lee) came in."[101]

Parterre garden scenes painted Cezanne-like by Florence Blood

It was well known in Paris and Florence that Jeanne Ghyka had a constant live-in companion and probable lover in Miss Florence Blood. Ghyka's companion was also reputed to be artistic. Living in Paris with Leo Stein, Gertrude Stein's homosexual brother, Blood gave painting lessons to a young Paul Cezanne. Later in Florence, Blood

55

painted several views of the water parterre garden at Gamberaia – all in the color style of Cezanne. She copied his works and was known as a reproductionist, specializing in faithful copies of the works of other artists-of-the-day, particularly the impressionist Paul Cezanne. Bernard Berenson called her a dilettante painter, her ability, "mediocre." As reproductions, however, her work was thought to be "astonishing. She copied very well."[102] "As the city of Florence was known for its remarkable reproductions (or fakes) of art, it is quite possible Miss Blood did these to provide personal support.

> "Li s'intrattensva Violet Paget, l'eccontrica scrittrice Inglese piu consciuta come Vernon Lee, che abitara al (villa) Palmerimo, i la vieccia lady Paget [la contessa Walburga Hoental, moglia d'al l'Amrascia Tore Englesse], che amava recarsi a passegiare nei giardina della Gamberaia."[103]
> Simonetta Angeli Festin

Miss Blood, as the equivalent of a dependable marriage partner, was a curious persona. She was a small dainty woman who along with Ghyka, wore long velvet dresses in the style of tunics. Blood was extremely fond of her magnificent blue-greenish angora cat. Miss Blood, counter to the impression she gave as a small figure, was aggressive, especially sexually so.[104] Miss Blood's personality may be best described by her name, an obvious pseudonym. Like so many of the lesbian artists living abroad,[105] Miss Blood changed her name, using a *nom de plume* to protect family identity back home. Her name was probably chosen for its generic and descriptive value. In order of their use; "Miss" connoted her preferred singleness; "Florence" the city she resided in; and, according to rumor, "Blood," her sado-masochistic behavior as a dominatrix.

Bernard Berenson told a story at one of his intellectual gatherings in 1912 of "a wonderful Balkan princess who lived in a beautiful old villa with a woman companion, and how she had gone to visit Janet Ross in deshabille."[106] Berenson's dinner guest, Miss Maud Cuttwell, the art historian, asked Berenson why a lady should take such pains to un-dress "for nobody." Berenson laughingly replied, "You are innocent. There are no men in her life but that doesn't mean that she undresses for nobody." When Cuttwell wondered how the Princess Ghyka could bear to live with Miss Blood, "such a commonplace person," Berenson laughed again and replied, "She isn't commonplace. Miss (Blood) is brutal and vulgar and wicked - but she isn't commonplace."

> "The aesthetic preoccupations of that liberated society on the Fiesole hillside inevitably fostered the worship of Eros in all degrees of intensity,

hidden lives / secret gardens

especially since it contained more unfulfilled women than men and British censors were far away."[107]

Ernest Samuels

The third social circle of the Gamberaia was the Florentine lesbian community. The Gamberaia with its lesbian couple in residence provided a discrete setting for like social gatherings. There was already a sizable lesbian community in Florence at the turn of the century that included many famous openly lesbian Brits in exile, including the novelist Radcliff Hall,[108] and others. Florence was known among gays as "the Pink Lily,"[109] a play on the city's epithet, "The City of the Lily." Nicky Marino, Bernard Berenson's secretary, records in her memoirs, her first observation of the Florentine lesbian community in 1914. "That far more interesting groups of foreigners existed in Florence and its surroundings I knew vaguely but had no access to them. Sometimes when the Fiesole tram stopped in San Gervasio, it was boarded by several manly looking women. One of them seemed to be the central figure. Her face in spite of its snout-like ugliness was fascinatingly witty and intelligent. Someone told me that her name was Violet Paget and that she wrote books as 'Vernon Lee'."[110]

Henry James, the noted English writer, who met Vernon Lee in Florence, described her as; "exceeding ugly, disputatious, contradictory and perverse." She was able to discuss "all things in any language, a superior talker with a mind."[111] Michael Fields[112] stated that Vernon Lee looked fifty, but was thirty-nine, and was a Sybil in tailor-made black dress. He said she was "very ugly, the face long...(marked with) ruthless features."[113] From other descriptions, she was strange looking, short sighted, a young woman in mannish clothes, had short boyish cropped hair, protruding teeth, gleaming eyes behind thick spectacles, and was a constant talker. "She talked like a steam engine" Bernard Berenson once noted.[114] Vernon Lee's life-long mate was the Sapphist, Kit Anstruther-Thomson. Berenson termed her "bovine."[115] They lived with Lee's mother, a grotesque deformed invalid; Lee's recluse father, a retired Polish-educated engineer who was aggressive, unpleasant, and sinister; and a mentally unstable brother who laid prostrate in perpetuity on the living room sofa with nervous disorders. Lee's villa, Il Palmerino, a *villa rustico* adjacent to Fiesole in Maiano, could be approached only through narrow, high-walled lanes that curved through olive orchards. Il Palmerino had become the chief meeting ground for intellectuals and aesthetes of Anglo-American society.[116] It was one of the most noted lesbian gathering places in Florence and one that Ghyka reportedly frequented. Conversely, Lee attended all Gamberaia functions.

A colorful community by the prevalent social standards of its time, stories abound about the lesbian circle. Ouide, the pseudonym of Marie-Louise de la Ramee, the Florentine writer of romances and children stories, was a fixture in the community, and hosted extravagant parties at her villa, Villa Farinola, where she placed a notice on the entrance door that morals, like umbrellas, were to be left in the hall. Ouide and Janet Ross fought outrageous battles for several years over the affections of a certain Marchese's[117] causing Mary Berenson to call them and their circle, ironically, the "Virgins of the Hills"[118]

Lesbian life in Florence at this time was partially known through the writings of travelers. Pensione Berticelli, located near the Ponte Vecchio, was known for its artistic crowd and was "lesbian friendly." The *pensione* was valued for its authentic Renaissance furniture and Grand Empire decoration. It was a perfect example of what Arron Betsky calls "queer space or queer architecture."[119] Its interiors were excessive in decor, its walls hung in gilded mirrors, and light levels were dark and moody. Its rooms were physically and symbolically closets. Baths were in the room and uniquely Italian. Only the toilet was in a separate room; the sink and shower, placed in a corner of the room, was walled off only by a self-drawn curtain. Single women traveling alone were often paired by the proprietress with other single women, a practice that was not adverse to its clientele.

The tea salon at the Piazzale Michelangelo was another place where lesbians would meet. Since identifying other lesbians was an essential need and a part of self affirmation, these centers held special importance. Cruising, an activity of gay males, was not possible for lesbians within the Italian culture. A single woman strolling would have been mistaken for a prostitute. Once known to each other, lesbian couples or groups could comfortably make the *passagata* along the newly constructed, Paris-like ring boulevard, especially between Porto San Gallo and Piazzale Donatello. Strolling, of course, was common along the Via Roma and the Calimala, the main shopping streets of their day, from Place Republica to the Straw Market, but one could not be openly affectionate as always there was the danger of being spotted by members of the foreign press and by paid informers whose work was to lurk, imagine rumors and report any societal "inversions." to those back home.[120] Rather than risk exposure, the expatriate lesbian community would retreat to the northern hillside of Florence, there to live openly and privately.

The need for a sense of self-identified community was noted in the studies on homosexuality done at the beginning of the twentieth century. While the case studies did have a detrimental effect on a true understanding of the subject, some very important discoveries emerged, among them the necessity of gay community life.

Finding and making contact in common gathering places was identified as a major need, not only to assure finding sexual partners, as exclusively thought before, but for affirmation of self identity - the sharing of one's common nature with others, and in return, confirming one's own self awareness. [121]

Lesbian couples felt comfortable at the Gamberaia with the Princess and Miss Blood. In 1910, Vita Sackville-West, then sixteen,[122] and her passionate lover Violet Trefusis, eighteen, made the Gamberaia their place of rendezvous when they planned their separate and discrete Italian travels.[123] Upon Violet's debut in society, she was presented on the arm of Marquis Orazio Pucci at a grand fete in his villa. That same evening, she was also feted in bed by "the Rubens lady," Rosamund Grosvenor, whose appearance Violet described as "pink and white and curvy."[124] Vita, with her gardening interests, had a perfect reason to be staying at the Gamberaia, but Violet's stay there could only be explained by her social interest in visiting Princess Ghyka, the reigning noble who ruled at the center of the expatriate lesbian community in Florence.

From Paris, the openly lesbian couple of Gertrude Stein and Alice Toklas visited Florence often, enjoying walks in the Fiesole hillside. They noted visiting Gamberaia, Princess Ghyka and Miss Blood on many occasions.

The lesbian community's parties were by nature selective and secluded. We would know nothing of their affairs except for a favorite dinner story by the raconteur Bernard Berenson, which, in turn, was told to him by an indiscreet Gamberaia attendee. It is made even more interesting when placed in its garden setting. A party of all ladies gathered at sunset in the south space of the wrap-around terrace, in front of the enclosed water parterre garden. As the sun sets at the Gamberaia, shadows from the house begin to envelop the south "flying arches." In the growing shadow, the villa's south façade is gradually enveloped in dusk, the shadow overtaking "the flying arches," one segment at a time, moving down its length until only the descending stairs at the end receives the last red rays of sunlight. Just at this point, Ghyka makes a dramatic entry from the second floor bedroom wearing only three rubies at essential positions on her body, walking the length of the arches, high above her friends. She then descends the spiral staircase into the garden to meet and greet her assembled guests.

Placci and Berenson were among the few Ghyka social contacts that were part of overlapping circles - the Fiesole aristocratic circle and the art circle.[125] Likewise, Vernon Lee and Janet Ross had overlapping contacts within her lesbian circle and her art circle. Except possibly for Mlle Di Montebello, there were no known crossover contacts between the nobles and the sisters of lesbos, as this would have breached the protocol of the day and exposed the Princess and the Serbian and Bulgarian crowns to international censors and probable scandal.

The privacy of the garden was a major concern for the Princess. Ghyka never responded to appeals to see her garden. The first few years, only Placci had access to the gardens and was allowed to show it off.[126] The Berensons were first shown the garden by Placci in March, 1896, and both were charmed. Later, after Ghyka's self-imposed seclusion, Berenson became the sole person permitted to respond affirmatively to the numerous requests he received to bring visitors to the Gamberaia,[127] and then, he could show the garden to guests only on Sunday afternoons.

Ghyka forbade any servants to open the blinds to the garden before ten in the morning and then they were to be shuttered by four in the afternoon of each day. Servants were not to go near the gardens except during the proscribed daytime hours.

Ghyka was known for her two exotic *maremmani*, white sheep dogs. They were part of her aesthetic, her self-identity as an artist. The two dogs are seen in many of the pictures taken at the time, including one with Berenson at the *belvedere*. So rare were these animals that the noted American architect, Stanford White, who visited the Gamberaia in 1905, asked Arthur Acton to arrange for a special mating so that he might ship a pup to his client, Mrs. Payne Whitney.[128] (It is quite possible that Ghyka raised these rare animals for additional financial support.) The Princess was a naturist and loved to walk the gardens in the nude and would not be disturbed during this activity. In the early morning, Ghyka would walk the "flying arches" dragging a white towel, her two white dogs trailing behind, and descend the spiral stair to swim in one of the four parterre pools. In the evening, again accompanied by her frisky white *maremmani*, she would walk the bowling green, end to end,[129] swimming in the pool of the nymphaeum at one end or standing nude at the *belvedere's* terrace with the entire Arno valley before her. The bowling green's lush grass was a space she loved for its verdant feel underfoot. She certainly spared no amount of water to keep it that way, even in the driest part of summer.

hidden lives / secret gardens

Berenson enjoying the gardens with the Princess's white sheep dogs

The garden possessed one element unique in any garden: The ability to be a part of the garden, yet suspended above it. The "flying arches" on the water parterre side allowed Gyhka to survey her creation on a daily basis, to leave the normal confines of a building and its limitation of windows and porches, and to view the garden in its entirety and in all its beauty. From above, laid out before her would be every pool, fountain, topiary, and plant, all to be studied in every detail. Cypresses, roses, water jets leapt up from the floor; the pools mirroring the sky receded, seemingly into infinity. Ghyka could stand above her creation and lavish adulation upon herself, for is not the creation but a reflection of the self? Obsessing over *ouevre* and self identity, Ghyka, with her garden below her very feet, was indeed, mistress and goddess-figure of all she surveyed.

Ghyka's water parterre garden was perhaps the first example of a designed garden "queer space." In its original form, the Ghyka composition contained the three main elements that Aaron Betsky defines as the architecture of same sex desire.[130] First, its "closet" or protected interior spatial definition. The Gamberaia garden is totally interior and not viewable from any of its external surrounds. Its high ramparts and enclosing hedges created the closet-like protection found in so many gay and lesbian establishments. Ghyka could have initially removed the defining western hedge, opening the garden to views of Florence and to fresh breezes, but instead she added further to its enclosure, completely walling-in the south garden area.

Second, the space is mirrored throughout, satisfying her all-consuming lesbian narcissism. The parterres and *exedra* end are pools of still water, reflecting the sky, as Harold Acton so poetically described, but also reflecting the viewer's image. Wherever Ghyka and her guests strolled in this enclosure, reflectivity of self abounded. Did not Psyche see her self and her inner-self peering into water?

The third aspect was the romance in the applied pastiche of historical objects. The garden itself was styled not after vegetable production or some other utilitarian program, nor was it an authentic historic reproduction, which would have been an easy genre. Ghyka, in fact, was in possession of the seventeenth century engraving illustrating its original form.Rather, she drew inspiration from all past periods, laying out unequal parterres with a mixture of architectural forms and reference elements (posted roses) that were never part of any classical period.[131] To this she added thin, free-standing Bernini spiral columns draped in trailing-roses, along with urns, and added other unrelated garden ornaments here and there. These all tended to make the water parterre a collection of objects with historical references but out of historical context, making the garden an object garden. The creation of the south garden's water parterres may have been that of Ghyka, the liberated woman, but the nature of the space, materials and design motifs was that of Ghyka, the gay liberated woman.

The Villa Gamberaia is undoubtedly one of the most elite, most beautiful and best-maintained Italian gardens. Since the turn of the twentieth century, writers and historians have visited and lavishly praised this garden. Since the first guide / garden books on Florence or on Italian gardens were published, the Villa has listed as "a must see." Although thought of as a fixed piece, reflective of its early history, the Villa Gamberaia has changed, not just once or twice in its five-hundred year history, but it has changed with each new owner at least six times, each change reflecting new needs and differing concepts of design and taste. It has been built, restored, remodeled and/or re-built anew.[132] In this century alone, the Gamberaia has undergone at least three major changes in site structure and concept, each further developing its Moderne composition. These interations have mostly been missed despite the abundant pictorial evidence of the new garden's Moderne era. Dozens of books have been written, each illustrating unconsciously the development of the Gamberaia from, the classical, Renaissance derivative and the Moderne – the period from Princess Ghyka forward.

These works still dwell mostly on documenting the chronological history of the classical periods, giving little attention to defining what constitutes the Moderne developments in the twentieth century Gamberaia, the new life philosophy of Princess Ghyka and Miss Blood definitely influenced or guided the garden's design.[133] It is thus the water parterre garden's historic development that reveals the dramatic change from an open expansive garden to a hidden garden for the owner's secret life.

The water parterre garden was the Princesses' love and required great effort to maintain in perfect condition. All elements of the gardens required constant fine-tuning, aesthetically and horticulturally. Gardens are perishable and have limited life expectancies. A Renaissance garden cannot outlive the four hundred plus years since its original creation, without both changes of ownership and without one or several re-plantings required by the varying life expectancies of each of its numerous plant species. Each re-planting would become an occasion for changes to the garden form. Add to this the natural inclination of new owners to incorporate new and personal needs, and more probably, new concepts of modern art and aesthetics. It is logical that many revisions would have naturally occurred since the Renaissance inception of the garden. If a superficial change were required at any one period, there is the likelihood that the pre-existing structural element would have been retained by the succeeding generation. Therefore, each successive garden was built upon the base of previousone. Today, the earlier classical gardens themselves have long vanished and only the structure of past iterations remain as hand-me-downs.[134]

For the water parterre garden of the Moderne period, four distinct and successive compositions emerge: 1) the Ghyka renaissance II object garden; 2) the Porcinai abstract classicism garden; 3) the Pinsent display garden and 4) the contemporary Marchi / Porcinai topiary gardens. The Pre-existing South Parterre Garden the Moderne water parterre garden was not built from a *tabula rasa*; it grew out of a pre-existing garden context. From comparisons of the *Giuseppe Zocchi 1774* engravings and the earlier *Cabreo (1718-1825)* the cadastre plan related to the transfer of a property, we can construct a composite of the pre-Ghyka remnant Renaissance Gamberaia. The house that we see today was located on the west side of a small knoll and was entered originally from the east,[135] through the space of what is essentially the grotto now. Flanking the entrance drive on both sides, the lemon garden and two *boschi* were on top of the knoll's retaining walls. The entrance was a direct line from the road to the front door and entry cortile. A broad terrace wrapped around the house like a donut, equal in width on all four sides, forming an urban terrace[136] At a later point, the long axis, lined with cypresses along its full length, was added in various stages, paralleling and in front of the main façade of the house. The full length was accomplished in stages. The first iteration had its first stage terminating on the south at the end of the bosque. Later the axis was expanded in a long cypress-lined *allee* emanating from a hill on the north, to a valley-overlook terrace on the south. A major fountain, over 10 meters high, centered the southern extension of the *allee*. Behind the *allee* - a new major compositional element - the house jutted out into the surrounding orchards with three sides of its former donut terrace fully exposed. The location of the water parterre garden was a full level down and was shown as agrarian fields. It should be noted here that from the south terminus of the *allee*, the terrace overlooks the upper Arno valley and not urban Florence. (The view of Florence, which was unbroken could only be had from the the wrap-around terrace of the villa.) The terrace, wrapping around the house on the north, west and south side, was open and utilitarian - forming arrival and staging areas for farm production. The terrace was built separately from the house as can be witnessed by its irregular shape, i.e., not paralleling the house geometry.

Plans, left and right, of the pre-Ghyka parterre garden showing the two part composition: embroidery parterres and an oval fountain with an island of rabbit hutches.

Sometime after 1744, the parterre garden area was raised to a height a half meter below the wrap around terrace and was planned as part of a new entry on the south, with a straight line continuation of the via del Loretino. We can still see this entrance's beautiful gates and entry drive.

The state of the garden at the time of Ghyka's purchase has been widely debated. From descriptions by several visitors before or at the time of purchase, the gardens were in pleasant-to-good conditions,[137] but the house, was in disrepair. The villa was often rented out to boarders, according to visitors during this period.[138] One account has Napoleon staying there for several months. Whether it was derelict or in a good state, a garden variously described to be either a vegetable garden, a rose garden, a fish pond or an apple orchard or all of the above were said to be in some state on the property.[139] A seventeenth century engraving, the Cabreo, found in the cellar below the terrace of the house, shows the form of the original parterre garden. A two-section composition, the first section closest to the house was a classical four-part *parterre de broderie* (parterre of embroidery)[140] typical of that century's French garden. The parterres were cited as filled with vegetables. The second part at the southern end was an oval pool utilized as a fish pond with a "*garenna*", a smaller center oval island containing a rabbit hutch, similar to that of the Villa Valsanbizio in the Veneto. The pool was surrounded by small trees of unknown type but believed to be fruit trees.

     The eastern edge has of the garden was changed during the 1744 to 1900 period. On the southern portion of the *allee*, the early photographs taken of the villa, 1901 and 1902, at the time of Edith Wharton's and Janet Ross's visits, and by Charles Latham in 1905, show well-established large topiary urns dividing the *allee* from the vegetable parterres and fish pond garden. These plant features pre-existed the Ghyka era by at least thirty to fifty years, as evidenced by their maturity. This, combined with the missing cypresses, allowed the parterre area to be open to the sky and to full sun, making the area perfect for vegetable production, which both visitors cited as a possible use for the space. Such a hedge treatment would block out the western storm winds, creating a micro-climate that would extend the production season.

     As was typical to all gardens of this period, walks were constructed of *terra battuta*, a layer of crushed stone or gravel tamped with a mixture of sand/clay and lime. The cedar-lined *allee* would have been treated in gravel paving as was the custom in all such Renaissance-period gardens. It addition to its occasional use for jousting, it was probably used daily as a countrified urban street for evening *passeggiate* or strolls. Similarly, the wrap-around terraces of the house would also have been paved in *terra battuta*, i.e., as at Villa Aldobrandini, Frascatti and other free-standing houses. The Gamberaia *allee*, wrap-around terrace and parts of the parterre garden were seen as totally carpeted in grass when Ghyka moved in.[141] Grass in the Renaissance was difficult to establish under the scorching Tuscan summer sun. Since equipment and techniques to maintain grass were non-existent until the late eighteenth century, its maintenance problems compounded its expansive use. The use of water, a precious commodity, was limited to small displays and agriculture uses. Maintenance of grass areas was of a lower priority to drinking, bathing and foodstuffs. The passion for grass

R. Terry Schnadelbach

came to the Italian garden with the arrival of the English during the early nineteenth century. At that time, the Brownings, Lord Byron, Percy Shelly and many others flocked to Florence and its idyllic countryside.[142] In it, they found an artistic paradise where they could enjoy a cultured and unrestrained libertine life. Here, in the Romantic period, numerous Renaissance villas were Anglicized; any semblance of classical structure was eradicated in favor of the informal, English pastoral scenes. With the English taste for grass came the equipment to maintain grass areas. It was in this period, probably, that the Gamberaia's cedar-lined allee and parterre garden were planted in grass. Gabrielle D'Annunzio in letters to Princess Ghyka prior to her buying the villa, visited the Gamberaia and records its green appearance.[143] And the allee's name changed to the very un-Italian, Bowling Green. The creators of the Moderne garden accepted these major paradigm shifts without even a reflection on their paradise lost.

The Ghyka renaissance II Object Garden   Many historians have said that Princess Ghyka was the author of the Modern garden.[144] Since the Villa Gamberaia is surely one of the most photographed gardens in the world, careful examination of dates, records and photographs confirms Princess Giovanna Ghyka as the initial creator of the garden. The first known photographs taken in 1904, by Latham,[145] show the garden under construction. As this pre-dates any known hired assistance, the work shown must be attributed solely to the design of Princess Ghyka. In her youth, the Princess had studied art in Paris[146] and quite possibly had studied with Arthur Acton of the Villa La Pietra,[147] a point discussed later. Ghyka could have possessed the innate talent and artistic training to have designed the water parterre garden. The 1904 photograph shows the two parterres nearest the villa as completed and the remaining two southern parterres, along with the exedra end, a *teatro di verdura*, just under construction. The Ghyka design was accomplished by cutting the old fish pond in half and extending the parterre pattern of the old vegetable area into the area of the half-removed pond. This clearly explains the oddity of the unbalanced lengths of the parterres; the southern parterres being a third larger than the two northern ones.

There existed a sub-area within the Ghyka parterre garden for a dining table and eating area. The dining area occurs by the sudden widening of the central walk to accommodate a dining table which begins just where the end of the old parterre garden ended and the extended area began. To provide a sense of enclosure and perhaps some limited late afternoon shade, thin Bernini-like spiral columns were placed at the edge of the water parterres.

*Porcanai' refined garden eliminating the columned
dining space and simplified plantings*

In 1910 Cecil Pincent revised the garden to introduce a medium height denser planting seen here circa 1914

The post war Marchi topiary garden in 1965

hidden lives / secret gardens

The newly constructed southern edge to the south parterres was raised to form a seat walls for viewing performances in the new exedra.[148] It is the only architectural edge to any segment of the parterres. In the 1904 photograph, the remains of the old fish pond is clearly visible and empty, signaling its reconstruction. One can understand Ghyka's logic: the parterre garden must have been stifling during the summer days with full solar radiation and no breeze. Water, with its evaporation, had a cooling effect, both physically and psychologically. Any other climatic solution would have required the tearing out of the developed western hedges and the reestablishment of the tall cypress *allee* to the east, not a quick and easily achieved option.

Added to this composition were the numerous large flower pots. One sees the garden had a rhythmic feel, similar to the gardens of the classical Renaissance period. The rhythmic punctuation throughout the remaining water parterre garden that typically would have been provided by statuary, urns, and balustrades, was now carried out in the new renaissance II garden by rose standards planted in the borders of the parterre beds. Also, along its perimeter edge of the parterres, bands of irises paralleled the hedges and were to be seen across the pools where the evergreen hedge provided the dark-toned backdrop to the flowers typical to the English gardens of the earlier Arts and Crafts Period. Such floral design, i.e., the combined hedge and border of flowers, was not common to gardens of the Renaissance periods. It is a new device contributing to a language of "green architecture."

The effect of the Ghyka water parterres was atypical to the Renaissance period. Then, such water basins, which Sir Harold Acton termed "horizontal mirrors,"[149] would have begun at the path edge and would have filled the entire parterre area, such as those at Villa Lante, Villa d'Este or the Pratolino island within the Boboli gardens. Their edges would have been defined by architectonic elements - balustrades, sculpture, urns or clay pots. The introduction of plantings at the Villa Gamberaia, both hedge and a related flowering shrub border as defining the water areas, was an ingenious and original idea. It sets Villa Gamberaia apart from all other classical Italian gardens.

Simple large scale manicured and shaped vegetation or "green architecture" was yet another development of the renaissance II elements. It is interesting to speculate on the origins of the *exedra* as a new element in the garden. It has no precedent in any previous Gamberaia gardens.[150] In both the 1904 Latham and 1905 Triggs photographs, the newly established plants forming the exedra are splayed out at the top on iron rod armatures to begin the arched apsinal end to the garden. This garden feature correlates exactly with the beginning of the *exedra* end of the Acton gardens at Villa La Pietra.[151] It is interesting to note that Arthur Acton bought Villa La Pietra around the same time as

Princess Ghyka bought Villa Gamberaia and that Princess Ghyka's sister, Queen Natalia of Serbia, was in residence at one of Villa Pietra's outlying *villini* at this time. Conversations with Sir Harold Acton, Arthur's son and heir, reveal that his father, on several earlier occasions, discussed the possibility of buying a villa in Florence and, in that eventuality, the garden design he envisioned.[152] It is quite possible, then, that either Princess Ghyka or Queen Natalia told Acton of the Villa La Pietra's availability. Arthur, after acquiring La Pietra, began collecting sculptures and garden fragments to place within his garden. Two notable examples were the water balustrade from the Boboli garden, which was later copied, and the copies re-installed in the Boboli, and the free-standing stone peristyle which formed the *exedra* end at La Pietra.[153] Harold Acton cites the close collaborative nature of the Arthur Acton/Ghyka friendship.[154] Both Gamberaia and La Pietra have *teatro di verdura, exedra* forms that are elliptical in shape and act as termini to their gardens' main axes. Who had the originating idea is not important. The collaborative nature of the relationship and the simultaneous garden developments of these and other Florentine garden redevelopments is the important point to note. Ghyka, with topiary green architecture created a new distinct space unifying the whole composition. In this new space, an outline low concrete step created the impression of a sunken garden although the area drop is no more than 20 centimeters. Three lines of the miniature box at stepped heights were planted along the edge of the parterre garden and at the base of the *exedra* and are fist described in the notebooks of D'Annunzio in 1898.[155]

There was probably collaboration between Jeanne Ghyka and others, including other garden owners, designers and visiting enthusiasts. In photographs, we see Bernard Berenson visiting the Gamberaia gardens as construction was just underway. Berenson, Acton and Ghyka formed a cell of garden aesthetes, a Second Renaissance Circle, that later grew into an English and American circle of friends who bought outlying Florentine villas, remodeled gardens in an idealized renaissance II garden style and entertained in the gardens. The exchange of ideas was their *raison d'etre* and to this end their gardens were open to each other and visitors from around the world. Berenson was more than just a welcomed friend; he alone had the keys to the garden and showed it to inquiring visitors.

The 1898-1905 Ghyka garden was a boldly fresh, young water garden formed by hedges and flowering plants and rhythmically punctuated with oleander shrubs at the corners, spiral columns at the dining space and posted roses throughout. Its entire development was achieved though the skillful manipulation of plantings, its architecture was now "green architecture," the anthem of the renaissance II garden. This garden in its finished state is well illustrated in photographs in the Indigo Triggs book[156] taken around 1905-06. The garden contains one new element that is not evident in the earlier Latham photographs; jets of water in each of the four parterre beds were added to aid in the defining of the central space. This space was the crossing of the axes and contained a central, raised fountain as focal interest. These aided in the climatic cooling and animated the garden with sound, but when active, destroyed the sky mirror pools so loved by Acton.

The Porcinai Abstract Classicism Garden   In 1905, Martino Porcinai, a well-known local horticulturist, was hired to be the *capo giardinere* or head gardener.[157] He immediately made changes to the garden, emphasizing the plantings and simplifying the design. He became friends with Villa La Pietra's landscape architect, Diego Suarez,[158] who created most of the gardens at La Pietra without flowers or any seasonal display. The term landscape architect is used to describe Diago Suarez professionally, for he was formally educated in architecture but worked exclusively in gardens. Space and unity were his prime concern. The main element of the garden in its second rebirth by Acton and Suarez was "green architecture." Although Porcinai's background was horticultural, he must have been influenced by discussions with Suarez, for unity also became Porcinai's interest at Gamberaia. The first element eliminated by Porcinai was the Bernini-like fluted columns around the dining area. He continued the parterre plantings in their place and made them denser. He mixed annuals with the irises, in part to soften the hard stone edges (non-green architecture) of the pools. These became strong seasonal bands paralleling the herbaceous borders.

In 1908-09 photographs,[159] the *exedra* hedges were now well formed. The effect, coupled with the removal of the dining area columns, was to treat the whole south terrace garden as one complete space from the villa facade to the *exedra* end. It would be a space defined on the west by the simplicity of the straight high hedge; on the south by the *exedra* hedge with its arched gallery, of which only one arch at a time permitted a view of the panorama; and on the west, by large rounded laurel knobs, cited as large "urns" that gave enclosure while allowing a spatial flow into the adjacent *allee*. If this space contained any sub-spaces or features, it would be only the center fountain area, the Berensons' Villa I Tatti.

Porcinai's main contribution was the addition of a topiary rug between the semi-circular pool of the *exedra* and the last two pools of the water parterres. This low form of boxwoods has small topiary knobs at its corners, continuing the rhythms of the parterre's hedge borders. For once the entire garden was now structured in precise green architectural elements with little stonework. In photographs from this period, a person believed to be Martino Porcinai is pictured watering his new plantings. This rendition of

R. Terry Schnadelbach

the Moderne garden demonstrates the subtle adjustments that were made to define the space and unify the whole composition.

The Pinsent Display Garden: A few years later, photographs[160] show a dramatic change in the water parterre garden. The garden was planted with young flowering trees at the *exedra* forespace; additional shrub oleanders, in pots were added to define the central fountain area and renaissance-like garden architectonic elements lined the pool. The flowerbeds and urns were filled with seasonal blooms. The garden, pictured at the height of the spring season, takes on the character of a display garden. It appeared knobby and dense, lush and colorful. No longer a topiary rug, the center fountain area became a space within the garden, the viewing area in front of the *exedra* end. The garden was best perceived now from the air and the second floor balcony window of the house. This fenestration, the one connected to the free-standing arched wall with its secret staircase, became *the* place for seeing the composition in its entirety. Pedestrian views along the walks were semi-enclosed. A sketch drawing for the Villa,[161] by Cecil Ross Pinsent (1884-1963)[162] probably was the basis for these changes. It is done in a very similar pallet Pinsent used at Pinsent was influenced by his partner Geoffrey Scott (1883-1929), who was writing what many architectural historians have called the definitive thesis on architectural thought of the day.[163] And, too, there is a photograph where Cecil Pinsent is caught studying or sketching in the Gamberaia gardens.[164]

These changes could also have been aided and influenced by several other persons. Bernard Berenson's Villa I Tatti was simultaneously under construction and touted its renaissance inspiration, but in reality his garden, too, was a renaissance II creation, the third such sequential new garden employing these "green architecture" concepts and classical form. Any of the *anglo-becceri* (English boors), the circle of foreign aesthetes, could have influenced the changes. Among these were Bernard Berenson (Villa I Tatti), Janet Ross (Poggio Gherardo), Violet Paget / Vernon Lee (Villa il Palmerino, Maiano), Charles Strong (Villa Le Balze) and later, Sir Harold Acton (Villa La Pietra, 1904-1994). Dining in their gardens and attending their parties were numerous international landscape architects and designers who visited all three new renaissance II villas: Villas Gamberaia, I Tatti, and La Pietra. Among these were noted landscape architects Susan and Geoffrey Jellicoe, Gertrude Jekyll, Henry Vincent Hubbard; Rome Prize winning landscape architects from the American Academy in Rome, Charles Lawson, Ralph Griswold, Richard Webel, Norman T. Newton, and Ferruccio Vitale; garden historians such as Edith Wharton,[165] Peter Coates; and garden luminaries, Violet Trefusis and Vita Sackville-West (Sissinghurst), Lady Astor Cliveden, Lawrence Johnston (Hidcote). Any and all, including Bernard Berenson,[166] could have contributed to the refinement of the Ghyka plan. It was truly a time of a second renaissance in Florentine landscape architecture.

The water parterre garden remained essentially the same throughout the remaining ownership of Princess Ghyka. Among the few changes were further refinements or corrections to technical problems. For example, the urns along the seating wall at the south end of the parterre garden were removed in 1914-15, perhaps the one change that can be attributed to the period when Luigi Messeri was head gardener.[167] His departure in 1915 as head gardener coincided with the beginnings of the Great War. After the war, head gardeners were not hired and the gardens remained as before, except for the seasonal planting throughout the garden which returned primarily to irises.

Sometime during the war, Princess Ghyka is reported to have lost her beauty and to have become a recluse. She dressed in black, covering herself from head to toe. She was seldom seen in public and came out of the Villa building to walk the gardens only when it was cleared of all servants and when all house shutters were tightly closed.[168] This changed social life and a lack of interest in entertaining in the garden was the probable reason that a new head gardener was not hired after the war, and that we see in photographs from this period no changes to the water parterre garden.

In 1919, the villa and its gardens were accurately measured by the laureate of the Rome Prize in Landscape Architecture at the American Academy in Rome, Edward G. Lawson.[169] Lawson's drawings included a beautiful Beaux-Arts style watercolor rendered plan, sections through the villa and the gardens, and a planting plan with complete listing of all plants in the garden. It also included some interesting notations of horticultural practices.[170]

In 1923, the Jellicoes[171] "sketched" the plan of the villa. This was a beautiful sepia tone, water color plan and section of the garden accompanied by an ink line drawing from a "birds-eye" perspective. The work was not detailed in its rendering of the garden's elements and contained sparse descriptive writings. Together the two works, the Lawson and Jellicoe drawings, done about the same period, give a clear picture of the Pinsent Display Garden period.

Throughout the successive developments of the garden, the role of Miss Florence Blood in the design of the garden, is not clear. Harold Acton, who was very young at the time, stated that Miss Blood was also a designer. She is said to have advocated the planting of parasol pines. "You can never get enough of them," she is quoted. At that time, the garden contained only one pine tree - at the overlook terrace - and photographs show that this is where dining and outdoor sitting occurred. Miss Blood is cited in Leon Zach's guide as infirmed in 1921.[172] Her role was most probably advisory at best.

With the death of her long time companion Florence Blood in 1924, Princess Ghyka sold the Villa,[173] bringing an end to the Ghyka line of the Modernist garden. The Gamberaia was sold to the Baron Enrico von Ketteler and the Baroness Maud Ledyard Cass von Ketteler. Both were less flamboyant and were not members of the English / American Art community. Both lived quiet lives at the Villa and maintained the Ghyka era garden in all respects except one change.

It was Mrs. von Ketteler, who was responsible for that element of change to the Gamberaia. In the von Ketteler garden, the wrap around terrace was made to be an introductory landscape space, a part of the garden, a significant alteration to the sequence of approach to the water parterre gardens. The terrace's paved portion (north eastern corner roof to the storage rooms below) as seen in the Triggs series of photographs, was excavated and planted in grass making continuous the area, from the entrance drive around to the water parterre garden. Now it was a unified lawn terrace. The irregular geometry of this terrace was hardly noticeable. The von Kettelers then planted a new pine in the 1930s that has the exact same spatial relationship to the viewer who arrives on the terrace and turns right looking over the distant valley - the pine on the right framing the vista to the town, Settignano - as does the pine at the end of the Bowling Green's belvedere - again to the right, framing the vista of the overlook terrace out to the distant Arno valley. These two pines are diagonally opposite and lead the visitor through his initial impression of the garden.

The Marchi / Porcinai Topiary Garden: During the Second World War, German troops destroyed much of the gardens.[174] The water parterres were driven on by tanks and heavily damaged by bombs from the liberating armies. Luckily the main elements of the garden survived - the exedra and western perimeter hedges. In 1957, Marcello Marchi[175] rebuilt the water garden along the plan of Princess Ghyka, utilizing the Lawson drawings. But Marchi made major changes and it is his garden that we know today.

The rebuilt garden follows the Ghyka plan to a large extent, but Marchi changed the plantings of the parterre area. Throughout the garden he planted evergreen hedges to line the walks and border the pools. The usual pool edges now are wide, defined solely by hedges. Gone are the oleanders and flowering trees of Pinsent, or the irises of Princess Ghyka. Gone are the posted roses that gave the garden rhythm. Now the rhythm is achieved by geometric topiary forms emerging from the broad hedge line - domes, cones, and vertical cylinders. They mark the cross axes which form entries to each parterre area. Without the flowering trees, the scale and intimacy is achieved with large-scale topiary such as the huge globe at the terminus of the western path. All are evergreen; all Mannerist in scale, and all elements of the garden are now "green architecture." Now the seasons come and go and the garden remains a constant. The water parterre garden is now the ultimate expression of Renaissance unity.

Dr. Marchi did not create the new version of Villa Gamberaia alone. He was assisted by Pietro Porcinai[176] the son of the first *capo giardiniere*. In 1955, before the reconstruction of the gardens began, Pietro Porcinai drew up a planting plan. Porcinai the Younger, then, is the creative force for the final idealization of the garden in its evergreen form. How much else he contributed and if anyone else took part in advising Marcello Marchi, is still unknown. Cecil Pinsent was still alive at that time and had just finished the restoration of his earlier work at the war-damaged Villa Medici in Fiesole for Lady Iris Origo.[177] Certainly, the geometric handling of the topiary is similar to his other works, such as those at Villa Capponi.[178] Further research is needed to establish authorship and to define the intent of the new composition.

In conclusion, four periods of significant garden changes to the parterre garden that were reflective of the philosophy and taste of the modern time have been outlined. To the historian, such distinctions from one period to another must seem trivial, for indeed the garden is as originally laid out by Princess Ghyka. It is still her armature that the three later modeled variations have been laid over. To the writer of garden development, the garden remains as Sir Harold Acton describes it; the mirror pools still reflect the sky. But to an art critic and landscape architect, each garden permutation was a new composition, a new fresh clay piece modeled on its previous armature, embodying elements of earlier designs, yet also transforming them.

The Villa Gamberaia thus led to the banding together of the landscape architects / architects who worked on the three new Florentine gardens, Villas Gamberaia, La Pietra and I Tatti. Guided by the artistic direction of Geoffrey Scott, Cecil Pinsent, Diego Saurez, Martino and Pietro Porcaini during the period from 1910 to 1935, the Angliofied villa gardens were removed, reversing the trend toward the English picturesque landscape style. From the ruins of the English garden in Italy, there came a rebirth of humanistic philosophies of artistic composition where point, line, plane, mass, solid, void, color and texture - the classical elements - were the dominating aesthetic. It was a rebirth, or the "renaissance II."[179] These gardens did not copy the past; instead, through their abstraction and simplification of forms, they brought the beginnings of the Moderne style to landscape architecture design. In this modern version, they simplified all classical lines, minimized sculpture and stone and masonary architectural elements and emphasized plantings, especially unifying evergreens as architectural forms and elements. They developed a "green architecture" to define space and articulate its subdivisions. Green hedges, green topiary shapes and the ubiquitous green lawn as planes were substituted for balustrades, walls, urns, clay pots, *rocaille* and *terra battuata*. These new breed landscape architects used the word "restore," but their product was new - a Moderne intervention reflecting the modern taste which was occurring simultaneously in the other arts. Villa Gamberaia was one of the first of these Florentine "renaissance II" gardens.

The Gambaraia has been measured several times, but only in modern history. The first plan was recorded in 1906 by the English landscape architect, Indigo Triggs, and showed the new Ghyka water garden along with its classical armature.[180] There were, however, many inaccuracies in the drawing. It wasn't until 1919 that the villa and its gardens were accurately measured by Edward G. Lawson, the laureate of the Rome Prize in Landscape Architecture who was then in residence at the American Academy in Rome.[181] Lawson's drawings recorded the entire villa and recorded the garden at its peak of refinement and elegance.

> "For the student of Italian villas in general, the Villa Gamberaia offers several advantaged characteristics, not only because it expresses the perfection obtained by the Renaissance architects, but also because at the present day it practically retains its original design, both in the sub-division of parts and in the plantings. The original design and beauty of a villa can be completely changed or spoiled by the substitution of exotics or other plantings not intended by the original designers.....but in the case of the Villa Gamberaia, it is known from an old original print that the main planting exist essentially the same as when it was first designed. The formal garden, originally a parterre garden, is practically the only part of the villa that has undergone any radical change in design.
>
> "In the accompanying plan of the villa, there is given a complete list of the planting, and special attention is called to the small variety of different kinds of trees and shrubs employed. This conservative use of plant material is one of the chief elements of its beauty, and is a point which the landscape architect of today may well bear in mind."[182]
>
> Edward G. Lawson

Not all who saw the garden gave it positive reviews. The noted garden critic Edith Wharton, in 1902 thought the water parterres were "unrelated in style to its surroundings .. completely out of harmony with the rest of the villa. It was unrelated in style to any other part of the garden." Miss Blood rose to the garden's defense, charging Mrs. Wharton with the dubious fault of being "in-critical."[183] Wharton never was permitted to visit the garden again.

The renovations of Princess Giovanna Ghyka were precedent setting and began a new movement in the design of landscapes that heralded the Moderne movement of the early twentieth century. In her search to renewing Renaissance principles of design, Ghyka was joined in spirit by the art connoisseurs Bernard Berenson and Arthur Acton, who also sought to rejuvenate these concepts and joined with Ghyka to live the life of the aesthete, a life as art. Together with their life partners, their landscape architects, *capo giardineri,* and a coterie of friends - some in-residence in the Florentine environment and some habitual visitors – they developed the new mantra and life style. The landscape architects, Cecil Pinsent, Geoffrey Scott, Diego Suarez and Pietro Porcinai contributed greatly to the development of the design philosophy and pallette of this new landscape expression. Other English and American landscape architects conducted pilgrimages to Gamberaia to measure, sketch and study the villa's gardens. From the Gamberaia came an unwritten philosophy of garden aesthetics that was on a parity to that found in architecture and that became its own prevailing school of landscape architectural design.

Villa Gamberaia was used as a hospital from 1915 to 1917 because of World War I. Being expatriates, Ghyka and Blood were notified in 1917 that for their safety it would be better to leave Italy and the two went to Biarritz, a place they felt was at the farthest possible remove from the lines of battle. An interesting story is associated with their leaving Italy: While neither Ghyka nor Blood were noted for their "mannish dress," Acton, who saw them off on the train, recorded their attire in pants and military jackets, with hair hidden under manly caps. Writing to Bernard Berenson, Acton noted the surprise of the Italian customs when they reviewed the papers of the crossdressers.[184]

Ghyka and Blood stayed in," Queen Natalie's seaside chateau in Bidart. Little is know of their activities during this lengthy stay. Presumedly, Ghyka executed art works as she had in the past. This summer residence of European royals of warring nations, a stranger place of retreat, though, could not be imagined.

After 1917, and the end of Italy's active participation in the war, the returning Settignano residents' lifestyle changed dramatically. The Princess's beauty and good looks, we are told, were suddenly lost. Ghyka seldom gave parties and the villa grew dark and shuttered, its occupants living as recluses. Whenever the Princess appeared, she was covered head to toe by a veil or shroud. She became a mysterious figure to her former friends. Even when she walked in the garden, she was seen as a black veiled figure accompanied only by her two white dogs.

> "...... and I wondered about (Gamberaia's gardens) hoping that I might catch a glimpse of the place's owner, Princess Ghyka, a famous beauty who, from the day that she had lost her looks, had shut herself up in complete retirement with her English companion, refusing to let anyone see her unveiled face again. Sometimes, I was told, she would come out of the house at dawn to bathe in the pools of the water-garden, or would pace the long cypress avenue at night - but all I ever saw...was a glimpse of a veiled figure at an upper window."[185]
>
> Lady Sybil Cutting Scott Villa Medici, Fiesole

Possibly suffering from psoriasis, a genetic disease appearing mostly in adults in their forties (which was Ghyka's age at the time) or from another disfiguring illness, Ghyka remained veiled. An ailment little known then and considered incurable, psoriasis has only recently become known to be triggered in some cases by the presence of syphilis.[186] At about the same time, Miss Blood became ill and was bedridden. It is possible that they both had contracted syphilis, a disease that was noted for its affects on the brain and internal organs.[187] With both the Princess and her companion housebound, the supervision of the garden was then left to Bernard Berenson, who showed it to inquiring friends and allowed garden devotees to tour the villa grounds.

It was common knowledge to her remaining friends that after World War I Ghyka was strapped for funds. Her finances were thought to have contributed to her hermetic life. Her former benefactor, Carlos Placci, was no longer residing in Florence. In 1925, with financial strain increasing and with the death of her long time companion, Miss Blood, Princess Ghyka sold the villa to the American widow, Matilda Ledyard Cass, the Baroness von Ketteler,[188] and took up residence in a small rented apartment nearby in the center of Settignano. Several years later, Ghyka sold at auction in London, many of the prized objet d'art from the Gamberaia, including the last of her jewelry.[189] Ghyka left Florence in the late 1920s entering a convent in Paris, where she died in 1942. With the sale of the Gamberaia by Princess Ghyka, the early beginnings of the Moderne period of the second renaissance in garden design was brought to a close.

> "There is an air of loveliness about the Villa Gamberaia that lingers long in one's memory as an example of the formal gardens brought to a state of perfection under the influence of an owner who knows the charm that lies in the combination of well designed architecture with the beauty of flowers and foliage."[190]
>
> Indigo Trig

Mural of Villa laPietra as designed by Carlo Fontana in the early 1600s.

Chapter 2/ Largo

Villa La Pietra

"Villa La Pietra evokes the golden age of the aesthete."[191]
"Editorial," *Apollo*

MARIO ARTHUR ACTON BEFRIENDED Princess Ghyka in the early 1890s, during his student days at the Ecole des Beaux-Arts in Paris, where he studied art. His roommate was Guy Hamilton Mitchell, the son of a wealthy American, William Mitchell, who was founder of the Illinois Trust and Savings Company of Chicago. It was widely rumored that in his youth Acton was bisexual, having an intimate relationship with Guy and the two being thought of in Paris as a couple. When they completed their studies, the two toured Italy for a year, taking up residence in Florence.

When Acton first arrived in Florence in 1894 with Mitchell, he established an antique store at number 16 on the Borgo Ognissanti, just a block off the Arno River, to the west of Florence's historic center and around the corner from the tony Hotel Grand Britannia. He began selling *objet d'art* through several dealers in London and New York. Arthur felt comfortable with Italy and the language, and his family had connections in Naples where his grandfather and other Actons were members of the ruling aristocracy, at the title of Baron, under Napoleon. But the Neapolitan culture was very Catholic and sexually restrictive while, in Florence, culture was secular and libertine. A favorite city for gays at the turn of the century, Arthur and Guy decided to give Florence a try.

Mario Arthur Acton in Paris

As stated earlier with regard to lesbianism and herewith repeated in relationship to same-sex male pairings, homosexuality had become a heightened area of study for German scientists[192] and Viennese psychiatrists in the latter half of the nineteenth century. Previously unanalyzed,[193] published research reflected closer scrutiny of same-sex relationships. In these first-ever case-study reports, sodomy was carefully described, its practicing numbers estimated, and correlations proffered. Normal sexual activity was defined as strictly opposite sex attraction and fulfillment, while a person with a "predisposition" to same-sex relationships was described as pathological, having psycho-social aberrations, "sexual inversions" or "contrary sexual instinct." Although the phenomenon was found to exist in women, "men were clearly predisposed to this affection." The word "homosexual" was used for the first time. No interpersonal relationship was considered innocent or beyond study. Dreams, verbal language and inflection, dress and body language were all considered to communicate conscious as well as subconscious sexual desires. With greater research, more extreme cases were brought to the fore and social reaction quickly changed "social inversion" to "social perversion."

In England, bisexual relationships were believed to be a phenomenon of youth, a product of the all-boy English prep-school or all-male college environment. Clinical reports described the phenomena in quasi-scientific terms. It defined age as a factor, whereby older youth, typically an unmarried man in his twenties to early thirties, "the agens," engaged in sex with only younger boyfriends, commonly adolescents of sixteen to eighteen years-of-age, "the patiens." Such was the case between Guy and Arthur: Guy was six years older. On entering his twenties, a young "patiens" was expected to reverse and assume the active "agens" role with a new, younger boyfriend while the older "agens" were expected to marry, say after age thirty and abandon such homosexual behavior. This practice, while not socially accepted, was not condemned, nor considered unlawful. It was viewed as part of youthful experimentation and a product of the repressed Victorian heterosexual courtship. But if such practice persisted into adulthood, that is, an adult having anal intercourse with another adult, it was considered sodomy. Even then, sodomy was associated only with the adult receiver, the "patiens," and was seldom used to describe the "agens or penetrator," whose role in this sexual relation was considered the same as in any "normal" heterosexual act.[194] Boys who consented to penetration were never punished because of their youth.[195] In this milieu, Arthur and Guy's youthful relationship, if known in England or to their parents, would have been only alarming, but not thought of as being "permanent."

In England as in America, sodomy was illegal and sodomists were shunned in most social circles. Until 1861, buggery was punishable by castration or hanging in England. The revealing clinical reports caused many doctors and psychologists to champion repeal of the law.[196] Successful though the effort was, the old law was replaced by a similar law, the 1885 Criminal Law Amendment Act, codifying the act of sodomy to include both partners and imposing, jointly, only slightly less severe punishment of life imprisonment.

Same sex attraction, *inclinazione* in Italy, was described as broader and more inclusive. It was thought to be either/or exclusively male, or gay, "where the invert has a congenital absence of sexual feelings toward the opposite sex," as well as bi-sexual, where the "invert" was attracted to both sexes. The "invert" phenomenon was egalitarian, occurring in persons of all occupations and social levels, though it seemed to be "more prevenient among clerks, small businessmen and postal employees." [197]

In Italy, where the Catholic Church enforced the traditional gender and family roles and its limitations on "non-reproductive" sex, similar criminal laws on sodomy were not enacted until the 1889 *Codice Zanardelli*. Although laws were established, "*le vice Italian*" as the French termed it, or *"florenzen - florentinize,"* as called by the Germans, only the most flagrant cases of rape and seduction were prosecuted - *publicus et famosus sodimita*. In the more liberal north provinces and Tuscany, the *Codice* was rarely enforced, and when it was, punishment was exacted in fines.[198] With such a relaxed climate, gays felt less restricted in their behavior and less persecuted. This then became the attraction of Florence for gays and to couples such as Arthur and Guy.

Perhaps history made it possible for the Italians to accept, or accord, social legitimacy with respect to *inclinazione*. Homoerotic art and literature abounded in this Mediterranean region where homosexuality was common in Ancient Greek and Roman cultures. Hadrian and his male lover, Antinous, entertained lavishly and openly in the gardens of his Tivoli villa. Homosexuality was revived again in the Renaissance period - the list was long and well known: Michelangelo and his beloved, Tommaso Cavalieri, whom he immortalized in numerous sculptures in the guise of a David or a Cleopatra; the writer Boccaccio, a member of the Sienese circle of love poets who wrote on homosexual themes in the *Decameron*; Dante Alegheri, who extolled the virtues of his lover Brunetto Latini ("You are the radiance among men") and whom he specifically placed among the sodomites in his poem, *The Inferno*. These beloved examples of art were proudly and un-apologetically taught to all Italian children in all Italian schools. An analysis of fines for sodomy levied in Florence during the Renaissance shows an extraordinarily high incidence of *inclinazione* behavior among Florentine males.[199]

Homosexuality in the Italian culture was far more diverse than that of

R. Terry Schnadelbach

Germany and England and added to Florence's allure for gays. The Florentine practice of autoerotic and oral genital sex, like sodomy, while not socially or religiously accepted, was prevalent and not condemned through criminal prosecution.[200] Such common manifestations of sexual encounters were not the subject of German or American scientific case-studies (and therefore thought to be uncommon there), and such behavior was not considered then as part of the homosexual's "inverted" behavior.

Homosexuals were visible in the daily life of Florence: Composers like Tchaikovsky and Bellini took prominent roles in the *Balletto e Orchestra della Toscana*; artists presented homoerotic works in the Mostra Annale at the *Museo delle Belle Arte*, and the works of poets and playwrights such as Gabriele D'Annunzio were widely read and performed. Access to public places went unfettered for homosexuals, allowing them open contact for cruising or self-affirming socialization. Widely known among the homosexual community for this purpose, were the streets Borgo Santi Apostoli, and the Calimala behind the Piazza della Signoria. Gays could meet at any of the local *urbana taverna*. Then, too, they were known to openly engage in sex in the Park Cascine and its bulrushes along the Arno, in Florence's western suburbs, or in the shrubbery-with-a-view, at the Belvedere Fortress on the Arno's south bank

Similar to its lesbians, Florence's gays called the city the Pink Lily. So prevalent were the English and American homosexual couples seeking a libertine existence in Italy that the Italians gave a derogatory term to the *inglese italianizzato*, or *gli diavolo incarnato*, devils incarnate.[201]

Princess Giovanna Ghyka chose for her exile the Florence of sexual liberation; Guy and Arthur would choose similarly for the same reasons, making "The Pink Lily" theirs. It was the only real option they had to Paris, if the two were to continue living together. But within a year of settling in Florence, an event colored their continued cohabitation. The famous Oscar Wilde[202] criminal trial of 1895, the most celebrated trial under the then ten-year-old Sodomy Amendment Act, inflicted humiliation and a two-year prison incarceration on England's most prominent gay. It also resulted in unwanted public attention and intense scrutiny for any homosexual. Florence was abuzz with every new report from England. In central Florence, there were many morally self-righteous expatriates who delighted in reporting back to England suspected or known homosexuals in hope of seeing the named party prosecuted, or at least, embarrassed upon their return. While the Italians themselves were passive on the subject, Guy and Arthur were quite possibly fearful of such snoops and decided to take separate quarters

"One of the things (Harold) Acton most assiduously concealed was his homosexuality...... and threatened lawsuits to get all mention of his proclivities removed from published writings."

Beginning in 1896, just after his arrival in Florence, Arthur met socially with his old Parisian friend, Princess Ghyka, often having drinks on the Gamberaia terrace while discussing the possibilities for renting a Fiesole villa. Princess Ghyka's sister, Queen Natalije Obrenovic of Serbia,[203] was renting a major *villino* on the via Bologna just outside Florence's San Gallo Gate. The Villa Natalia, as it is now known, was part of the five villa La Pietra 23 hectare complex and *podere*. The main villa, at 130 via Bolognese, was owned by the family of the former ambassador of Prussia, and had been a center of Austro-Hungarian culture in Florence. The Queen informed Acton that the main villa at the La Pietra had become available.[204] Acton visited the pale ochre building, viewed its idyllic setting across from a *fosso,* (dry creek bed), toured its extensive park-like grounds on the ridge amidst a light grey-green olive grove, and inspected its threadbare, stripped interiors. It was all charm to Arthur Acton; he rented it for five years.[205] Guy, in turn, purchased the Villa il Giullarino across the way.

With mounting pressure from both sets of parents to get on with their lives as adults, Arthur and Guy, now in their thirties, were both pushed to make heterosexual marriages and families. To assuage family demands and offer some comfort, Guy suggested that Arthur marry his sister, Hortense, adding legitimacy to their relationship while affording them even better reason to continue seeing each other. Hortense Lenore Mitchell and Arthur Acton were married in Chicago in June 1903, providing the necessary social respectability to Arthur, and a "cover" for Arthur and Guy. Guy was not only Arthur's lover, but now his brother-in-law.[206] But with the marriage, Arthur seemed to change, becoming repressed and closeted, concealing any further homosexual relationships. Guy Mitchell, less conflicted in his homosexuality as an adult, remained unmarried and lived a private gay life in the Villa il Giullarino .

While pretending he was from a prominent English family, Arthur Mario Acton was unrelated to the Neopolitan Lord Acton family whom are decendents of great-great-grandfather Commodore Sir John Acton, who was prime minister of Naples under Ferdinand IV. He was born out of wedlock and pretended to be of threadbare nobility. His marriage to Hortense could have been more than a marriage of social convenience. Arthur, it would seem, desired to marry into the Mitchell money. Upon the marriage, William Mitchell bought the Villa La Pietra for his daughter, Hortense Mitchell Acton, as a wedding present.[207] It is interesting to note that the property was placed in the name of

Hortense Mitchell, a precautionary move taken by the elder Mitchell. (The Mitchell-Acton courtship was swift and conducted by letter exchanges.) At the time of the wedding, Guy Mitchell's Villa il Giullarino[208] was undergoing renovation, courtesy of Mitchell Sr's funding. Following suit, the Arthur Actons began to make major improvements to La Pietra - both the house and site - further utilizing financial gifts from the elder Mitchell for the substantial remodeling. There was not a year that Acton did not build, modify, or rebuild his beloved gardens. He pruned, pampered, and petted them to perfection and loved their beauty for more than fifty years, until his death.

An incised marble plaque, fabricated and hung by Don Giovanni Guiso[209] in 1954 on the Southwestern corner of La Pietra's *Vasca di Diana*, cites six architects as consultants to the building's rehabilitation. The list includes the American architects, Stanford White of McKim Mead and White, and Charles Platt, both of New York.[210] It included also H. (Henry) O. Watson, who was not an architect but a noted New York art dealer. Henry, Arthur Acton's uncle, helped Arthur establish himself as an art dealer. None of these men listed on the plaque were involved in the architectural renovations of La Pietra. Rather, they were all involved with Arthur Acton in his primary line of international business, the sale and resale of European art objects.

Arthur Acton had positioned his career on the new and growing art market in America. The great industrial expansion at the end of the nineteenth Century brought great wealth to a number of families seemingly overnight. Oil's discovery in eastern Pennsylvania and its refinement made John D. Rockefeller a millionaire at a time when the standard wage was $58 per month. Andrew Carnegie, already wealthy from the manufacture of steel, invested and controlled a vast railroad empire necessary to ship his product. In the process, he accumulated even greater wealth - far beyond any possible human use. The Mellons, Kresses, Wanamakers, Gardners, et al., had millions of dollars in expendable income. After acquiring jewels, dresses and stables of new automobiles, they spent their considerable money on new homes that were designed by America's best architects and landscape architects, in America's best suburbs, planned and designed to fulfill the new ideal of country living for the elite. These country places, as they were called, were enormous mansions in the style of architecture familiar to Europe's nobility. They were furnished exquisitely with European furniture and art, chosen by "experts," men of taste - for the client, poor dears, who had neither the taste, education, nor family backgrounds to ever fully appreciate the objects to be purchased, themselves. Mansions were designed almost overnight, built and furnished almost as quickly. Instant mature landscapes, the trademark of landscape architect Ferruccio Vitale, a Florentine immigrant whose name was synonymous with Country Place era estates, were put in place.[211]

George W. Vanderbilt set the watermark to match with his Biltmore estate outside Asheville, North Carolina. Hortense as a young debutant visited Biltmore returning to Chicago with a firm vision for a similar villa sometime in her married future. In 1888,[212] Frederick Law Olmsted, Sr., the nationally prominent American landscape architect who, with the architect Calvin Vaux had created and designed Central Park in New York, was commissioned to conceive and plan Biltmore, the 125,000 acre Vanderbilt estate.[213] Olmsted, the consummate social reformer, treated the commission of the private estate with innovative design and technologically advanced management systems. Initially, he structured two teams for the commission, the first headed by the New York architect Richard Morris Hunt. This team was comprised of a cadre of sculptors and artists who would work on the main portion of the primary site, where the chateau was located. The second team consisted of a collection of natural scientists, i.e., botanist, horticulturists, agronomists, etc., who were engaged in the real interest of Olmsted, Sr., the management of the remaining vast acreage. The latter was far less interesting to Vanderbilt.

Olmsted, Sr. relied heavily on his partners, John Charles Olmsted and Frederick Law Olmsted, Jr., to work with the architects in carrying out the design of the thirty-five-acre house area. They, in turn, brought in the second-generation staff member, Warren Manning to manage and execute the design concepts in detail.[214] Richard Morris Hunt was the first American architect to have studied architecture at the Ecole des Beaux-Arts in Paris, and while in Paris he worked for the French Architect Hector-Martin Lefuel, who had been in charge of a major addition to the Louvre. Upon his return to America, Hunt designed a French Renaissance chateau reminiscent of the Louvre for the Vanderbilts. It consisted of 250 rooms in a massive, multifaceted building. The architecture was an eclectic collection of elements copied from French chateaus; the beautifully proportioned spiral staircase from the *Chateau de Blois* was copied exactly and was the main feature of the Biltmore's facade.[215]

Broad terraces associated with the Biltmore house were reminiscent of those of the French landscape architect Andre Le Notre. These terraces descended steeply sloped terrain, ending in exquisite formal herb and cut-flower gardens. The rose garden, just one section of the total space, was reported to contain over 2,500 varieties. Although the Olmsted firm's design of these formal gardens is judged by some to be wonderful, the design was, in fact, crudely proportioned and rigidly mechanical,[216] with the house off-axis and the spaces ill-defined. As the first "classical" landscape by a firm known for its Central Park-like naturalistic and rural designs, the execution was clearly a learning experience, for the professionals involved lacked understanding, experience and depth in this European idiom. Biltmore's 250 rooms had to be furnished and decorated, its interiors fitted with appropriate period furniture, drapes, tapestries, carpets, object d'art and art pieces. Vanderbilt and his architect Hunt sent scouts to Europe on "buying trips," often paying top dollar for major works. These scouts were known for buying the furnishings of entire castles and chateaus from cash-poor nobility. In a practiced *modus operandi*, the scouts would first set aside major furnishings after prices were negotiated and fixed, and after a suitable number of pieces had been amassed, the patron and his architect would be called in to view them prior to confirming their purchase. The purchases thus became wonderful excuses for expensive trips abroad.

Accompanying the furnishings were art pieces, paintings and sculptures to adorn every room and every architectural niche. Art from all periods was bought to complement room themes - an Italian Renaissance room next to a French Baroque, followed by an English Mannerist, then perhaps a Hapsburg room to be then followed by the Louises - XIII, XIV, XV, and XVI. It became the mark of a civilized man to acquire a broad array of periods and styles. What took generations for Europeans royals to achieve in their palaces, an American magnate might accomplish overnight. With the completion of Biltmore, it became the standard to emulate and America's captains of industry and finance began a competition to create ever greater country place estates. Located in the rural suburbs of every major American city and in every tony resort, hundreds of impressive eclectic mansions were built and furnished with antiques and *objects d'art*. The mansions and gardens of the wealthy were built in New York City's exclusive suburban communities of Long Island's Gold Coast, Westchester and the Connecticut shore, in Philadelphia and its Main Line, Brandywine and Chestnut Hill, in Pittsburgh and its Squirrel Hill district, in Cleveland's shore front area, and on Chicago's Lakeshore Drive and the Lake Forest community.[217] Stanford White, utilizing his Ecole de Beaux-Arts architectural education, designed many of the mansions, especially those found in New York City and on Long Island.

To furnish his eclectic urban and country place mansions, Stanford White began to make annual trips to Europe. The first occurred on November 20, 1890 with his clients the Payne Whitneys. They visited the major art dealers of the day: In London, the Duveen Brothers and Arthur J. Sully, (15 Bond Street); in Paris, E. Lowengard; Rome, Godfrey Kopp and Galerie Sangiorge, Palais Borghese; and in Florence, Stefano Bardini (Piazza Mozzi 1).[218] White's trips were primarily for interior architectural acquisitions, but the process of discovery was equally part of the fun. On such trips, White assembled draperies, furniture, paneled walls, stone mantels, entire ceilings, swords and armor. On a June 1905 trip, White's partner, Charles Follen McKim, traveling alone, remarked in a letter to his wife on the many purchases he had made, finding the "antique scene in Florence sizzled....fine things at awful prices."[219]

While still at the Ecole des Beaux-Arts, Acton, through his New York art dealer uncle, Watson, recognized the opportunity to be found and high profits to be made in the emerging art market. Watson was prospering as an art dealer and, possibly assessing his own talents and prospects as a painter, Acton decided to enter the newly emerging profession.[220] Arthur was introduced to Stanford White by Watson,[221] who was one of several art agents doing business for the McKim, Mead and White firm. In a letter of September 9, 1897, White wrote Acton introducing himself[222] and engaged Acton as his agent, offering to pay him a fee and all expenses. After their initial exchange of letters in 1897, Arthur Acton became one of Stanford White's most highly regarded art agents, among several American and European agents, and one through whom White most often made purchases. White's letters often asked personal favors from Acton, to be done "on the dead quiet:" To buy a FIAT (like Arthur's) at the Italian price and ship the car to White in New York,[223] to provide architectural tours to members of the firm on the "Grand Tour" of European architecture, or "to assist Mrs. Potter Palmer in finding antiques, at no costs to S.W."[224]

The White contract provided Acton some small degree of financial security in the fluid commercial art world. Arthur provided certificates of authenticity as well as acquisition information for White's purchases and resales. From the numerous letters and cables, we know that White was interested in Acton's finding entire interiors to have built into his eclectic buildings. Arthur would arrange discussions with the owners for settling on price, and send photographs to White for review. White most often rejected these as being inappropriate in size, scale or detail. The service, however, was not limited to architectural elements. Arthur made numerous purchases of *objects d'art* - vases, paintings, lamps, armor and heraldry. Always, there was much bickering over price and one suspects White had a strong profit motive in his dealings, even though he denied such. "I am only getting these things for houses we build for our clients, and should never think of selling them, to outsiders, nor do I in any way buy them to make profit on them, as they are always turned into clients at practically their costs."[225]

During their eight-year association, Stanford White visited Florence to meet with Arthur Acton only once, that in 1904 on an arranged buying trip. The White party did not stay at the La Pietra but in a hotel in the center of Florence.[226] White and party may not have even visited the villa and there is no evidence of any participation by White in the design of La Pietra's remodeling, which by this time was well underway.

R. Terry Schnadelbach

Over fifteen years, White, with the assistance of Acton and a dozen other European art dealer, amassed a large collection of paintings, carvings, pieces of furniture and *objects d'art*. So vast was his collection that White had to rent an entire warehouse to house it. The "placing" of these acquired pieces in the homes of his many clients became an exclusive service of the McKim, Mead and White firm's Italian style commissions, making that firm "the" source for beaux-arts architecture. The Payne Whitney house on Gramercy Square,[227] the Joseph Pulitzer house on Fifth Avenue, and the J. P. Morgan house and library on Madison Avenue, all in New York City, are notable examples.

In 1905, a fire in the warehouse holding the White collection destroyed it and priceless treasures were lost. Holbein portraits of Henry VII and Edward VI were among the treasures consumed in flames. In 1906, Stanford White was murdered in a much-publicized assassination, brought about by his philandering. With his death, and the dissemination of the White collection by fire the previous year, Acton's connection with the McKim, Mead and White firm[228] seems to have ended.

Charles Platt, the American landscape architect / architect, was referred to Arthur Acton[229] by Stanford White. Acton and Platt corresponded regularly regarding art purchases – "garden urns, railings statues, etc." and though Platt is listed on the 1954 Guiso wall plaque as an architectural consultant on La Pietra's remodeling, he never visited La Pietra and was not known to have produced any sketches or drawings for the villa's remodeling. His bound photographic archives[230] on Italian architecture and gardens does not even contain photographs of Villa La Pietra, however, a review of Platt's many classical-derived gardens shows many a garden architectural element, sculpture or copy that might have been purchased through Arthur Acton.

While purchases for White and other American architects centered on architectural assemblages, *objet d'art* and furnishings, Acton's real interest was in sculpture, an art that White seemed to have no real interest in, nor affinity for. The fees earned through Acton's dealings with White, however, enabled Arthur to make purchases of sculpture for La Pietra's gardens, which he did unceasingly, amassing over 180 pieces. Quite possibly, it is the largest and most important collection of garden sculpture in Italy today. Acton's collection of historic sixteenth to eighteenth century sculpture was acquired over a fifteen year period. Acton traveled the Veneto, a region then untouched by collectors, and bought the entire contents of villas, including garden sculpture. Centering on Vicenza and the Brenta River, he was able to buy entire estates, including the sculpture of the gardens, for the price of a single piece in Florence.

In the more northerly zone, the *serena* stone was harder than that of Florence and weathered better. At some villas, Acton promised to replace old "weathered" statuary with fresh new versions, all crisper copies of the original. The originals were then incorporated into the new gardens at Villa Acton which, as idealized Renaissance gardens, were structured by architectural elements and rhythmically filled with sculpture. Acton's sculptures would be reproduced yet again, to be sold through Stanford White, Charles Platt, William Wells Boswell, Ferruccio Vitale and other American architects then designing estates for wealthy clients.

Acton's showroom in central Florence, first at 16 Borgo Ognissanti and later at 9 Vialle Umberto, was in continuous operation throughout his life. It housed *objet d'art,* primarily, fabrics and decorative items. Large art pieces - paintings and sculpture - were kept and displayed as part of the furnishings at his villa. He also used a house in London's fashionable Lancaster Gate section as a showroom. This house was furnished with Florentine antiques, almost all of which were for sale. The London house, an inheritance, became Hortense's residence for most of each year after the births in Florence of their two sons, Harold (1904) and William (1906).[231]

Primarily, Arthur Acton became a collector and dealer in Italian Renaissance art. Both the London and Florence houses held works collected up to the First World War, before prices for such works skyrocketed. "There was not a day that Arthur did not add to his collection with a purchase of some piece."[232] William Mitchell's money made the Acton collection possible as there is no record of Acton affording any of his numerous purchases. The collection's strength was in Sienese Primitives, paintings by such artists as Jacopo del Casento. It also featured a magnificent gold coin collection of the Papacy by the famous Italian artist, Benvenuto Cellini. Although Acton traveled Italy in search of acquisitions, his painting collection expanded dramatically with a singular purchase at a distress sale in 1917 of the collection amassed by the American painter Francis Alexander, a Florentine resident.[233]

As a student in Paris, Arthur Acton struck a dashing figure, tall, with a slim face that sported a mustache. At the time he married Hortense, he had filled out considerable, and was tall and stocky. He was a full head-and-a-half taller than the petite Hortense, and his moon shaped face sported a high forehead with the eyes of an awakened owl. His ebony moustache was bushy. With age, his features broadened and his figure grew portly. Acton always had those behavioral characteristics that have stereotyped gays everywhere - well dressed, fastidious and intensely artistic. His dress was always a three-piece suit with a cravat or bow tie. For sport, Acton was a skilled fencer.

"....he collects and sells. Was Stanford White's agent here but since then has married a very rich Chicago woman. He is a 'bounder' but he has a flair for good things."[234]

Bernard Berenson

Arthur Acton's character was not above question, and was considered by some to be of questionable standard. We catch a rare glimpse of Acton's reputation from Bernard Berenson's letter of introduction to his Boston patron Isabella Gardner. Acton was visiting America at the time. Berenson, in using the term, "bounder," was, in essence describing a low life, a trashy man of dubious honesty and personal character. In the only other use of the term by Berenson, he was describing Oscar Wilde, the internationally renowned homosexual. Berenson was alluding to Arthur's rumored double philandering life, widely assumed among the expatriate community in Florence.[235]

Arthur and Hortense circa 1910.

Arthur Acton was equally rumored to have had numerous heterosexual affairs. He was reported to have brought secretaries from his offices in England for romantic week-long trysts at the villa. Shortly after his marriage while at his dentist, Arthur met Ersilla Beacci, an unemployed beautiful girl in her twenties. He invited her to the villa beginning a long-standing affair. In short time Ersilla became his personal secretary and moved into one of the empty villas on site. This illissit affair was common knowledge around the expatriate community and Hortense had to live with it. Within a few years Arthur and Ersilla had a baby girl at which time Hortense moved out.and was reported to live most of the year in London. Arthur, it was assumed, was given free reign in Florence to live as he wished; his sexual appetite unfettered. A paternity suit over the parentage of Ersilla's daughter has been in litigation and has been settled with the daughter given legitimate claim. The recent bequest of La Pietra and its collections to New York University has proceeded nonetheless with compensation made, one presumes, to the co-heir. Knowledge of Arthur Acton's bisexual philandering, nor the homosexuality of his sons, William and Harold, was widely known outside of Italy.

Ersilla Beacci, in the garden

hidden lives / secret gardens

In his relations with others, Arthur Acton's behavior was almost bi-polar. He was overly felicitous to his clients, as his correspondence with White illustrates, falling over backwards to provide personal services far afield from those associated with the business of being an art dealer. On the other hand, he was verbally abusive to family and servants, providing ample reason and excuse for Hortense's London residency. Beyond their need for schooling in Britain's finest schools, Arthur drove away his sons through his verbal abuse, attacking their character and demanding lifestyle changes. Arthur's conversation with his workers was vulgar, strident and overly demanding. He complained bitterly of the poor skills of Italian packers and shippers and often displayed colonial airs of superiority.

It was well known that Acton was in the reproduction business. He made contracts for the copy of many *objet d'art*, the famous Galileo's lamp among them. In a letter instructing Acton to proceed with a copy, Stanford White says he "wants the real 'make-believe' candelabra such as your Uncle Mr. Watson's." White then questions the quality of the past copies: "I do not know why it is they do not seem to be copied as well as when they sell them to you as the real imitation thing." This criticism is found again in reviews of Guy Mitchell's Villa il Giullarino , which was reported to have "poor quality of sculptures from Vicenza," referring to copies from Acton's made after Acton's forays into the Veneto.[236] In several instances Acton lied, or at least practiced deceptions, regarding the reproductions. In negotiations with owners, he was less than forthright in the replacement of their art, and was even less so in the resale of copies to American buyers. He copied many architectural components and sculptures from the Boboli garden, keeping the originals for La Pietra's gardens while returning reproductions. He is believed to have sold as "originals" to American architects such as Ferruccio Vitale and William Wells Boswell.

His erratic behavior appears often in his writings. In correspondences with Stanford White over a period of time, one can see the extremes of personality. From time to time, his normal prep school-perfect neatness and penmanship contrasts with periodic correspondence that is chaotic, neither neat nor artistic,[237] his own name shakily written. The corners of the paper are eaten or broken away and the page organization is erratic, with horizontal lines at angles and varied vertical alignment from one line to another. While Acton was able to maintain a business tone throughout the letters, one suspects inner rage.

Living mostly alone in the villa, except for short buying trips throughout Italy, Acton led a solitary life. He spent little time in his London townhouse, but regularly, each summer, took a cure at the Aix Les Bains spa.

R. Terry Schnadelbach

To the eye of the first-time visitor, the landscape architecture of Villa La Pietra might appear to be historically derived and cut from a single piece of cloth. Often the landscape is described by essayists on villa gardens as illustrative of authentic Renaissance design. To art historians, the landscapes are uninteresting, as there is little of historic value. To this eye, the landscapes are predominately Moderne creations, encapsulating fragments of times past. All these impressions are real. To discern the fullness of this landscape complex, one must strip away the layers of time, thereby revealing the shards of past landscape compositions strewn throughout the site.

The history of the Villa La Pietra gardens can be found in four periods, and are not easily discernable to the eye even when on-site. The Villa dates back to the Sassetti family in the fifteenth and early sixteenth centuries when several developments made it a significant Renaissance country seat. It was owned and improved by the Capponi family from the mid-sixteenth century to the mid-nineteenth century. In the nineteenth century, the villa fell into the neglectful hands of the Incontri family, who abandoned it during the Austro-Hungarian period. The gardens were substantially altered at this time and were Anglocized by the Prussians who were then tenants on the property, adding all the pastiche of the English garden style. Some of the major clumping of trees remains from this picturesque period. The fourth phase of garden development was the Acton period.

Arthur Acton rehabilitated the remaining historic, sixteenth-century enclosed garden and re-established the renaissance-like garden around the main house, eradicating any trace of the then out-of-fashion Anglo style. The new re-development was based on the philosophy of an idealized and utopian Tuscan garden, following the precepts of garden design being established at the Villa Gamberaia, and as such, was to become the second renaissance garden in Florence.

The main villa building contains remnants of the Sassetti family's initial development begun in 1459 and completed in 1466. Francesco di Tommaso Sassetti built most of the main house and several of the outlying farm structures. The site was located in the hamlet of La Pietra, named after the first milestone on the road to Bologna - a stone marking the contemporary first measure of distance, (approximately 1.5 kilometers). Sassetti, the general manager to Lorenzo the Magnificent's Medici bank, was also a philanthropist. His younger son, also a banker, was the director of the Medici banks in Lyon and Avignon, both cities then a part of France. Francesco Sassetti set up the La Pietra property as a *podere* under the cooperative farming *mezzadria system*, its production to be in olives, grapes and lemons of the region and specializing in the commercial production of olive oil, wine, flowers and citrus extracts.[238]

hidden lives / secret gardens

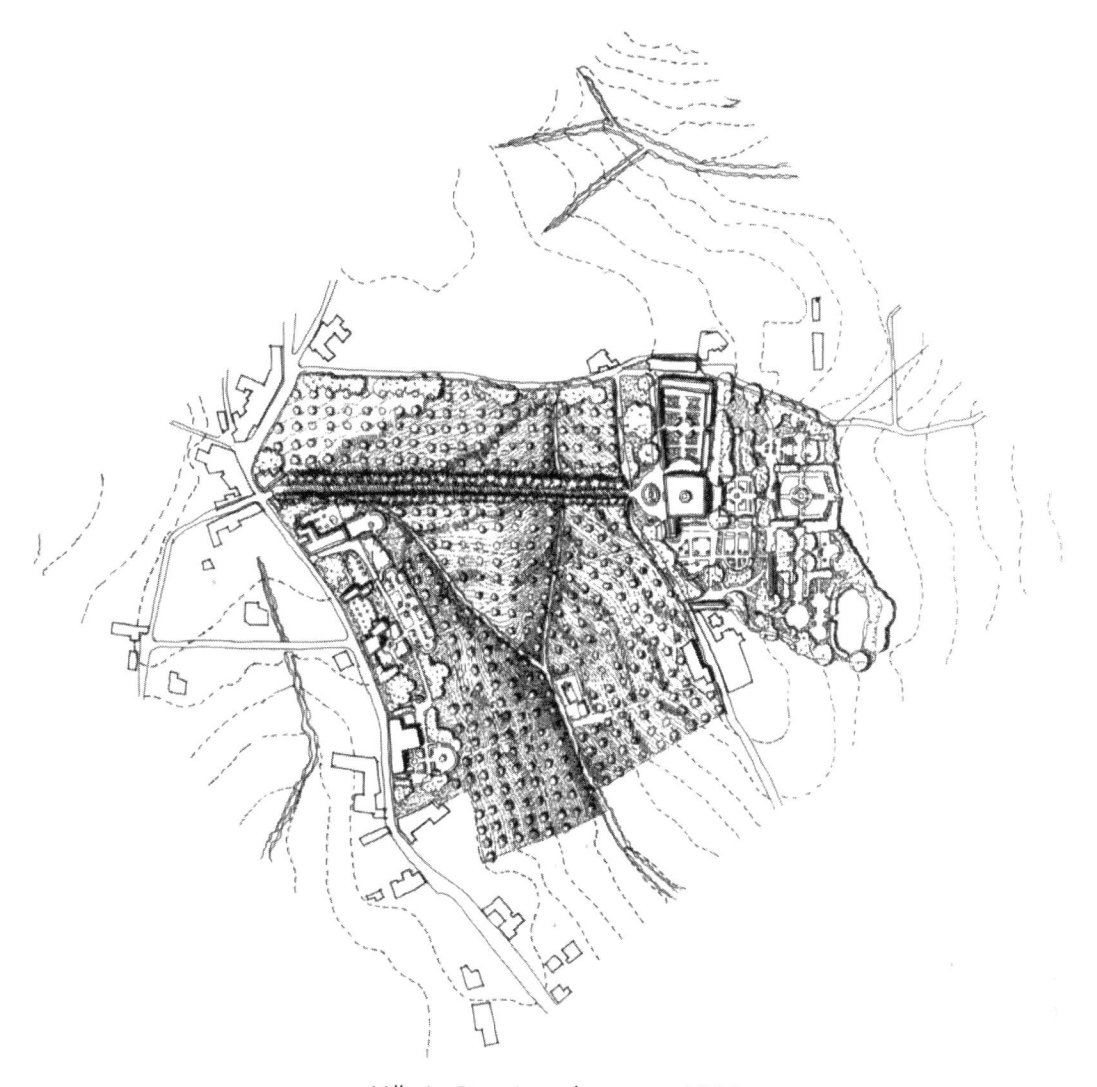

Villa La Pietra's podere circa 2000

"What is Florence without its encircling hills, and what are its hills without their terraced villas and cypress avenues and vineyards leading serenely into the Tuscan countryside?"[239]

Sir Harold Acton

Villa La Pietra dominates its crest line along the Montughi Ridge, the far western land form of the Mugello hillside. It is a complex containing five working *podere* that still produce a strong independent revenue stream. The complex included four additional *villini* - Colletta, Natalia (named after Ghyka's sister, the Serbian Queen), Ulivi and Sassetti - all stretched along thevia Bologna. The four *villini* are known separately as "Oriuolo." Each of the l'Oriuolo's *poderes* slopes to the east and ends at the *fosso* (dry creek bed), separating the four *villini* from the main villa. Villa Acton, the name now given the main villa, the largest and grandest *podere,* sits squarely in the middle of its productive fields straddling both the eastern and western slopes of its crest line.

Altogether, the La Pietra complex contains about 57 acres. The organization of this *mazzadrini* differs from that of the Gamberaia in that it's layout resembles a valley floor villa where topography cannot be used to differentiate the functional and communal areas from those of the *padrone*. At the Villa Acton, the *mazzadrine* space and the *padrone* space are organized on the same level. The *mazzadrine* area was approached from the local farm roads, via dei Bruni and vicolo di San Marco to the north, arriving at the far northern end of Villa Acton's *pomario* in an area behind the *lemonaia*. It is an area with utilitarian structures, one of which must have functioned as the office of the *factorre* and for storage of the *podere*'s equipment and produce. This northern area of the villa's grounds contained all the *mezzadrine*'s and *podere*'s production areas, freeing the remaining area around the villa for the *pradrone*'s or owner's private use.

Water, as ever, was the largest issue and controlled La Pietra's life and its *mazzadrini*'s productivity. Typically, there are four types of villa sites in the Florentine region - all based on water availability. The valley floor villas, like the famous Villas Medici Castello and La Petraia, utilized permanent springs located at the base of the Fiesole hills. The second type is the fluvial villa, which was built adjacent to *torrenti*, the rivers, and diverted run off into their agrarian fields. Only the Terzzolina and Faldi on the Torrenti Mugnone, are fluvial villas. Villa I Tatti is a typical smaller version of these. The third type is that of spring-fed or spring-supported sites, where a geological aquifer strata surfaces. There are several known areas where springs abound. Villa Medici at Fiesole is believed to be located on top of such a spring. The Villa Gamberaia, as we have seen, harnessed several springs, one a "sacred" spring, upland to the northwest, to supply its water. The diverted waters were routed through channels and aqueducts to the upper terrace of the *lemonaia* and through the long allee, to the house and its gardens. Without a doubt, the water rights acquired made the Villa Gamberaia

Mural depicting the villa during the Sassetti period 1466

productive and unique among all Florentine villas. The fourth and last type of villa location is the most common, but also the most problematic. It is a cistern system and not dependent on any specific site location for its water. It simply gathers all available runoff from building roofs and paved surfaces for on-site storage in cisterns.

Villa Acton and its four other *villini* all required run-off collection with cistern storage. Terraces were built around three of Villa Acton's facades solely for the purpose of collecting rain water. Cisterns were built either under or adjacent to the north and south terraces and were tied directly to the house and to the family's production gardens. If a year's rainfall should be deficient, the *podere*'s crops suffered, causing losses to both the *contadini* and *padrone* alike. Ultimately, in periods of drought, the *contadini* families suffered the most. (In earlier times, the *padrone* would simply abandon their seasonal home.) In the Moderne villa, however, where occupancy was year round, in severe droughts water was on-site. Water rationing in the summer months was a common occurrence.

The first house of Francesco di Tommaso Sassetti was a simple two-story farm house called *alle Citine*. It was arranged in an open "U" plan and was set in the location of the present Villa Acton.[240] Later, after his successful appointment as Cosimo de Medici's banking partner in Lyon and Avignon, Sassetti *fili* expanded the house into a Renaissance cube by filling the open area at the north side of the "U" and adding a third floor. It was at that time terraces were added to the eastern and western facades.

Villa's terrace façade during the Capponi era, 1550

"Why if you were to see Sassetti's palace at Montughi, you would think it is the work of a king."[241]
                          Ugolino Verino, a contemporary of Sassetti

In 1545, Piero di Nicolo Capponi bought the La Pietra *podere* and kept the main villa much the same. His nephew Scipione Capponi, who was deeded the property in 1650, spent over 2000 florins on projects in the gardens, of which only parts of the *pomario* remain. The house was further elongated by extension walls along the villa's east and west facades enclosing gardens on the north and south. On the north side, Scipione built a magnificent *pomario*, or walled vegetable / fruit garden exclusively for his family's use. Its surrounding walls tied the villa to the stables and *lemonaia* on the north and kept views of the *padrone*'s opulence from the *contradini*. This sixteenth century garden was a classical example of a *hortus conclusus,* (or enclosed garden,) and is today perfectly preserved. The south-enclosed garden, a walled-in flower and herb parterre garden, was destroyed in the nineteenth century as part of a road building project and the formal gardens were changed to the English picturesque plan. Parts of the walls at the southern terminus were retained, as they contained a much needed cistern. (These architectural components were intact when Arthur Acton leased the property.) Named il Villa Montughi by Scipione Capponi after the name of its ridge, the expanded villa development better resembled a countryfied urban *palazzo* than a true villa, as in the buildings that the Medici were building at that time. Montughi's blocky mass prevented the ease of transitions of inside spaces to exterior terraces and gardens, and also the villa's main *salas* were located on the *piano nobile* or second floor, typical of the urban *palazzo*.

The south and east gardens outside the walled *hortus conclusus,* elements illustrated in a circa 1600s plan by Giorgio Vasari il Giovane,[242] have all vanished. They were thought to have descended the slopes in a series of terraces and quadrangles, all informally formed by banked earth, hedges and vegetation. It is this motif from which Acton allegedly drew inspiration for his "reconstruction" of the villa's landscape. Within this garden area, there was a distinct absence of architectural walls and built structures. Further from the house, the eastern slopes were probably left in the productive lands of the *podere*.

Later in the early seventeenth century, the villa was given to Cardinal Luigi Caponi who added numerous barogue elements to the exterior architecture, all designed by the noted Roman architect, Carlo Fontana.[243] In 1760, the Marchesi Incontri inherited the villa complex from her husband, the historian Marchese Gino Capponi. In the 1800s, the villa complex was rented to the Prussian government and used as their embassy. As was the fashion of the period, the Prussians remade the Villa Acton gardens into *il giardino all' Inglese*, in the English landscape style. The southern and eastern sides of the house were re-graded, the southern *hortus conclusus* was torn down, the formal terraces were removed, and the slopes were reshaped to feature meadow and specimen trees in a composition of sweeping curvilinear walks. In the new *prato* (or meadows), clumps of exotic trees were surrounded by mixed woodland trees, as was the fashionable pallette of this period. The vistas were focused to the southeast where, in the lowest corner, an oval lawn had a spectacular view toward Florence and Brunelleschi's *Duomo,* Giotto's *Campanili* and the *torre de pallazo signori*.

> "Sometimes when the air is very, very clear, you can see it all like a miniature painting."[244]
>
> Arthur Acton

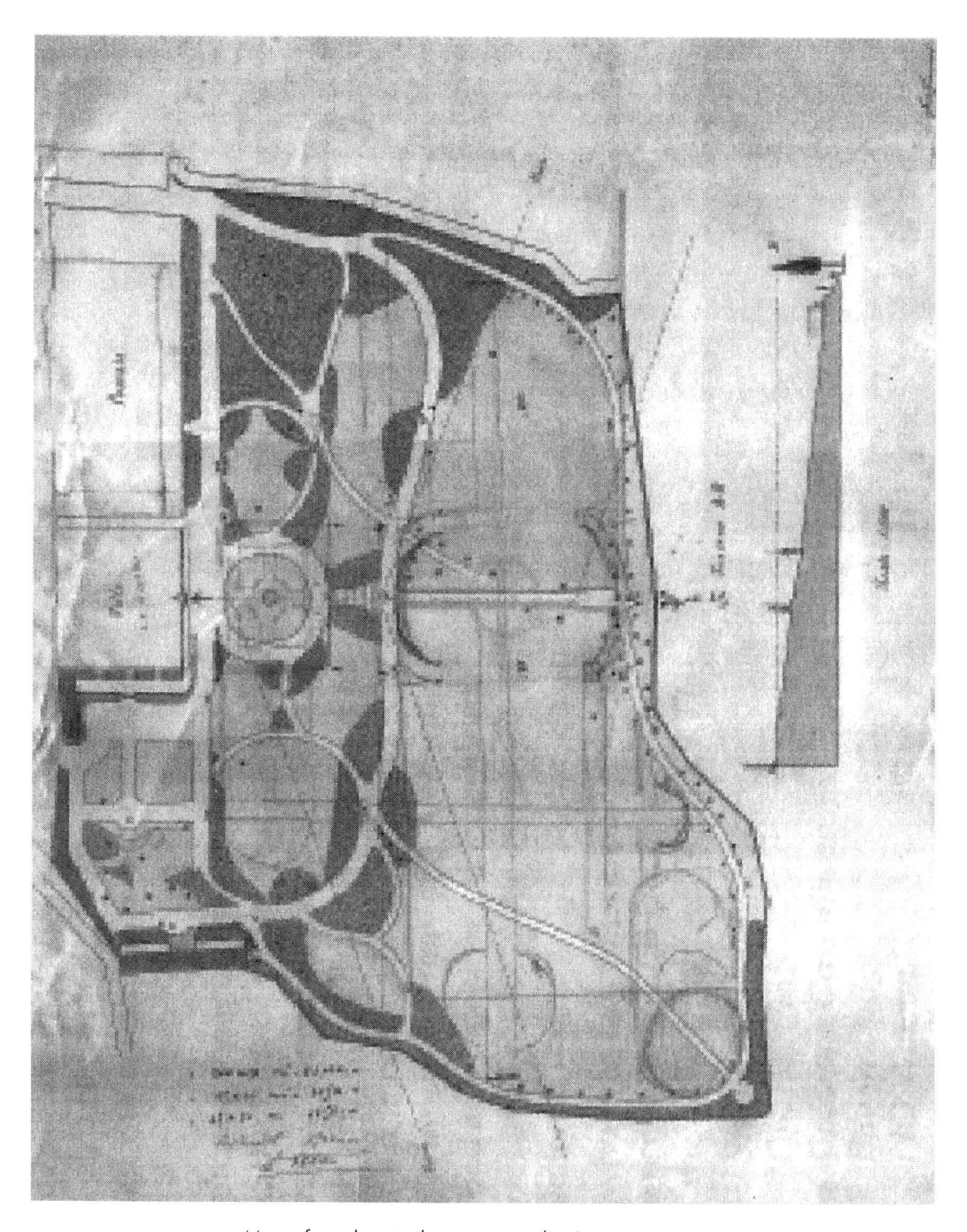

Map of gardino inglese, prior to the Acton renovations

The *giardino Inglese* in Italy is a strange stylistic perversion of the original Repton model. In Italy, it would contain a complete assortment of plant material used singularly to display every decorative aspect of the plant. Strident contrasts - purple leaf plum against a chartreuse-leaf maple, fastigiate elm next to pendulous posted mulberry, copper beech contrasted to a blue Atlantic cedar - would be the featured design motif. Remnants of the Prussian garden remain sprinkled among several of the enclosed spaces of the current garden. Such trees as the stately Atlantic cedar stood to the south side of the central garden;[245] others formed the small space at the southeast corner of the current garden. On the walls of one room inside the villa[246] are seven painted scenes of Capponi villas in the region. In each scene, villas are depicted as set in English landscapes. The paintings vary in size, but are similar in purpose to the Utens lunettes of Medici villas that recorded the wealth of that distinguished Florentine family. The Capponi villa illustrations are artistically lacking, crudely painted with off-colors, poor perspective, and sloppy brush strokes,[247] but the illustration of the Incontri La Pietra gives a glimpse of what the original Prussian *giardino Inglese* was like.

> "When Florence became the capitol of Italy, it (La Pietra) was taken over by the Prussian Embassy and (the gardens) converted into English like woods."

With the advent of Italian nationhood, the Prussians gave up the villa, and the Incontri family, finding its upkeep difficult, abandoned the villa and its gardens in the 1880s, while keeping the *podere* in production. A couple of the *villini* were used as cheap housing or hotels; as previously stated, one was rented to the Queen of Serbia. The main villa was left unoccupied until 1896.[248]

In 1903, after buying the La Pietra property, Arthur Acton embarked on a course typical of any new owner. Repeating the steps that the Princess Ghyka undertook at Villa Gamberaia, he began to repair La Pietra's water system. Again with partial if not complete financial support from his father-in-law, Acton commenced repairs and enlargement of the south terrace's cistern in the old *giardino inclusivo*. Using the remaining historic wall that had enclosed the garden at one border, Acton placed behind it a thin two-story volume, a cistern that would hold vastly more water and provide much needed water pressure to the upper floors of the house.

Arthur initiated a sizable interior renovation at this time. The central courtyard of the square building was glassed over to form a two-story main reception *sala*, and a grand central stairway, elliptical in plan and cantilevered from the wall, was added to reach the *piano noble*'s *salas.* The first floor rooms were improved to be more villa-like major *salas*, but their relationship to the outside was still denied as new *fenetre, logia* and porches would have severely changed the villa's facade.

Except for the historic northern *pomario*, the exterior site was totally restructured. For the new gardens, Acton first engaged an *ideatori*, a noted French garden historian and restoration expert, Henri Duchene.[249] In training with him at that time, was his son Archile. A scholar and artist, the elder Duchene had achieved notoriety in France by restoring many of Le Notre's garden, among them, Vaux-le-Vicomte, Courance, and Maintenon. Acton knew of Duchene's reputation from his studies at the Ecole des Beaux-Arts. Father and son, Archille, visited La Pietra many times. Henri's first visit went unrecorded, but occurred sometime before 1902 and any work was done on the gardens. After the older Duchene's death, Archile continued the Duchene involvement with the garden, consulting between 1908 and 1910 and again in 1912. It is uncertain as to what parts of the plan, if any, were specifically done by the Duchenes.

The final garden plan consisted of spaces as series of enclosed garden rooms, a trademark of Henri Duchene's new, non-historic, rehabilitated landscapes. The placement of sculpture defining the primary spaces replicated many of Le Notre's employments of alternating urns and figurines in his central gardens. While there are no Duchene plans for La Pietra, there is a 1908[250] plan attributed to Arthur Acton himself, sketching out a concept for the garden. It was drawn over a survey of the prior *gardino Inglese* and shows the newly intended axis and general areas for the various garden spaces. The locations of axes and garden developments are carefully located to fit the major structure of the *giardino Inglese*, selectively saving the garden's central stairs and many of the mature evergreen tree stands.[251] These ideas could have been the result of the Duchene collaborations.

> "Mr. Acton was a disciple, you might say, of the great Henri Duchene ..... he taught me Duchene's ideals."[252]
>
> Diego Suarez

While the credit for the design and layout of the garden is attributed to Arthur Acton, its execution was in collaboration with the young, talented architect / landscape architect from Bogata, Columbia, Diego Suarez.[253] Diego's mother was of Italian and Latin American parentage; she was a descendant of San Martine, the South American patriot. His father was Columbian and believed to be part of Columbia's Italian diplomatic corps. Born in Bogota, Diego grew up in Paris[254] in the area near the Rond

Point, its adjacent circular streets then a Latin American in-city colony.[255] Diego moved to Florence with his family as a young adult and there began the study of architecture at the Accademia di Belle Arte.[256]

Diego Suarez was a very attractive fellow with good social connections. "He moved in a special world."[257] By the time he had met Arthur Acton in 1904, who had been married less than a year, Suarez, was in his mid-twenties, and as architect / landscape architect was astonishingly reported to have already completed eight other Italian villa restorations. In Florence he is known to have restored the Villa Loeser,[258] the Villa Schiffanoia and the Villa Selva e Guasto.[259] Suarez spent from 1904 to 1921 working with Acton on the villa. He was Acton's constant companion during this time, often traveling to the Brenta Riveria and to Vicenza in the Veneto region on sculpture buying expeditions. The Acton - Suarez relationship seemed to be more than just close, and perhaps was modeled on the standard older / younger homosexual relationship of the time. The usual abusive manner attributed to Acton with regards to staff does not seem to have existed with Suarez. On at least one instance, Suarez listed himself as the designer of the garden restorations at Villa La Pietra[260] and in another instance, he credits Acton. Because of their long relationship, probably both attributions were correct.

> "Mr. Acton had been engaged for several years in restoring the superb Renaissance gardens on his estate, some parts of them going back to the seventeenth century. They had been destroyed during the stupid craze for naturalistic English gardens, Arthur Acton was my tutor. I went to his villa four or five times a week while he was at work carefully supervising the restoration. He gave me my teaching in classical Italian garden design." [261]

Even though it is certain that Arthur Acton and Diego Suarez were the day-to-day creators of La Pietra during the initial decade, there were many other *ideatori* or design consultants to the gardens.[262] We know that between 1905 and 1914, Acton and Suarez often visited Villa Gamberaia to discuss landscape design issues with Princess Ghyka and her *capo giardineo*, Martino Porcinai. Acton had abundant opportunities for these visits as the Topolino quarries of Settignano was the location for many noted stone carvers and sculpture reproduction houses. Utilizing the harder limestone of this particular Mugello foothill, seven prominent families set up shop. It is the most probable location for Arthur to have arranged and supervised the reproduction of his Brenta acquisitions. A social visit to the Gamberaia after business was finished was not out of the question on such occasions.

> "Their head gardener and ours became close friends: they belong to a vanishing species whose passion for horticulture was religion and all-embracing."[263]
>
> Sir Harold Acton

Between 1910 and 1915, Berenson often invited Arthur Acton to lunch at Villa I Tatti while its gardens were under construction. Possibly, Cecil Pinsent and / or Geoffrey Scott were included on these occasions. Discussions and issues raised in Scott's writings on the humanism of Renaissance architecture were akin to the sort of design expression being employed by Suarez and Acton in the gardens at La Pietria. Together, this group sought both the ideals of humanist architecture and *"il processo di Toscanizzare,"* or the process of developing a Tuscanized design vocabulary. The pallettes of I Tatti and La Pietra, with their green architecture, clearly defined architectonic spaces, and gardens in series are too similar to not have emerged from the same "cloth." In 1911, Cecil Pinsent and Geoffrey Scott were specifically asked by Acton to design a new *contadino* or farmhouse at the western edge of the topiary gardens on the south side of Villa Acton.[264] Cecil Pinsent was in charge. He designed an elaborate two-story structure with a baroque facade that was accessible on two levels - from the house / garden level, and from the farm road below. The structure was probably proposed to house the *mezzadrini*'s functioning spaces - an office for the *factore* and storage rooms for the *podere*'s equipment and produce. He probably went beyond his assignment, making recommendations to expand the topiary garden located across the sunken road into the *podere* orchards to the west. The Pinsent plans were not executed.

> "....era da aspettarsi che lo stilo Barrocco sarebbe vento a regione indiscusso nel giardino e nel teatro - le due province che permettono la maggior liberta di disegno." [265]
>
> Geoffrey Scott

Geoffrey Scott was much enamored with the Acton garden and studied their composition. He found its multi-axial arrangement unique to any humanist garden heretofore studied by him. Perhaps the Boboli garden with its two differing sections and their corresponding separate axis was a precedent - one, the central axis, circus to amphitheater, and the second, the long *viale* to the Pratolino - but in both cases, it was topography that dictated their complete separation. Villa Valzambizio in the Veneto, certainly familiar to Arthur Acton, could also have been an inspiration. This late seventeenth century villa has one central axis but many cross axes and side *vascas*.[266] This layout would differ still from the in-line *vascas*, the multi-axial and multi-direction axes' composition of Villa Acton. Perhaps, too, the Villa d'Este, Tivoli, could be cited as a precedent, as this villa has three north south-axes and three east - west axes. The villa though, in its original form, was one totally open room with these axes as mere dividing paths for the garden's huge parterres. The axes were not used conceptually as the organizing elements of enclosed rooms connected in series. There is a rare painting, *Villa d'Este, Tivoli*.[267] in the collection of Sir Harold Acton by an unknown seventeenth century artist that shows in perspective the villa's original Renaissance garden development. As Harold inherited this work from his father, Villa d'Este could very well have been a source of inspiration in the garden's new compositional structure. (Although, in the English Garden period of the Villa d'Este, the hillside parterres were planted in the naturalistic fashion, thereby destroying the spatial unity in its natural/classical fusion, the garden could have provided the inspiration for Acton's garden composition.) Importantly, Scott's comments show that the elements of composition were discussed by the three groups of designers and were formulated into a landscape architectural coda, mutually confirmed, if not acted on.

A number of major garden designers and garden *afficionados* toured or visited the gardens of Villa Acton, but far fewer than those who visited Villa Gamberaia's. Any of these visitors could have contributed ideas for the garden's development. Florentines, such as Sir George Sitwell, were also frequent visitors. During the formative years, guests included foreign owners and designers of famous gardens, among them Vita Sackville-West of Sissinghurst (sans Violet); Lady Astor Cliveden and Lawrence Johnston of Hidcote. Gertrude Jekyll, stayed at the villa,[268] but alas, none of her famous sketches that she often made while a guest at other villas were left behind for her host at Villa Acton.[269]

By the beginning of the First World War in 1914, the Acton gardens were still generally unknown. The finished gardens post-date the death of Stanford White and were known to very few American architects. The gardens also post-date the most influential American books on Italian gardens; those by Janet Ross and Edith Wharton. The first book describing La Pietra in text and photographs was not published until 1922 and was by the English author Harold Eberling.[270] By this period the gardens were mostly complete. Visitors were drawn there either as a result of visiting the Gamberaia or by word-of-mouth references. John Deering, the Chicago financier, visited La Pietra in 1914 at the suggestion of William Mitchell, Hortense's father, and John's young lover, Paul Chalfin, an American art expert[271] and would-be painter who studied in Paris under

Whistler, was brought along in-tow. Chalfin was friends with Bernard Berenson and Isabella Gardner, and had been to I Tatti in 1907 before the completion of any of the major renovations to Villa Acton. Mitchell was probably trying to connect Deering to Acton for the expansion of Deering's Chicago art collection. Arthur delegated Diego to show them around the gardens. They were stunned at its beauty and Acton's use of sculpture to structure spaces.[272] Over lunch, Arthur invited them along on a buying foray in the Veneto. The two couples, Acton, Suarez, and Deering, Chalfin traveled the Brenta region acquiring sculpture.[273] It was a fateful trip for Arthur Acton as Suarez, on a later trip to America, decided to remain and become the designer of *Viscaya*, Deering's new mansion and gardens in Miami, one of America's most elaborate and beautiful gardens of the Country Place era. Perhaps, Suarez felt that the gardens of La Pietra were essentially completed and saw a creative challenge at *Viscaya*, or perhaps Suarez had a romantic attachment to Chalfin

> "It was there (Florence) that Diego Suarez, America's greatest living landscape architect, did his first gardens, revealing the genius that was to produce the magnificent gardens of *Villa Vizcaya* in Miami."[274]
>
> Henry Hope Reed

From photographs, Villa Acton's development continued under Acton's sole direction, but with a striking difference in its design. It was as if the second renaissance landscape architectural design had been transformed into the topiary expressions of the English Arts and Crafts movement. In 1921, perhaps to replace Suarez, Acton hired a Polish immigrant, Mariano Ambroziewicz, as his *capo giardinero*.[275] His "brilliant" Mariano headed the maintenance of the garden until 1942, the beginning of the Second World War in the area. But Mariano had no training in design of any type and provided solely horticultural expertise. The garden's changes were guided by Acton's design skills alone, for the most part, and little was changed during this period. Few visitors are recorded as having come to the gardens during this period, but garden historians Georgina Masson, and in 1923, the Jellicoes visited the gardens and offered advice. They may have critiqued or proffered design ideas to Acton, but specific suggestions are not known to have contributed significantly to the garden's development.

It is interesting to note that none of the Fellows in Landscape Architecture from the American Academy in Rome sketched or measured the gardens as they had done at the Gamberaia. Only Lawson photographed the gardens, in 1919, to provide us with an excellent record of the Acton / Suarez era. The only early garden historian to publish La Pietra within his compendium on the subject was the English landscape architect, Geoffrey Jellicoe. Even here, Jellicoe produced no measured drawings, and furnished only a small aerial perspective sketch and a very minimal description, one paragraph long. La Pietra's gardens in the Arthur Acton years went unmeasured, unrecorded and certainly unstudied.

The frozen music of Villa Acton's landscape architectural composition is a choreographic/symphonic poem in three parts:[276] An entry processional; a *pomario* scherzo - *sotta voce*; and a largo *brillante*. Like Modeste Mussorgsky's symphonic poem, *Pictures at an Exhibition*,[277] the garden is a composition of tightly defined outdoor rooms, each like a landscape painting, one connected to the other. The first movement, as in the Mousorgky composition, begins with a processional theme that propels the visitor through interconnected axes, from movement to movement and from room to room. The second, a scherzo, is rapidly moving, a light hearted piece, half a jest of fanciful foodstuffs and half a play of geometric tricks, positioned as tradition would require, in the middle of the composition. The first two movements present singular images, while in the final movement, multiple images are presented, their sequence dependent on the choice made by your host as guide or made at random by the viewer, himself. In the largo *brillante*, each scene is a room with a story told by the Acton sculptures and topiary; each room connected by the repeated theme, the informal composition of trees and shrubs that are reminiscent of the earlier *giardino inglese*.

Acton hated the crude color discords of the English garden style; instead his rooms were composed as romantic Tuscan passages, where a mixture of evergreens formed a lyrical *bosequetto*-like (or small wood-like) setting. Here, he employed Holm oaks, Italian cypresses and stone and umbrella pines, some as regal as those imagined in Respighi's *Pines of Rome*.

The Processional: *Il Viale*   Arriving at La Pietra was a particular delight. Having left the noisy crowded streets of urban Florence and driven exactly one mile along a road solidly lined with yellow-ochre two meter high walls, the arrival at the villa was marked by a high point in the road. At a small indentation on the right, beautiful iron gates, flanked by two *portinerie*(or gate-keepers' houses) announce one's arrival. The entrance could be

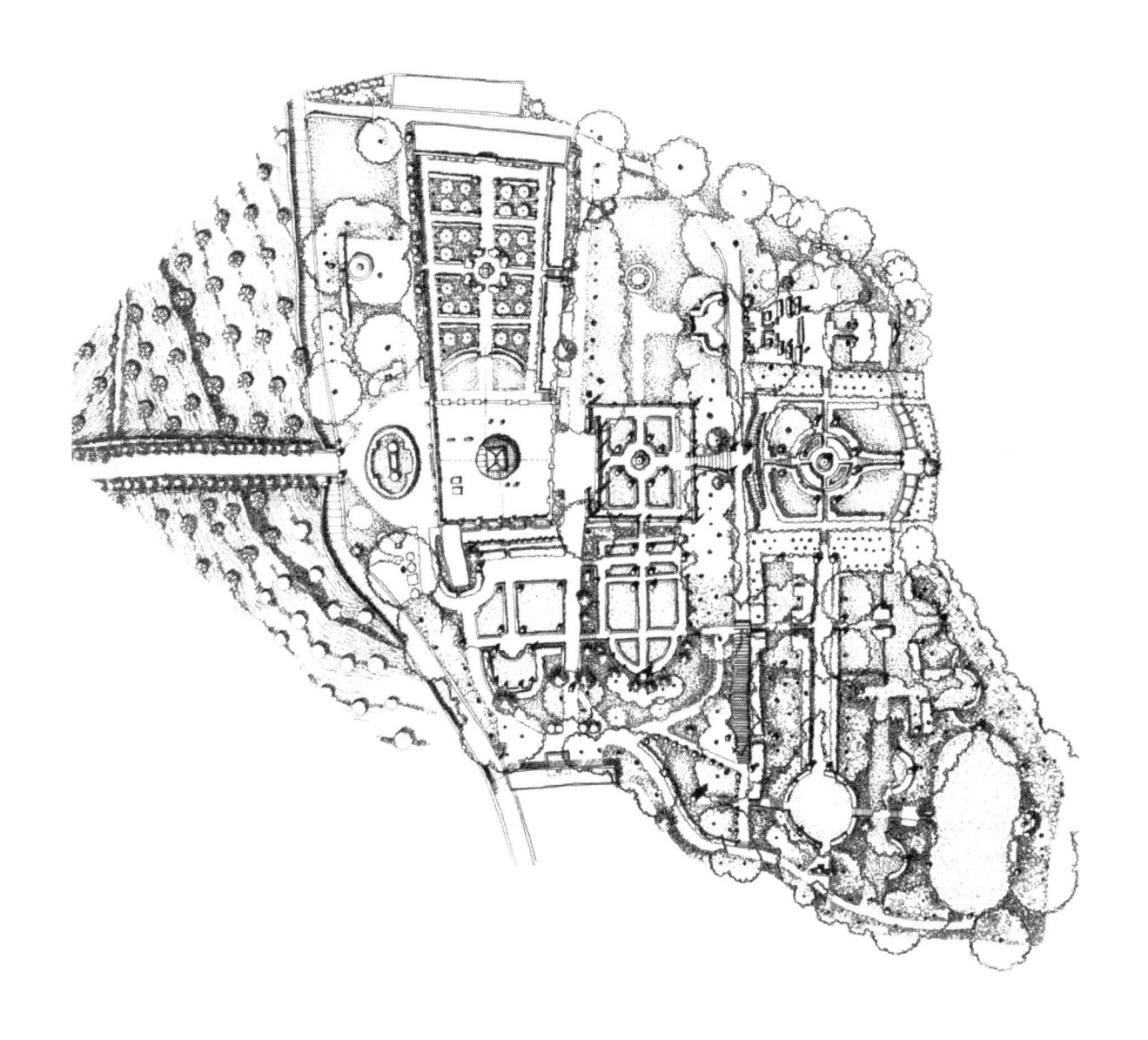

Illustrative Plan of Villa Acton of La Pietra, 1999

missed with a blink of the eye, but once through the gates, the noise and congestion of the city road was behind and the first vista of the villa's main house, at the end of a straight allee of Italian cypresses, lay ahead. The perspective, with subtle changes in grade to the arrival point, becomes immediately apparent. With the processional following a gradually descent to the allee's midpoint before rising again at its conclusion, the forecourt of the house and the feeling of arrival seems both grand and inevitable. The road was built in *terra battuta*, a particular Italian invention - a mixture of coarse sands and fine aggregate that are stabilized by the addition of dry cement. Over time the cement, picking up ground moisture, forms a dirt roads. The 260-meter long road was edged by a 30 cm high, raised solid balustrade behind which a trailing form of roses (*Rosa chinensis*), clumps of deep blue irises, and the Italian cypresses were planted. The dramatic line of cypress would purposely and completely block any view to the adjacent olive orchards of the *podere* located to the side.

The procession down this impressive allee was constantly bathed in bands of brilliant sunlight and deep shadow cast by the cypresses. Side views over the adjacent orchards were startling as one became aware that the transit was taking place on a raised viaduct, rampart or causeway. The constant dramatic light / shadow rhythm continued as the road would finally reverse its descent and begin to rise as one approached the looming house at its terminus. Exactly upon reaching the gates to the villa's forecourt, the prospect of the full width view of the western facade came into view. In the process of arriving, one may have missed a side revealing the crossing of the via dei Bruni, a major local farm road, passing though a tunnel four meters below the level of the allee.

The entry viaduct is a marvelous piece of engineering that existed before Acton's arrival. The new entry from the west dated back to Sciopione Capponi who installed the route and lined it with low hedges,[278] but left it to rise and fall with its natural grades. It was in the 1880s that the Incontri heirs raised the route by building the viaduct of pointed stone buttress piers and brick arches infilled with stones to form the road's base. It had a tunnel for the *fosso* in the route's center and one for the now-suppressed via dei Bruni. The suppression of the road made the adjacent countryside raw and unappealing. The omission of any lining shrubs and with only fields of olive orchards along the road, its former glory was lost.

Acton began his new landscape developments with replanting the entrance allee in cypress trees, installing irises and roses along its base. The roses and native iris were perfect species (tried and proven at the Gamberaia) to cope with the dry climate, the limited depth of soil on top of the viaduct, and the competition from the roots of adjacent cypresses. Villa Acton was now approached along a stately avenue of cypresses typical of Tuscan villas and lined with seasonal flowers. So impressive was the change that Guy Mitchell would copy the roadway, the Incontri family removed the walls of the southern *hortus conclusus* and razed the Baroque parterres incorporating this area into the new *giardino inglese*. They built the viaduct wider than the road so as to include strips on both sides for vegetation, planting its entire length with the tree-form of Robinia. When Acton arrived, the original planted allee presented a hot dry landscape that lacked drama. With lack of maintenance, the appearance idea for the redesign of his gardens at the Villa il Giullarino. The cypress trees at La Pietra, however, have suffered ever since Acton planted them and have had to be replaced several times on an on-going basis. In this particular region of low-lying valleys adjacent to urban populations and grandeur of the procession remains intact.

Piazzale   As the finale to the processional, the *piazzale* was a fitting terminus to the allee. After traveling the shadow-striped cypress lined causeway, one entered the *piazzale* through a gateway, emerging into the full sunlight of the entry court, a simple oval space featuring beautifully proportioned façade of the house. As originally designed by Sassetti's architect, Giorgio Vasari, the facade was a perfect cube, its windows and moldings in thin shallow relief, giving the impression of a flat, solid mass. The stucco walls of the exterior were a brownish-grey color, the shutters light green, and the stone trim of the doors and windows a brown-toned *pietra serena*. The entry gates, dating from the Incontri era, were unadorned elements standing before an unadorned facade. To the gate's pillars, Acton added a matched pair of mythical hunters/gatherers bought during one of his forays into the Veneto region. Decorative raised fountains to the sides of the low gate walls, were an Acton addition.

The earlier arrival court was a rectangular space that stretched the length of the house and its attached *pomario*. In the Prussian's anglofication, the western edge was lined with a mixture of trees and shrubbery, *anghuillare*, and the entire surface area was planted as lawn. The simplicity of the space matched that of the facade and must have been most striking in itsserenity. In even greater Anglo zeal, the Incontri family added islands of *anghuillare* to modulate the length of the lawn and further dotted the space with one or two specimen trees. Even as a renter, Acton was displeased with the effect of such an inharmonious space and refocused the entire composition onto the building's facade. To achieve this end, he planted massive hedges defining the northern and southern limits of the forecourt and created a *parcheggio,* or utilitarian parking area behind, screening the remaining area to the north.

The articulation of the new forecourt space evolved over time and changed in nature. The attendant pollution, the cypresses are susceptible to disease and must be constantly protected and treated if they are to survive. Even with their irregularity in age and size, the of the space. In the first iteration, Acton placed a large stone tub from antiquity at the oval's center and surrounded the wide circle of *terra battuta* by low clipped boxwood (*Buxu ssempervirens*) hedges. The side spaces to the north and south were planted in English yews, the first use of this plant in Italy. It was a simple and effective treatment for the terminus of the grand processional *viale*. A second and later iteration, achieved in collaboration with Diego Suarez, included newly designed north and south planted sculpture gardens, with large figurative pieces flanked and backed by an assortment of topiary evergreens. The southern garden contained a statue of Diane, the huntress, set into a clipped green architectural niche of yews, *Taxus baccata*, and a background of tall mixed evergreens. The simplicity of the new green architectural room coincided with similar garden developments at Villa Gamberaia, in the 1910s, and was part of the new pallette of the second renaissance gardens.

A later iteration, in the 1930s, shows Acton's singular and unrestrained design hand. He flanked the central stone tub with English yews, *Taxus baccata*, that were trained into the shape of topiary urns. Along the tops of the yew hedges, peacocks sprouted and were silhouetted. They were joined by two topiary peacocks, facing each other, that were placed in the lawn in front of each of the two sculptures - all tacky and needless elements. Down the side drives to the *parcheggio* and service areas, topiary columns sprouting topiary urns and more peacocks were added. These topiary features were distinctly reminiscent of the English Arts and Craft garden style of the later part of the nineteenth century and were used here by Acton in what was reputed to be the first employment of the Arts and Crafts style in Italy.[279]

The *piazzale* contained the key to the pallette used throughout the new Acton gardens: It was a complex jumble of styles, using landscape elements to define rooms of green architecture, punctuated by sculptures that defined the geometry of the room. Plants were employed to spatially define the sculptures, or to add background to them. The composition of plant material was a subtle mixture of textures and hues, expressing, in part, either the newly emerging simplicity of forms begun at the Villa Gamberaia (in cases where the work was designed during the Acton/ Suarez era) or the introduction of the topiary expressions of the Arts and Crafts movement from England (after the mid 1920s, when Arthur acted independently.)

The Processional: Il Viale

The entry gate and Piazzlea beyond

Cortile looking to the entrance allee

The entrance Piazzale and Viale beyond

The Piazzale

Pomerio's enclosing wall surfaced in rocaille.

Center of the pomerio space7

The main axis of the Green Parterre Garden as seen from the Terrace

The Prima Vasca

Cross axis and defing edge of the Prima Vasca

The Prima Vasca looking toward the house

The Secunda Vasca from the Prima Vasca

The Secunda Vasca and its exedra

The Tempieto from the Secunda Vasca

Il Teatrino Verde,

The western end of the Processional

Brochetto

il Vialone

Vista del Colosso

Pergola Della Rose

Rose Parterres

The Terrace from the Prima Vasca

The Cypress Allee

Pomerio   The *pomario*, located to the north of the house in this choreographic poem, was a delightful scherzo and represented a perfect example of *hortus conclusus*, or walled secret garden, rare to any of the present day survivors of the Renaissance garden. Traditionally, these gardens were more than production areas for household medical and foodstuffs – the *sotta voce* of possible garden types - and were private protective retreats, embellished so totally as to represent a separate art form. Their perfect geometries were this scherzo's jest, overstated to the point where vegetables, such as beans, were structured in circles, and fruit trees were espaliered into beautiful structural patterns. Water, here, was used not just for irrigation but for its animating and musical sounds and the garden's walls were elaborately dressed in *rocaille* mosaics of mussels, clams, scallops and shell waste from domestic consumption.[280]

> "The *pomario* is probably the oldest surviving part of the garden. The walls of the garden are suggested by Vasari's plan for Francesco Capponi (c1600) and the *limonaia* at its northern end would appear to date back to the *'nuova conserva'* built for Scipione Capponi in 1654. The garden would have been used as a productive space for fruit (pears, peaches and citrus) and vegetables and probably divided into axial quadrants, similar to today's layout."[281]

The *pomario*, like all other gardens of the villa, changed over time. In the Francesco Capponi form, it was called *giardino grande*, and was a much smaller parterre garden comprising of about a third of the present front *pomario*. It was expanded to its full length by Scipoini Capponi in a curious geometry, wider at its far end and narrow at the house, indicating the use of the device of false perspective. Its internal form is unknown for certain, but it was thought to be typical of other Renaissance *hortus conclusus* of the period, that is, in some pattern of parterres.[282] Enclosed gardens typically featured a complete mixture of pleached, posted and espaliered fruit trees, herbs and seasonal vegetables filling two quartered-parterres. The north enclosing far wall was usually the facade of the south facing *lemonaia*, as is the case here. Different internal development is shown, one similar to that of the Capponi plan of In a 1896 plan at Pianta della Citta di Florence, Instituto Geografico Militare,[283] a garden where the oval is formed by small trees, some frost intolerant and others that require the protection of the adjacent *lemonaia*. It is so incredibly similar in plan that one could imagine a pool in the oval. (Water, we know, was used later in a central fountain). This then becomes yet another example of the typical Tuscan gardens that the Florentine architect Filarete spoke of in a 1470 description of the Villa Badia in Florence. As already noted, that villa was an antecedent to the original parterre garden at the Gamberaia. It described a fish pond, fed by crystal clear waters from a nearby spring, filled with fish of all types, and surrounded by fruit trees whose fruit conveniently fell into the pond, feeding the fish.[284] Add to this the nutrients from the runoff of a rabbit island, and the scene describes a perfectly balanced, self-sustaining ecological garden. This wonderfully efficient household-type production garden appeared to be favored by the Capponi family. Unrecorded in the survey of the *giardino all'inglese,* commissioned by Acton when he bought the villa, nor evident in photographs of the period when Acton rented the villa, the garden was probably eradicated by an Incontri for what would be considered a more traditional *giardino inclusiva,* a plan of eight parterres arranged around a central fountain, as in the present plan. *"Cabreo Villa Gamberaia:*[285] It shows a two-part development, the first some sort of central walk lined with border bedded plants leading to the second rear development, that of an oval.

Acton spent an incredible amount of money and time "restoring" the *pomario* to the refined culmination of what he thought such a garden could be. His first repairs were to the underground cistern along its southern edge, this to better supply water to the house and garden. The work necessitated reshaping the terrace area into a semicircular space. He added stone piers to frame an ornate wrought iron gate, placing atop, statues of dwarfs holding cornucopia. He lined the space with hedges and oleanders in tubs and planted hydrangeas, fronting the hedges. Kim Wilkie noted: "hydrangeas - known as *ortensia* in Italian, a nice echo on the Italian pronunciation of Hortense's name."[286] Rather curiously unsanitary, Acton used this space as a kennel for his Bernese mountain dogs. Similar to the *maremmani* white sheep dogs of Princess Ghyka at the Gamberaia, both breeds were the signature of a cultured life and were raised for their commercial value. But in Acton's case, their location over the house's major cistern posed a potential problem of water contamination.

In rebuilding the *pomario*'s enclosing walls, Acton installed a cross axis at mid-point, with ornate entry gates at either end, providing cross circulation through the garden. The gate on the east required a bank of steps for the sharp grade change, and buttresses to support the end-wall segments. Columns and niches were implanted in the wall's elevation in new *rocaille,* mimicking that of the preserved *lemonaia* at the northern end. Atop the walls, Arthur assembled urns, vases and busts, reproductions from originals gleaned from other gardens. To strengthen the new cross axis, he placed statues of the four seasons in the parterre corners, backed by hedges. Additionally, outside the walls in the *parcheggio,* he placed the old discarded pool and fountains from the *giardino inglese* period as a visual terminus to the new axis. The complete renovation was accomplished with funds provided by his father-in-law, William Mitchell, who was probably enlisted to Acton's cause on his 1903 visit to the property.

Inside the *pomerio* space, Acton lined the parterres with the new pallette of the Second Renaissance landscape - hedges of alternating color - green boxwood, *Buxus sempervirens var. suffuticosa,* and a reddish leaf plant. He accentuated the central space with a meter-high laurel hedge, *Myrtus communis.* Within the parterres, he planted a variety of fruit trees including, just as an example, twenty-eight differing pear trees, with vegetable crops as a ground cover below. Many of the vegetable seeds were imported from America, including sweet corn and lima beans.[287] During the summer, citrus trees would have been moved out of the *lemonaia,* filling the space with sweet scented flowers and bright shiny fruit.

In the 1930s iteration, Acton allowed the central laurel hedges to grow tall, forming a semicircular half-domed hood over the four statues which he humorously turned to face away from the fountain and toward the individual parterres. (One can only imagine what antics Acton was saving the sculpted figures from having to witness.) The laurel mass was articulated into an English Arts and Crafts grotto-like topiary form, all four in combination making a most unusual central space to mark any known garden.

The Largo – The Eastern Garden   The new "eastern gardens" created by Acton and Suarez were a largo composition of cross axes extended, expanded and repeated brilliantly and crisply, in differing colors, textures, shapes and volumes in all its sub-parts.[288] The second renaissance vocabulary, enclosed green architectural spaces defined and enhanced by stone architectural accents, was used throughout the largo and in its entirety provided a most effective setting for advantageously showcasing Acton's sculpture collection.

> "Ultimately everything at home revolved around the collection, of which the garden was an open-air extension." [289]
>
> Kim Wilkie

> "Most visitors think the statues have been here forever, but they were bought at a time when statue-less English gardens were the rage and Arthur had his choice of the finest available."[290]
>
> Patricia Schultz

The "eastern gardens" were in the shape of a fat, reversed "L" in plan, wrapping around the east and south facades of the house. The garden was constructed with the new terraces reportedly derived, in general, from a historic plan reported to be reposited in the Uffizi Gallery.[291] But in all likelihood, it was structured using the survey that was commissioned earlier by Acton, probably at the time of his purchase of the villa in 1903, when the Prussian *giardino ingleses* was still very much intact. Over this survey, Acton would have sketched out the center lines of the largo's primary and sub-axes, indicating where major terracing would occur, thus organizing the garden's structure. Using two cross axes as the organizing elements, a series of gardens were laid out, one after the other. One axis is an extension of the main axis through the house, the descending sloped central axis, (the *vasche*), and the other, an all landscape axis,(the *vialone,)* which is on a flat that parallels the primary facade of the house. From each of these axes, other cross axes spring leading to other gardens of various sizes and uses. The simple palette of elements carry the largo's melody throughout: Stone balustrades and sculptures amidst clipped green hedges, walls, and sculptural topiary, surrounded by plane trees, stone pines and cypresses. Each passage is separated by the romantic melody of informal evergreens composed like those of the prior romantic English garden. The processional landscapes are played in dark and somber tones, the *vascas* remaining in brilliant sun-light hues of green.

"Restored by my father as he imagined it might have been,"

Harold Acton

" My father refined upon the traces of the former garden and its retaining walls, with the creative ingenuity of a Cinquecento architect."[292]

Harold Acton

The multi-axial connection of garden rooms is the brilliant aspect of the largo of the Villa Acton. In creating the compositional device, a visitor was presented with options in all directions. After a tour of the central *vasche*, a logical beginning, there were choices all along the way, as seductive vistas through opened doors in their green walls offered new possibilities. It was the perfect dream space for a *flaneur,* or aimless wanderer in the French, sense, except of course, not if one was on an always hasty Acton guided tour. The *flaneur* however, would have had the opportunity to muse upon a Bacchus sculpture, to study the intricate *rocaille* work of the *pomario*, gaze upon slopes of lavender, dwell on the perfect symmetry of the *secunda vasca*, to fantasize a Moliere play in the *teatrino,* or be startled by the sudden view of a sculptural colossus. In the largo it was easy to get lost; the garden was immense and full of surprises. Although the largo by its multi-axial nature, could have been toured as the *flaneur* might have, that is, in any number of combinations, it is presented here as the structured tour that would have been the proud undertaking of Arthur Acton for the benefit of his compliant guests.

> "The garden became an architectural expansion of the house, a series of open-air rooms, descending the hillside with broad flights of pebble-patterned steps from one suite to another."[293]
>
> Sir Harold Acton

> "Laid out on a sloping site as a series of garden rooms, complete with green theater, this aspect of the garden is typically Tuscan. But the extensive use of topiary and the introduction of motifs in the classical style and Venetian garden sculpture has given the garden a curiously individual character. It can best be described as a foreigner's conception of an ideal Italian garden, but as such it is not at all out of place in a city that is one of the meccas of the foreign traveler in Italy."[294]
>
> Georgina Masson

The Central Axis, *Terrazza*   His largo began at the house and its *terrazza (terrace)*, with the central and primary axis extending down the eastern slopes in a series of *vascas* (rooms) forming the *vasche,* or central axis. It was continued through the house and extended westerly by the cypress-lined entry road. The simple terrace, paved in travertine, was created by carving out the slope and adding a retaining wall and grand taircase to the *prima vasca* below. The sandstone balustrade began the main series of gardens stepping down the steep hillside. It was also the center of a cross axis paralleling the main eastern facade, extending the axis to the south, into the Italian topiary garden, and to north onto the grand avenue fronting the *pomario*'s enclosing wall. It was here that the visitor could survey the gardens below and to the sides, understanding the compositional order of the Villa Acton largo - the central *vasche* immediately in front, the *tempietto e teatrino* area to the left, the *boschetto* to the right and, to the far right around the side of the house, the *giardino topiario*. find Athena, Bacchus, Hercules and Apollo.[295] The sculptures frame the panoramic view across the valley or the view down, into the consecutively descending gardens, or can be seen in silhouette against sky from below. It is important to realize that this terrace offered the only long, panoramic views over the olive orchards to the adjacent parallel ridge line. (The view was closed off in each of the sequentially lower gardens.) One of the striking features of the Acton / Suarez plan, differing dramatically from the Gamberaia with its belvedere or wrap-around terrace, was that, with the exception of one window at the end of the south property line in the bottom-most *vasca*, there were no distant views nor large panoramas to the Arno valley or distant hills. The spectacular panoramic view from the Incontri era terrace has long since been lost to a line of romantic holm oaks and pines that continued to grow, changing what once was the short passage of the *scalene,* into a dark, prolonged passage. Now these romantic evergreens, with the new oaks and pines planted by Acton / Suarez, have enclosed the space, eliminating the distant skyline from the terrace and enclosing, in truth, the entire largo. Perhaps this was for the better, as the olive fields, the signature element in the view, have long since been sold off, replaced by blocks of undistinguished suburban housing.

> "The garden became an architectural expansion of the house, a series of salons descending the hillside with broad flights of pebble-patterned steps."[296]
>
> Sir Harold Acton

Prima Vasca From the *terrazza*, one descends flights of architectural stairs onto the very first garden space created by Acton in the 1910s, the *prima vasca.* The beginning space in the long east/west cross axis that contains a number of garden rooms in series, the *prima vasca* is a wide, square space, exactly the width of the house, enclosed by low walls, lined with alternating figurative sculptures and mannerist urns, with its corners defined by short stone obelisks. (Placed inside the *prima vasca,* on a pedestal to the side and near its end, was a statue of Eros and Psyche, serving as symbols of the primary reasons for this and the other second renaissance garden spaces. One other major figurative piece is the remorseless stone Salome holding the head of John the Baptist, an Acton and Diego acquisition from northern Italy.) The walks of the *prima vasca* are paved in mosaics of colored pebbles, and its parteres are filled with topiary hedge columns with arched niches at their corners. A fountain and fish pond filled with water lilies and long-tailed goldfish, descendants of those brought back from China after the Boxer Rebellion by Janet Ross's estranged husband, stand at the center of the garden. This fountain is a copy of the one at the center of the *Pomario.* The *prima vasca* contains the only water to be found in the largo movement. Water, as we have seen was a precious commodity and was not to be wasted, although ironically, and irrationally, the water necessary to maintain the grass and the evergreen hedges throughout the gardens more than consumed the amount that would have been necessary for a water parterre garden. Water usage was such that in the summer months it was often brought into the household from the *villini* below.

Of especial interest is the use of plants in the four center parterres of the *prima vasca.* Within a space that would normally have been planted in a single evergreen species, so small was its size, the topiary elements employed are planted instead in a number of differing evergreens, providing the space with a wide variety of textures, and most startling, colors. Defining the limits of each parterre, the low hedges are planted in *Buxas semprivirens cultiva,* with its small fine glossy leaf; the central diagonal hedges backing the stone *poltrone* or benches, are *Taxus braccata,* dark green needled; the eight cylinders marking the central space are columns of *Taxus baccata >golden,'* cut off at two meters, forming a crisp geometry; and on both sides of the downhill steps, arched-over *Cupressus sempervirens sp.,* a brownish-green, fine-needled plant. Each plant was chosen to contrast with the others so as to reveal its role in the composition. The golden columns were electric when compared to their somber neighbors and played a key role in defining stone walls and statuary of the space. The parterre's centers were originally filled with white daises, which completed the full range of tones.

The *prima vasca* illustrated the difference in taste of the Acton/Suarez team and later variations of Acton acting solo occurred in the manner of its plantings' trimming to the geometry of the topiary forms. During the Acton /Suarez period, the hedges were simple, never over one-meter tall, and emphasized the horizontal lines of the space. The late Acton period provided variations that showed the accentuation of vertical elements, with the center forms rising to two meters in height, the central space becoming a separate sub-space within the whole. The corners and entries were arched-over, completely enclosing the room and offering only a tunnel view into the next space beyond. In the later Acton period, the role of Mariano Ambroziewicz, the *capo giardinero*, provide additional variations. This can be seen in changing the contrasting hued evergreens into more adaptive local varieties. The columns of *Taxus baccata 'golden'* were replaced with the common, and far coarser, dark green bay laurel; the daisy-filled parterre replaced by grass. Ambroziewicz was practical and expedient, but had no eye for aesthetics.

"The prima vasca is the climax of the main vista from the villa."[297]

Scalone   The *scalone,* the processional stair between the *primavasca* and the next descending garden space, was a space in itself, and had to accommodate the major grade change that existed even in the romantic Prussian plan. The fluid and expanding *scalone,* made of grey and white pebble mosaics in geometric patterns, was marked by side bands of Holm oaks, *Quercus ilex.* They were retained by Acton in their extant condition, only to be embellished by a pair of lion sculptures. Adjacent to the sun-soaked rooms, the dense dark woods provided highly contrasting background. Suarez recommended adding bay laurel to edge of the *scalone* to conceal the untidy adjacent slopes where the colonization of ground covers had proven to be difficult, due to the surface-rooted oaks, but it was Acton, in his late period, who allowed the laurel to grow and arch over the stairway, forming a dark tunnel that heightened the contrast to the sun-filled *vascas.*

Continued descent along the central axis, led to the *seconda vasca,* a spectacular elliptical space. Like the Ghyka cadenza at the Gamberaia, this *vasca* is a cadenza showing the virtuosity of Acton and Suarez. The *seconda vasca,* the last space on the central axis was preceded by the *Scalone* which provided the cadenza a perfect fermata. Completed in 1920 by the Acton and Suarez team - the last space completed by the team- it derived its form from combining two classical themes, the standard parterre garden and the *exedra* form. The *seconda vasca* was formed by tall, green, clipped architectural hedges, rectanglar on to opposing sides and exedral on the other two the side terminating the eastern side and thus the central axis is formed also by a pergola *exedra* in stone. The four corners of the space, probably at the suggestion of Villa Gamberaia's Miss Blood, are planted with parasol pines. She was known to have advised Acton on pines, reminding him: "You can never plant enough." The pergola, a *peristilio della glicine* (or peristyle) was built by placing thin stone lintels atop paired Corinthian columns that, in turn, were topped with stone urns acquired by Acton/Suarez on their northern Italian forays. The roof of the pergola was formed with wire in a cross weave on which banksiana roses were trained. In a later veriations, Ambroziewicz changed the roses, which required intense maintenance, to the denser spreading wisteria; yet another insensitive change made by the *capo gardiniere.* Behind the pergola, giving it full enclosure, was a two-meter, coarse-textured laurel hedge, followed by a densely planted mass of Holm oaks. The hedge originally was grown only to the height of the peristyle, giving it a dark interior wall. In the 1930s, Acton allowed it to grow two meters higher, changing the nature of the peristyle from a solid architectural form to architectural tracery. A pair of existing cypresses leftover from a late Capponi period ended the axial development on center. Below, in the center bay of the *exedra*, is a prized Acton acquisition, a statue of Hercules. Four other stone figures filled the *peristillo della glicine*'s architectural bays.

As architecture, the *exedra* peristyle was poorly conceived and executed, neither Suarez nor Acton showing competence as architects. The concave and convex curved facades of the peristyle were built from gathered thin flat stone pieces and applied as a facing over stucco-covered metal beams that rested on top of their support columns. The stone fascia pieces themselves were not sized to fit the spaces and overlapped crudely at the joints of each bay. The cornice lines from one piece to another often did not line up, reflecting the diverse and collected nature of the material's source. Crude detailing and patched over structural ties abound. The pergola appears to have been more of an opera stage set than a piece of permanent architecture. The low level of detailing and execution is reflected throughout the largo, as architectural niches, terminating the end of axes and framing major pieces of sculpture, are a mere ten-centimeters in depth and show the crudest of structural buttressing for the architectural pieces

The *seconda vasca*'s paired column gateways, adorned by a figurative sculpture, and its wide curvilinear steps and balustrade was Arthur Acton's pride. On one of his trips to the Boboli Gardens, he persuaded officials to allow him to replace what he termed as "worn", the Baroque water cascade balustrade lining the two sides of a small staircase, and to replace a damaged pair of entry columns for the Isolo de Pratto.[298] The Boboli's chain watercourse was typical of many Baroque gardens and similar to those at Villas Aldobrandini, Caparora and Lante. Comprised of a series of raised water troughs that formed overlapping pool segments, allowing water to spill from one segment into the next along the way, the chain watercourse was a sensual pleasure both for its playful visual effects and the water music it provided. Acton had the Boboli elements copied in Settignano's stone shops and re-installed the copies in place of the originals in the Boboli, retaining the originals for La Pietra's *seconda vasca*. As installed at the villa, the original Boboli balustrade was placed on a curve to edge Acton's elliptical staircase, bending at each joint to accommodate the arc of the stair. Pleasing enough aesthetically, this one time fountain was now kept dry, as the spreading joints required to make the curve would no longer hold water, and even if they were able, little of that commodity could be spared at the water-short La Pietra site. Furthermore, the beautiful original balustrade, had since been overgrown with "Dorothy Parker" trailing roses, concealing its form and beauty.[299] Similarly, the paired columns atop the entry stairs were copied many times and sold to American landscape architects, Ferrucio Vitale - possibly for use at Villa Carola, the estate of Solomon Guggenheim on Long Island - and to William Wells Bosworth for installation at Greystone, the estate of Samuel Untermeyer at Yonkers, New York. The centerpiece of the *seconda vasca* space is a tapestry parterre of intricately patterned, concentric hedge circles, clipped to a uniform height, forming what appears to be a deeply inscribed flat plane. The effect, in fact, is deceptive as the whole composition appears level when, in fact, the ground is sloping dramatically. The topiary itself, bearing a slight downhill cant, conceals a far greater drop in grade. The parterres are on two separate terraced levels, adjoined by a set of steps at the center that from the uphill side are shielded from view by a central stone fountain. Between the rows of the hedges, Acton planted pink dahlias, only later to change to pink and blue larkspurs during his Arts and Crafts period when he raised the height of the topiary. Photographs from 1937 indicate meter-high cypress cylinders, rounded boxwood globes, conical taxus cones and other topiary forms inserted into the space. In all phases, the center was held constant, marked by *terra batuatta* paving around the simple stone fountain which, like the baroque chain water course, is kept dry.

Processional   There are a number of processional routes that could be taken to tour the remaining sections of the largo. Side axes abound to the left and right of the central axis and occur at mid spaces of each *vasca*. Regardless of which path would be taken, there would remain constant the commonality of a dark dense vegetation providing a distinct break from one sun-filled room to the next. Most of these divisions would be formed by Holm oaks, although a few would consist of a dense planting of laurel hedges. We will, however, follow the route that Acton himself might have taken when leading his guests before a particularly festive luncheon, "of salons descending the hillside with broad flights of pebble-patterned steps."[300]

Tempieto E Teatrino, Il Teatrino   Acton would have proceeded by leading the entourage down the central axis as we have just done, commenting on the prior state of the garden, on the sculptures, their origins and subject matter or on the unusual assortment of his green architecture. Waiting at the end, under the *peristilio della glicine,* for stragglers, he would have led the party northward along the rose/wisteria-covered arcade, through an extra dense planting of high laurels and into the audience area of a surprise garden, *il teatrino*. Entering the hidden green *il teatrino* (theater) aroused surprise and awe. This green room presented an elongated space with fabulous sculptures set among a green topiary stage set - complete with clipped yew wings and globed boxwood footlights. The sculptures represented a frozen moment in time, a scene, as if part of some eternal play. The theater, which Acton called not by its generic Italian name, *teatro verde,* but by an affectionate equivalent, *teatrino,* or little theater, was more a space meant for after-dinner poetry readings by his son, Sir Harold Acton, or Italian folk tales performed by the blind Esther Frances (Francesca) Alexander. Occasionally, there would be a *quarteto di corde* played by Acton's musical friends.

> "The whole garden is essentially green; other colors are episodic and incidental. Sunlight and shade are as carefully distributed as the fountains, terraces and statues, and in no other private Florentine garden have I seen statues of such individual strength and grace, from the colossus by Orazio Marinali to the Venetian figures by Francesco Bonazza which have stepped on to the open air theater as for one of Goldoni's comedies."[301]
>   Sir Harold Acton

The *teatrino* was in the form of a classical outdoor Renaissance garden theater. The nave space was on two levels separated by a set of stairs (corresponding, parallel and

R. Terry Schnadelbach

adjacent to the two *vascas* and their transitional *scalino*). Two beautifully branched pear trees framed the entry perspective. The lower space was a reception space for refreshments enjoyed before and between acts. Occasionally, though the area was depressed, it accommodated overflow seating. Stairs led to the upper level where the main seating and stage areas were located. Upon this terraced stage, Acton created a "V" to the audience (indented center at the rear of the stage), using four Bonazza statues, a pair of balustrades, and a terminal architectural niche housing a fifth and smaller figurine. The sculptures of peasants in native costume carrying bounty of the harvests, were placed male on one side and female opposite.

    Clipped wings of receding hedges were worked around the sculptures to provide a false perspective, exaggerating the depth of the small stage area. The wings, as in a typical stage set, concealed the actors and their props. The addition of "footlight" topiary balls that actually were used to conceal the limelights was an unusual and inventive addition.

    Built at about the same time as the *seconda vasca,* and possibly in collaboration with Diego Suarez, the *teatrino* showed Acton's experimentation with topiary forms. The initial 1920s theater employed only two simply cut, one-meter high hedges for the stage wings. The backdrop was an existing planting in a naturalistic style from the Prussian *giardino inglese.* In the mid 1930s, Acton added a second line of topiary, a two-meter high hedge that created a strong enclosure to the theater space. Within two years, he completely rearranged the *teatrino* yet again, adding two topiary columns in front of the stage to create a proscenium-like effect and an additional pair of figurines of equal size to the side of the columns that thrust out into the audience area. Still in the "V" formation, this further elongated the perspective. He sculpted these vegetative columns, as well as the stage wings, into Arts and Crafts style topiary. Each proscenium column began from a square base, cut at the same height as the stage floor, rising to a fat circular shaft of two meters in height, and continued as a thinner column a half-meter higher. The next set of wings were trimmed in an opposite form, square columns with two widths, fat and thin, stepped back at correlating levels. The next receding pair of wings returned to the rounded columnar forms. This mixture of forms added mystery and intrigue to the space, as it appeared that actors would and could appear from any niche and cranny of the stage. The whole created a clear and unified form and a beautifully structured space. The final iteration, created in the 1950s, after the Second World War, removed the stone balustrades, leaving the figurines floating in the stage space, and equally destructive, sculpted all the topiary elements into the same form - a wide fat column base and a thin domed topping - both unfortunate design changes.

    Il Tempietto After the applause of a performance died down, guests would find their way onto the stage in front where, re-grouped, they would follow Acton uphill to the *tempietto* to meet the actors. Then, after appropriate kudos, guests would say their thank-you's and exit through the *pomario*'s cross axis to the *parcheggio*.

Boschetto But if one were on Acton's complete tour of the gardens, (sans performance), one would view the *tempietto* from a distance and the largo would continue from the nave of the *teatrino* - trailhead of the *vialone*, the largo's center and most important of three north-south axes - into the vast garden area called the *boschetto*. In its entirety, the *boschetto* was designed as a series of rooms strung along the multiple east-west and north-south axes beneath the canopy of romantic woodland species. It consists of two closely spaced north-south cross axes, the *vialone* and the *pergola della rose*; and two east-west axes, the *vista dell'arco* and the *vista del colosso* that were roughly spaced in equal units to the south of the largo's *vasche,* or central axis. In Acton's original sketch, these latter axes were spaced equally and parallel to one another, but the installed lattice differed, the last space being expanded further south and the two axes splayed apart at their far eastern end. These differences were the result of the design of each axis being made *en situ,* responding on site to the particular design intent for each separate axis. Between the axes, the *boschetto* is chopped into short mini-axes and mini-cross axes as changes in design intent dictated, with a most confusing effect.

The *Boschetto's* major axis, *il vialone* actually begins slightly to the north of the *Boschetto*, in the *Tempietto / Teatrino* sector, with the green architectural niche defined by a baroque stone window of unknown origin. Placed in the niche is yet another figure collected by Acton and Suarez from the Brenta region. From this point, the tour heads south, crossing through the shadow-filled, dense laurel *bosci* (*Laurus nobilis*) that defined the *teatrino* from the *Secunda Vasca*. One would now see the *seconda vasca* anew, cross slope from green side to green side, as opposed to the first impressions of it which were seen through the architectural elements of the twin-columned gateway stair and the *peristilio della glicine*. Suddenly, an abundance of avian life found in the *boschetto* becomes apparent. Overhead, the flutter and chirping of songbirds can be heard at any hour, a cacophony of morning and evening song to be followed by the lonely, but beautiful song of the nightingale. Across the sun-filled *vasca,* the tour group would enter the *boschetto* through another defining passage of the dark laurel *bosco,* and descending a small staircase, would find themselves on the *vialone*.

Il Vialone The *vialone*, the central north-south axis of the *boschetto*, is an area that is anything but woods-like, although it has the most trees of any section of the largo. It is really the main piece of a lattice connecting a hillside of small terraces, some of which were completed as early as late 1910s by the Acton / Suarez team. The *vialone* descends the *boschetto* slope in small gradients, while its cross axes, those running east-west, changes grade via dramatic stairs. A grass floor surface throughout adds to the *boschetto*'s soft and low-key character. The wooded impression of the *vialone* emanates from the tall, mixed trees that separate one room from the other and provides shade to the whole - *Pinus pinea, Quercus ilex, Quercus petraea, and cupressus sempervirens*. Here, the largo is played in quick-changing rhythms and in dark and somber tones.

> "So rapidly did the stone pines and evergreens shoot up that after sixty-years the garden had assumed the patina of a seventeenth-century pleasance."[302]
>
> Sir Harold Acton

Perhaps, Acton was influenced by the grand cypress allee of the Villa Gamberaia, for the *vialone* speaks of a similar but not exact copy of the Gamberaia's central organizing space. Its long green architectural space crisply articulated and defined by clipped hedges, the *vialone*, too, forms a hall-like space from which green architectural rooms unfold to both sides, each separated by dark *bosci*.

The *vialone*'s length, defined by half-meter-high laurel hedges, is backed by fragrant, white-blooming viburnum, and topped by a mixture of umbrella pines and Holm oaks. At each end, statues of semi-clad women holding objects - probably reflecting a four seasons theme - were placed in pairs. The ends were treated as gateways, again, each slightly different at any time in the history of the gardens at La Pietra. In Acton's first iteration of the 1910s, the gateway was nothing more than the simple turning of a corner and backed the statuary with the room-defining laurel hedge. In the 1920s, cypresses were added at the terminus of the hedges, forming a vertical gate. In the late 1930s, the cypresses were rimmed in the Arts and Crafts mode, cut-off columns that were modified twice by Arthur's son, Harold Acton, first in the 1960s, into square columns and later as larger square end walls surrounding the sculpture figures.

Vista dell'Arco One third of the way along the *vialone,* an opening in the wall revealed the first east-west cross axis, the *Vista dell'Arco*. Through the hedge doors of the *vialone*, stairs rising steeply uphill to the west were edged with lavender, ending in a stone arch, perhaps the remnant of some historic monument's doorway. Climbing this inviting set of stairs, the party would arrive at the lawn plateau and look back. A most remarkable change has taken place: Acton's guests would find themselves in a larger room comprised of a series of descending terraces bathed in the dappled light of umbrella pines.

Acton and Suarez masterfully achieved a false perspective mimicking that of the *teatrino*'s, which was located in the same position on the other side of the largo's central axis. This false perspective can be read in two directions: From the terrace down, the space opens out to a veiled but enclosed landscape vista of the adjacent ridge line and in reverse, in the uphill direction, a diminishing perspective increases the apparent length of the garden. This is skillfully done by splaying the end walls and the alignment of the pairs of umbrella pines set on each terrace. From the top terrace the space below appears as two terraces defined by the cross lines of low hedges that terminate in the inset balustrade *exedra* space. The oval *exedra,* half inset into the bottom-most terrace and half jutting out from it into the abutting woodlands, is terminated by a semicircular wall of cypresses, similar to that of the Gamberaia. Within the inset oval, urns and figurine statuary are rhythmically placed on top of the continuous balustrade fronting the oval. From the bottom of the *exedra,* the view uphill is one of horizontal lines – stone balustrades behind which are three sloping horizontal bands of purple blooming lavender - contrasted against dark laurel hedges, all under the umbrella pines that frame the perspective to the stone arch. Lavender, planted *en masse*, is never part of the humanist garden and here represent a unique plant material introduction. This vista must have been a most dramatic and unique Tuscan scene when, in late spring, the lavender would be in full bloom.

How this space was used or what purpose it served during Acton's days is unknown. The terraces of the *Vista dell'Arco* could have been yet another opportunity for Acton to feature his sculpture collection or it could have been created solely as landscape architecture art, a part of the largo's composition.

Another third of the way along the axis, a deeply cut recess in the hedge appears to mark yet another cross axis, but instead, only another paired set of sculptures appear. Running out of space for yet another largo garden to be added to the composition, Acton had to settle on this aborted substitute.

Vista del Colosso   Ending the *vialone* axis was a circular space, *il tondo*, from which the largo's final cross axis, the *Vista del Colosso,* emanated. A circular hedge enclosed the space and was purposely designed to "turn" the visitor in either 90-degree direction, aligning him with the new axis. This last axis was yet another surprise. From the circular *tondo*, the downhill / eastern side was the most inviting direction. A subtle planting device also directed the visitor to that choice, as the north side was densely planted with *philadelphus*, a fragrant blooming shrub tree that arched over the lower hedge, partially blocking any uphill view. The reverse occurred on the downhill side, where one could see into the lower terrace spaces and their parallel mini-axes.

Descending a short flight of stairs to the east, one arrived in a small complex space of no distinction that at first caused confusion; it was devoid of garden features or sculpture. The axis continued downhill via stairs that descended into yet another space, but if one were to choose this path one would miss a very important garden surprise. In a small semicircular side niche, a small window opens up on a diagonal to the south-east affording a spectacular framed view of the dome of the Duomo in Florence. This niche, *il Vista del Domo,* is the only location in the entire garden that took advantage of the remarkable opportunity for views to central Florence or the Arno valley.

There are many small, limited axes to side spaces, mini-*giardini segrettti* between the major spaces. Everywhere, figurative sculptures are to be found, tucked away amid other elements of stone urns and arches, and green hedge niches enveloping stone doorframes. It is almost without relief. Overhead, branches form the separating *bosci* and shade these tiny rooms. The floor is sparsely grassed as the deep shade, competing roots and dry conditions make grass-growing difficult. Some have felt that despite the magnificent display of garden art and architectural detail, this "is a ratty and confusing part of the garden."[303]

Il Pratone   If Acton were to choose to descend the final set of stairs, which are in two flights - the first wide and the second puzzlingly narrow - one would arrive in the enormous *pratone*, ironically translated as little meadow. This southern-most space, an oval at cross axis to the *Vista de Colosso,* is yet another subtle surprise. A green architecture space enclosed by smoothly-clipped cypresses, it is surrounded by umbrella pines that define its un-mowed grass form. It is the only space in the garden entirely defined by pines and most probably the result of Miss Blood's predilection for the tree. The *pratone's* real charm is that it is the one natural passage - a wild meadowland - to be found in the largo. Comprised of myriad blue-flowering wild thyme, *Thymus serpyllum*, a sprinkling of yellow-flowering bird's trefoil, *Lotus corniculatus,* and white blooming wild dwarf orchids that mix in with the grasses and sporadically bloom throughout the summer, its expanse provides a haven for fireflies that rise up from the un-mowed grass at dusk, an effect made more dramatic by its large scale. This space was used for picnics and lawn games, tennis and croquete. Acton was known to don his white fencing suit and steel screen mask and challenge a competitor to a "friendly" but aggressive match here.

Colossus   Uphill, the axis fulfilled its name, *Vista de Colosso*. From the *pratone*, a narrow slot allowed re-entry through the previously visited *la vista del Duomo* and *tondo,* through the small *philadelphus* trees, wood-like plantings of pine and evergreens and, seen for the first time in the largo, the *Calocedrus decurrens*. Continuing up yet another flight of stairs, one emerged to a grassy knoll, and there a huge threatening Colossus, club in hand, loomed from the high point of the mound. Sculpted by the seventeenth century sculptor, Orazio Marinali, Acton tried placing the over-scaled figure in several other locations before settling on its placement on the crown of the knoll, where it recalls a similar placement of a similar colossus, Apennines, found at the Villa Pratolino, just a kilometer north of La Pietra, on the very same ridge line. But Arthur missed an essential compositional trick in the sitting of his Colossus, that of its silhouette against the skyline. The immense, looming nature of a colossus would have been greatly heightened if only Acton had reduced or eliminated the planted backdrop, allowing the form to be silhouetted against the sky. Mistakenly, Acton placed Marinali's *Colosso* amidst a *boschetto* of mixed trees and a clump of vertical cypresses and even at one time bent thin cypress trees to create an arch over the sculpture, further containing it.

Throughout this *boschetto* or lower largo gardens, the *capo giardinero*, Mariano Ambroziewicz, replaced aged or dying vegetation with a mixture of flowering cherries, azaleas, rhodendrons, magnolias and other exotics. These showy varieties distracted from the simple green and white scheme of the second renaissance garden, and are exotic species to the Florence area. How or why Acton allowed these changes is puzzling.

Pergola Della Rose   Having climbed up to inspect the Colossus, one arrived at a long north-south allee where, at the middle, a wonderfully long *pergola della rose* had been built. Built from gathered material, Acton found simple round columns from a ruined structure. Their weathered sections lent romance to the garden structure, as their pieces were often precariously held together by iron straps and pins. The pergola was roofed by rough-hewn poles that were covered by old *Rosa banksiana* vines. The floor was paved in stabilized crushed *terra battuta*, (beaten earth,) and was generously covered over time in fallen leaves. It was a charming space, cool and intimate.

One of the first terraces and structures built by Acton in the new largo gardens, the *pergola della rose*, was used for lunch parties during the hot months from May to October. Guests were seated on one side of the tables *alla compagnia*, the long boards of the table placed on top of wooden horses. Each guest, therefore, had exceptional views of the garden during the repast, - views through the shrubbery into the various *boschetto*'s gardens below. The *pergola della rose* was the usual destination of Acton's garden tour sequence, prompting him to serve light refreshment there even at a non-lunch hours. The *pergola della rose* was another of the garden features Guy Mitchell copied for his gardens in Villa il Giullarino .[304]

Processional   The *Vista dell'Arco* cross axis was just to the right of the last bay of the *pergola della rose*. The cross axis would have provided Acton a short cut should the tour become too long and his guest too hungry. Continuing on this axis, however, the tour would leave the shade of the *boschetto*, arrive at the base of the *scolone*, return through the shade of one of the original passages in the romantic *bosco di giardino inglese*, and traverse across, ending at the top of the stage area where guests could take their leave by turning at the *templetto* to traverse the *pomeario* for the *parcheggio*. But the long Acton tour of the largo would continue by turning west onto the *Vista dell'Arco*. Here, Acton could display the plants of the wood's floor under both pines and oaks and introduce a new evergreen, the *Cedrus atlanticum*. Passing under this magnificent specimen, the grass path turned to gravel as the tour group entered a large sun drenched space, the *giardino topiario*.

Giardino Topiario   Designed as three separate but integrated sub-areas, the *giardino topiario* was comprised by the *giardino segreto*, the *vasca di Diana* and the *prato del cedro*. The three, although differing in dates of design, detail and construction, flow into one another and are unified as one. The *Visto del'Arco* axis organizes the centers of the two main spaces of the *giardino topiario* - first the *prato del cedro* and then, the slightly uphill, the *giardino segreto*.

Prato del Cedro   The lower garden, the *Prato del Cedro*, which was the first to be entered and is the more important of the two, was centered on a cross axis from the *prima vasca* that continued from the *tempietto*. Clearly visible from the main terrace of the house,

Acton could enter directly into the *prato del cedro* via the front *Terrazza*. A broad, south-facing formal parterre garden, the *prato* was lined by a continuous stone balustrade that held free-standing sculptures placed at regular intervals. At the terminus of each path between the parterres, an important piece was on display. The exceptional sculpture, Eridano, the river god, terminated the central axis and was the *prato's* primary focus when viewed from the terrace of the house. From morning until noon, Eridano remained in full sunlight while other space-defining statues were in contrasting shade. In late afternoon, equally dramatic illumination occurred, when the declining sun again illuminated the full figure of Eridano along with the garden's enclosing statuaries. The *prato del cedro* provided a dramatic setting for Acton's cocktail receptions.

> "The giardino topiario demonstrates Arthur's special talent for displaying sculpture."[305]
>
> Kim Wilkie

The *prato del cedro* was an all green garden, a nubby rug of clipped low hedges with interior panels of grass. At the center of the panels, at the intersection of the two major axes, topiary knobs and urns were placed, giving the garden its nubby feel. To the eastern side, the majestic *Cedrus atlanticum*, which gives the garden its name, began a line of cypresses that randomly edge the garden's curved terminus. Developed in the late 1910s as an Acton/Suarez collaboration, the garden features diverse floral planting that might have adorned the Renaissance Villa Lante, and were considered, even in their day, to be in poor taste, as the new idealized garden was known for using only clipped hedges and grass. Harold Acton, Arthur's son, put it best: "Statues are the flowers of Italian gardens."[306]

Giardino Segreto   As the *giardino topiario* continued to wrap around to the east facade, the second garden to be entered was the *giardino segreto*, the site of the former historic walled garden, *the hortus conclusus*. It had matched the *pomario* on the north side of the house which was torn down by the Incontri heirs. In the *giardino segreto*, the terrace that had been raised but a half meter marked a small section of the reconstructed cistern that was attached to the house. Acton faced the new wall with *rocaille* similar to that employed in the *pomario* and incorporated a nymphaea grotto. Here a particularly attractive Neptune ruled.

At the base of the south facade of the house, along a narrow travertine terrace, an outer, freestanding perimeter ledge held a collection that included sculptures of various sizes and periods, historic fragments of stone decoration, and pots containing seasonal flowers. The sculptures were mythological gods and goddesses; Athena, Hercules and Apollo, their randomness similar to a display at an ancient *sciave* (excavation site). Spaced evenly along this terrace wall was a "pillar capstone" that Arthur had made especially for the villa, possibly designed to be used as the identifying Acton icon, much as the Barbarini bees, the Farnesi's six-pointed *fleur des lys*, or the Chigi eight-pointed star. Acton's element was a squat pyramid-like obelisk placed on lion-clawed corners and topped by a ball emitting iron flames. A stranger combination of parts could not be imagined, but some how it was a handsome garden element.

Like the *Prato del Cedro*, the *giardino segreto,* created in the early 1930s, was all hedged panels of grass featuring a handsome architectural arch of Palladian motif. Its mannerist scroll-like wings aligned with a centerline axis from the house. As the focus of the garden, the arch housed an expressive Bacchus, drunk with the pleasure of the setting, if nothing else. In the front two panels, facing each other from opposite sides of the central axis, Acton placed two large topiary peacocks - a most bizarre element, especially when seen with the composition of the adjacent topiary gardens. Originally the upper garden was created by the Acton/Suarez team as a rose garden, square in plan and featuring a wide border of roses and sweet alyssum surrounding a large grass plain. This simpler form gave purpose to the two differing gardens and provided for the garden's one area of seasonal color. In the 1930s version, however, the roses were set into the grass panels, dotting the edges just behind the parterre's hedges.

Vasca di Diana   Between the two gardens, the main axis of the *giardino topario* led to the *vasca di Diana* at the far south end of the garden. This space contained the remaining parts of the historic walls of the *hortus conclusus* that Acton expanded in creating the cistern that was probably meant to irrigate the gardens, but doubtfully, was ever used. Acton dressed the new face of the cistern with *rocaille* and housed in its grotto a masterpiece sculpture of Diana, the goddess of the hunt. The relationship of the grotto is tenuous to the other two garden spaces of the topiary garden, for it occurs downhill and is in a space of its own. Diana's grotto, located in the middle of the wall, does not align with any path or axis, and to further isolate this garden space, Acton left the existing trees in place, retained from the prior romantic landscape. These trees masked the impact of the wall as part of the *giardion topario* and shaded the lovely statue of Diana.

To end the main axis linking the house terrace to the *Vasca di Diana*, Acton placed a sculpture of Daphne turning to stone in the grip of a particularly muscular Apollo. The dynamic couple sits within the path of the axis, framed by woodland trees.

Promenade Finale   On the Acton tour, the master of the villa would then turn 180-degrees from the *Vasca di Diana*, and follow the axis as it left the *giardino segreto*, crossing the terrace of the house and entering an allee paralleling the wall of the *pomario*. Treed on one side and vine-clad on the other, the allee led to a sloped lawn on the right, where a beautiful stone *tiempieto* was sited. The *tiempieto* was a fitting spot in the garden for Acton to end any tour. The beautifully proportioned circular structure was set in the only romantic passage within the largo, and recalled what the gardens might have been before the second renaissance hands of Acton and Suarez were applied. The *tiempieto*, like the other garden stonework, was the product of an Acton purchase, brought in and sited by Acton, himself. From here, the visitor might take leave through the *pomario*.

"Villa La Pietra is significant because it was one of the most exceptional and influential turn-of-the-century gardens."[307]

The Villa Acton's largo is another example of what Arron Betsky calls "queer space or queer architecture."[308] Like the water parterre gardens of Villa Gamberaia, La Pietra's landscape rooms are physically and symbolically closets, their interiors shut from public view and, in reverse, excluding the world outside, even the adjacent Tuscan landscape and the magnificent views of Florence. The *boschetto*, like the romantic Florentine Park Cascine, is dark and moody, a place suggestive and inviting to secret liaisons. Like the "gay and lesbian friendly" Pensione Berticelli in Florence, La Pietra's interiors spaces were excessive in decor, and supercilious in pastiche, its garden architecture an applique lacking in structural integrity. Sculpture populated its every room, terminated its every axis, and filled its every void. Like the explicitly gay d'Annunzio interiors at Villa La Capponicina in Settignano, it was a composition of forms on top of forms, historic periods on top of each other, objects such as urns, spheres, figurines, cylinders, cones, and nude statuary incongruously mixed together. Many of the sculptures were homoerotic, emphasizing full genitalia. How many statues of Diana, of Bacchus, or Pan were enough, or how many figurines of nude women and naked men were needed to make the point of this garden? The gardens were designed during a period when the ubiquitous fig-leaf was in fashion and the absence of such was considered lewd. Acton, one would think, made his point.

> "Our nurse disapproved of most of the garden statues and kept dinning into my ears that they were shameful."[309]
>
> Sir Harold Acton

Arthur Acton was always in constant need of money for his projects. With the improvements to the house and its gardens and his insatiable appetite for art acquisitions, there was never enough money. Revenue from the *podere* was a small but dependable source of income. Its vineyards and orchards to this day still supply an abundance of commercial product and it must have supplied much of the daily needs for the villa and financial support for the staff. The leases associated with the purchase of the entire property of La Pietra were a major source of steady income for Acton. With the purchase, Acton became manager of the *l'Oriuolo*, the complex of the four smaller villas, or *villini*, on the property. Leased by his close friend, Princess Ghyka's sister Natalie Obrenovic, the former queen of Serbia, Villa Natalie produced a steady rent. Information about the occupancy of the other three - Villas Colletta, Sassetti and Ulivi - go unrecorded. They must have provided some sort of income, as Acton spent time and money on their improvement. It was far easier and less costly for Acton to "dress-up" these properties with landscape improvements than to have altered their structure and provided modern baths and kitchens which they needed. However, each of the *villini* were given "Tuscan" gardens "*all'Italiana*"[310] by the Acton / Suarez team.

The Villa Natalie, an imposing structure of four-stories, abutted the edge of the property on via Bolognese. Its facade treatment was high Renaissance, with excellent architectural detailing in the cornice moldings and fenestration trim. "L" shaped in plan, the shortest leg extended to the rear of the building. To make Queen's residence regal,

R. Terry Schnadelbach

Arthur Acton provided the villa with a Baroque parterre garden in the semi-enclosed space in the "L". It consisted of grass panels edged by straight and curved sections of low boxwood hedges that were shaded by four stone pines, each centered within each of the parterres. The corners of the garden were marked by huge Baroque urns on pedestals, a simple but elegant touch. From this semi-private space, its axis connected to a terrace overlook with views to the east across the ravine to the Villa La Pietra. Following Queen Natalie's period of residence, the *villino* has housed many noted English authors. Novelists Evelyn Waugh, Graham Green, and James Lord lived and wrote at Villa Natalie.

Acton provided similar but less elaborate landscape architecture for the remaining three *l'Oriuolo villini*. At the Villa Colletta, also in the shape of an "L", an enlarged, simple two-story farm building formally used as a *lemonaia* for the Villa Natalie, Acton provided a similar four-part parterre garden, defined here by topiary boxwood spheres. At its far end, Acton provided a small stone *exedra* decorated with urns similar to the *exedra* in Villa Acton's *secunda vasca*. It separated the two *villini*. On the Villa Colletta facade, Acton planted vines and masses of two-meter-high hedges to screen the unattractive parts of the farm building.

But Acton's most brilliant entrepreneurial idea was to combine these separate and distinct parcels and incongruent buildings of the *l'Oriuolo* together into one development. He did this by designing from the first villa, Villa Natalie, a curving entry road that swept around to the rear of that building, and paralleling via Bolognese, continued north to the last villa, Villa Ulivi, then exited back to the via Bolognese. In this way he treated *l'Oriuolo* as a residential complex similar to a present-day condominium or office park development.

Along the new internal drive, Acton provided for a garden landscape that would unify the four *villini*, organizing the whole into one development while retaining the private nature of each *villini* space. He designed a linear garden as an overlook terrace between the road and the edge of the ravine, employing the same second renaissance landscape vocabulary as found in the new gardens of Villa Acton. Designed as a series of open *vasce*, each consisted of simple box parterres around a dry fountain as sculpture, each connected in series to the other. But unique to these gardens, was their openness to views across the ravine that focused on the *padrone*'s house, Villa Acton. These gardens presented a charming panoramic composition impossible to find in the gardens of the main house - an open terrace overlooking an enclosed, serene agrarian valley of olive trees set amid wild Tuscan grasses.

The improvements made by Acton to his real estate holdings quite definitely provided Acton with a sizeable monthly income. But Acton had other sources of revenue, among them, in the early years, his steady monthly fee from his arrangement as agent for Stanford White. In the beginning of 1903, White began to think that their business arrangement was too expensive and billing payments, in the form of international drafts, too difficult to arrange. On Arthur's wedding trip to America in June 1903, Acton met with White in New York to cement their relationship. At that time White gave Acton the authority to draft directly from an account with a Florentine bank. Even with that ease of payment, periods of financial difficulty still followed for Acton. One period was in December 1903, just after his marriage to Hortense, when he wrote urgently to White asking for an advance fee payment. "I find myself rather pressed for money. A man for whom I was doing a great deal of work failed last fall and as another result of his failure some New York clients of mine upon whom I depend for a large share of my annual business will not come over this winter. Under such circumstances, you will I am sure, see your way to help me out with a draft."[311]

Another date was April 1904. Acton cited his "taking the liberty to draw a check of $250 on account as business is not good and I am feeling the pinch a good deal. If at the same time you could see your way to letting me have some more cash on account, it would be doing me a great favor."[312] Much of the money from art dealing was used for living expenses as well as in the acquisition of his private sculpture collection.

Even with his multi-source income, and with support from his other art dealings, the income never proved adequate. Acton, as we have seen, involved William Mitchell in the renovation of the gardens of the villa - the elaborate *rocaille* work in the restoration of the historic *pomario* was but one example. For Acton, meeting the villa financial requirements was a constant scramble for funds.

When at La Pietra, the Actons were diligent and gracious hosts. They belonged to no one circle but mixed in many - the Ghyka/Natalie circle of nobility, the Berenson aesthete circle (though the Berenson's did not like Arthur much), the Charles Loeser circle of American expatriates, and their own, consisting of art dealers from around Italy.

> "Few of the professional critics were on speaking terms, but nearly all of them (Bernard Berenson, George Gronau, Herbert Horn, Edward Hutton, Charles Loeser, Mason Perkins, Janet Ross, Geoffrey Scott, and George Sitwell) were welcomed by my parents.
>
> "I recall how they glared at one another when they happened to collide

in the drawing room: One retired in a rage on spotting an enemy, another stood by to mutter sarcasms. Some offered their attributions spontaneously with a smile: others remained silent until they published them in a journal."[313]

Sir Harold Acton

Arthur and Hortense were very sociable, but disliked intellectuals. Arthur's artistic and intellectual interests went as far as to accumulate knowledge specific only to the art pieces he held or marketed. He was, therefore, ill equipped to hold in-depth discussions on many of the discoveries and theories then being advanced on Renaissance art. He wrote no professional articles or books. Acton found Bernard Berenson arrogant, condescending, and anally compulsive; Berenson found conversation with Acton painful. Although Acton thought of Bernard and Mary Berenson as friends, the opposite was not true. As previously mentioned, Bernard, in his letter of introduction to Isabella Gardner, called Arthur by the unflattering term, "a bounder." Mary, in her diary, expressed their feelings toward Arthur:

"Late October 1898, Common friends: Miss Blood (companion to Princess Ghyka), Placci, Janet Ross.   No Acton." [314]

When Hortense was visiting, Acton used the *villini* for social contacts and to host guests that would come to stay in them. She was noted for her "wicked martinis."[315] Arthur used these occasions to develop strong Serbian connections through Princess Ghyka and Queen Natalie Obrenovic. The Serbian connection continued during the First World War with Prince Alexis Karageorgevitch, then a war refugee in exile, housed along with his entire Serbian entourage in the *villino* Villa Sassetti. To demonstrate his political neutrality, Acton housed in the adjacent *villino,* Villa Ulivi, convalescing British army officers who reportedly "flirted and danced with Florentine girls who were not too closely chaperoned."[316] Former Queen Natalie lived until 1929 in exile and quietude, either in Biarritz, France, or in Florence at the Villa Natalie. After 1929, she entered the convent Notre Dame de Sion in Paris.

Acton, like Berenson, entertained all the notables who visited Florence, holding *grand salons* in the Villa Acton in the evenings and *pranzo di tavolo longo* in the garden for lunch. Dinner was always a formal affair that typically started with early drinks and introductions on the *vasche's* upper terrace, an Arthur tour through the largo, pausing here and there to discuss one of the sculptures or some new acquisition, then, re-gathering in the villa's central glass *sala,* and a processional up the cantilevered

hidden lives / secret gardens

staircase for dinner in the grand salon. Lunch was always an informal affair that began with the Arthur tour of the garden, winding up at the long rose-covered pergola. After lunch the guests might enjoy a stroll, a game of croquette or bowling on the *Prato's* large oval lawn, or perhaps, a poetry reading in the *teatrino*.

"We gave frequent luncheons and visitors came to see the house and gardens almost every afternoon."[317]

Sir Harold Acton

By the late 1930s, the gardens were largely completed and were revised for the final time. During the Second World War, Acton, who was known to be opposed to the Italian Fascist regime, abandoned the villa, fled to London and lived in an apartment house on Piccadilly Circus. After the war, life resumed at La Pietra in somber times. Villa Acton was saved from destruction by the Italian Monte Dei Paschi but the gardens were in shambles. The *vascas* were pockmarked by munitions; unexploded bombs lie among the fallen statuary. After its reconstruction, Acton graciously entertained such notables as Winston Churchill in the largo gardens

Arthur Action and his two sons, William on left and Harold on the right, circa 1915

At the same time, Arthur's conflicted views on homosexuality had finally caused an estrangement with his sons, as both were gays[318] who refused the cover of heterosexual marriages. In the dysfunctional Acton family, both Harold and Willian were sent to prestigious private schools in England. Both were known to have homosexual encounters under the prep school environment. Upon graduation from college, Harold, the older of the two, had chosen to live in Paris and China in order to escape from his father's condemnation and constant carping on the "family disgrace." William lived n the United States and kept a house in London for a monthly visit each year. Arthur forbid any discussions or acknowledgement of their homosexuality. In 1942, William on a visit to La Pietra and while his father was in London, committed suicide. He could not reconcile his lifes and family. But in the 1950s, bedridden and in poor health, Arthur reversed course, and asked Harold to return to La Pietra to manage and preserve his life's work. Harold promised his father that he would do so for as long as he lived, no doubt making the now enfeebled Arthur Acton somewhat comforted in his final days. As he observed daily and seasonal changes of his beloved gardens from his second floor bedroom windows, Arthur Acton

R. Terry Schnadelbach

had to marvel to see the sunrise, the early morning flush of birds, the changes of color and hue as the sun swooped over the topiary forms whose shadows swung circular from their fixed positions; to see the evening's orange glow and the final flush of birds, to be followed by the nightingales as the garden's evergreens grew from dark to black, the night's moonlight alone illuminating his collected figurines, their pale, eerie reflected light setting them apart, as if ghosts in the landscape.

> "For fifty years my father's life was mainly devoted to embellishing the villa and the garden, which except for the walled orchard and lemon house was his creation." [319]
>
> Sir Harold Acton

Arthur Acton died in 1953.

Cecil Pinsent's sketch for the new stairs from the lemonaia into the green garden

Chapter 3/ Fugue

Villa I Tatti

> "Villa I Tatti is not just a shelter to house Berenson's art collection, books and papers, it is a shelter to house Berenson as art. For Berenson, life was really his art. The location, the site, the house and its architecture, the extensive gardens, his wife, his mistress / manager, his staff, the audience of ever changing visitors and the daily regimen as tableau, all comprise a strange but beautiful art form."[320]
>
> Nicky Mariano

BERNARD BERENSON, "BB," LOVED the Tuscan landscape. His Italian stay began in 1887, after Harvard, when as a young man he took up residence in Florence's historic central area, daily making trips into the Tuscan countryside. Noting the changes of light, the unique coloration of the sky, and the crops growing there, he tried to imagine the Renaissance artists capturing these very same landscape images.[321] True to his inner soul, Berenson eventually left the dense urban center of Florence and made his home in the bucolic beauty of the Fiesole hills. Walks into the adjacent countryside of the Mugello foothills near Fiesole were to become a part of his adult life until when in 1959, when, weakened and dying, he was no longer physically able to continue.

In 1890, Berenson left the center city and moved to a single room in the Villa Kraus in Fiesole. His letters noted how lovely the gardens were, "filled with blooming roses, wisteria and lilacs." Here, the harshness of central Florence's summer was moderated. The Fiesole days were merely "warm" while their nights were "balmy" and "filled with the sounds of the nightingale."[322] In the countryside, BB took up bicycling and increasing his range, came to experience even more of the Mugello hills and valley. With money earned from lecturing and conducting art tours, and better financial prospects, Berenson moved, in 1898, into a suite of rooms in a boarding house in the small settlement of San Domenico di Fiesole. Mary, his love, then Mrs. Mary Smith Costello, joined him in the hillside country, taking a room three doors away at Il Frullino, another local guesthouse. BB, Mary and her brother, Logan Pearsall Smith, would explore the countryside by bike, cycling the narrow walled lanes of the hillside, investigating the numerous villas and remarking on the beauty of the landscape with its native cypresses that spiked the skyline, or on the pungent aromas of pine and roses that hung in the air as they pedaled the roads. It was on one of these outings that Bernard first met the idiosyncratic Mrs. Janet Ross who lived in the crenelated and towered villa, located in the lower part of the neighboring village of Settignano. Ross, noted for her abusive and hostile tongue, was a novelist and avid gardener. Her style of gardening was very informal and leaned to usable products. She shocked many of the foreign community by setting up a roadside stand to sell her surplus vegetables, something unknown to the neighboring *contadini* who sold theirs in the urban piazzas on market days, and something unthinkable to Anglo Americans of her status. It was Ross who told Berenson of the villino "next door" that was owned by a British eccentric and was unoccupied. Walking the site's perimeter, Berenson was smitten; he found for himself - as he wrote to his patron, Mrs. Isabella Gardner – "the perfect site." A small sixteenth-century villa, the main house of a *podere*, it was set on the hillside adjacent to Ross's Poggio Gherardo, and downhill from Ghyka's Gamberaia. Here, Berenson envisioned a monastic environment run under the concept of Altamura - a colony of aesthetic perfection, possessed by ITness, a term coined by Berenson to represent[323] the perfection of Altamurian beauty. ITness would be the unifying theme of the aesthetic, architecture and culture of I Tatti.

Bernard Berenson and Mary Costello picnicking in the Mugello hillsides.

hidden lives / secret gardens

> "[We will] dwell in the contemplation of eternal essences...behold Beauty with the eye of the mind and... feed on the shadows of perfection."[324]
> Bernard Berenson

A combination of unexpected events provided Berenson the opportunity for a new life in the Florence countryside. Mary Costello's divorce-denying Catholic husband, Frank, died suddenly, liberating her to remarry. At about the same time, Janet Ross reported to Berenson that the villa was for rent. By coincidence, both BB's and Mary's separate leases were coming up for renewal. Deciding that this most fortunate confluence of events could not be denied, the couple made a total commitment, married and secured a lease for the villa, I Tatti. The wedding took place in the small chapel in the adjacent hillside fields of Poggio Gherardo with Janet Ross supplying the fresh garden flowers and the "lucky" marriage rings.

I Tatti at the time of Berenson's purchase.

I Tatti was a rural villa in dilapidated condition and in need of much work. The original house was a simple building, rectangular in plan, and classical in its exterior appearance. Its name, I Tatti, was probably derived from a corruption of I Zatti, it's thirteenth century owners being the Zatti family.[325] At the time of Berenson's marriage, the villa was owned by the British archeologist, John Temple Leader, who lived at the very highest crest of the long Settignano ridge in the Castle Vincigliata. In England, Leader had been a liberal politician. Out-of-favor, he had exiled himself to Italy where he devoted his life to archeological work.[326] He bought the Vicigliata in a state of ruins, and made it habitable while at the same time reconstructing major portions of it in the Dante-esque style.[327]

I Tatti, located at the bottom of the Vincigliata *collina* (hillside,) was a three-stories-high box with the main rooms found on the *piano noble* (or main floor), which in this case was at grade on the east and north sides. The main facade faced the east, fronting onto a parallel road that ran steeply uphill from the village of Ponte a Menosa, just off the road between Florence and Settignano. There was a *piano terreno* (or ground floor) accessible from the southern and western sides. I Tatti's south facade faced onto a small, enclosed sloping garden that was edged by abutting farm buildings. (It was a vegetable plot for the previous household.) At a low angle over the rooftop, a framed view could be had of the Arno River and valley. Between the village and I Tatti, lay the fields of the Ross's Poggio Gherardo *podere*. (Janet and her husband were among the few people in the expatriate Florentine community with whom the Berensons were not at war.) Bernard wrote to his patron, Isabella Gardner, that he dreamt of bringing I Tatti back to its former "radiant" life, planting flowers in its overgrown garden, restoring its stones and trees and finally, in its restored state, contemplating in solitude the "eternal poets."[328] For Bernard Berenson, I Tatti's environment was ITness perfection.

Bernard Berenson at the Gardner's residence

"…. at the very entrance to the most beautiful strip of rock and forest country that we have near Florence."

"You scarcely have an idea what a paradise are the environs of Florence."[329]

Bernard Berenson

The only son of immigrant parents, Bernard Berenson was keenly aware of his background; but he was young, ambitious and eager to succeed in spite of it. As a student in his last year at Harvard College, he was invited, through his professor, Charles Eliot Norton, the famous professor of fine arts, to meet the professor's close friend, Isabella Stewart Gardner, the famous art collector and Back Bay Boston social figure. Her husband John "Jack" Gardner was a wealthy Boston industrialist who had made his fortune in coal. Isabella, the daughter of a New York grocer, played with Jack's money, buying expensive *haute couture* dresses, jewels and houses. She was brash, tasteful, if on the radical side, and oh so *au currante*. In the Boston Brahmin milieu, she was thought to be outrageous. Preoccupied with his business affairs, Jack Gardner left Isabella free to do as she liked. She was known to go to parties and afterwards hit the town's ritziest, glitziest spots, dancing until three in the morning. Her dress was flamboyant and, with her svelte body, she was able to model to her advantage off-the-shoulder, deeply plunging

hidden lives / secret gardens

necklines and slit skirts that caused the more matronly Bostonians to gasp. Bejewelled hands, wrists and neck were her signature; Isabella swooped in and out of every event, the focus of attention.

For the most part, she was happily addicted to young men. She loved their "physical pre-eminence," and the "grace and symmetry of young athletes." At one event, a ladies luncheon, Isabella brought in young prizefighters in their boxing shorts to display their powerful physiques.[330]

> "The younger and handsomer, the better. She was never pretty. Her white skin, sandy red hair, trim waistline were the only physical characteristics of which she was proud."[331]
>
> Meryle Secrest

She had a personality that played events and meetings. A sense of drama was a part of her every appearance. She was a genius at self-dramatization, traveling with a bevy of young men who swarmed around her - her escorts, admirers, "males-in-waiting" as the newspapers of the day called them. At forty years of age, and under the disguise of supporting emerging talent and intelligence, the "Isabella Club" included only the most gifted, intelligent, and socially poised men whom she had ordained to be the stars of tomorrow. More often than not, her instincts were correct. Among her young lovers were F. Marion Crawford, the future noted romance novelist; Clayton Johns, the future acclaimed concert pianist; Charles Loeffler, the American composer; Morris Carter, the later museum director of her own Gardner Museum; and Ellery Sedgwick, the future editor of *Atlantic Monthly*. Bernard Berenson, himself now a member of the Isabella Club, called her: "a sun in that heaven of my own boyhood."[332] With Prof. Norton as her guide, Isabella Gardner began to immerse herself into the arts. Gardner was

Isabella Stewart Gardner

a regular attendee to Norton's lectures in Boston. It was customary for Isabelle to scan the crowd for handsome, intelligent and interesting young men she might like to meet and afterwards to invite, one or more at a time, to her house. At one of these lectures,[333] she spotted Berenson, a handsome youth who was not shy about posing questions to the distinguished Prof. Norton. Berenson, then eighteen years old, with dark unkempt curly hair and soft broad facial features, caught Gardner's eye. A discrete note was passed to Norton and after the lecture, the introduction was made. Accepting her invitation,

Berenson spent a quiet evening with the cultured lady who was more than twice his age.

Bernard Berenson, the son of poor Lithuanian Jews from the Pale, was born Bernhard Valvrojenski, but after arriving in America changed his last name to better assimilate into the culture of his new country. With many social barriers limiting his prospects, the ambitious Bernhard Berenson, on entering Harvard in 1884, changed his name again, this time from Bernhard to Bernard, and he dropped all connection to both his Jewish faith and its culture. He was baptized one year later, in the famous Trinity Church in Copley Square, Boston, by its famous Pastor, Phillip Brooks.[334] Later, he would allow his name to be shortened by his friends to the very Protestant-like initials, BB. Assimilation was a constant goal for Bernard and his befriending only the most noted of Harvard's professors was a conscious strategy. He typically jollied" them along with his particular method of flattery, starting with a personal letter stating his desire to bathe in their friendship, as each one was "the one man in his life that he longed to see again."[335] He added to his letter to Norton, that he (Norton) had come to play an important role in his life, referring to the Gardner introduction. Norton, though, was not fooled by such importance being place in his person. Berenson has more ambition than ability,"[336] he once remarked to Berenson personally.

Berenson at Harvard

After the first meeting, Berenson became a regular member of the "Isabella Club" of young men. Her parties, *fiestas* as she called them, were themed productions held in her Back Bay mansion or in the Japanese garden of her country home in Brookline. There would be Italian peasants in traditional ethnic dress serving native cuisine, orchestras playing Italian classics and Italian art featured, some purchased just for the occasion. Berenson was as impressed by the events as he was of those attending, the social register of the very elite. For him to be able to break from both the confines of his Jewish past and from the limitations of his college environment, and become one of the "chosen" in society, albeit the society of Isabella Gardner, was the zenith, the highest possible point of assimilation for this son-of-an-immigrant.

"The female element is strong here, and I succumb to it. Only this distinguishes me from most other fools: I am well aware of my folly."[337]
Bernard Berenson

For his remaining year at Harvard, Berenson was a sometime lover of Gardner and was rewarded by introductions to other prominent socialites - Boston's cultural elite, persons of later importance to Berenson, such as art collectors and buyers. He was given references that would aid him in his hoped for post-graduation Grand Tour of Europe. When his much hoped for Harvard traveling fellowship was won by another, Mrs. Gardner provided the funds for the young Berenson to travel, by making small contributions that were quietly channeled through Berenson's Harvard professors as cover.[338] After graduation, Berenson met one last time with Isabella and broke off their affair, departing for Europe in June1887. Symbolically, it was the great break with his youth.

Subsequently, he wrote Isabella of travels and sought additional funds to extend his tour, but after two years, she evidently lost faith in the promising youth and asked him not to correspond further.[339] During this time, Berenson was a prolific letter writer, corresponding with a broad array of family, friends and scholars, all with the ultimate purpose of procuring additional funds. In 1894, five years into his European experience, and on the publication of his first book, *The Venetian Painters of the Renaissance*, Isabella and Bernard simultaneously wrote to each other, their correspondence crossing at sea. BB proudly transmitted a copy of his book along with a guarded personal letter; Isabella congratulated him and plainly stated that during the absence, she had often wanted to write him "on art, on literature and many other things."[340] With their friendship renewed, Berenson resumed his tone of familiarity in their correspondence as if it was only yesterday that he had broken off their relationship. He felt that their previous intimacies gave him the right to scold her, to critique her as well as to share personal details. In doing such, Isabella must have felt that their relationships might be rekindled, if only as an occasional fling. She spoke of traveling to visit him in Florence, but Berenson responded by saying he would be on a "long planned trip" and instead, limited himself to suggesting that she should and must visit on her trip. He thus was able to avoid her advances, all the while still pushing his own agenda, that of acting as her agent for future art purchases. Though their letters flirted and inferred, Isabella and Bernard were never romantically involved again. Berenson skillfully played their intimate correspondence into the business of research and acquisitions for Isabella's burgeoning collection of art, now housed at the Gardner Museum of Art in Boston. With his book, Berenson's career as an art historian was established; the six books that followed only cemented his reputation. He usually wrote weekly letters to Isabella of his art discoveries and his involvement in the then current art scene of Florence; sometimes as many as two and three letters per week were sent. He escalated their relationship from his being authorized to make specific buys to *carte blanche* for small works; major works were acquired only with Jack Gardner's approval. In all these transactions Berenson received an undisclosed percentage as a commission. These purchases paid the bills for his effusive parties, his numerous extended travels in first class, and his continual Villa I Tatti renovations. Jack Gardner was quite aware of Berenson's relationship with Isabella and often threatened to stop her Berenson dealings, but the Museum's prominence as well as the notorious and scandalous reputations of other art dealers, left the Gardners little room to redirect this linkage.

Later in life, BB wrote Isabella an indirect, passionate letter (at this point, he was married to Mary and had already bought most of Mrs. Gardner's Renaissance collection). He had heard of a portrait of her painted by the noted American, John Singer Sargent, a former member of the Isabella Club, and had requested a copy of Sargent's sensual masterpiece. As painted by Sargent, Isabella's slim figure was clad in a stunning green evening gown on which she wore a string of pearls around her slim waistline. The dress featured a daring and revealing neckline the press called "shocking." On receiving the copy, Bernard wrote her: "It is a great work of art, but could my hand follow my brain, my portrait of you would be greater."[341]

Mary and Bernard were at first inseparable. From the time of her arrival in Florence in 1891, they toured all of Italy together, including the major Italian cities - Tuscan hill towns, agrarian villages in the Po valley, and even the smallest chapels in the rural provinces of Italy. Berenson would take meticulous notes on the works found and provided on-the-site analyses of the pieces. Always, he was the professor, and she the student.[342] Together they were consumed by their historic discoveries and classifications of Italian art. Later, his notes would become part of his detailed art histories, or be found as a critical ingredient in the overarching system of classification of various periods of art history, a Berenson invention and self-learned tool that only he possessed.

There were times of relaxation, too. They took strolls in the hills above Florence, through groves of cypresses, over needle-covered paths beneath the umbrella pines, across meadows of wild flowers and *ginestra*. They visited many of the Renaissance gardens that BB knew so well: Villa Prato, and Villas Medici at Poggia and at Fiesole.[343] All the while, Mary Costello, wife of Frank and mother of two children, studied Bernard as much as she studied the art under consideration. Back home, Mary's Florence trip was officially described as one of instruction in art history, her relationship to Bernard, the instructor, platonic. The reality was that only one of their two rented hotel rooms was ever occupied. In museums and galleries, their demeanor was such that they were viewed as romantically involved, *"stanno per baciarsi."*[344] "They talk to each other as if they are about to kiss," was a remark overheard by one gallery visitor. In reality, Mary Costello was a married woman who had abandoned her two small children, Ray and Karen, to travel to Italy to seduce and conquer the acclaimed, brilliant aesthete, Bernard Berenson.

They had met in their youth, but love had to wait. Mary Whitall Smith, a Philadelphia Quaker, had met Bernard in 1885, at a Harvard concert, while she was at the Harvard Annex for Women, a Harvard-associated school. Mary was one of a small group of radical women determined to avail themselves of a Harvard education despite its all male strictures. The Annex, whose students included Gertrude Stein, was to become well known as Radcliffe College.[345] While able to attend most major lectures, the women were denied entry to Harvard's small tutorial classes. Mary was attending a concert at Sanders Theater, as was Bernard, when they met. A Harvard College senior, Berenson had already noticed Mary Smith, whose self-assertive walk crossing the yard had caught his eye. Regarded by Harvard men as beautiful, she had attracted many male admirers. Berenson knew little about her. From Radcliffe friend, Gertrude Burton, her views on feminism and women's suffrage; and from his own Harvard connections, Berenson knew well her homosexual brother, Logan Pearsall Smith[346], who was BB's classmate. On the night of the concert, Berenson was directed to observe Mary by a friend, who remarked that she was the "most brilliant" in her class. After the concert, the introduction was made by Logan, but the chance meeting passed by uneventfully. After her marriage to Frank Costello, Mary began to follow, through her brother and mutual friend Gertude Burton, the development of Berenson's career as a connoisseur of Renaissance art.[347]

On his European tour in the fall of 1887, BB had met Logan Smith while traveling through Paris and learned of Mary's new family life. Married to an upcoming English barrister, Benjamin Francis Conn "Frank" Costello, the Smith family had relocated to Sussex, England to be close. It was with this background that, in the early Spring 1888, on a trip to London, three years after their initial meeting, Bernard planned a visit to the Smith's country house, Friday's Hill, in Fernhurst, Sussex. Calling himself "an old friend of Logan's," he left his calling card. Mary, always a free sprit, was delighted at the reappearance of her earlier fantasy beaux. She invited Bernard to attend the Smith family's Easter dinner, for which she wore an especially seductive pink satin dress and, during the dinner, made all the seductive moves of a siren. Mary recorded in her diary and letters, by way of innuendo, a fulfilled intimate encounter. Their behavior to follow, taken on face value, certainly confirms more than a flirtation. After the Easter dinner,

R. Terry Schnadelbach

Bernard extended his stay by several days. He was always the dilettante whose skill as a raconteur could charm his audience on any subject and he conscientiously chose topics that would create instant, but separate bonds with Mary and her husband Frank Costello.

> "Therefore when this beautiful and mysterious youth appeared, for whom nothing in the world existed except a few lines of poetry which he held to be perfect, and the pictures and music he held to be beautiful, I felt like a dry sponge that was put into water. Instinctively I recognized that those were the real values for me, however wicked and self-indulgent they might be." [348]
>
> Mary Costello

> " For Mary, it was love at first sight." [349]
> Sylvia Sprigge

As was the Berenson trait, Bernard developed separate but equal friendships with both Costellos, playing the role of the unproductive, undirected intellectual, terribly in need of their personal assistance. Mary claimed for herself the mission of converting this extremely knowledgeable art lover into a productive writer on art history and an expert on institutional collections. Frank, a fanatical Catholic, saw a Jew-cum-Protestant who could be converted to Catholicism.[350] Exposed to the true meaning of the Catholic mass and the church's iconography of religious art through his contact with Frank, Bernard let his mentor think him nearly converted. In turn, Berenson thought that Mary could be converted into a serious and talented art history scholar. On leaving, Bernard wrote Mary every day and sometimes three or four letters a day; Mary was Bernard's new Isabella. Mary responded in kind. Their talk was of art and artist, but their emotions were clearly about each other. Mary hid almost all BB's letters from Frank for "fear that he would discover their emotional relationship." The three met many times over the course of a year, and while leaving behind daughters Ray and Karen with Mary's mother, they often traveled together as a *menage a trois*. Between these trips, there would be a constant flood of "art" letters.

Bernard Berenson, 1898

"Were ever stranger love letters written?" [351]
Sylvia Sprigge

After more than a year of this strange triangle, the ever-willful Mary planned and perfectly executed a personal nervous breakdown. Known to be willful, she outdid herself. The doctor, summoned to her home, prescribed nothing less than a year of rest and a change from her restricted domestic situation.[352] Frank, a barrister who after three unsuccessful attempts had finally won a seat on the London Council, would not be able to join her.[353] She immediately left her husband, children, mother and rainy London for sun-filled Florence, Italy.

Mary arrived on Berenson's Florence apartment doorstep, suitcase in hand, unannounced. Berenson was caught off guard. Flattered, surprised and elated as he was, he still refused her wish to move in. Instead, she would have to establish a more discrete residence two doors down the street.[354] For the world's consumption, this was to be a professor of twenty-seven -years-of-age teaching the world of art to a new student of twenty-eight; and in fact, it was just that. Bernard taught Mary how to see a work of art and to scan the whole painting for those passages that were spontaneous, usually those far from the primary subject of the painting. It was here, BB maintained, that each's artist's thumbprint was evident, as its creator would unselfconsciously and quickly render the passage without thought as to technique or stroke. Surely, BB posited, the spontaneous passage of one artist could be compared to that of another and in that way, through each artist's "thumbprint", the true identification of the artist would make itself known. Artists' signatures, which could be easily faked, need no longer be relied upon; verification could now be found in the spontaneous strokes found in the painting. Mary took copious notes of BB's judgements and attributions, piece by piece. The more she learned, the more Berenson put her to work. They talked only about aesthetics. When one gallery was finished, they would begin the next; when one city's art treasury was expired, they would move on to the next. They scoured any small Italian town large enough to have a primary church, and even stopped at wayside shrines.

".....in Paris, Bernard and Mary, as was their practice, he taking lodging at the Hotel Voltaire and she at a hotel in the rue de Beaune."[355]

Mary Castellos, 1898

Ernest Samuels

They became a couple running away from both their families and any sense of reality. Mary-sightings, though, brought problems at home.[356] Her principled Quaker parents, who were now raising her two daughters, disapproved of her apparent behavior. Dealing with political fallout from his constituency over Mary's absence, Frank tried to be generous, saying that Mary was still ill and "finding herself," maintaining that she would return. Besides, it was Frank's understanding that Berenson had converted to Catholicism, and surely, he thought, BB would not violate their friendship nor church strictures. Frank believed the double hotel room and double apartment story. But when after more than a year, Mary did not return, Frank became furious. In December 1893, he demanded Mary's return. Mary complied with a visit, telling him that she wanted a separation, if not a divorce. Frank's wrath exploded; he filed for and gained full custody of the children,[357] claiming Mary an absent and unfit mother. Saddened but unfazed, Mary returned to Florence to continue her relationship with Berenson, whom she now openly declared as her lover. At Berenson's insistence, they still kept separate houses.

Remarriage for Mary was out of the question. Frank, a good Catholic, vowed never to give Mary her desired divorce. BB was not really concerned with making a marriage or with raising a family, but Mary's seductive skills drew him gradually into what he thought would be safe under the circumstances, a marriage commitment at some future date. Fate again struck an opportune note for Mary. Quite unexpectedly, Frank developed bone cancer in 1899 [358] and died within three months. Frank's will left nothing to Mary, but his death left her free from their destroyed marriage and free to marry her true love, Bernard Berenson. On December 27, 1900, one year after Frank's death, Mary and Bernard were quietly married in the chapel adjacent to their new joint home, *I Tatti*. The news was devastating to Isabella Gardner.

> "Why then, did Berenson marry? There is the prosaic, if undeniable, fact that Mary was indispensable as secretary, librarian, filing clerk, and a main picture scout.
>
> Mary wrote many of his letters, spent four or five hours a day correcting his proofs and in the laborious and thankless task of indexing his books. She read, commented upon, and helped revise his manuscripts. She organized his photo collection, supervised the library, and even acted as preliminary reader, weeding out the new books not worth his trouble to read." [359]
>
> Meryle Secrest

"She accompanied him on his tours of museums and private homes to study Renaissance painting, and as a skilled and vivid writer she edited his manuscripts, bringing to them the liveliness and polish which Berenson's English lacked."

Richard Dunn

"(Mary) was the determining factor in the rest of my life and career."[360]

Bernard Berenson

The burgeoning American art phenomena created the art dealer overnight, with collectors buying at greatly inflated prices any art discovery that came from abroad. Many art dealers, Acton included, were of dubious moral standing, selling unauthenticated items or known fakes. The need for expert authenticators able to assign attribution became paramount.

Through his studies, travels and writings, Berenson had developed a system of determining style and authorship through tactile values. Connoisseurship and attribution, fields that did not exist prior to Berenson, but that have became common place in the art world post World War I, were his invention. Tactile values were a systematic set of conditions that described the sense of weight and texture that made a two-dimensional image appear three-dimensional, so real it seemed that one could touch it.[361] Style was defined as a set of common characteristics that could be set in iconographic terms as having a common meaning.[362]

For example, style may be the defining characteristic of Impressionism where common elements - the use of atmosphere, light and brush strokes are similarly employed. Attribution was defined by Berenson as the determination of a work to a particular artist or from the school of an artist, i.e., work done under the skillful direction of the artist. Such attribution was based on stylistic evidence and on the notion that an artist, consciously or unconsciously, expressed his individuality through his work to such an extent that the expert eye could correlate repetitive external evidence such as signatures, paint strokes, color and pigment comparisons, and by detailed elements, such as the way fingers were consistently painted, etc.[363] Connoisseurship was developed by Berenson to describe the ability to deduce simply from a work of art alone, its period, aesthetic merit and possible relationship to other art works.

The three learned skills had important financial as well as scholarly consequences. Through connoisseurship, Berenson was able to define the style of entire schools of art, artistic periods, and their primary artists. A work could then be authenticated, even without definitive signatures, contacts or contemporary accounts, and in turn, such attribution would elevate the value of the work. Utilizing his system, Berenson became the primary authority on Italian art, the unquestioned arbiter of authenticity. His word was considered final when it came to determining the period, style, and specific artist or school for any particular Italian work of art. Berenson parlayed his expertise in the new market in numerous ways. As a scholar, he would be asked to confirm, for a fee, the attribution of a specific work. Also, he was asked to buy works from reputable art dealers, for which he would receive a commission from the dealer as well as an attribution fee from the buyer. But Berenson also roamed the countryside discovering works by obscure or totally unknown artists. He would buy these works, publish articles exulting the discovery and then, having created a market for the works, sell them at incredibly high prices. But of greater importance, Berenson founded a new field of marketable art - religious art - works on ecclesiastical subjects found in churches and shrines, not previously thought of as works of art. In wayside chapels, or paintings found in side chapels, apses and alters of both major and minor churches, Berenson discovered and identified Pesellinos, Sassettis, Caravaggios, and works of other prominent Renaissance artists. He bought these from the impoverished churches, as Arthur Action noted on at least one occasion: "(The work) belonged to a church which needs money."[364] Having cornered the market, Berenson was able to establish their authenticity and merit and sell them at a great profit. The art market at the turn of the century was such that Italian art was in great demand. The better pieces were sold within a period of but a few days, often with no more than telegraph notices changing hands between patron and agent. Berenson would hear of a work, or would discover a work and plead for the reservation, i.e, of it not being sold to another for a day or two. He would then telegraph his patron, most often Mrs. Gardner, who would then wire back her approval for the purchase. On many an occasion, any hesitation meant the loss of the work to a competitor, or worse, the beginning of a bidding war.

    Isabella Gardner built her famous home and museum between 1899 and 1902 alongside the Fens, a part of the Olmsted designed "Emerald Necklace" park system in Boston. The mansion was designed in the Venetian Renaissance style with ground floor grand salons for recitals and entertaining. In truth, these salons were really museum spaces to show off Gardner's art collection. Isabella personally selected or decided on every piece in the collection of paintings, sculpture, drawings, prints, furniture, textiles, ceramics, glassware and books.[365] Berenson's purchases for Gardner included such important works as Titian's *Rape of Europa*, which is considered the greatest Renaissance painting in America, or the three paintings by the then unknown fifteenth century artist, Pesellino, a contemporary of Botticelli, the only works by this artist in America. Berenson alone is responsible for all of the Gardner Museum's Italian Renaissance collection plus some significant work from other periods; several Rembrandts, a Vermeer, and several Impressionists.

For just one of the years that we can document, 1898, the year that Berenson moved into I Tatti, he bought over $300,000 worth of paintings, receiving from this source of income alone, more than $30,000 in fees. This was an upper middle class income in the U.S. at the time. In impoverished Italy, it was a rich man's income and out-stripped that of Arthur Acton and other Florentine dealers. Other fees that year came from Herbert Horn, who had a London collection of paintings that included some Botticellis. Berenson helped in the sale of a painting, sharing the profits with a London dealer. Yet another fee was earned from the American collector, F. Mason Perkins, who lived in Siena and had amassed a collection of Sienese paintings that on Berenson's attribution, was sold with Berenson sharing in the profits.[366] Altogether, one could hypothesize that Berenson lived more than comfortably and that he was awash in cash. This enabled not just the lavish life style, numerous trips, etc, but also extensive book purchases, the acquisition of more works of art and, equally important, the improvements to the Villa I Tatti.

Berenson's first client (beyond Isabella Gardner, who would always be the first among "firsts") was Theodore Davis, a "billionaire" as Berenson put it. He acquired a few small painting from Berenson for which Berenson was paid a small consultant's fee of $100. Davis's mansion, "The Reef," in Newport, Rhode Island, was considered the *creme de la creme* among many such edifices in that elite resort. On Davis's tab, Berenson visited Newport and New York, where he was put up at the Union League Club, a wonderful beaux-arts building across from St. Patrick Cathedral on Fifth Avenue and the home of its own recently acquired art collection. Berenson was astonished at the scale of the buildings and the enormity of the personal wealth of its members. "People seemed to talk only in millions."[367] Through connections of Mary's Philadelphia-rooted family, Berenson became a consultant to Peter Arrell Brown Widener, a magnate of U.S. Steel, American Tobacco Company, Pennsylvania Railroad and light rail systems in numerous U.S. cities.[368] Berenson's work for Widener included attribution of Italian paintings within the collection, which resulted in published descriptions and biographical notes for each painting and artist.[369] This greatly elevated the worth of the collection which, in turn, provided Berenson with an important reference. The Widener consultation was just one of several such attributions or purchases made for wealthy collectors during the early years.[370] Even with ample income and fees, cash flow was always erratic and often the Berensons lived as if their lifestyle were unrelated to their actual means. Seemingly in a state of constant poverty, they always needed supplemental funds from family and friends.

In December 1907, Bernard Berenson was once again presented with an important opportunity. A contract for consulting services with the London art dealer Lord Joseph Duveen was presented. It would provide Berenson with a steady income of 20,000 pounds a year plus commissions on all art sold through the Duveen gallery. For his role in the contract, BB was to sign certificates of authenticity, thereby reassuring the largely unknowledgeable Duveen clientele that their purchases were genuine. In numerous cases, Berenson was simply restating his original finding, reached through his own methods of connoisseurship or attribution that he had stated when he first sold the work to Joseph Duveen. In this circular process, there were no challenges and the fees were paid, undisputed.

The Duveen contract also provided an initial professional fee, a signing bonus that was ample down payment to buy I Tatti. Again by chance, the owner of the villa, Leader, had just incurred huge losses at the casinos of Monte Carlo. BB was able to negotiate a purchase price for I Tatti at a considerably reduced price of $28,000, that for the entire Villa - the main house and its seven *poderes*.[371] Henry White Cannon, president and chairman of Chase National Bank, an avid art collector and resident of Settignano, helped arrange for a very unusual Chase loan in an amount larger than the purchase price and at the very favorable rate of six percent. It would cover the purchase and projected remodeling costs of I Tatti.[372] Part of the basis for the financing was the consideration that I Tatti, like the Villas Gamberaia and La Pietra, was a working *podere*, having a steady stream of income.

Joseph Duveen

Once belonging to Leader, I Tatti's *mezzadria* now became BB's to manage. It contained seven functioning but small *poderes* with their vineyards, olive orchards and vegetable fields plus several small *contadini* houses for the peasants who worked the *patrone's mezzadria*. These houses were strung out, village-like, at the base of their property's slope. Parts of the site were rich in alluvial soils of an intermittent stream's or *torrente's* flood plain. Unusual as it was for a villa to have both severe slopes and flat plain, I Tatti was situated alongside the Torrenti Mensole that, in reality, should have been called a *fosso*, (or a dry or sporadic stream,) as its flow of water in the late summer months was minimal or nonexistent. The upstream *laghetto*, or small lake, formed by a small dam, was an attempt to store water for use in the drier season, but the watershed of the *torrente* was too small and there was never enough water to irrigate the *podere* past late spring. The Berensons would have to conserve water for most of the year. The house, itself, could survive off the diverted stream, but in the arid summer months, it would have to be supplied from a cistern system. Even with I Tatti's water supply problems, the Berensons, as new owners, were able to enjoy a swim in the small *laghetto* just uphill from the house.

The *podere I Tatti*, pre Berenson

In 1908, Bernard, as the *padrone*, found himself looking after buildings, roads and crops and supplying the *poderes* with seed, cattle and tools. BB commented on his first meeting with his consultant team of the *mezzadria*:

> "I have been walking my estate with the *fattore* (farm controller), *ragioniere* (accountant), *ingegnere* (engineer) and *maestro di cassa* (Pinsent) and inspecting one's cows and oxen with knowing looks of ignorance. I'm planting fruit trees everywhere with the view of spring blossoms, but I fear that our agriculture is not very useful. Doubtless, the *contadini* will go in the tradition of centuries, no matter what we advise."[373]

The life of the art collector or dealer, and that of expert authenticator even more so, was best located in Europe, near the source of the work then in demand. Florence was the undisputed center of that world, the optimum location, and the lifestyle of choice was to be found in the large gracious villas, preferably still in a state disrepair so that they could be renovated to accommodate the art dealer's collection. In addition, it was best to suitably equip the buildings for entertaining and lodging visiting patrons.

R. Terry Schnadelbach

To entertain, one needed friends to fill the tables and to broaden the conversation. Intellectuals and aesthetes were highly sought after in this regard, the rarified villa life, and Florence itself, attracting scores.

At the time, promising, talented young men, fresh from graduation at top universities were expected to go on a Grand Tour of Europe. In fact, one was not considered truly educated or cultured without having done so. They would arrive on a villa's doorstep with letters of recommendation from leading professors and scholars in hand. Those that succeeded at their first lunch or dinner with BB – "who were quite up to Bernard's startling paradoxes,"[374] - were invited again. Conversation, wit, self-assuredness, and a special area of interest, were the required personal attributes. This practice, over the years, produced a guest-oriented, open life style revolving around lunches, teas and dinner, where long standing locals and visiting old intelligentsia would mingle with new art patrons and young cultured prospects. The social occasions were lively, animated affairs.

Each villa had its circle of close acquaintances and its own cultural slant. The Gamberaia had its royals; the Villa Acton, its art dealers. The circle of one villa would sometimes overlap another, but different circles, and a network of interconnected cliques, or entanglements, might better describe the resultant Fiesole hillside community. I Tatti became known as a mecca for the *cognoscenti,* or center for intellectuals to gather. To accommodate guests and provide a suitable, learned domestic environment, I Tatti would undergo dramatic transformation.

If a villa's architecture and its interior rooms were authentically appointed and demonstrated a knowledge and breadth of collection, the architectural exterior should not be less authentic, or so went the reasoning of the day. The exterior had to confirm the proprietor's cultured status, and the garden development complementing the complex was no less included as one of the important elements. Florentine collectors Arthur Acton, Charles Loeser, and others were building considerable gardens to their villas, and so Berenson, like Acton, felt compelled to have an authentic house and garden, a villa worthy of a cultured and knowledgeable connoisseur.

Even as a renter in 1900, Mary Berenson immediately began repairs and remodeling to bring back the dilapidated old villa, to make it habitable and to achieve what Berenson termed "ITness" perfection. In her zeal, she embarked on a course that would change I Tatti from a modest house into a huge and money-devouring institution. The first improvement to the site was Mary's initiative to organize the chaotic south garden and repair the derelict farm building lining the garden's downhill opposite side. She took the first of three small terraces within the space and introduced a simple grass lawn. For the second terrace, she organized potted lemon trees and introduced exquisite small statues in a semi-formal arrangement, perhaps inspired or directed by Arthur Acton. And on the third terrace, she created an informal cottage garden and planted its stone urns with tulips, hyacinths, wild narcissus, sweet freesia and native pinks. It was charming in a British sort of way, but not very Florentine. The whole space was enclosed by walls, either high garden walls or the painfully long wall of the farm building along the south side. For the latter, Mary hired an English architect, Herbert Horn,[375] who lived in Florence, to design a new garden facade and an entrance to the building, despite its floor being almost two levels below the lowest garden terrace and originally accessible only at the far ends. Horn provided a large door and new stairs, at the building's mid point and on center with the garden's axis. Mary now called the building the *lemonaia*, or lemon house, although it would require herculean men to lift any lemon tree tub the two stories necessary to set them in the garden. Modest in dimensions and scope of effort, I Tatti's first garden renovation provided an air of informality in a Tuscan-like landscape. It was a spring, summer and fall retreat, a tea-terrace, a summer evening exterior dining room and an area for entertaining and socializing with I Tatti's many guests.[376]

> "The upper terraces at I Tatti recalls an 'English' Jekyllesque interest in old fashioned and cottage garden flowers."[377]
>
> David Ottewill

At first, Mary did very little inside that was cosmetic and focused instead on getting the plumbing in order and repairing the leaks.[378] Her first project was to provide a bathroom for the second floor and remodel the others, bringing modern plumbing to Italy and the villa. As the Berensons now had grave doubts about continuing with Herbert Horn, who had become a competitor art dealer, Mary hired a group of Italian architects to draw up renovation plans. While not considered normally a difficult project, it was a challenge to the Italians at the time. Their understanding of plumbing was still rudimentary; through-the-wall plumbing was unheard of, as Italian plumbing was normally done with exposed piping snaked along ceilings and walls. A full year later, little had been completed, and after the typical Bernard Berenson outburst of rage, Mary fired these "incompetents," noting a long list of reasons - shoddy work, cost overruns, thievery and chronic absenteeism.

Settled of sorts into their own house, the Berensons began to perfect their new life together, focusing it around the monastic lifestyle of BB's invented cult of Altamura[379]. Altamura was the art of living a perfected cultured life in which the all arts flourished and excelled. Love for Bernard was "idealized" and his love for Mary was "eternal."[380] Sleeping in separate bedrooms, Bernard would visit Mary's chambers for lovemaking, but never remained the whole night. Mary, in turn, declared her search for free love and her liberal views on sex outside of marriage. These they discussed as part of their search for a perfect love. Mary found willing partners among her young guests and the garden a perfect place for such intimacies. Whether it was Greek lessons, or art history discussions, serious conversation always took a break for frank personal views on love and, ultimately, Mary's revelation of a personal desire for her current love interest.[381] For Mary, free sex was part of life and part of an art to be perfected.

Mary Berenson, like Isabella Gardener, was exclusively attracted to young men. She instinctively knew how to play them, how to stroke their young insecure egos and how to commence the warm-up that was required for young men to be attracted to older women. A woman in her forties, as was Mary, was old enough to be their mother. Aided by the libertine setting of Florence, so remote and foreign, they were more open to the possibilities of taking a mature, knowing partner - an Oedipus fantasies fulfilled.

Even throughout her early married years, Mary had had numerous flings with men in their early twenties. First, there was Bertrand Russell, the noted philosopher who was engaged at the time to marry Mary's sister, Alys. Mary shared adjoining rooms with Bertrand at the Paris Hotel Vouillemont. Bertrand, in his letters, described Mary as continually asking him frank questions and as being "interested in all questions of love." She then began a series of "brother and sisterly kisses"[382] that soon grew more passionate. While Berenson was in America in 1894, Mary traveled to Germany with Hermann Obrist, a "young dashing" German sculptor who had befriended Bernard on one of his visits to Florence. It was, as she wrote Bernard, a travel-study tour of galleries. Her involvement on the surface was professional, but she confessed to Bernard of achieving intense admiration and "platonic" intimacies. The descriptions of the "intimacies" sounded too similar in comparison to their own relationship, and Bernard became upset. A series of trans-Atlantic discussions took place on the subject of "comparative monogamy and comparative promiscuity." Berenson stated that he believed that promiscuity led to "greater and greater animalism and farther and farther away from what is the highest attainable pleasure - the sexual act as an expression of one's utmost yearning for union with what is not oneself."[383] Mary, for the sake of their marriage did not advance the discussion, thinking it doctrinaire, and offered to wipe the slate clean if he would, implying that she was knowledgeable of Berenson's side affairs. Mary confided to her husband's sister, Rachel Berenson, "Generally, after some years of married life, people know each other too well, bodily and spiritually, to weave romance of any kind about each other."[384]

With Bernard traveling a good deal and consumed by his work, attending parties, letter writing and of course, the main activity, finding and selling art, Mary knew well of her husband's many "distractions."

Over the years, Mary proselytized and practiced freer, more open sexual mores than did her husband. Among Mary's affairs there was the brief encounter in 1896 with Wilfrid T. Blaydes.[385] Blaydes, a young philosopher who had innocently sent a chapter from his book in progress, *Epicure and Death*, for Berenson's review, was an alleged bi-sexual, a concerned friend and probable lover of the notoriously gay Oscar Wilde.[386] Although he came to I Tatti to talk with Berenson, he befriended Mary and for two weeks they "were emotionally swept into each other's arms."[387] Mary was a gifted listener with a ready sympathetic ear. They spent the day in I Tatti's gardens "lying in the grass listening to readings of Renan and Shelley."[388] Then there was Carl Hamilton, a young American orphan who was traveling through Europe using a *nom de plume*.[389] He was neat, slim, of medium height and debonair. There also was an unnamed youth that Mary seduced. He had come to I Tatti to paint Bernard's portrait. "A mixture of Dionysus and Saint Francis," quipped Geoffrey Scott.[390] Mary thought him a prodigy and was to teach him Greek and other pleasures on the side. Every afternoon they went into the garden, away from the activities of the main house and away from the constant arrival of foreigners who were visiting her internationally recognized art historian husband. In breaks from teaching, Mary would make inquiries into his personal life, his activities, his views on love, and the more they met, the more personal the conversations became. Quickly, the conversations became seductions; the villa gardens the site for trysts and sexual encounters. The garden grottos, bathing places for Venus, Diana, Europa, and other mythical Greek figures, were both great sculpture gardens and sources of evocative suggestion.

Hermann Obrist, Design for a Memorial, c. 1895

After the Blaydes affair, Mary was intent not to repeat the mistake of telling

Bernard of her desires or conquest of other young men. In the spring of 1906, Mary cleverly concealed an elaborate scheme of seduction built around an Italian Easter Holiday *festa* for her two abandoned daughters Ray and Karin, who were attending colleges in England. Willful, Mary was certain her constructs could be made to work. It took planning and hard work to bring to fuition her plan to have a schoolgirl-like spring fling in a seductive sun-filled foreign setting. For the Easter Holiday *festa*, Mary planned to invite several handsome and promising young men, ostensively as escorts for her two college-age daughters, but more possibly to be her intimates. Researching the names of possible candidates through her friends and relatives in England, and later on one of Bernard's trips to England, she personally interviewed each candidate. Requiring good-looking young men from England's finest institutions, she chose Maynard Keynes, a manly figure with red hair and a strong build, and the equally attractive, Geoffrey Scott, a tall, lanky, and quirkey youth. They both possessed good backgrounds and would provide her daughters with suitable "escorts, companions or company" for all their 1906 Easter/Spring Break functions.[391] And Mary would be pleased, too.

Rachel "Ray" Costello, the older of Mary's two daughters from her previous marriage, attended Cambridge and was the physical, rather than the intellectual, type. She had just written her first novel, had literary ambitions, and was a champion swimmer, with a beautiful athletic build. Mary's younger daughter, Karin Costello was just emerging at seventeen, into the social world. Handicapped, she was losing her hearing and surgery to correct the condition had been unsuccessful.[392] Mary was known to be excellent at pairing people, but her approach to finding real matches for her two daughters was not her prime concern at just that moment.[393]

John Maynard Keynes was twenty-two and a graduate of Cambridge, excelling in finance. He was muscular and possessed angular features, "but looks like an incarnation of Mephistopheles."[394] Geoffrey Scott was a completely different type; long legged, slim, of fair complexion, with brown hair, and definitely afflicted with nearsightedness. He presented within himself a dichotomy in appearance - casual, constantly rumpled, with a nervous twitch – " a quivering freak."[395] He wore prim circular-framed glasses, was clean-shaven and well-groomed, with oiled hair neatly combed. Keynes described Scott as having "perfect Botticellian good looks."[396]

Scott was born 11 June, 1884 at Hempstead, London, into a family of prosperous flooring manufacturers. His uncle was C. P. Scott, the noted editor of the *Manchester Guardian*.[397] Geoffrey was said to have inherited talents in architecture from unknown family sources, and in journalism from his uncle. He was a self-declared aesthete

hidden lives / secret gardens

with a desire to be a noted architect and critic. He had just finished his education at New College, Oxford and was going to have a holiday before starting his career.

First, Mary found Maynard most attractive and immediately made time to have a tete-a-tete with him.[398] Maynard appreciated Mary's easy personality and jovial disposition, remarking: "(Mary) roars with laughter the whole time, allows you to laugh at her and never worries one."[399] Maynard might have found the older daughter Ray, interesting and, as a hedge, he politely professed to be in love with Ray, "a little bit."[400] But Mary's eager attention was personally directed and flattering to Maynard's young ego. The seduction was a success. It is from Maynard that we discover Mary Berenson was a sodomist and *patiens*.[401]

Geoffrey Scott

Maynard, though, quickly found the relationship difficult and a courtesy at best. Aware of his sexual interest in men - he had several serious relationships with fellow students at Oxford - he was becoming convinced of his homosexuality. On the train to Florence with Scott "he discussed ethics and sodomy," and may have had a set or two with Scott during his I Tatti stay.[402]

Mary then turned her interests to the egocentric Geoffrey Scott, and found another willing young man in him. He presented himself as an intellectual, possessed an easy and agreeable personality, was self absorbed, witty, and loved to postulate grand ideas. He was a near-constant talker, and it was easy for Mary to stroke his ego. Geoffrey was Mary's and she developed, much to her own surprise, quite a romantic attachment to him.[403]

"Scott had all the earmarks of her favorite kind of lame duck; young, handsome, highly educated and very neurotic."[404]

Richard Dunn

Cecil Pinsent

And what of the daughters? Too young to know or even suspect, they were blissfully unaware of Mary Berenson's ultimate game. Protective of their own young virtue which schooling in England had instilled in them, Mary's daughters found little mutual attraction with either of the two young men.[405] The holiday passed without any of the youths developing love interests in one

183

another. In fact the boys were openly trans sexual, holding a drag soirée where Maynard wore a chiffon gown and a pink ribbon headdress and Scott dressed in one of Mary's black dresses. Finding no response from the two young men to their tentative first attempts, Karin, the younger of Mary's two daughters, made the following assessment to her mother on departing: "You do not provide young men likely to carry hearts by storm."[406] Mary's plan was a complete success.

At the end of the Easter holiday, the daughters returned to school and Maynard to England,[407] but Geoffrey Scott had loved the holiday and would not leave. Seduced by Mary, Scott became infatuated with the lifestyle and the Berenson intellectual circle. Like a moth drawn to the light, he dropped his architectural studies and apprenticeship in England and remained in Florence, much to the delight of Mary Berenson. Mary schemed that Scott could become BB's librarian, a job made necessary by Bernard's lack of literary or librarian skills. In college, Scott had won the Newgate Poetry Prize and Chancellor's English Essay Prize[408] with his article entitled "The National Character of English Architecture." Being a winner of England's prestigious contest was certainly an honor that would garner interest and accolades in their circle of aesthete friends.

It was Mary's idea to create the position, but to have it actually realized, it would have to be conceived by Bernard, himself. She announced to Bernard, Scott's interest and talents in literature and the arts and convinced BB to interview the young man. Bernard was delighted with the prospect of developing his library, the centerpiece of his I Tatti academy. As Bernard was a compulsive collector of books and prints, he would have in Scott someone to sort his archival material. Berenson, through conversations with Scott, became aware of his English education and his rapid on the spot development in the native Italian sensibilities, a characteristic BB thought the job required, and hired him.[409]

> "On my visits to the churches and galleries of Florence, I had as my companion, Geoffrey Scott.... Dark-eyed and pale, he looked strikingly like a Botticelli portrait; indeed, he was more Italian than English in appearance. Scott had come to stay at I Tatti for a week; but after several months he was still there, no wonder; he was the most inspiring and entertaining guests. I for my part have met no one, not himself a painter, who appreciated painting more than did Scott. A wonderful talker, his talk at the Berensons' was something to be remembered."[410]
>
> William Rothenstein

To have Scott easily available to her, Mary had to find a place for him to live outside of I Tatti. While previously in London, she had met Cecil Pinsent, a young architect who aspired to become a master garden architect. Pinsent, recently returned to Florence from a short work stint in London and was living in the center of the city. He had been given a small commission to be the architect on the remodeling Villa Gattaia owned by Charles Loeser, Berenson's Harvard colleague.

Pinsent, twenty-two, was a graduate in architecture from the Royal Academy in London, and had developed his own love triangle. He first arrived in Florence in the summer of 1905. While sketching one day at the Renaissance monument, the Palazzo Nonfinito, adistinguished older English gentlemen approached, wanting to see his sketches. The man was Edmund Houghton,[411] a forty-ish English resident of the city. He showed interest in Cecil and his drawing and, and on discovering that Cecil was an aspiring architect, suggested that Cecil was wasting his time at the Nonfinito and should instead be sketching the Pazzi Chapel.[412] Cecil had known about the Pazzi, that wonderful Renaissance jewel, from his architectural history classes, and taking the suggestion, followed Houghton through the streets of Florence and into the cloister of Santa Croce where the chapel is located. At twenty-five years Pinsent's senior, Houghton instructed the naive Brit about Renaissance Florence and how he, Houghton, had modeled his life after the humanist concept of the Renaissance man, i.e., well educated in all the arts and in science. He had even built his own astronomy observatory in the roof of his Florentine house. The invitation to gaze at the stars soon followed. It probably was in the course of such an evening that Cecil and Edmond became intimates. For Cecil Pinsent, Edmond Houghton "was the first person... to open windows on to new horizons."[413]

In the weeks that followed, Pinsent was invited to dinner to meet Edmund's daughter, Alice, and his wife, Mary, a jewelry designer, novelist and author of *In the Enemies Country*. Alice, who was a year younger than Pinsent, and quite attractive, aroused his interest, and unwisely Pinsent confided to Mary Houghton his feelings. Mary H., herself interested in Pinsent, would have none of it. Shortly thereafter, Cecil and Mary H. became romantically intimate in an Oedipal-like relationship,[414] a relationship made all the more strange by her frumpish appearance of full figure and unkempt hair. Matters developed from the Edmond-Mary H. relationship to an Edmond-Cecil relationship, to a Mary-Cecil relationship and finally, to an Edmond-Cecil-Mary relationship.[415] Pinsent's own triangle had been established. To the Florentine, the Houghtons were very queer people who lived queer lives in a Florentine castle. From then on, Cecil was introduced in Florence as the Houghton's "adopted son."

To replenish Cecil's diminishing funds caused by his extended stay in Florence, Houghton gave Pinsent his first architectural commission - the design of his spinster sister's house in Bournemouth, England.[416] Cecil returned to London to execute the commission and to gain practical experience in an architectural office there, but as strong a professional start as the position and commission were, Florence was still far more seductive and he returned shortly after completing the work. He rented an office-apartment in the via della Terme, in the vicinity of numerous Florentine landmarks.[417] In coming back to Florence, he would be able to live and work away from the scrutiny of his family in England.[418]

Edmund Houghton belonged to a circle of Florentine aesthetes who were frequent guests at I Tatti. Known as "The Souls, a small circle of 15 aristocratic, wealthy, intellectual Brits. These men and women spent weekends at great country houses, talking constantly about philosophy, literature, and politics. They included Charles Loeser, a noted art historian and classmate of Berenson at Harvard who had just purchased the Villa Gattaia in Florence. Houghton introduced Pinsent to Loeser who engaged the young architect in his first Florentine commission - renovations to his villa and the design of a new adjacent "lodge." On a later occasion, Houghton brought Pinsent, who now had a reference from Loeser, to meet the Berensons. In presenting Loeser's recommendation to Berenson, Pinsent was probably hurting his effort in obtaining the I Tatti commission. Forever careful when it came to socializing with a competition, which is how he viewed all other Florentine art dealers,[419] Berenson would have preferred Pinsent to have been free of the connection. Loeser nontheless had been Berenson's mentor on his arrival in Florence and had introduced him into the tight art historian community, even loaning BB money (never repaid) when Mrs. Gardner stopped her support. Their relationship however, subsequently grew cool and Loeser's recommendation of Pinsent probably dampened BB's otherwise enthusiastic reception.

On the other hand, Houghton's recommendation was probably more influential, as BB knew and respected Houghton's sincere advice. While Houghton had considered himself a Renaissance man, he was really a dabbler. He developed interests one at a time and pursued them until boredom or fatigue set in; then his interests would shift to something new. During this period, he began to pursue an interest in photography and rapidly became accomplished in it. Because of this skill, known well among "The Souls," he was approached by Berenson and asked to photograph some of the Berenson art acquisitions. (The I Tatti collection has many fine quality photographic reproductions of pieces taken by Edmond Houghton.) Hearing of difficulties the Berensons were having with Italian architects and their workers on the remodeling of I Tatti, Houghton offered to introduce Berenson to the talented Pinsent. Perhaps, Pinsent could "help out" he suggested.[420]

At first, Mary did not like Pinsent. He seemed detached from their aesthete interests. But with her twin needs to get I Tatti remodeled and to find a place for her young romantic interest, Geoffrey Scott, to live, she reconciled herself to re-introducing the two. She invited both young architects to a lunch and they got along so well that she commented, jokingly but prophetically, that they might want to form an architectural partnership "someday, maybe here in Florence."[421] With the successful luncheon, Pinsent had found a room-mate with whom he could share the cost of his apartment. He would have a friend, of similar age, with whom he could share common interests. Their romantic attraction was instant and their friendship grew naturally into what would become a lifelong intimate relationship.

Already, on several occasions, Scott had related his inner-most homosexual passions to Mary[422] saying, "he liked girls as pictures, but they seemed to him to be lacking in promise, and he did not feel drawn to them."[423] Knowing her own predisposition to free love, he spoke of his homoerotic fantasies with the confidence that he would not be repulsed, and further revealed himself by telling her of his past homosexual relationships. Finally, having gained her sympathy, if not support, he told her of his and Pinsent's romantic homosexual relationship and Pinsent's strange love triangle with the Houghtons. With the full disclosure, an open agreement was accepted by all participants, forming yet another intertwined triangle of Mary Berenson, Scott and Pinsent, and Mary and Edward Houghton and Pinsent. From that point forward it was understood that Mary Berenson would create work for the two; her young lover, Scott, and his lover, Pinsent.[424]

> "We have not solved them [entanglements] because it seems a waste of time to try to square the circle."[425]
>
> Mary Berenson

Geoffrey Scott was exuberant and flamboyant; Cecil Pinsent was quiet and reserved. Some even described him as cold and impersonal. Pinsent was either bisexual, or his same sex preferences were yet to become exclusive. Scott's attraction to men, and sodomy, was always a troubling problem for him and he was in constant denial.[426] Through his constant and available partner, Pinsent, Scott would find the outlet for satisfying his own homosexual needs, while allowing his relationship with Mary to fulfill the heterosexual self-image he so desperately wished for. At one point Scott called Mary affectionately, "Chere Mere," acknowledging his Oedipal neurosis.[427] Pinsent, on the other hand, possessed with the very same demons, did not wish to be discovered in either of his relationships, that with the Houghtons nor with Scott, and was content to have Scott as his secret lover, available but discretely hidden. They lived together for twelve years in the following manner: During weekdays, they were tied up in their external relationships, Scott with Mary Berenson; Cecil, with Edmund and Mary Houghton; on weekends, they lived together in the center of Florence, entertaining at small parties hosted at their apartment on via delle Terme.[428] Although they lived in the midst of Florence's flourishing gay life, from all accounts the two had little interest in the burgeoning homosexual community, the "cult of Florence."

Cecil Pinsent and Geofrey Scott on a trip to America

Mary Berenson found that her needs were met, despite her lover's other attachments. She had long ago established her independent bedroom far from Bernard's. He would awake at all hours to work on his papers or think his ponderous thoughts - such as whose idea of love was aesthetic. Their spheres were different. Bernard ran the art business and Mary the house and household staff. It was she who administered to the numerous guests. Scott gave Mary emotional, sexual and romantic gratification that was no longer offered by Bernard. Either Bernard was unaware of the whole Mary-Scott affair, or he simply did not care. Similarly, we have to presume that so long as Mary's needs were met, she did not object to whatever relationship existed between Cecil and Geoffrey. Besides, Mary felt that because of her age and maturing figure, she wasn't in any position to be possessive in her relationship with Scott.

At the start of their formal professional relationship, Mary simply informed Bernard that the young architect, Cecil Pinsent, was being engaged to solve the problems left by the Italian architects who had been dismissed. Upon Bernard's agreement, Cecil was brought in. He immediately jumped into the floor construction pits and had the non-functioning drains properly refitted. Mary proclaimed success: "He loves going down there and getting thoroughly dirty."[429]

When one small project was finished, Mary would invent another. Cecil

hidden lives / secret gardens

next worked on I Tatti's new kitchen; then, a pantry room, a larder and servant's quarters; and then, upstairs, several guests rooms, which included a second bathroom. Downstairs, he was asked to remodel the *salotto*, or sitting room, in the Venetian style. Here, Mary had Cecil design the architectural work, but inserted Geoffrey into the project, as Cecil's partner, for his decorating and furnishing skills. Geoffrey was chiefly responsible for working with Bernard on the hanging of the art pieces. Here, with BB's approval, Scott hung ecclesiastical and secular works of art together.

> "Though I lived in partnership with him, (Pinsent), for four or five years, ours was a partnership of opposites, complementary gifts, each one having what the other did not have."[430]
>
> Geoffrey Scott

> "Geoffrey Scott [was] intellectual, literary and brilliant, with the gift of words, but unpractical and impractical, inventive, with an aptitude for things visible to the eye, but dumb."[431]
>
> Cecil Pinsent

The notion of a utopian life style had its beginning early in Berenson's career. Dandyism was well known throughout Europe, where gentlemen of taste and artistic education proffered a unique speech, dress, and posture - often posing. They tried to perfect these affectations into a lifestyle, imbuing them with recognition and notoriety. While dandyism largely garnered a reputation for homosexuality, the ideas of dandyism were picked up by a non-gay group who called themselves, "Aesthetes,"[432] They tried to perfect their lifestyles into a life as high art. Every part of life was analyzed in aesthetic terms and was "designed" to reflect aesthetic tastes of the times.

In 1898, BB, Mary and Mary's gay brother, Logan Pearsall Smith, a writer and classicist, founded a journal on aesthetics entitled, *The Golden Urn*. It was dedicated to the cult of perfection and featured in its articles anthologies of perfect *"sacred"* images, perfection in passages culled from the Bible; perfection "quotations" from England's literary greats, such as Shakespeare, Keats, and Milton; and perfection quotations from Walter Pater's *The Renaissance*,[433] which discussed the way in which a painting obtains greatness by the perfect fusion of subject and form. Its third and last issue was devoted to the new religious cult of Altamura. It's convoluted premise centered on the philosophies expressed in the book, *Marius, the Epicurean*, which expounded salvation through moderation in all acts and through a cultured life. With Logan's help, Bernard prepared a manifesto that proffered the tenets of the new religion - what was to be worshipped, "life in its beauty and essence" - and a formal code of conduct best suited to its ends. Altamura was to result in a stylized society that lived a monastic life.

> "To this end he started a non-deist cult, Altamura, which proffered humanistic values and an elevated life of art."[434]
>
> Meryle Secrest

This religion was to be devoted to the Spirit of Delight, to the art of living. It would have its own quiet sanctuary, housing books on art and instruction in the cult. It's motto would be: *"Nil dulcius est, bene quam munitia tenere/Edita doctrina sapientum templa serena."*[435]

Altamura, though, in its monastic lifestyle, was to create an environment untainted by worldly concerns, a state of mind where followers were free to pursue enduring truths. It was "hoped that by devout enjoyment, the burden of the world's joylessness can in some degree be lightened."[436] For Berenson, Altamura was a way of life befitting an Aesthete, offering a religious philosophy that embraced the transported[437] state produced by art and culture, and a monastic environment giving sanctuary for this new lifestyle. Berenson was converted, and the Altamura fantasy was the constant goal of his life at I Tatti, guiding his life style to the end.

Life in the Altamura monastery - where certain acceptable lifestyles were practiced and other excluded,[438] - was to revolve around seasonal themes. In addition, the Altamura year was to be broken down into the many "eternal" themes of a cultured life, one featured each month as a meditation. Beginning with spring, representative of the beginning of life,[439] the year's themes were set as follows:

Spring represented all the themes of youth

March:	dedicated to the gods of the Deists, the moralist and gnomic poets
April:	featured the contemplation of youth in its springtime innocence
May:	devoted to lovers

Summer featured the developed world or worldliness

June:	a review of the world's great achievers and contemplation of the forces they embodied.
July:	celebrated the rich life and allowed monarchs to visit selected cloisters of the monastery, bringing gold and monetary treasures.

August: praised pastoral beauty and rural landscapes.

Fall featured the mature and aged phases of life

September: dedicated to the somber contemplation of elegiac regret
October: celebrated mature hedonism and "the acceptance of what life has to give."
November: examined the inevitability of decay

Winter celebrated the riches of culture

December: rejoiced in human brotherhood
January: evoked the glories of all art
February: studied religion (non-organized) and metaphysics

Raised as a Jew, Berenson knew Judaism's moral and social values. Having rejected it in prep school before attending college, he then converted to Catholicism in Italy, studying its iconography, traditions and beliefs. Berenson, in turn, became disenchanted with Catholicism and rejected all religion only a few years later. Mary was a Quaker. Their search for the spiritual in life was a fundamental part of their intellectual search for meaning. BB had articulated the spiritual connections in art, and sought to transpose into a non-deist religion, his sentiments on the subject. At about this same time, several new forms of non-deist religions had surfaced and, perhaps, had captured his attention. The Altamura monastery they envisioned at I Tatti, seemed to the Berensons comparable in its genesis to those of other non-deist cults of their day.

In 1909, Mary devised the perfect project to keep Cecil and Geoffrey happily productive and within her sphere of influence, i.e., to build the ultimate Altamura library. It was the perfect project, fostering Scott's career as architect/librarian and Pinsent's as architect/practitioner. The two would have equal interest in the project and would be the basis for forming their long prophesied partnership. The library would be larger and more refined than the existing one within the villa. Bernard would be keen for the idea as the library was his love and Geoffrey, who was bringing order to the collection, had an architectural background, and was a natural to collaborate with Cecil. On hearing the plan, Bernard was ecstatic that Mary, at long last, would help him in advancing his Altamura goal. BB saw the library as the centerpiece of the monastic aesthete retreat.

Cecil Pinsent's sketch for the lower parterre garden

Cecil produced wonderful sketches and the project was begun. His first major architectural work was not without problems, ones that greater professional experience would have cured. It brought all the traumas that working in Italy would typically bring. Bernard, lacking patience and seeing "their mistakes, their sloppiness, their laziness and their extravagance,"[440] their long periods of inactivity and the indecisiveness of the inexperienced Cecil, wanted to fire Pinsent a thousand times. Or Berenson, not finding a needed reference book, or seeing books that he had circled for ordering not yet ordered, or not finding the order and discipline he expected in his library, would fly into a rage over Scott's work or lack thereof. He continually wanted Scott terminated. The continued employment of the two was a source of endless contentious dispute between the Berensons.[441] BB believed Mary was favoring them, not for their talents but for other, strictly personal reasons.[442] Mary always interceded and re-established a reasoned, more decorous dialogue. As so many had attested, Bernard Berenson was a difficult man with whom to work. His need to control everything and his irritability were blocks to any personal relationship, other than with Mary. Mary always found a way to soothe Bernard's rages and to keep the two young men involved and on the job at I Tatti. Meanwhile, the late night oil burned in Mary's bedroom during the week and at the Pinsent-Scott apartment on weekends. This love triangle colored every aspect of their lives and caused entanglements few others could understand.[443]

The first library, on the ground floor, was to do double duty as a sitting and reading room space. In true remodeling fashion, the work would affect more than just the library space itself. While the existing house was being torn up anyway, Mary reasoned that it was a good time "re-wire the electricity throughout the villa, whitewash the walls, and restore all floors."[444] Because of this, the Berensons temporarily moved into one of the villa's empty *villini,* or travelled away from I Tatti.

This project had even greater problems in construction than did the one previous. Along the way, the cistern's water system broke, flooding and ruining the floors. The break required the replacement of the villa's entire water system. The combined opening of walls for pipes, tearing out all existing flooring, and through-the-wall electrical rewiring produced so much noise, dirt and debris, that the Berensons abandoned staying anywhere near I Tatti. They moved in with Janet Ross at Poggio Gherardo temporarily. Bernard was constantly frustrated with all aspects of the project.

> "Almost all of 1909, from Jan to June, (I Tatti) was un-unhabitable as by the interior construction, mostly on the library."
>
> "Trouble upon trouble in the house"'
>
> "I wish to goodness we had attempted nothing but left the house and grounds as they were."[445]
>
> Bernard Berenson

The second main library space was begun only after the completion of the first and after the Berenson's returned to I Tatti. It consisted of a smaller room to serve as Bernard's retreat while the library space itself was in construction, with an expansion off the north side of the house. Completed in 1912, this proved very popular with Bernard and contained most of the book collection. A third large library space was created in 1915 that contained a small space called "a recess" which became a very private study for Berenson. At no time during this five-year period was there an absence of work devoted to Berenson's personal love, the library. In its ultimate form, Berenson collected and built a library of over forty thousand volumes, and research archives of over seven thousand photographs of paintings and sculpture. "ITness" was, and still is, the heart of I Tatti.

Mary did not want the triangle to end, but about the time that Bernard's patience was at its limit with the construction mess, Scott's own contribution in architectural writing was taking hold. He was writing the manuscript *The Architecture of Humanism.* Mary agreed to the hiring of a professional librarian, freeing Geoffrey to return to the Pinsent / Scott Partnership. The artichokes, as both Bernard and Mary called them when they were less than pleased with their work, now needed a real project. Since all other small interior remodeling projects had been completed, Mary focused her thoughts, and their's, on the garden. As we know, like wine, gardens take time to plan, construct, and grow to maturity. To Mary's way of thinking the time required would keep Cecil and Geoffrey engaged at I Tatti for the indeterminate future.[446]

In the winter of 1911, Mary took the two architects aside and charged them with creating a new and extensive garden, to complement and finish the design work already accomplished at the villa. It was to be a fitting "Renaissance" garden to accompany the ever more refined and restored house. The Villa Gamberaia's gardens were complete and a wonderful success. Villa La Pietra's gardens were under construction and already, its cypress entrance allee complete and the Italian garden, with its fantastic collection of sculptures, a finishing touch useful to Acton in his enterprise. Should I Tatti be less? Bernard knew nothing of Mary's plans for a similar garden.

Both Scott and Pinsent were becoming permanent fixtures at the Villa I Tatti. The Villa's ITness environment itself was seductive. The daily life was unique, and more than one visitor remarked on the unusual domestic scene. Maynard Keynes wrote of his stay; "The comfort here, [at I Tatti] is incredible; the cypresses and sun and moon and the amazing gardens and villas in which we picnic every day high above Florence have reduced me to a lump of Italian idleness."[447]

Edmund Houghton, in a moment of mercurial passion, bought one of the first Fiat cars in Italy and became an expert motorist. The auto-enamored three amors, Edmund, Mary H. and Cecil, would take off on a holiday weekend in the heretofore inaccessible Italian countryside. To supply him with pocket money when he needed it, or just for his company, the Houghtons hired Cecil to drive on their week-long excursions. There are a number of tender photographs of the threesome lying affectionately together on a Tuscan hillside covered in hay. BB, seeing the efficiencies of this new form of travel, was quite eager to utilize Edmund's car for touring the remote regions of Italy.[448] Berenson's travels by bike were arduous and time consuming, especially when compared to the territory the Houghtons were able to cover in a single weekend.[449] Engaging Edmund and his Fiat, BB began exploring the hillsides by car, studying and acquiring in areas previously beyond reach. The Berenson art tours would always be conducted with a complete entourage, filling the car to capacity. Included were Edmund Houghton with Bernard and Mary B., and either Cecil or Geoffrey filling in the extra seat, depending on whose romance took precedence.

The signature domestic scene at I Tatti was this: Edmund, with his polished car sitting in the driveway, ready to be useful; Mary Berenson inside bustling around, running the house; outside the window, down below, Scott's half-naked, lanky form laid out on a garden chaises, airing in the full Tuscan sun; in the distance, amid the heap of construction, Cecil and his team of gardeners, happily at work building the landscapes of I Tatti. "[Scott] held morning receptions in his bed and poured out his length on garden chairs," remarked Will Rothenstein, on his spring of 1908 return.

The romantic entanglements of the Berensons, while typical of other expatriate lives in the Mugello hillsides outside Florence, happened at a time of unique convergence. It was at a time when sexual desires and sexual freedom became a primary driving force shaping a new lifestyle - the life of the Florentine aesthete. It was at a time when art had become an economic force and one of its major production centers revolved around a few people gathered in one place. It was at a time when cash-flushed aesthetes lived "life-as-art" and integrated all the arts - painting, sculpture, architecture and landscape architecture - to produce a humanistic expression unique to that moment in history. It was at that unique moment in time, at the turn of the century and the early part of the twentieth century, when an isolated community of English and American expatriates drawn to the hillsides surrounding Florence, lived a sexually free life, amassed and sold art collections, and rehabilitated historic villas and built renaissance-like gardens. It was then that the classical garden, an integral part of the aesthete's lifestyle, was reborn again in a new and Modern expression - the second renaissance of Italian gardens.

Berenson loved the garden at the Gamberaia, and as the sole person allowed to open it to visitors and scholars, he was a proud custodian. He routinely brought I Tatti guests who knew nothing of Gambaraia gardens, declaring them to be the finest in Italy. Berenson knew them to be Moderne and to possess little more historically than their Renaissance structure.

After Mary commissioned the garden project in the winter of 1911, Cecil did a plasticine model of the proposed new garden.[450] The garden project began with the logical first elements that were necessary in any event - a new gardener's house at the base of the hill and an extension to the Villino Corbignano. The work, again, was predominately Cecil Pinsent's, as Geoffrey Scott was still Bernard's personal librarian.

On the creation of I Tatti's new gardens, Mary attempted adding another person to the design "team." She had become acquainted with a "pennyless" young painter and horticulturist, Aubrey Waterfield, who was staying with her neighbor, Janet Ross.[451] Thinking she could be of financial help to him, she asked him to contribute his horticultural skills to the project. She introduced him to Cecil in hopes that the two would form a "partnership." Aware of Cecil's deficiency in horticulture, she felt the suggestion to be beneficial to all parties.

> "Aubrey Waterfield, who lunched with us, was helpful in criticizing Cecil's plan... The general scheme is his. Aubrey approves Cecil's general plan. I engaged Aubrey here, to add the flowers and trees. I think we shall get on very well. More, BB can hardly bear it; but he has to."
>
> Mary Berenson

The partnership did not work well; Aubrey proved to be a problem almost immediately. Eventually, he proposed a different plan than Cecil's, one that utilized the current craze in England for a picturesque landscape of meadow grasses and specimen trees in an informal arrangement.[452] Both Mary and Cecil disapproved of such a concept and discussed with him their philosophy for a renaissance-like garden that would extend the lines of the architecture down the hillside and ultimately recreate a new-renaissance garden.

> "I had been very wrong in trying to patch up a situation that wasn't possible, but I had always kept hoping Aubrey would understand that I meant what I said when I expressed a desire for grass and ilexes or cypresses and box, and would not approve his idea of a wild garden on English lines. Aubry was thus very bitter with me and Cecil had to come to the rescue and remind him that when he came down last autumn, he was ill, depressed, and that only a friend could have had the heart..... and say ' I want you only for a flower list.' That I kept hoping he would..... yield to my wishes, but that instead I had encountered obstruction, and insistence on his own ideas, and great touchiness. He was sulking and awful and full of conceit - as difficult as a person could be. Aubrey was so sure he was right, he just couldn't hear it. And he said, to save his reputation, he must go on with it."[453]
>
> Mary Berenson

Meanwhile, Cecil had begun construction on the garden according to his early model.[454] The work went painfully slow with massive re- grading and extensive new retaining walls. About this time, Bernard looked up from his books and discovered Scott spending time "out in the garden." He only discovered the project one day, after hearing unusual noises on the other side of the *lemonaia*, - which was blocked from view from the house by construction. He investigated the lower property where, for the first time, he saw the massive regrading and installation of an allee of cypresses. By coincidence, Scott, as well as Pinsent - who was hard at work- were both present. BB was given a verbal tour by the talker Scott (describing Pinsent's composition) and was shown the plasticine model. To everyone's surprise, BB liked it, saying the scheme was "promising." But due to the numerous tussles with Aubrey that Mary now conveyed to him, he refused to see the full potential of the scheme and threw numerous angry rages at the destruction of the lands.[455]

Scott greeting Berenson who had just discovered his new south parterre garden.

> "I just came home a month ago...Outside, it is too horrible. We have wasted a small fortune on the garden with the results of turning what was a dear Tuscan *podere* into a miserable potter's field. And destined to look like that for many years to come."[456]

Finally, the Aubrey Waterfield conflict grew to enormous proportions and Mary realized that she had to extricate herself from the problem. She concocted a plan that would prevent Aubrey from finding any way to stay involved in the project - she would fire both designers, dismissing and dissolving their partnership. Then, later, after the dust settled, she would re-engage Cecil to finish his design. In the meantime, Cecil was to complete a formal design for the full extent of the gardens.

> "I went down early and got Cecil and brought him here for our final settling-up with Aubrey. We went to the Villinos, where he was painting. He was so cross he would hardly speak to us, but when Cecil began to investigate the chimney of the drawing room, he came in and said a few contemptuous things about its being the business of the architect to make chimneys that didn't smoke. He was so black and horrible that I felt like running away, but at least I took my courage in my hands and said: ' Aubrey, Cecil and I have a horrible thing to say to you. I think the garden is awful and I have come to the conclusion that it can only be done by a man who combines what Aubrey has, a knowledge of flowers and plants and what Cecil has, a knowledge of design and the ability to sketch out. The partnership hasn't been a success so I'm going to take over the garden ...... and relieve you both from all further responsibility. At this Aubrey burst out into heavy and nonsensical complaints about its 'not being fair to him,' of how Cecil hadn't carried out his scheme, etc. Cecil then, for the third time, produced the scheme which had Aubrey's approval marked on it and showed he had carried it out, but Aubrey was very nasty and obstinate about it."
>
> "Cecil said he thought it was true and that he was quite ready to retire. This put Aubrey in the hole for he knew nothing of the technicalities of garden design and had said that Cecil must continue to help him. I said I would not allow it."[457]
>
> Mary Berenson

Cecil had found and installed a competent *capo giardinere* named Capecchi. Mary found him a knowledgeable and cooperative spirit and continued the construction without her designers.

> "I have been busy out in the garden where I am amazed to find all going so well, without ME! Capecchi is a real gardener. The only thing that have gone wrong are the things that Cecil hindered him from doing. Cecil understands nothing of gardening - or of making a garden - but he is cocksure and I fear he has upset some of my nicest plans for another year. *Patzienza*! Then again, after starting the work with fury, he left me half way through and I have no instructions to go on with. It is most unfortunate temperament. However, in general the garden is really alive and Carpecchi is doing extremely well."

> "That cursed Aubrey, had he left it all a nice, easy-to-take-care-of *podere*..."[458]
>
> Mary Berenson

By the end of the growing season of 1911, much of Cecil's plan had been installed and the design intent became apparent. Mary's attitude toward the garden changed from reservation to praise for the first time, lauding Cecil's accomplishment.

> "Logan, I am anxious for thee to see the garden... The second *bosco* of ilexes has been going in this week, to complete the scheme which now embraces al lthe land in front of the *salone*.
>
> "I think the garden is going to be a great resource. It is curiously soothing. I go about and see things growing, your own things in your own land. All our wire netting is being covered with roses and honeysuckle and all sorts of creepers. Another year it will be very beautiful. Various kinds of clematis, too, are running up lots of the trees. Our tulips have been a great show. Capricchi has had hundreds of them in the house as well as the garden, for me, the last few weeks. And peonies and all sorts of things. The balcony outside of BB's room is a great bower of yellow banksiana, a nice kind of rose. The order comes into the library and the sound of bees humming. Certainly this is a paradise."[459]
>
> Mary Berenson

It is rare to find such detailed writings by a client on the pains and tribulations encountered in the construction of a garden, especially one as large as I Tatti's. But the accomplishments found at I Tatti stand out when reviewed by professionals and landscape architectural critics. The available correspondence is that of Mary Berenson, a singular point of view. She was not the easiest client to satisfy and Bernard Berenson was even more demanding and critical. Cecil Pinsent did not leave records of the project's planning and design. It is clear that he was able to achieve a great garden, fulfilling most of his design ideas at his own creative pace. It was a great artistic achievement.

> "Pinsent was exceptionally sensitive to landscape and had a sound knowledge of Renaissance design. Sir Geoffrey Jellicoe recalls that in 1923, he spent a day in Fiesole with Pinsent, who he came to regard as his first 'maestro' in the art of placing buildings in the landscape. The gardens of I Tatti and La Balze are adequate testimony to Pinsent's talent, the buildings and gardens complementing each other perfectly and uniting sympathetically with the surrounding landscape."[460]
>
> Ethne Clarke

If the Gamberaia was a waltz of a choreographic poem, and La Pietra the *largo brilliant,* then I Tatti was a fugue.[461] This composition's theme was a simple one; several separate but thematically similar axes perpendicular to the hillside slope, each utilizing the drama of vertical change. The composition was organized into two sections, the southern gardens and the western gardens. The garden fugue theme was played out in the southern garden by a hillside axis repeated in series, side by side, descending the slope, and generally parallel to each other. The axes were looped at their ends so that the slope down could be experienced in reverse, from the bottom of the hill up to the top. There were three separate axes forming this series and they are bundled together, working off the southern and the eastern facades, the main facades of the house. These are sometimes linked, intermittently, with paths paralleling the slopes.

Each axis has a definite measure and tonality, yet each repeats the theme in a variation, distinct from the other. The first axis was one long unit of measure, a cedar allee with two enclosed architectural spaces at each end; one, as entry to the gardens at the bottom of the hill, and the other at the top, as an entry to the house. Paralleling this first axis is a wooded oak *bosco* that was a half division of the cypress allee. It was a dark and secluded passage used for summer dining. The third axis, primary in emphasis, was a complex division of a full length allee, and was called the "Green Garden." Like the plan itself, the green garden axis was a composition of connected independent garden spaces and not one unified whole. Each garden of the "Green Garden" axis contained differing and un-related elements. Windows or doorways offered framed vistas from space to space, and it was through this device that the whole was comprehended. There were three main parts: The upper house terrace; the *lemonaia* building and its hillside, a sloped parterre formal garden; and the flat pleached *bosco* at the bottom of the hill. Each in turn was subdivided and changed in character, offering many variations of the main theme.

The upper terraces that had existed before were divided into three levels. They were structurally preserved but redesigned to relate to the composition of the whole Green Garden axis. Next, the *lemonaia* / parterre garden, also, consisted of three parts, the building and its entry stairs, the sloped parterres, and the flat water basin formal space. The lower *bosco,* again in three parts, had an entry space with descending staircase and fountain, the main *bosco* area and the third and culminating element, the grotto niche.

Looking away, down the Cypress Allee

Stairways ending the Cypress Allee

The wire frame exedra within the Oak Bosque

The Lemonaia Terrace and the green garden's central axis

The Oval window in the stair down into the Green Garden's Parterre Terraces

View of the Green Garden and its parterre terraces from below

The French Bosco Garden looking toward the central axis's stairs to the Green Garden

The Breakfast Garden

The Western Garden

The Secret Garden

The Secret Garden

There was a possible south axis, an oak-lined allee, in the opposite direction, that was formed with various materials. The main space of the western gardens, adjacent to the house, reflected the interior functions. The oak allee repeated the measure of the first axis and was so different that it was almost not recognizable as similar to, and a repetition of, the original theme.

> "Besides this green garden there were two long avenues of trees and three 'other gardens', all very good to walk in."
>
> Ethne Clarke

Throughout the garden's composition, the voices of this fugue were all Cecil Pinsent's. Mary, as we noted from her letters, remarked only on Cecil's limited use of plant materials – "grass and ilexes or cypresses and box."[462] Cecil utilized these to create architectural forms and spaces and for their internal articulation.

I Tatti's Altamura gardens were "ITness," meant to be the perfection of the humanist garden. They contained all the classical garden elements - terrace gardens, *lemonaia*, grottos, allees of cedars at the entrances, pleached tree allees, water stairs, and wooded oak *bosco*s. They also utilized the play of sunlight masterfully in classic variations of change, from dark to light, frontal to back lighting. This was obviously done by the hand of a designer, and that designer was Cecil Pinsent.[463] To walk through the composition now, is to experience this garden's delightful fugue:

The Cypress Allee   The entrance allee is the main space connecting the villa house to the fugue's outside world. It parallels the ridge line, shortcutting a wide loop in the adjacent ridge line road, and is parallel to other southern axial gardens. Formed by tall vertical *Cupressus*/cypresses lining both sides of the narrow space, the allee is carpeted in grass with a center strip of gravel as a walk. It is obviously modeled after the Bowling Green at Villa Gamberaia and copies the intent of the typical Tuscan Villa entry allee, which had just been recreated at La Pietra. It was the first garden space created at I Tatti, a year before Mary Berenson gave any thought to creating a major garden, and was intended as a space to the bottom of the road to the front entry of the house while avoiding the tedious switch backs required if one followed the roadway. It was Pinsent's decision to plant cypresses defining the space – "an architectural cornice" and block out the surrounding *podere* orchards. Several disasters occurred that completely killed the first cypress installation,[464] hereby necessitating further work and providing the impetus for a more comprehensive and extensive new garden development.[465]

A colossus sculpture terminates the allee's southern end, while the north is ended in an architectural walled terrace. The I Tatti colossus, a much smaller "me-too" sculpture whose placement at the end of the axis is inspired by the similar colossus of the Villa La Pietra, is a reverse of the general rule for such placements in the Renaissance garden; it is placed down hill, thereby dwarfing its full visual height.

> "The long cypress avenue, the first addition made by the Berensons was growing up well but looked puny against the majestic old cypresses near the house." [466]
>
> Nicky Mariano

    The most ingenious elements of the space are the architectural connectors at both ends. These are baroque, curvilinear and oval architectural rooms, utilizing, in part, existing walls while also building additional ones - retaining and free standing - to form the architecturally defined spaces. In conjunction with the walls, doorways and stairs that are employed for changed grade levels and are the thresholds from one space or level to the next. The top architectural room is entered from a terrace-as-balcony overlooking the cypress allee. Its base contains a central stairway up to a mid-level landing and is formed by paired cylinder retaining walls supporting the upper terrace. On top of each cylindrical form are huge clay tubs/pots of azaleas. The other end of the terrace is defined by a curved, two-story wall with a central niche and two flanking arched doorways leading to a second series of stairs, here circular, that join midway and continue in a straight direction to arrive atop in the entrance garden of the house. This niche wall rises to a height of one story above the entrance to both enclose the entrance garden and to conceal the view into the long allee. In reverse, one must enter the space at the top, and descend down curved stairways to burst onto the terrace overlook with its spectacular vista of the long cypress allee.

    The bottom architectural garden entry space contains a similar measure as its entry process. From the street at the far end of the site, one enters an oval-walled space at sub-grade to the cypress allee. It is covered by a high, one-story pergola of widely spaced columns. Passing through a narrow entry to begin a short, straight line of stairs - which again, as in the upper architectural room, split mid-way into two circular stairs - one arrives on an upper terrace and the beginning of the long allee. The colossus is centered between these circular stairs and seems twice as tall to the viewer from the entrance stairs as one rises up to the level of the allee. Architectural ends to simple green spaces are a Pinsent design formula and key to understanding the rest of I Tatti's gardens.

> "One of the avenues was the main approach on foot to the house, with cypresses thirty feet high, the other a gentle affair of ilex trees descending to another round pool, surmounted and enclosed by trellis crowned with a trellis cupola open to the sky. An evergreen jasmine grew on this trellis. The

reflection in the water, as you looked over the stone ledge of the pool, made you think of Mantegna's ceiling in the wedding chamber in the Palazzo Ducale in Mantua."[467]

Silvia Sprigge

Oak Brosco Allee   The next axis lies to the west, and is the oak *bosco* allee. Its length is equal to that of the cypress allee, but without its architectural *termini*. It is uphill from the Cypress Allee, and is built on a rounded knoll-like land form. Topography and dense evergreen Holm oaks are meant to provide a visual separation between I Tatti's Cypress Allee and the main Green Garden axis. The dense oaks are trimmed to form a grand interior, a lofty hall-like space while their outer edges provide a separating and enclosing "wall." Inside, the space is magical with intersecting dark twisted limbs and dappled light penetrating the evergreen mass. The *bosco* ended in a wire frame *exedra*, no longer extant. Additional branches were grafted onto the shaped trees - the work of the gardener, Capricchi, - to fill in any void and to totally enclose the *bosco*'s exterior "wall."

The oak *bosco* houses the garden's incredible collection of song birds, overheard at all times of day. This *giardini segretti* was a cool respite from the openness of the adjacent Green Garden or the Cypress Allee, a place where many raucous summer lunches were had under the cool shade of the oak trees.

The Green Garden   Next in the series of fugues, is the main garden axis, the Green Garden. A composition organized off the central axis of the south facade of the house, it begins a series of linearly arranged gardens that descend the full length of the hillside.

"To visualize this garden one must imagine it falling away at the sides and in front of I Tatti, downhill on every side. The green garden, evergreen with box and yew, ran down straight from the center of the house by a path through the orangery where lemons and oranges were sheltered from the frost in winter. The path then became a double stone staircase surrounding a pool and rapidly descended in a flight of broad pebbled stairs to two simple long stone pools far away at the bottom. On either side of this descent there were terraces upon which box bushes formed patterns and the whole wide descending green pattern was enclosed by what became a gigantic yew hedge in flat broad tiers on either side, like some giant's stepping stone into the valley. Papyrus and lotus grew in the pools and grey benches and statues, at some distance from them, formed another frame beneath the yew hedge to these airy spaces."[468]

Silvia Sprigge

The Green Garden is a series of separate sun-filled gardens arranged in series, carrying the central theme of the fugue - axial aligned architectural rooms descending down the sloped hillside. It's components along this axis are the following individual gardens:

The Lemonaia Terrace   A short, but wide space adjacent to the house is terraced forming three shallow levels. The original Mary Berenson garden, first created when she was a renter, was modified to the palette of the new fugue's elements of composition. Originally an English cottage garden, the changes were necessary to achieve unity in the Tuscan landscape pallette,"*Il processo di Toscanizzare.*" The first terrace is a predominately paved terrace with sculptures. The second is a series of four topiary parterres in line, each containing a major flowering and fruiting shade tree. The parterre pattern, planted with boxwood, employed a circle within a square centered on the trees. The two trees at the outer parterres are persimmons and are striking in the fall with their orange red fruits on bare branches. The other two trees forming the garden's center are peaches, lovely in spring and summer. This space is two feet below the level of the paved terrace and is box trimmed to the same height so that the terrace appears to be a continuation of the upper level. One descends from the hard material space into this green environment. The third terrace is a mixture of sitting benches, sculpture and small lemon pots brought from the adjacent *lemonaia*. It is a wonderful jumble. The space is formed on the south end by a continuous facade of what appears to be a one-story building, the *lemonaia*. A wide door, almost always open, provides a glimpse into the *lemonaia* and beyond, to the formal topiary gardens.

The *Lemonaia* Building   From the *lemonaia* terrace, one decends a massive wide flight of stairs located at the center of the two-storey *lemonaia* building below. It has a paved floor with finished and well-appointed interiors. Originally the space was used for storing farm equipment and was crude and roughly finished. Atypical, the new version is finer than any traditional *lemonaia,* and architecturally well appointed, but then no typical *lemonaia* would have had the difficult grade changes to the exterior adjacent terraces / gardens which would have required extremely difficult movement of heavy potted lemon trees, stored in the winter, to be carried up the flight of steep stairs for the spring and summer. Winter lunches were often held here on cool sunny days when the space was naturally heated by the sun. The *lemonaia*'s new south facade is punctured by tall arched windows that flood the interior with warming sunlight. These, along with a new, flat-arched central door, a sweeping roof line parapet, and engaged columns capped by urns, were the work of Cecil Pinsent. Curiously, a few years after its remodeling, the elegant facade was covered with wire mesh and planted with ivy. As Mary wrote in her descriptions of the garden to her brother Logan, "the creepers were covering the facade nicely."[469]

The central door of the south façade opens to a small balcony landing whose solid balustrade is pierced with a huge oval opening. From the doorway, the view over the terrace and through the oval is the second controlled view, revealing the formal topiary garden beyond. A dramatic circular stair descends from the terrace around a pool and sculpture grotto, acting as an overlook terrace to the formal gardens. The whole effect of the warped ivy meshed facade, curved windows, oval and curved staircase, like the entrance spaces of the cypress allee, is rather art nouveau.

> "Cecil Pinsent had used the underlying lemon house as a connecting link between the enclosed garden and the new formal one descending in terraces to an ilex wood. All this was in its infancy and looked out of proportion, the statues in the new formal garden ridicously large compared with the tiny box and cypress hedges."[470]
>
> Nicky Mariano

> "This series of stairs and terraces are a complete surprise as they are hidden from view from the house by the lemonaia building, yet they are the organizing backbone and celebrated feature of the whole garden. The astonishing drop, its depth, and the crafted perspective, breathtaking in its beauty and its studied details, produce one of the villa garden's most refined and elegant spaces. When the stairs were formed and the masonry walls were in place, Pinsent proudly announced: 'the garden will not be a failure after all.'"[471]

The Topiary Garden   The featured space of the whole I Tatti garden is this terraced topiary garden. It is divided into two parts, the first a series of three terraces with sloped banks and stairs; the second a central lawn terrace containing two pools designed as one. The terraces are each lined with box hedges, as is the sloped banks between. Within each of the box parterres are grass planes creating a knobby green slope. The center walk is patterned beautifully with *rocaille* stone work, while the terraces side paths and dividing parterre walks are paved simply with gravel. The success of the *rocaille* is due in part Pinsent's craftsmanship and the skill of the workers he trained on the site. The initial planting included posted roses (rose standards) at the corners of the parterres lining the central walk. Without doubt, they were inspired by the same rose standards lining the water parterres at Villa Gamberaia. These give height and enclosure to the central walk, something that the Pinsent redesign of the Gamberaia's water parterre garden of 1910 accomplished. It created a subtle space within a space. In photographs of I Tatti, two years later, the rose standards are removed and the corners are shown as trimmed into topiary pyramids growing out of the lines of box. This was a more uniform landscape expression, more in sympathy with the concept of a rug or *tapis* unfolding from the top terrace to the bottom reflecting pools.

The lowest space is enclosed by stone benches, hedges and pillars defining the edges. This is the brightest space in the whole fugue composition. The sky is omnipresent in this space. The entire terrace is comprised of formal green lawn into which is incised the bifurcated pool. Divided into two parts by the central walk, the "mirrors to the sky" pay a small homage to Ghyka's Gamberaia creation, with all their elements, edging and water level elegantly flush with the adjacent lawn.

Pinsent's pallette for this space was shades of green. From the sloped parterres to the flat reflecting pool area, the entire topiary space is formed by green walls of two different types of hedges. One is a tall tree, possibly little-leaf lindens, trained as an architectural wall. Their tops are trimmed to slope for the full garden's length. Interior to this tree hedge is another lower hedge of Italian needle cypresses that are trimmed to step down in crenelated levels corresponding to the drops in level of each parterre terrace. This hedge, when corresponding to the level of the pool area, is trimmed as one horizontal line enclosing this lower space. With this double hedge of contrasting green tones, Pinsent was able to clearly establish both the garden's architectural room and the specific sub-areas of each level change within.

> "The gardens at I Tatti, which are perfectly attuned with their setting and devoid of unnecessary detail, are evident of the breadth of vision of their architect, Cecil Pinsent. To balance the patterning of the box hedges and the traditional stone mosaic work of the paving, he (Pinsent) filled the parterres with plain grass rather than brightly colored flowers."[472]
>
> Ethne Clarke

The French Bosco Garden   From the topiary garden, one passes through the defining hedges of the parterre terrace, onto an open balustrade overlook. Immediately, one notices the clipped green walls of vegetation of what appears to be the continuation of the previous pool-enclosing hedge; but then the topography drops away, and the green walls are shown to be supported on tree trunks. One then realizes that below is a trimmed ilex *bosco*, closely grown to attain thin, column-like tree trunks with a uniform canopy. Cecil Pinsent sketched the exact form and gave the *capo giardinere,* Capricchi, the trimming instructions to achieve this deceptive perspective device. From this landing, a series of stairs descends along the retaining walls of the upper parterre garden onto the *bosco*'s floor, a leaf-littered mat. One is then plunged into the dark *bosco* of trees organized formally on a grid pattern. A centerline of this grove is omitted to form the central axis traversing the *bosco,* terminating at the southern property line in a grotto dedicated to Venus, the god of worldly beauty.

> "And there was a wood of young ilexes growing in rugs of moss, with a grotto with more water and a statue. Looking back from that grotto and upward, one saw I Tatti high in the distance, too far to read the time on the clock Mary had built into the stone cornice over the center of the facade. The whole garden was a bird sanctuary on a hill's side."[473]
>
> Sylvia Sprigge

The southern gardens contain well-placed sculptures of generally undistinguished quality. None are cited as originating from the Renaissance periods, none are from other respected villas gardens and none are attributed. The initial sculptures were Dionysus, placed within the northern niche of the French *bosco* garden, the Hercules colossus at the south end of the Cypress Allee, and Venus in the terminus grotto of the green garden allee. On the east side and the entrance terrace is Ceres near the front door along the east facade, and a bust of Semiramis on a pedestal by the chapel.[474] As there is no correspondence on these sculptures, they could be originals, or reproductions purchased from the Berensons' friend, Arthur Acton. As the I Tatti, La Pietra, and Gambaraia gardens were being developed at about the same time, and ideas seemed to float from garden to garden, it is quite possible that so did garden sculpture. But in no way is sculpture made an essential part of the garden's composition, as it was in the gardens of Villa La Pietra.

From these three garden axes, an informal rustic walk leads through a so-called kitchen garden to the western part of the site and its gardens. A very un-Italian rail fence lined a grass path that gradually climbs the slopes through remnant orchards of olive and fruit trees planted by Berenson himself when he first became *il padrone*.[475] The fence is heavily planted in wisteria vines and must be sensational in the spring when laden with purple racines. The orchard is typically Tuscan, with gnarly dark cork trunks rising out of brown tufted unmown field grasses. The walk is one of I Tatti's few garden flaws. As lovely as the plantings are and as well-maintained, and verdantly green and florally beautiful as the walk is, this landscape passage, with its contrast to the adjacent rural, unkempt Tuscan orchards, is simply too jarring to both mind and eye.

> "The others were a kitchen garden dotted with fruit trees whence the southern views to the hillside of Corbignano and distant Vallombrosa were constantly delighting the eye. There was a meadow too- as English

a meadow in springtime as one might ever hope to see south of the Alps. In spring, its grass slopes were dotted with anemones and daffodils, and fritillary. From it, in summer, came the smell of new cut hay."[476]

Silvia Sprigge

The Western Garden   The centerpiece of the western gardens is the oak-lined allee. A broad walk is cut into the sloping hillside forming a narrow terraced allee which is planted in laurel oak. It is a very shady and delightful space that runs east and west, through the sloping hillside's olive orchard. A secret stand of bamboo (again, very un-Italian) lies to the allee's north, offering a backdrop to the other western gardens and providing the structural "poles" for the upkeep of the formal hedges and pollarded plants. It was also Mary Berenson's favorite spot for Greek lessons, a place where one would not easily be disturbed.

The allee ends in a mucky flat area adjacent to the lower stream that was obviously a former flood plane. These lower flats are not particularly well suited for olive production or the oak allee, both preferring dryer soils. Instead, vegetable and grain crops were raised there in annual rotation. A small *tiempolo*, or circular columned garden pavilion, smaller but similar to the one at Villa La Pietra, ends the axis.

> "The sound of running water in this garden came from a steam, a tributary of the so-called torrent, the Mensola, whose waters formed a boundary to the property. Beyond the Mensola, the land rose again in olive-clad hills belonging to the neighboring castle of Poggio Gherardo [Mrs Janet Ross and later inherited by her niece Mrs. Aubrey Wakefield].
>
> "I had farms and fields beyond the garden whence came the wine which was drunk at meals and some of the flour used for making bread."[477]

Silvia Sprigge

The Breakfast Garden   Just north and uphill from the oak allee is a breakfast garden, of contemporary design, adjacent to the *piano terreno* pantry. This garden is almost the pre-curser of a Thomas Church, of contemporary California composition. It is a quarter round transition space terraced into the hillside. Its north edge is the high retaining walls of the Grotto terrace above, covered with a trimmed espalier of bay laurel. The area is lawn and the outer garden edge is formed by tall pine trees offering shade to a *terra battuta*, or earthen area below. This space is used for informal dining, bar-bqueuing and relaxing.

The Secret Garden   The grotto space, known as the Secret Garden, just above the informal breakfast garden, is one of the most serene and traditional spaces in the whole garden. Ending the garden processional, it is a cadenza demonstrating Cecil Pinsent's

R. Terry Schnadelbach

landscape architectural virtuosity. (It has just recently been refurbished - cleaned and replanted as originally designed by Pinsent.) The terrace is a three-sided architectural room formed on the west by the house, a wing volume that is part of the library on the north, and a free-standing enclosure wall containing the grotto. The south side is open but defined by the high balustrades of a retaining wall. Views to the informal breakfast space below are not easily accessible.

This space closely resembles the historic *pomario* of Villa La Pietra. It is similar in its position, extending the house out into the landscape and dividing the garden from the *podere's* functional building complex further to the west. Although considerably smaller than the garden at La Pietra, the materials defining the space are similar. The I Tatti grotto terrace is filled with herb parterres and paved with stone pebble mosaics, some geometric and some thematic - the east side walk space defined with a *fleur de lis,* a rational choice as it is the symbol of Florence. The parterres are three squares, each divided into four smaller parterres - perhaps a recall from the *lemonaia* terraces. All parterres are lined with box and the center spaces planted with a silver color, rosemary-like herb. The four parterres forming the three squares are shaped by higher trimmed box on the outer edges and have topiary nobs growing out of the low box borders at the central corner - a recall of the sloped topiary garden. The alternating of trimmed and natural plants with color changes from lush green to silver green produces a very interesting composition which, when aligned with the mosaic paving, form a rich tapestry floor to the space. The north wall is an unbroken facade that is treated with vegetation and provides a green link to the west and east grotto facades. Here, the north wall is planted with espalier wisteria that blooms in the spring and early summer, and arching sprays of light purple racines. At its base is a border of lavender, silver in color to match the parterre beds that also bloom in purple spike flowers. The unification of plant colors is striking.

This garden contains the same Pinsent design predilection - strong architectural elements at the garden's ends and well-designed green spaces in between. It is a fitting end to the I Tatti garden fugue. The cadenza and the whole garden fugue ends at the very entrance to Altamura's heart, the Berenson library.

> "Cecil Pinsent, the gentlest of men, with powerful imagination about plants, trees, views and flowers, performed the miracle of laying out the garden at I Tatti in such a way that after fifty years of steady growth, the sight of its evergreen spaces in the heart of the 'Tatti' landscape was as varied and as satisfying as a Bach fugue.
>
> "I have walked round that garden with him several times. I never asked the acreage: perhaps no more than fifty acres. Within it he and Berenson

> imagined that a man might take a fairly long and varied walk passing from one landscape and mood to another, not with violent change but imperceptibly. The walker might have to take a zigzag route (fifty acres is no great area for a half-hour walk) but there would be a choice of routes, again imperceptibly. Suggested - few paths, no fences. At first, when the trees were young and small, Berenson believed the miracle would never happen. As they grew mightily there was fear that the garden would get out of hand. But it never did. Four gardeners tended it. Through the years Pinsent came to see it grow and to legislate about the trimming of the great yew hedges and ilex trees, and to establish the placing of those statues and grey stone benches in dark shady places where one might sit and read."[478]
>
> Silvia Sprigge

All the axes, walks, or paths in the Altamura garden were given names, some for friends, some for visitors and some for "ITness," honoring other Aesthetes. Both the new gardens and the house were raised to "ITness," i.e., the Altamura level of aesthetic perfection. The construction provided spaces clearly set for specific Altamura purposes. There was the sitting room where guests arrived and awaited the appropriate hour for lunch, tea, or dinner, and where "majically" (both magically and majestically) BB would appear for introductions, afterwards to lead the group in procession into the new dining room or the garden's various seasonal dining spaces. There were the new guest rooms, each with its own sitting room / study and "modern convenience." I Tatti's hallways functioned as galleries for the Berenson Collection, where Bernard's held" artwork[479] were displayed, undistinguished with pieces BB wished to sell. All rooms were electrified, with new color-coordinated plastering and moldings, setting the villa clearly back into the earlier classical periods. The new furnishings throughout were "simplicity,"[480] - classical but not all of any particular period.

> "My house, I trust, does express my needs, my tastes, and aspirations. It is a library with living rooms attached. These are both spacious and comfortable yet with a touch of old Italian severity that might depress the happy victims of our 'interior decorators.' When the house was at long last finished and the works of art in their place, ... It took the scattering of most private collections all over Europe to make me realize that mine was one of the best remaining."[481]
>
> Bernard Berenson

For all these improvements the Berensons spent, by their own admission, "a small fortune." The operations and gracious hospitality cost them another fortune. The predominant impression, that the Berensons were from gentile families and independently wealthy, was a huge deception on the public. Even with a steady income from the art dealer, Duveen, of over one hundred thousands dollars yearly,[482] many a night was spent worrying about foreclosure on the bank loans or on funds necessary to cover their overdrawn accounts.

As mentioned earlier, Berenson was totally skilled and well-versed in European art, was expressly knowledgeable in all Italian art, and was the unchallenged authority on Italian Renaissance painting. His systematic cataloging, analyzing and traveling to the smallest *citta* gave no slack to his peers. His authentications were not just his word, but were backed up with page after page of documentation dealing with everything from composition to brush stroke analysis. When he spotted fakes, he would indicate the painter's natural style, tracing the indicators that did not comply; he searched the painter's development and noted discrepancies; he showed the painter's influence and indicated false reflections, and finally, he would give the name, place and owner of the original.[483]

On one occasion, in late 1899, Berenson discovered a specific dealer of the artist Benvenuto di Giovanni and reasoned that it was highly unlikely that there could be so many "discoveries" at this one location. He decided to visit the art dealer, Federico Joni, at his remote farmhouse. On arrival, they were met by "a rollicking band of young men, cousins and friends, who ran the forgery workshop."[484] It became obvious to Berenson that much of the Italian Renaissance art of the day was newly minted in copy houses.

Many of Berenson's attributions have since been reversed as inaccurate or fake. Most notorious are the paintings of the Samuel H. Kress Foundation, set up by the American five-and-dime billionaire "to promote the moral, physical and mental welfare of the human race." Kress's philanthropy included the purchase of art to be given to existing or newly established museums of art in cities all across America. For the National Gallery of Art, Washington, D.C., the Foundation donated in 1930, 375 paintings and eighteen sculptures. Cities like New Orleans, Cleveland, Oklahoma City, Saint Louis, to mention but a few of the more than 25, were given sizable number of Renaissance works, Kress's passion and major interest. Samuel H. Kress (1863-1955) was a personal friend of Berenson, but bought his art through the Duveen London gallery. Among the notable works purchased this way was, in 1938, *Allendale*, painted by Giorgione. Duveen purchased the work for $315,000, and then, with an attribution by Berenson, sold it to Samuel Kress for $516,000.[485] Bernard, as per his agreement with Duveen, shared in the profits. At one point in their relationship, Berenson tried to renegotiate partnership in the Duveen firm. Bernard later admitted that many of these attributions were rubber stamped. He also admitted that his financial relationship with Duveen influenced his judgements. Hired by Kress to give a closer look at one of his recent acquisitions, Bernard wrote only: "It is by Titian." and collected a handsome fee.[486] The value of Kress's purchase escalated considerably, as did the value of the collection. A large portion of the Kress Foundation collection has since been reviewed by scholars and appraisers and has been found to be forged, minted in the "back streets of Florence," if not the Fiesole hills. Many believed that Berenson, if not part of this game, knew about the sham. His "holier-than-thou" posture in his writings and public pronouncements often turned out to be just that - posturing.

The Berensons conducted separate love lives, discreet from each other. Mary's flamboyant affairs with young men were matched by Bernard's flirtations with women. Mary's encounters were sometimes planned and sometimes happenstance, but either way, the end was always self gratification. Bernard's desires were ambivalent and seemingly contradictory, and when BB was assertive, some of his advances were successes and others not. Gladys Deacon, Duchess of Marlbourough, Lady Sassoon, Gabrielle La Caze and Countess Hortense Serristori - were equal matches for Mary's ventures in young, free love, kept on some undisclosed scorecard between the two. The fact that Bernard and Mary slept every night in separate bedrooms, distant from one another, made outside liaisons possible. Bernard cited a hypocritical reason for this - the prohibition of strict orthodox Jewish husbands in Eastern Europe from sleeping the whole night in the wife's bed. Before their marriage, the reason for their having separate apartments and hotel rooms could have been out of public concern for Mary's family, but the practice continued throughout their marriage. As Bernard had long since cast off any espoused Jewishness, this reasoning is lame and only conceals his own unresolved sexuality.

BB and Mary separate personage

> "The slender evidence suggests that sex [for Bernard] was never very satisfying and that, by 1900, it ceased to be important."[487]
>
> Meryle Secrest

> "The Berenson marriage... was entered into on that familiar but precarious principle that each would be free to go his (or her) own course, if such a situation should arise."[488]
>
> Sylvia Sprigge

Of BB's flirtatious advances that fell on deaf ears, the prior mentioned seduction of the notorious American, Miss Blood,[489] a sadistic lesbian, were futile from the start, and Bernard quickly learned of the new, open lesbian community of Florence. Others, including his advances to Edith Wharton, one of America's leading novelist and authors on Renaissance Italian gardens; they were among Berenson's failed attempts. Edith was in the midst of a torrid affair with the journalist Morton Fullerton, a classmate of Berenson's who worked with him on the *Harvard Monthly*, but their flirtation resulted in a close personal friendship that lasted over forty years.

While he mixed socially, he never was seen as a sexual man, but rather as a man of intellect who sought the pleasures of anaesthetic life above all carnal pleasures. His early adult life, like his Apollonian boy-like appearance, was indicative of an androgynous nature. He liked the company of women, but only those who stroked his ego. He was never assertive and waited instead for their approaches, which seldom occurred. Berenson believed intelligent, beautiful and self-realized women to be his equals, endowing them with mythical traits he learned from art. They became Dianes, Primaveras or Valkyries - all on pedestals and unapproachable. Sex would violate his sacred, ideal image of them; it would be like violating a work of art.

> "Later, after puberty, when love began to glow within me but for years remained unmixed with lust, my yearnings were of a mystic being in youthful female shape with whom I could aspire to unite myself."[490]

> "Fundamentally sex is indifferent to its object. As a French saying has it: All wines are good enough. So with sex."[491]

> "And there is quite a house party, there is not one woman I could be in

love with at it. And when I am not hard at work, I must have women I *might*, and I would, be in love with."[492]

Bernard Berenson

Berenson therefore, distinguished between worldly and attainable sex for-hire and the unattainable idealized goddesses who took him into a protected land of the gods and seduced him to submission. Sex and love were thus different. Sex itself was a disgusting necessity, a submission to his human frailness. While most colleagues believed him asexual, he admitted, privately, to his humanness and acknowledged that throughout his life he frequented prostitutes, even when married and especially when traveling.

"His ambivalent views about sex, disguised as morality, make it unlikely that he would have been a skillful lover, however brilliantly satisfying he might prove as a companion."[493]

Meryle Secrest

Berenson called his genitals and his sexuality by the same term, his volcano.

"I have never got over my disgust with everything that comes out of the body, whether from nose, mouth, bladder or bowels. Even the supermost of all physical pleasures is somewhat spoiled for me by the ejaculation it ends with."[494]

Bernard Berenson

Belle da Costa Green, by everyone's assessment was an outrageous person. She had been librarian for J. P Morgan as well as his mistress. A stunning beauty of mixed Negro / Caucasian blood, she had thick sensuous lips, face and figure. She had pronounced green eyes, a slim waist, and flamboyant but impeccable taste. She reminded Berenson of another belle, Isabelle Gardner. She was an open seductress with stories circulating that she would slip men that interested her, her key on introduction. Rumors abounded as to her wild sex life; some said that after Morgan's death, she overcompensated with many lovers; others said these were flirtations to cover her same-sex affairs.

It is true that Belle Greene loved amusement of all sort - cocktail parties, dances, campaign suppers - all with cigarettes, cigarettes and more cigarettes. At these, she never would miss the opportunity to stun the conservative set with her exhibitionist behavior. First citing the primitivism of Rousseau, she would then sit on the floor and eat with her fingers, a la Rousseau. A gifted scholar, Green was an avid lover of rare manuscripts.

> "He is always in love and I put up with it all right, except when his mistress is an out and out vulgarian, like Belle Greene."[495]
> Mary Berenson

Bernard met Belle Greene on his 1908-1909 journey to New York and Boston. The trip was ostensibly made to deal with Gardner Museum matters, but when he met Greene he was immediately captivated by her beauty and searing intellect. Her first impression of Bernard was not flattering – "as to your friend, BB, irritating and annoying."[496] By all accounts Bernard was love struck and saw her constantly. He confided that he felt as if he had been struck by the sun. They had a sporadic, long-distance relationship, sending passionate trans-Atlantic letters (over 600 by Berenson alone) and seeing each other on visits to New York by Berenson, or in Florence, with Belle in residence at I Tatti. This was the one relationship that troubled Mary, for she thought it so serious that Bernard might leave her - but then again, she was into a deep relationship at this time with Geoffrey Scott. The affair between Belle and Bernard lasted four to five years, dying a gradual death. Some historians cite that Belle eventually loved Bernard.

> "A wonderful lover. She was the only woman for whom he would have left Mary."[497]
> Meryle Secrest

Through a convoluted scheme, Mary was responsible for Berenson's final love. It wasn't in accordance with her calculated plan and it was not immediate, but the result was a *menage a trois*. And it was, in the end, after Mary's death and Bernard's impotency, the idealized love that Bernard had dreamed of his entire adult life.

hidden lives / secret gardens

Belle da Costa Green

Nicky Mariano had visited Florence in 1913, staying with her family at the Villa Rondinelli in Fiesole, when she met a thin, long legged, bespeckled Brit who talked constantly about art, architecture and the philosophy of aesthetics. He had "long black hair swept back, his voice, his laughter, his sense of fun, his whimsical expression, his choice of words, all appealed to me."[498] She nicknamed him *Gambe Lunghe*, or Long Legs, in Italian. Writing in her autobiography, *Forty Years with Berenson*, Nicky, a Russian youth of twenty-something, was quite taken by this more mature man of thirty-something. Together, they toured galleries, churches, the hillsides of Florence and a very special garden, under construction, that he proudly claimed he and a friend were responsible for. These tours occurred while the owners, the Berensons, were away in America. The man was Geoffrey Scott. On Mary's return she met Nicky and liked her immediately, only to discover a problem - Scott was romantically in love with Nicky - seriously in love. Mary and Scott's own relationship, after seven years, was now faltering. Scott was interested in people his own age, as Mary was now a matronly-figured woman of fifty-something. The Scott / Mariano flirtation ended shortly, however, when Nicky left to return to Russia.

A year later, Nicky returned to Florence. Mary, knowing of Scott's lingering fantasy, realized she would eventually lose him to a younger person. Berenson had now found out about the long-standing Scott / Mary affair, and fired Scott as his librarian, forbidding him at I Tatti. Mary was eager to get the library back in shape and keep Berenson happy, and quite frankly, she agreed that Scott had done an abysmal job. Why not, Mary thought, rekindle the Scott / Mariano romance, keeping Scott around as a "handy man," beholden to her? She would give Nicky the job as librarian at I Tatti. The arrangement would leave open the possibility that Scott could advance the relationship to having Nicky marry him. All parties would be satisfied.

> "[I] saw Mary repeatedly. She became almost importunate in her eagerness to bring Geoffrey and me together, made all sorts of proposals, wanted me to change my plans and to join her and Geoffrey on a trip to the Dolomites instead of leaving for the Baltic provinces. It was a little bewildering and seemed to me to have no relation to the length of our acquaintance."[499]
>
> Nicky Maraino

BB and Nicky Marino

But this plan hopelessly backfired, as all of Europe went to war. On trying to meet Nicky, Scott was turned away at the door of I Tatti; and told that Nicky had returned to Russia. In need of employment, unwelcome at I Tatti, and wanting to stay in Italy, Scott went to Rome and got a job as a secretary in the British Consulate. There, he received the news that Nicky Mariano had been killed. It threw him into a suicidal depression. Irrationally, and impulsively, during this period, he married the widow Lady Sibyl Cutting, a former Pinsent/Scott client at Villa Medici in Fiesole.[500] On hearing of the wedding, Mary Berenson became furious.

Life in the hills of Florence stood still during the war. Mary and Bernard were sheltered in London. After the war, the impoverished Mariano family fled the Boshivics and returned to Florence. Russia and most of Eastern Europe was devastated and finding employment was a hopeless exercise in futility. Italy was spared much of the physical destruction and economic recovery efforts looked more promising there. A still very much alive Nicky Marino resurfaced in Switzerland, where she and a friend were seeking employment. Mary, who was sympathetic to the plight of the cultured Russians who were particularly hurt by the war, wanted to help. She inquired about Nicky, whom she remembered as a very nice person, and devised a complex, mutually beneficial plan. Wanting to dangle the rediscovered Nicky as a carrot in front of Scott, she announced that she had kept her side of this convoluted bargain; a job for Nicky was to be had as Bernard's archivist. Mary was well aware that the Scott-Cutting marriage at the Villa Medici, was not going well.

After her return to Florence and her acceptance of Mary's job offer, Nicky did initially meet Geoffrey, who did invite her to the Villa Medici where she met the Lady Sybil Cutting Scott. And Scott did, on other occasions, take Nicky to the upper terrace gardens where they relaxed while he read her some of his favorite love poems. Nicky was "deeply stirred by them."[501] But Scott was now too embittered by Mary's manipulation to ever see her again.

> "When in 1917, Geoffrey had decided to marry Lady Sybil, Mary's disappointment, disapproval and even rage had been so great that she had written very offensive letters both to Geoffrey and to Lady Sybil."
> Nicky Mariano

When Bernard first met Nicky Marino it was as his librarian and archivist. Their relationship eventually grew to complete intimacy. He did not like Nicky at first; he found her silence and quiet movements disconcerting and her intellect less than stunning. For Nicky, Berenson every utterance became magical. Was there a subject upon which he could not speak eloquently? Over a period of time and growing familiarity, Nicky gradually fell in love with Berenson - his mind at least, if not his body.

> "Most art critics are limited by the exigencies of their profession, but Berenson's mind ranged far beyond it."[502]
> Harold Acton

> "Berenson, with his astonishing intellect, delighted in the play of ideas; he could illuminate regions, however remote, not of art, only, but also of literature, philosophy, politics, history, ethics and psychology."
> William Rothenstein

Nicky's and Bernard's work led to a joint, intertwined life meted out in schedules and the business of buying and selling art; meeting with wealthy buyers or their art agents, and out-maneuvering other dealers trying to secure the same important pieces. Together at I Tatti, or traveling to major world cities, they worked as a team to make deals, see a gallery's collection or advise on future purchases. Their travels developed from short to lengthier stays, not all of which were consumed by business. Quite separate from Mary, BB vacationed together with Nicky and they were known as a couple, even while Bernard continued his marriage with Mary.

In royal England, this was possible. For example, it was a public knowledge that Mrs. Kepple was King George's "Queen in Waiting." She attended all functions at his side and was his companion at every afternoon's tea. She was his kept mistress in every sense of the word, given expensive budgets for clothing and house upkeep, and allowed to invest her savings with the King's in lucrative ventures, e.g., America's emerging and profitable railroad industry. The Queen attended all state functions and maintained her status as wife in the royal family, ran the palace and dined every evening with the king. Lady Kepple did the same in her marriage to her husband, George Kepple, who, publicly, was an understanding husband. Privately, he was known to love young men. With some, he built long term relationships as strong as a marriage. Their daughter, Violet, was the lesbian lover of Vita Sackville-West, both avid gardeners and friends with both Ghyka and Berenson.[503]

So too, Bernard Berenson's marriage became polygamous in form, involving two women, each having separate and critical functions in the operations of the enterprise. One became his sexual partner and love object, the other his soul-mate and alter ego.

The Florentine community had a long-standing liberal acceptance for same sex relationships in their various forms. Bisexuality among men was common. Where it occurred, the preferred homosexual relationship was more often between two young men while the heterosexual relationship was between a young man and an older woman. Such was the case with the young Arthur Jeremy Monteney Jephson, a young lover of Isabella S. Gardner. She had sent Jephson to see Bernard Berenson on his trip to Florence in the fall of 1900. Berenson, as a courtesy to Isabella, accepted Jephson, having him to tea and to many of his famous lunches at I Tatti. In successive letters to Isabella between November and late December of that year, Berenson reported that Jephson was now more of a ladies' man than a man's man and that he (Jephson) and Mary were spending much time together. Berenson gradually confessed to Isabella of this affair and that he

hidden lives / secret gardens

was letting them have their time together.⁵⁰⁴ Later, Mary acknowledged the affair, referring to Jephson as "this marvelously beautiful youth."

But Jephson's homosexual preferences took precedence and he was scandalously caught soliciting the "favors" of young boys in front of a Florentine theater. The particular youth was a florist who was leading a very open gay life. The informer tried black-mail, warning of public scandal, but Berenson came to Jephson's aid and, reporting back to Isabella Gardner, formulated an acceptable explanation of Jephson's "innocent" actions. He was simply offering assistance to this young man who was planning a horticultural trip to England and was presenting his card to his new friend. It was all misconstrued by one of the puritan; "foul-tongued Anglo-Americans who live here, God knows why,"⁵⁰⁵ Berenson accused the rumor-monger of a rush to judgment and inferred he was eager to make a profit from the incident. Berenson claimed not to have engaged in homosexual experiences although, with his Apollo-like youthful looks, he was exposed often to solicitations. Although Berenson was friends with Oscar Wilde, the notorious English homosexual playwright,⁵⁰⁶ he was always uncomfortable around him even though, when they traveled together, they shared hotel rooms. Fearing guilt-by-association, that he would be called a sodomist,⁵⁰⁷ he emphatically stated that he did not like the idea of sexual relations among men. But Berenson proudly acknowledged to the Philadelphia art dealer, Henry P. McIlhenny that Wilde had made advances on him and even worse, fell in love with him. "It was love at first sight."⁵⁰⁸ Of these approaches, Berenson observed; "And Lord knows that at the time, young as I was, I made homosexuals' mouths water." He recorded that in 1984, after a particularly strong Wilde advance, made while visiting in Florence, which Berenson again refused. Wilde exclaimed that Berenson "was completely without feeling; made of stone."⁵⁰⁹

Arthur Jeremy Montenev Jephson

Throughout his life in Florence, Berenson met and knew many from the "Brotherhood of Sodomites," or just "Sodomites,"⁵¹⁰ as he referred to all gays. He seemed compassionate and accepting of their sexual orientation. He even seemed to understand and admit to homosexual leanings in his own life. He strongly disapproved of the harsh laws that harassed them in their home countries. Mary was more conflicted. On one occasion, traveling through Florence with Geoffrey, she spotted that "awful" man, Balfour, one of the "cult of Florence" and warned Scott of what a sad state this life style was in old age.[511] But on hearing the news of Wilde's sentence of two years imprisonment and hard labor for being a homosexual, Mary Berenson, reflecting the jointly held Berenson view, stated; "It is sickening to think the punishment has fallen on the most brilliant of them all."[512]

Late in life, Berenson was asked to give his opinion on homosexuality. His long reply dealt with his this subject as well as on heterosexual love, which he had idealized in aesthetic terms. While he did not choose it on rational grounds, he said, he did not condemn it or its practitioners as social outcasts, which was the prevalent attitude of the day. The passage is remarkable for what it includes - his views on heterosexual sex- and what practices of the heterosexual that it does not include - monogamy, prostitution and sex for ambitious aims.

> "All emotions whatever seem to be physical that is to say a matter of sense. Insofar as we have feelings towards a person as distinct from a mere scientific estimate, that feeling is necessarily a physical feeling. Training, habit, respect may keep that feeling - as they do towards parents and elders and sisters and brothers - from producing sexual stimulation. But where there are no such hindrances, the tendency of all feelings of warmth toward a person is to a sexual discharge. It is obvious that between the man and a woman such discharge is normal and desirable. If it does not take place, it is for social and hygienic-economic reasons which reasons in the bulk we can call moral. But the same tendency holds between persons of the same sex. If it does not reach consummation, it is in the young because *ils ne servant pas comment s'y prendre,* and in older people either because of the artificial horror and disgust inspired by taboo, or because the sexual discharge is so complete elsewhere that the tendency dies in a mere ideation - as is the case with most men and a majority of women, thanks to their rich intersexual life.
>
> "It is pure superstition to talk of love between persons of the same sex as if it were unnatural from any physiological or physical standpoint. But everything that is natural is reasonable and desirable. The reasonable and desirable are questions of social need and ideal. Now there are obvious reasons why society must encourage love between the sexes and condemn love in the same sex. And condemning it as society does, and we being social beings, if we act against the taboos of society, we feel, if not at fault, at least singularized; we tend to keep with those who have the same tastes, we grow mysterious, we lose our ease of frank discourse with the run of mortals, and end by becoming a sort of

unnatural abnormal being - in the sense that we are not striving to live in harmony with our social environment.

"I therefore, with a delight in the beauty of the male that can seldom have been surpassed, and with an almost unfortunate attractiveness for other men, have not only never yielded to any temptations, but have deliberately not allowed temptations to come near me. And yet how well I understand! I have spoken of the facts from the outside. Now let me speak from the inside. When one is young - and only when one is young - love possesses one completely. This early love is something so shy, so sacred, and so awe-inspiring, that it lacks all conscious sexual concomitant. And when it gets to a pitch where the union occurs, it is an infinite longing to become one with the beloved, to mingle with it in every way, to leave no effort of interpenetration untried. Hence the extraordinary play of young lovers - a play which may be in actuality as monstrous as any *jeux de Venus* ever invented, and yet be not only free from lust, but as mystical and poetic as the ecstasies of St. Theresa. Nor does it seem to me in the essence of things that this physical effort in mystical union, when inspired by as intense a love should not take place between people of the same sex. It is to be avoided, and severely avoided, for the social consequences. It is not to be totally suppressed, but kept in tight reign. After all, it is a delightful thing to keep one's self in hand. I have enjoyed the effort not to possess, no less than the delight in possession. Think of the hundreds of women one has desired without love, and refrained from, even when one could have had them. Such suppressed desire immensely enriches life - and so it should, even when the desire is man for man or woman for woman."[513]

Bernard Berenson

Bernard Berenson's views are quite liberal for a time when society was particularly offended by overt sexual practices deemed deviant, but society was no less offended by polygamous relationships, affairs among married people, wide age differences and free love among heterosexuals, all practiced by Berenson in his liaisons. His argument on the effects of going against social strictures, with its predictable end results of separation from society and secretive behavior, apply equally for heterosexuals involved in socially unacceptable behavior as among inverts and same sex partners. This point is amply illustrated in the lives of the expatriate homosexual and heterosexual community of Florence. This particular isolation produced a unique community of Anglo-Americans all bound by art, gardens, and away from public view, a lifestyle that allowed freedom for all forms of sexual expressions.

R. Terry Schnadelbach

Daily life at I Tatti was conducted at a swift and deliberate pace. In the early years, Bernard and guests alike spent a good part of the day working in their rooms or in crude and makeshift library cubicles. The house was eerily quiet during these times. For Bernard, the library was the center of Altamura, a fountain of knowledge where all came to drink. He might have derived his concept for the Altamura library from his familiarity with the private collections of many of the social clubs of London, New York and Boston, especially the Boston Atheneum with its famous private library. BB only dreamt of such a library for I Tatti and began the long process of ordering books weekly to build his collection, cataloging books and photographic prints, and expanding the collection to become a full academic institution.

All guests and "residents" emerged from their individual pursuits for meals. Lunch was often in the garden, weather permitting. In the summer, with its mild weather and long twilight hours, dinner was outside under the lower terrace's cypresses. During the rest of the year, dinner was always inside and a formal affair. The dining and sitting rooms would have a blazing wood fire adding to the festivity. At these gatherings, the conversation centered on "ITness" was perfected to a level of art and was more important than food. The atmosphere always formed in quiet discussions, emerging into light and jovial stories during the main course and serious discussion on some particular topic late in the meal, usually directed and introduced by Bernard. One cannot help but suspect that the topics were chosen by Bernard to fit the monthly Altamura themes, as Bernard, himself controlled the subject matter.

Visitors came to I Tatti especially to bathe in the aura of Bernard Berenson's vast knowledge. Here, discussions could be had in five languages, and often they would become heated, with many a guest challenging the master. But almost always, Bernard's skills in logic, his articulate presentation technique and his detailed memory of physical settings, visual content and literary quotations would win the discussion. After lunch, a walk through the adjacent hillside cooled any ruffled feelings and was followed by "good-by" to visitors and a siesta for resident guests. This repetitious pattern was perfected, down to the minute.

Saturday was a special time and featured an "ITness" musical event in the afternoon following lunch, or later in the early evening, before dinner. In the beginning, a Miss Cracroff, from England, regularly played piano music by Bach, Beethoven and Gluck. These later became concerts by string quartets. Occasionally, they would feature music from a string orchestra. At eleven o'clock every evening, Berenson would automatically rise and leave for bed signaling all guest to follow suit. I Tatti, the monastery, once again became eerily quiet.

Bernard Berenson identifying authorship

    With a reputation for perfection - an emerging "ITness" collection of art, the wit and intelligence of Bernard and the hospitality and libertine morals of Mary - I Tatti quickly gained an international reputation. A constant stream of visitors began to arrive, among them museum directors, art collectors and men of arts and letters. But, only a few scholars and intimate friends knew of I Tatti as Altamura.

    Mary's informality and flexibility made accommodating guests easy. She perfected arranging the house and fitting the numerous guest rooms as academic studies with writing desks and study furniture. The decor was plain; chintz for wall paper and chairs alike. The rest of the house was equally restrained. The stucco walls were painted in a single cool neutral color, – the dining room a blue green, the drawing room a pale yellow, the library blue. The walls contained delicate old embroidery hangings Mary would acquire in the market, or an occasional work" acquired by Bernard of some little known or yet to-be-discovered Renaissance painter. The stone floors were covered in part by Aubusson and Oriental carpets. The furniture was unmatched; aged Italian and French pieces were chosen for their simplicity. The interiors of I Tatti were a perfection of understated elegance.[514]

> "The villa faces an ideal landscape where all the delicate trees and growths are like filigree....we basked in the garden which is more pleasant than beautiful, whilst the lizards crept about. After tea Berenson showed us his house which is spacious, cool, pleasant in wall color, white grey, grey-green, decorated with old furniture, some of which is exquisite."[515]
> Charles Ricket

As people came for lunch, tea and dinner, Mary organized the staff to have food available for any occasion. The kitchen could always be counted on to provide an abundance of fresh fruit, vegetables, pasta, wine and bread. Even the smallest amount of meat could be expanded to accommodate the unexpected. If a guest suddenly appeared, another plate was discretely added to the table. Similarly, if an anticipated guest failed to arrive, a plate would be swiftly removed.

During the first five years, the list of I Tatti's Florentine regulars included the lesbian writer couple, Vernon Lee and Kit Anstruther Thompson; the Florentine social dandy; Carlo Placci; the young, unkempt Italian historian, Gaerano Salvemini; the thespian, Gabriele d'Annunzio (until he turned Fascist); the Gamberaia's Miss Blood; the newspaper commentator and Jewish historian, Hutchins Hapgood, along with his playwright / novelist wife, Neith Boyce; Miss Maud Gruttwell, an art historian; art critic and architect Herbert Horn (until he became a competitor); the unpredictable and vulgar Janet Ross, and an "elderly English scholar named Alfred Benn, Berenson's wedding's best-man, who was a consummate gossip."[516]

Members of this Florentine family called the daily life at I Tatti, "fossilized."[517] Berenson had envisioned a lay monastery of leisurely culture, but Mary, with her self-deprecating humor described it more as a "wayside inn for loafing scholars."[518] BB, realizing the way that his aesthete and monastic lifestyle was perceived by others, in a moment of his own self deprecation, called I Tatti an "institootion."

" I have become an institootion - one of the sights - which the traveler to Florence has to see. [519]

Bernard Berenson

The I Tatti staff was ITness" perfection itself. It was vastly expanded to take care of the increased hospitality and maintenance. At its peak, the staff numbered over twenty, with four gardeners alone to take care of the trimming, staking and shaping of the green masses, grass areas and replacement propagation. As there were little or no floral displays typical of other Florentine gardens, this was an amazing number of support gardeners.

Punctually the staff went through the day's paces more efficiently than Napoleon's legendary army in drill. Daily life at I Tatti[520] was an open-house most of the day but run like a monastery, with strict rules of order. The day began at 6:30 a.m. sharp. Staff would have drawn a bath at a Bernard-preferred, perfect temperature. Bernard arose and began with a comprehensive grooming that took close to one hour.

He took no breakfast. Mary arose and after a simple toilette, would meet with the staff and organize the work of the day. After, she would begin her prolific correspondence, accepting requests for future scholars and dignitaries, scheduling their reception, writing family and loves and corresponding with the growing list of foreign friends. Visitors, staying in the house, awoke with breakfast served in their study while a warm bath was drawn and the visitor was expected to rise and begin their toilette and the day. They were "invited" to remain in their rooms until eleven o'clock, engaged in the quiet pleasures of reading and writing. Mary's youthful guests were invited to the library to read, or to the garden to sketch and paint.

At eleven the visitor was offered the opportunity to join Bernard on his morning outing. Berenson would descend the stairs, greeted by a butler, choose from among his favorite camel hair coats, gloves, scarves and hats and select a flower for his boutonniere from the nearby vase of daily fresh-picked flowers. The outing would be either a stroll in the garden or a drive up one of Settignano's spectacular country lanes, to be dropped for a walk through the Tuscan landscape. Each time, the location varied within a number of set options. The car trips were by chauffeur-driven *machina* - a jeep rebuilt with the top of a station wagon. The routes led to differing scenic beauty spots - crest walk, quarry walk, cross country walk, tree walk. A favorite trip, the tree walk, was to an ancient tree growing out of the hillside slopes north of Fiesole. The heavily weathered tree with its splintered trunk and expressive upturned branches would cause BB to stand in silence for an endless period of time, contemplating its subtle beauty. The airing ended promptly at noon. From noon to one, Bernard remained in his study and handled his correspondence.[521]

Guests for lunch would gather in the *salotto* and await the one o'clock "magical," hour, Bernard's precise time for entrance and introductions. Within two minutes, no more, no less, introductory conversation was deemed sufficient and the processional to lunch began. There was always a maximum of only ten for lunch and, never planned, odd numbers were often the case as chairs were added or taken away quickly when the "final" number could be determined. They were limited so that Bernard could "lead," or control the conversation, the latter more usually the case. In good weather, most of the year, lunch was in the garden under the oak allee or, on a rare warm, sunny winter's day, in the *lemonaia,* overlooking the topiary garden

Coffee and liqueurs were served after lunch, usually at two-thirty, in any number of garden spaces such as the ilex grove in summer and warm weather- "The ilex grove at the end of the formal garden was still in its youth and the view over the Arno valley was not yet hidden nor spoilt by ugly buildings;"[522] in the *lemonaia* in the cool of spring and fall where guests were treated, without wind, to the open view of the panorama and the topiary garden below; or in the lower terrace of the *lemonaia* garden in the winter. After coffee, no later than 2:45, "everyone retired," and visitors were expected to take their leave and speedily depart. Guests were offered a siesta in their rooms where the staff had already prepared their beds, turning down the covers. Bernard retired to his chambers for his "nap." It was during this rest period that Mary, whenever possible, would teach some young-person art, Greek and a myriad of other subjects, often in the secluded parts of the garden. The bamboo area behind the western grotto's walls was a favorite spot.

Four p.m. there was the return to work. The staff ran through the *cameras* remaking all beds, even those unslept-in. Bernard entered his private study and guests were shown the garden and the library. Five-thirty was tea time and everyone gathered on the upper terraces for a spot, where conversation usually focused on the discoveries of the day. A new crop of invited guest were often a part of tea, ones that the Berensons did not wish to entertain for the longer mealtimes. From six to nine, Bernard returned to the library or study, and I Tatti was quiet again. Occasionally, if the atmosphere was conducive, Bernard would offer to continue discussions from tea with a particular guest in his study for a short time before beginning the evening's work session which was devoted to his work with his librarian/personal secretary.

At eight-thirty, the evening visitors began to arrive and aperitifs were offered with resident guests joining in. The drink was always *martini bianci* (the vermouth, not the mixed drink). Knowledgeable guests brought their own favorites. At nine precisely, BB again "magically" entered to greet the new seating and make introductions. Within minutes, the processional to the dining room commenced and Bernard would lead off with the evening's subject of conversation. BB would talk through the entire meal - hors d'oeuvre, entree, salad and cheese, fruit and coffee. "In general, Mr. Berenson talked without interruption except for shouts of laughter and applause."[523] Dinner in the fall, winter and spring was always indoors, while on warm summer nights, it was held in the long cypress allee where strings of lights, hung from tree to tree, lit the affair. I Tatti cuisine was not "ITness". Instead, it was "club fare," undistinguished and unpretentious. Berenson did not eat the daily menu but rather had the same foods specially prepared for him, every meal, every day, and every year of his life. "He ate a thimbleful of rice, two drops of wine and a sliver of steamed fish."[524]

Ten-thirty was cordials and coffee accompanying a stroll through the garden by moonlight. There were occasions where BB would dismiss everyone early and with Mary in arm, enjoy the empty moonlit garden alone together.[525] At eleven o'clock exactly, all monks and acolytes became pumpkins once again. Everyone was expected to be gone, or in their bedrooms, and the villa was shrouded in total quiet, another day in the Altamura paradise completed.

> "Sir John Pope-Hennessy found the monastic life inside Altamura, despite the presence of great works of art, a little daunting...The most unnerving feature of the house in those days was the quietness. It was a temple where the prevailing silence was never, save at mealtimes, broken by the human voice."[526]
>
> Christopher Hibbert

The daily regimen that the Berensons evolved was exactly like that of the beaux-arts academies of various nations housed in Rome. The French Academy, in Villa Medici, the British School, near the Borghese Gardens and the American Academy in Rome, on the Gianicolo, had exactly the same time table and meal procedures. Bernard Berenson was personal friends with the American Academy's then director, Chester Aldrich. I Tatti was the only such academy ever created as a private institution.

Habitués of I Tatti changed dramatically from period to period, due to a number of external factors. First and foremost was the beginning of the Great War in 1914, almost on the heels of the completion of construction.[527] Bernard's stature in the art world had risen and in the process he had alienated many of his former intellectual friends. Many Anglo-American Florentines, such as Charles Strong, were disenfranchised by BB's superior intellect or, as was the case with Vernon Lee, his attack on her credentials (to comment on art) as well as her character, accusing her of plagiarism. Bernard became paranoid about any of the new over-night art dealers, such as the architect Horne, fearing that they wanted to associate with him in order to gain some advantage by his superior knowledge.[528] After the end of the war, there were very few of the original Florentine intellectual circle that were welcome at meal times at I Tatti. Cecil Scott, having married Lady Sybil Cutting, was definitely *persona non grata* for breaking Mary's heart. Princess Ghyka was now a hermit and Miss Blood, seriously ill. Janet Ross was old and crotchety; her constant cursing did not make for exciting conversation. Bernard considered Arthur Acton a "bounder" and saw little of Cecil Pinsent and the Houghtons.

The friends of Altamura post World War I were internationals who frequently visited the villa. Members of the Bloomsbury Group, the London-based circle of artists and writers who Berenson derogatorily called "the Gloomsbury Set-up," were constantly passing through on any excuse. Often called by their critics, "snobs, egotists, neurotic bisexuals" and a "junta of aesthetes," they were Berenson's intellectual meat course.

Duncan Grant, with his lover Maynard Keynes, Clive Bell, Lytton Strachey, all visited many times.[529] Duncan Grant was the most frequent visitor of the group. His work between 1910 and 1925 was termed Cezanne-like and his stays occurred during the early part of this period corresponded with visits of Miss Blood, an I Tatti regular, who was doing her Cezanne fakes. Edith Wharton visited yearly and the Berensons likewise visited her villa in Hyeres, France.

> "[I Tatti] was no mere parterre of heaven; it is the very *'cielo della quieta'* that Dante found above the seventh heaven. I've found the Great Good Place."[530]
>
> Edith Wharton

Since the Berensons' life was so public, we get special glimpses of how the gardens were used. Eugenie Sellers, a French writer wrote:

> "Madam Berenson, swathed in furs was stretched out on her chaise lounge, etc. Groups of young people broke away to discuss Italian politics. A young nobleman... violently discussed the theories of Karl Marx with another person who had just concluded a romantic union, etc. etc, here and there one saw people amusing themselves leafing through albums of photographs selected by the celebrated connoisseur Mr. Berenson - and a group of adorable young girls leaned over the balcony admiring the valley of the Arno and Florence stretched out at their feet, etc., etc., From time to time all conversation stopped while musicians of rare talent evoked the melodies of Tristan on the grand piano, etc, etc."[531]

At one springtime lunch gathering in the garden, one of the young aesthetes, a woman guest, disrobed and posed nude standing on the stone balustrade posing as various Greek statues. The guests, including the English poet Alfred Austin, and the Berensons "were in raptures over her beauty," and "her most delicious simplicity,"[532] One hot summer day in 1919, Hugh Trevor-Roper was chatting with the Bloomsbury artist Duncan Grant, who was doing a painting in the central space of the topiary garden with its pools, when Trevy decided to cool himself off by taking a plunge - nude. After, he aired himself to dry by jumping up and down and twirling around as fast as possible, to shake off the water. "A visiting guest, Fernande Salvemini was coming up from the lower garden gate for lunch and entered the garden as Trevy was doing his thing. Shrieks and howls of laughter were exchanged all lunch long."[533] Fernande, the wife of Gaetano

hidden lives / secret gardens

Salvemini, was shocked and spread the tales of wild debauched happenings – "nudes were everywhere in I Tatti's gardens."[534]

One of the most memorable events at I Tatti was Gertrude Stein's visit in 1908. She was there with her gay brother and art dealer, Leo Stein. Leo has acknowledged profiting from his BB connection. Through his sister's Paris circle of artist friends, Leo became the primary dealer in works by Picasso and many other famous Cubists of the day. At least one painting, perhaps others, was sold to the Gardner collection through Berenson. Gertrude, the famous literary lesbian, on this occasion without her constant mate, Alice B. Toklas, went for a swim in the small lake in the Torrente Mensole, at the "Ladies Only" time "clothed in nothing but her fat." Mary Berenson commented she didn't know such enormities existed."[535]

"Who can enjoy what I enjoy more than I enjoy."[536]

Bernard Berenson

For many guests, I Tatti was a daunting experience. The formality, the possibility of a confrontation or a snub by Bernard, or the heightened expectation of the moment could evoke anguish in the most humble traveler. In a letter, Kenyon Cox, the wife of the famous American painter who was staying in Fiesole in 1898, commented on being: "too afraid, yet, to go visit the Berensons."[537] Henry Hope Reed, who wrote the "Forward" to Geoffrey Scott's book, *Humanism in Architecture*, froths that his "audience" with Berenson was a "Horror...pompous...a pain in the neck - the worshiping. [As if] I was taken to a high priest."[538]

"Norah Lindsay and Lawrence Johnson, Vita Sackville-West, Harold Peto, Thomas Mawson, Edwin Lutyens and countless others made the Florentine pilgrimage and brought home visions of enclosed garden rooms, pergola-covered walks, long avenues ending in distant views, formal parterres of clipped box and landmark plantings of ilex and cypress."[539]

Ethne Clarke

Bernard Berenson was proud of his accomplishments at his Villa I Tatti, especially the gardens. He spoke of the difficulty finding the right garden "fit," utilizing a metaphor more aptly applied to having a suit made-to-order.

"I require many fittings from my tailor. Not that I as much as think of looking elegant or wishing to be smart or dressy in my clothes. I want to look and feel myself. So it was, so it is, with my house [and its gardens]. Although I had so gifted an architect as Cecil Pinsent, who often understood my wants better than I did. It half killed me to get it into shape and it was not, when I gave up the struggle. With the years I got used to it, stopped seeing blemishes or defects, stopped bothering about fading, damage, moths, decay, and now after many years, I love it as much as one can love any object or complex of objects not human."[540]
Bernard Berenson

Berenson in his garden

On other occasions, he waxed poetic at some aspects of the garden's beauty. At night, it was particularly special. He stated on one occasion that he and Mary were: "plato-nized in the moonlight with the odors of violets and roses to sooth us, for hours and hours."[541]

"I have a garden too, Unless it pours with rain, I run through it at least once a day, to taste the air, to listen to the sound of birds and streams, to admire the flowers and trees....Each day as I look, I wonder where my eyes were yesterday. Why did I not perceive the beauty of the lichen-trimmed tree-trunk as gorgeous as an Aztec or Maya mosaic; of that moss of a soft emerald that beds your eyes as reposefully as the greens in a Giorgione [painting]"

"So as I walk in the garden, I look at the flowers and shrubs and trees and discover in them an exquisiteness of contour, a vitality of edge or a vigor of spring as well as an infinite variety of color that no artifact I have seen in the last sixty years can rival. And beyond the garden, as I walk on the olive-crowned, pine-plumed, cypress-guarded hills, I enjoy the effects of clouds under the high and spacious dome of sky, the hazes between me and the horizon."

"I had planted a garden with nooks where I was going to sit and take pleasure in my favorite *Dichter*. By the time it had grown and could be enjoyed, hurry seized me; and for arbors and fountain curbs where I

hidden lives / secret gardens

was to sit and listen to the nightingales, blackbirds, thrushes and larks, and draw in the fragrance of roses, lotuses and lime blossoms, I never found the leisure. I could only glance and pass on.

"For every morning, every afternoon as I go out of doors, I discover more than enough newness to suffice for the day."[542]

Bernard Berenson

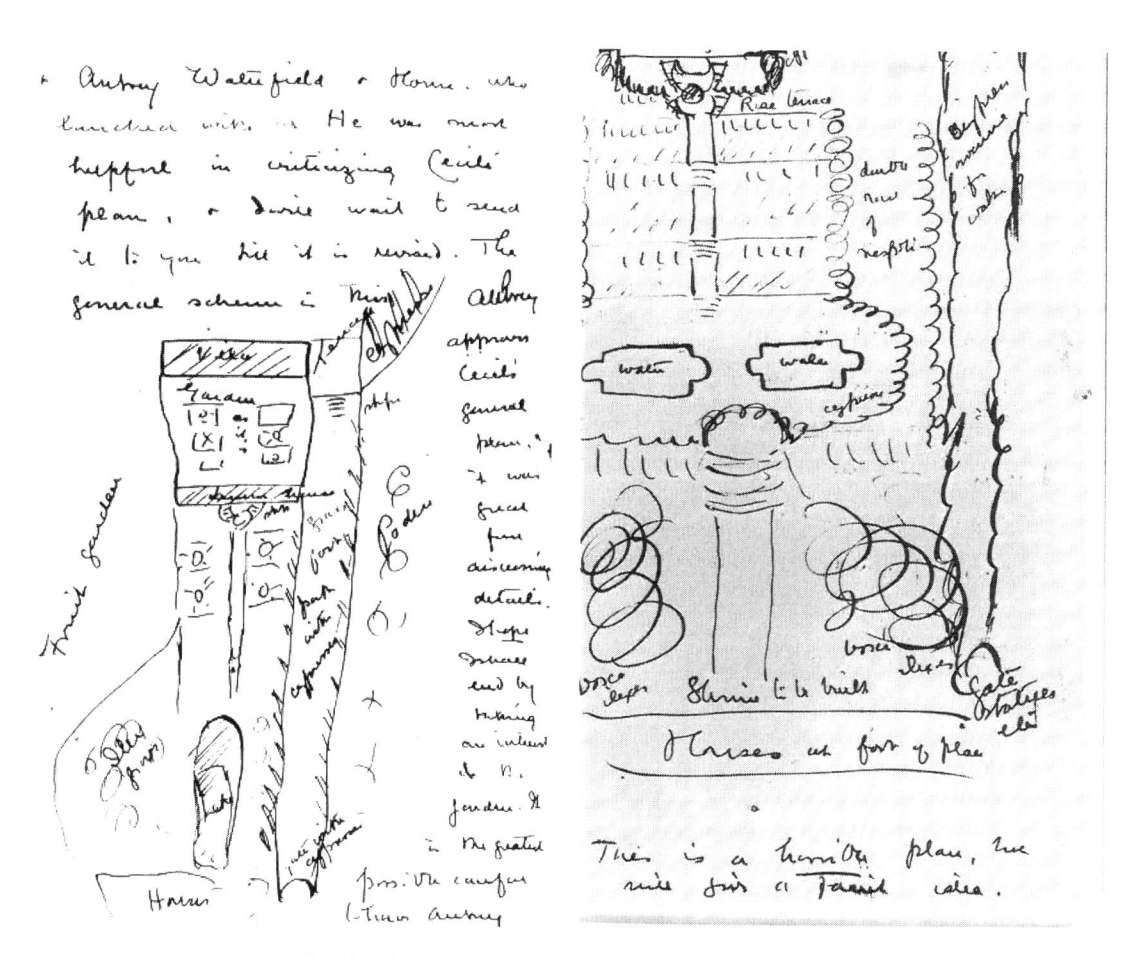

Sketches by Mary Berenson in letters to Cecil Pinsent

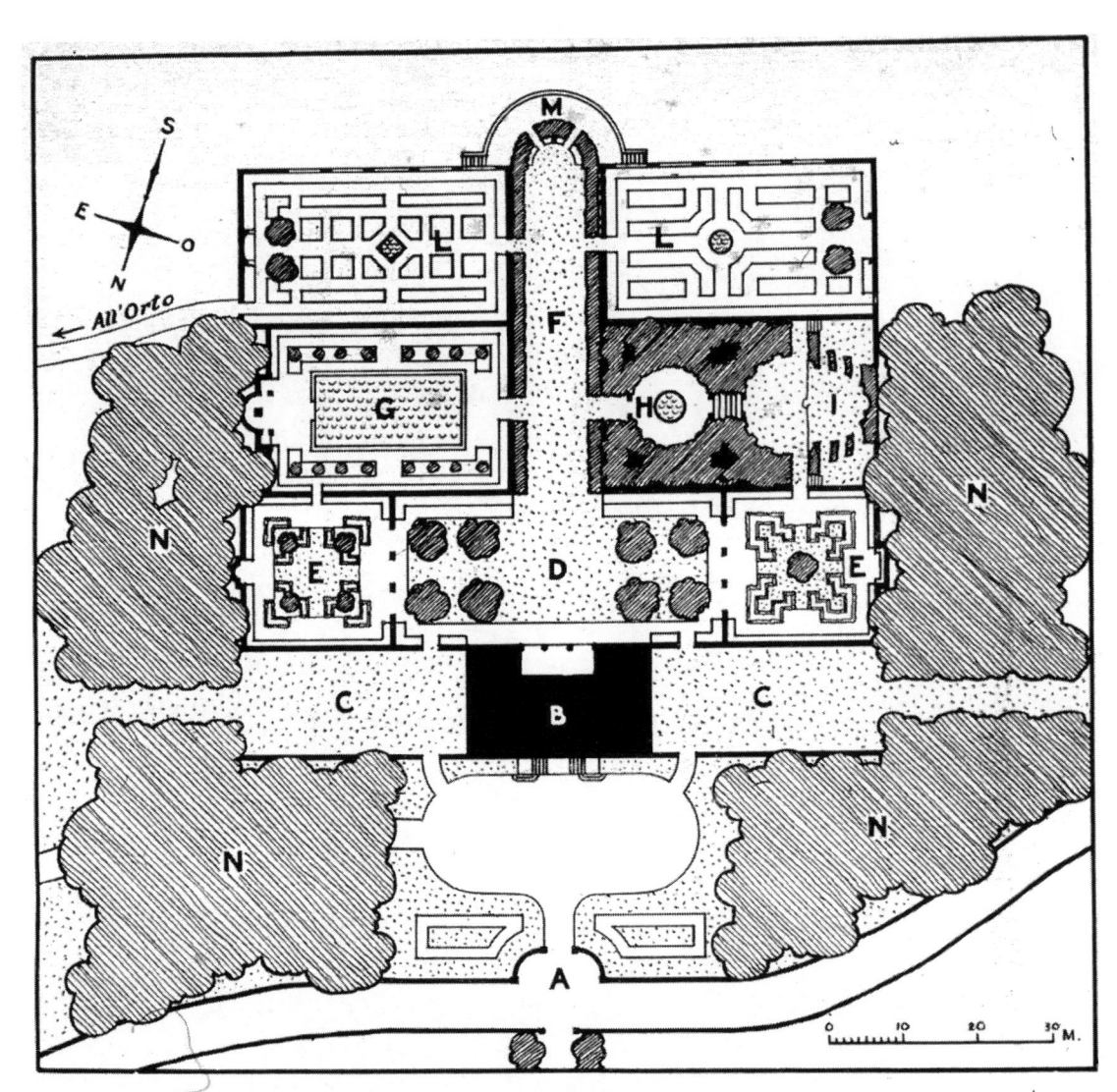

Fig. 2. — Giardino per una villa di media grandezza.

A. — Ingresso.
B. — Villa.
C. — Prati di erba.
D. — Parterre con magnolie.
E. — Parterre con bossolo e fiori.
F. — Viale fiancheggiato da pareti di cipressi potati.
G. — Laghetto.
H. — Vaschetta.
I. — Scenario verde.
L. — Giardini da fiori.
M. — Terrazza.
N. — Boschi di leccio.

An early drawing for the terraces at I Tatti by Cecil Pinsent

Continuo

THE SECOND RENAISSANCE CIRCLE[543] - Princess Giovanna Ghyka, Martino and Pietro Porcinai, Arthur Mario Acton, Diego Suarez, Geoffrey Scott and Cecil Pinsent - never intended to be landscape architects, yet their design innovations and skills honed at their Villas - Gamberaia, La Pietra and I Tatti - garnered them this professional title. Ghyka was a naif to gardens, although she possessed artistic talents and general training in the arts. Only Martino Porcinai received traditional horticultural training, but he was unskilled in formal design. On the other hand, Acton, Suarez, Scott and Pinsent had some architectural educations, albeit lacking in any landscape design or horticulture training. Only Pinsent and Suarez were fully trained and apprenticed in the profession of architecture. Acton studied historic landscapes and amassed a small but important engraving collection of historic villas supplemented by a large collection of photographs taken on his villa tours. Yet, together the Second Renaissance Circle acquired these collective skills on the job, in the field, or on-site. It was as if they each contributed individual skills to the common good. Through the many meetings and discussions that took place in each other's gardens, they were able to explore solutions to common problems of design, and in doing so, create a new language in landscape architecture.

Unlike the others, Princess Ghyka had not traveled extensively in order to acquire first hand garden experience. In fact, it is doubtful that she visited other gardens in the Florence area, as she was self-consumed. With the exceptions of Janet Ross's and Vernon Lee's gardens, we know of no other gardens visited by her. Acton on the other hand, knew all the major French gardens of Le Notre and of Henry Duchene's efforts in their restoration. He gathered historic prints and paintings that featured isometric views of villa designs. He trained Diego Suarez in Duchene's theories and together they traveled widely around Florence and the Veneto region, stripping the gardens bare of all sculpture as they went. Surely, though, even as they stripped the gardens, they observed their design and landscape techniques. Martino Porcinai was trained solely in one German garden, Sans Souci in Potsdam, gaining experience there in horticultural propagation. He trained his son, Pietro, in both horticulture and design and allowed him direct access to the second renaissance designers. Pinsent was totally unfamiliar with Italian gardens before he began his work at I Tatti. In circular exposure, he gathered his garden references by initially studying the Gamberaia and then the Acton /Suarez composition at La Pietra. Geoffrey Scott had only the briefest architectural education, but he had the privilege to be tutored in art composition and art history by the master, Bernard Berenson. Scott knew nothing of gardens and is known to have studied only one garden, La Pietra, before participating in the design of I Tatti. The discussions and exchanges of these seven, often accompanied in the early years by Bernard Berenson, were rich, on-site explorations of a new garden design and its development. Up to that time, no individual or collaborative committee had developed a whole new set of compositional elements, design vocabulary, and philosophic outlook on Italian villa garden design. No doubt, the changing programmatic basis for the villa was an impetus, but the seven of Florence were the progenitors.

The gardens of the Gamberaia, La Pietra and I Tatti show amazing correlation of design elements, compositional principles and landscape palette. It is impossible to miss their common root. This common set of expressed design philosophies is the basis for identifying them as forming a common school of thought, and since they are based on the precepts of the earlier humanistic Renaissance, or the classical Tuscan garden - but with distinctly Moderne changes made - they, therefore, become renaissance-revival gardens or gardens of the second renaissance.

Having visited and experienced through their histories and descriptive tours these three "new" gardens, several overall design ideas become evident and begin to coalesce as the common philosophy of the second renaissance Florentine garden:

First, unity is the key element of the whole composition. Throughout its numerous spaces and allees, the sameness of materials and their common usage produces a consistency throughout the entire design. There are no abrupt contrasts here between rooms or axes, such as in the relic Renaissance-of-old space that previously existed at the Gamberaia in, say, the grotto room with its hard *rocaille*, or the totally exposed *lemonaia*, or the walled and shaded *bosci*. With the exception of these and the Villa Acton's historically preserved *pomario*, all second renaissance spaces are musically harmonious throughout. They are based on simple plant material compositions, as exhibited in the Gamberaia's water parterre garden, and the totally new gardens of La Pietra and I Tatti.

> "The [Tuscany] garden changed from a secret garden rich in flowers to an architectonic garden defined by evergreens."[544]

The second design idea is the development of abstract classicism. One notices that all second renaissance gardens appear to be classical in form and design detail, but a more careful inspection reveals that these landscapes lack the complexity and flourishes of past classical gardens. It is as if the forms and elements of a classical space were stripped of any complexity and reduced to their essential expression. It is a form of classical minimalism. They are abstracted versions of their former models.

The *exedra* at the Gamberaia is the simplest clipped-hedge form possible. It contains none of the top topiary decorations of its classical prototypes, and being of the same height and plant material as the long, western-enclosing hedge, it is an abstraction of an enclosing Renaissance form that could not be reduced further. Other spaces of the Villa Acton - the *viale*, the topiary garden, the *teatrino*, and the *Vista del'Arco,* and of the Villa I Tatti - the Cypress Allee, the Green Garden and the French Bosco garden, show similar stripped-down or abstracted classical forms. It is also interesting to note the experimentations in Arthur Acton's gardens, where the spaces were developed in their simplest forms and later, topiary elements were incrementally added or modified to more complex or decorative forms. Each space was studied and evaluated so as not to exceed the unified composition. Even in the most decorative of spaces at Villa Acton, the *Prima* and *Seconda Vasca,* considerable restraint and simplicity are shown as compared to its classical model.

With abstract classicism comes the third principle, metaphysical design.

> "The Villa Gamberaia, [when viewed from the Villas's upstairs loggia], seems like an elaborate table top elevated above the country side. It could be the deck of an aircraft carrier"[545]
>
> John Stubbs, Architectural Historian

The other-worldly aspect of the Moderne design palette was exactly the removal and isolation of place that the owners, and designers of the villas, sought. They had taken the vocabulary of the classical orders and remade them into something new, and in this way had transcended the mere physical and historical nature of the employed elements. They sought the spiritual connection of an art object with the participant, to transcend the physical and thereby to attain the spiritual. The metaphysical garden had been invented.

Altamura, with its artistic spirituality, was not an accident, but a conscious goal to strive for. There reality metamorphosed into symbolic logic, which in turn morphs into metaphysics. The true nature of the objects are no longer the material but the immaterial - trees are no longer recognizable as trees but as walls, arches, topiary forms, all without scale, which would enable them to relate to man. The spaces became more universal to all design, and they lost their connection of real gardening, to real landscape design or to any real site. Thus the more the second renaissance designers succeeded in the Tuscanization of the garden, the more they failed in making them Tuscan specific.[546] When abstraction or modernity dominates the design, reality is lost and the design becomes dream-like. More than one garden critic has commented on the surreal-like aspects to all three of these gardens. For many visitors, the Moderne Florentine gardens have become other-worldly, transposed environments, conjured illusions.

The fourth principle defining the second renaissance garden is the predominance of enclosed spaces in their compositions. Each of the new spaces in the three villas I self- contained and connected by landscape doorways. They are organized in series of green rooms structured as in-line (sometimes referred to as "shot-gun" or "railroad") allees. The realm of the exterior is reversed; the gardens rooms become interior spaces, unlike Renaissance or Baroque gardens where the long view is prized and spaces are opened fully to the view. At Villa d'Este, for example, the view of the axis generated from the house, like that from the water organ's cross axis, is un-enclosed, open to the countryside beyond and its vast panorama. Also, in the Renaissance garden there is a sense of the large unified space with sub-rooms, sub-spaces or sub-areas within. Anywhere from within the original Renaissance design of Villa d'Este, one was able to take in the whole space, both its multi-axes and its related sub-parts before descending into the garden's many sub-sections. There are no overviews of the whole composition at La Pietra and I Tatti. The Gamberaia's unique suspended view from the flying arches was utilized only by its creator, a private perch as it were, to pose, adore, and be adored. Even the central axes of the three villas deny the long view. Further, the terraces of each of the three villas are fully enclosed spaces, accessible only through framed doors, grade changes, and steps, breaking the spatial flow that might otherwise have been achieved.

When one creates defined rooms, the fifth precept then occurs: The enclosed spaces become receptacles for objects and "things." There is a tendency to fill these rooms with material goods, and less with people, thereby de-emphasizing the humanistic. The spaces become wonderful museums for Acton's and Suarez's sculpture collections, Ghyka's water "mirrors," Pinsent's architectural gateways or Porcinai's or Acton's topiary. Where in the water parterre garden of the Gamberaia can one assemble a group of fifty or more? One cannot. Instead, a wrap-around terrace or the great bowling green must be utilized, and both are the design vocabulary of a different era.

hidden lives / secret gardens

The way these rooms are filled can have strong psychological connotations, and as we have seen, can be identified as "queer" or same-sex space. Many of these rooms are closeted, and designed for narcissistic and fetish activities. "Fetish merchandising" as Karl Marx termed the consumption in particular extremes, was borne out by the sculpture at La Pietra, the fetish of mirroring water at Gamberaia and the general excesses (topiary, rocaille etc.) in all three of these gardens. In all three gardens, the sharp contrasts of light and shade that created mystery and transmitted deep sexual feelings that were just then being studied by psychiatrists at the turn of the century, are significant and startling design motifs.

The sixth precept of the second renaissance designs is the adoption of *the rationale* design vocabulary and philosophy of the Beaux-Arts design education.[547] Entailing the use of classical styles from the Greco-Roman eras, the architectural orders of each period were utilized to compose new works that closely resembled, if not directly copied, the original. Accompanying any one period or style were sets of artistic compositional tools or aids that were used to order and embellish the work. With clear rules on structure and design thought, there was a clear moving away from arbitrary design. The second renaissance designers did not embrace the spectrum of the Beaux-Arts eclecticism, rather, if they borrowed from any historic period, they limited it to a melange of the best of Italian Renaissance or Baroque villa design. Cecil Pinsant and Geoffrey Scott were interested only in an idealized prototype of a classical garden, not in any actual garden. They used the analytical design tools of the Beaux-Arts, focusing on the methodology behind the historic style. As no accepted name for this concept is commonly used, the author has called this design paradigm the *"rationale* design methodology."[548]

> "[Scott stated] ..... by the direct agency of mass and space, line and coherence upon physical consciousness, architecture communicates its value as art.' For the future, Scott's book signals a turning in the classical tradition toward a stripped classicism unshackled by the beaux-arts tradition - toward an architecture of classicizing innovation." [549]
> Michael Greenhalgh

These designers discussed their gardens using the analytical elements of the Beaux-Arts: point, line, plane, solid, void, light, shadow, scale, and then secondarily, elements of tone, shade, color, texture, pattern. This analytical methodology is evident in Arthur Acton's 1908 design layout of his gardens and surely was shown and discussed by Suarez and other second renaissance designers.

R. Terry Schnadelbach

The seventh precept is color. As Harold Acton aptly stated about the *teatrino*, and applicable to the compositions of all three villa gardens: "The whole garden is essentially green." Mary Berenson wrote of Cecil's palette: "a desire for grass and ilexes, cypresses and box."[550] It is green architecture. Sculptures are the only other element of color and they contribute white or a neutral color that act as spatial accents. The floor is green grass, the walks are edged in green clipped hedges and the space is enclosed by green walls and canopy. As limited though it may seem, there is a surprising degree of variety in this green palette. Acton used a wide range of topiary materials from yellow green to dusty blue green, plus the normal array of close-range green, greens - from bright glossy to dark matte green.

This aspect of limited color is actually contrary to the designer's stated desire to "Tuscanize the gardens. Rich hued color was inherent in Tuscan materials, especially the numerous possibilities of *terra batutta* - from white marl, sand, terracotta, yellow ochre, umbra and burnt sienna. Blocked out are the color-rich, far views of the olive colored groves with their yellow ochre fields or burnt umber soil. Nor are there terra cotta pots, stucco walls of sienna red or any other earthy Tuscan colors found typically in original Tuscan gardens. The total enclosed green spaces ruled out bringing these Tuscan-colored elements into the composition

The eighth precept is one unique to the turn of the century with its women's suffrage and liberation in the forefront; it is the pan-feminization of landscape architecture. Although marginalized in the fields of architecture and sculpture, women were beginning to be fully accepted as equals into the professions of painting and landscape architecture. Gardening and landscape architecture, even more so than painting, had many trained professional women within their ranks. With the repeal of restrictive laws against women owning property, women developed legitimate concerns and responses to the design of their exterior spaces. In the Florentine expatriate community, we see an open society of female and male gardeners working and communicating about design issues. More importantly, we see a group of designers intent on advancing the art, meeting and discussing art and landscape theories without any gender identification and more strikingly, without any sexual prejudice. The second renaissance circle represents, perhaps for the first time, such a liberal and equitable professional group.

These eight design percepts are found exclusively in the Princess Ghyka new water parterre garden at the Villa Gamberaia and in Villas Acton and I Tatti. They become the accepted design philosophy and palette for the second renaissance gardens of Florence. Giovanna Ghyka, Arthur Acton, and Bernard Berenson - with their partners, landscape architects, *capo giardineri* and a coterie of friends, some in-residence in the Florentine environment and some habitual visitors - picked up the new mantra and lifestyle.

The art of Renaissance Florence was termed humanistic art. Its values were based on the human experience and the individual's expressions in art. What held such individual artistic expressions together were a set of formalistic rules on composition. Many such formalistic rules, such as those on perspective, proportional formulas of the golden mean or rhythmic modular repetitions from music, were highly technical in nature. In the rebirth of the Renaissance, as art pieces and their artists were re-discovered, these original rules, *"rationales,"* were discussed and codified in books. The overnight art collector was faced with a need for an instant education in art in order to recognize and evaluate works of art competitively. Bernard Berenson was foremost in this field, cataloguing paintings of the Renaissance and codifying the aesthetics. He believed art to be mentally elevating, mystical and hallucinogenic and he termed art in one's life to be "The Art-of-Life."

Geoffrey Scott developed the same "rationales" for architecture. His book, *The Architecture of Humanism*, is the definitive work on the subject to this day. George Sitwell, Edith Wharton and Janet Ross, all members of the Berenson and Villa I Tatti circle, had written the early theses on the Renaissance art of garden-making or landscape architecture. They awoke the passions of this earlier art form and aided the rebellion from the passé English garden style. Geoffrey Scott began to write at the same time as the three gardens were under development, his thesis on Renaissance architecture heralding its strengths and advocating a return to its aesthetic methodologies and principles. Writing in close scrutiny with Mary Berenson and while consulting Bernard, Scott explored the historic development's of architecture, discussing each period of architectural development in terms of "fallacies" or fallacious logic - all periods that is, except the Renaissance, which Scott illustrated to be the only period / style to be true and of "humanist" value. Scott stated: "The art of Renaissance Florence was termed humanistic art. Its values were based on the human experience and the individual's expressions in art."[551] For Scott, the Renaissance was a broad period that incorporated the eras that most historians separate into the Renaissance, Baroque and Mannerist styles. For Scott these were all one and the same and therefore, in the new second renaissance's humanist revival philosophy, were freely drawn from in any combination.

Maria Pasolini Ponti, a landscape historian residing in Rome, met Geoffrey Scott who, after his book was finished, worked in Rome's British Embassy. She found in Scott and in his book a sympathetic *amiato* and began a book that would set, in landscape architectural terms, the very same humanist theories. In 1915 she published *Il Gardino Italino*. It defined the design philosophy behind the forms and aesthetics of the Italian Renaissance garden. Through Scott, she was able to spend a considerable time at the Villa Gamberaia and seemed to formulate the essence of Renaissance design from its design:

"The basis of abstract design, running through history like a silver thread, are independent of race and age. Their unchanging expression is through pattern... a sturdy foundation from which afterwards to build. Pattern is the architectural prototype of formality of life and in the same way is modified by the circumstances of the moment, principally those governing the relationship of formality to informality. In any design where nature is admitted, such as the garden, this relationship is the first consideration."

"The most general conscious principle suggested that the lines of the garden should grow less defined as they left the house, like water ripples spreading from the center to die gradually in their surroundings - lines always formal but less and less emphasized."

"The psychological purpose of the garden was to give pure contentment to its owner. As two individual temperaments are never the same, every garden varied according to the light in which this purpose was regarded. The Villa Gamberaia set out deliberately to please and refresh ...and is great for being so human...... In the grander gardens (Villa Acton and I Tatti), which were primarily for entertainment, this personal expression of feeling was lost in a more general expression."

"All important cohesion was (uniquely) accomplished in the asymmetrical plan of the Villa Gamberaia. Here was an elongated irregular site in which had to be fitted nearly a dozen differing elements. A broad band, the "bowling alley," was stretched across from one extreme end to the other, and in cross axis bound to the house by an equally broad band of grass (the wrap around terrace). To such a formal combination only could be attached all the variety of features which makes the place unique"

"So dazzling is the light in Italy that the bright colors of flowers are greatly missed. Glare calls for cool tones and response was found in delicate contrasts of green and grey, used simply or with a variety of shade. At Gamberaia the aim of elaborate variety was extended into the color scheme which begins in the ivory and brown tones of the house, changes to all the shades of green, from deep cypress through varieties of box, yew, ilex, and privet to light green of lemon trees and grass."

hidden lives / secret gardens

"The most practical need for enjoyment of the garden was shade, and this was the reason for elaborating the treatment of trees and hedges. An avenue of cypresses, trees in themselves that reciprocate the idea of formality, makes not only a shaded approach to the house, but a very magnificent one as well. The *bosci* of the Villa Gamberaia are weird, ghostly things in themselves, but they are carefully placed. "

"Water was essential to the garden to suggest coolness both by sight and sound. Reflecting pools are designed solely for peace and rest, in surroundings beautiful enough to be mirrored. "

"Parterre, a carpet of low clipped box lacking the varied interest of colored flowers, was designed in pattern of form, and generally placed so as to be looked upon from above."

"Effect in three dimension naturally governs the plan of every garden, but often advantage was deliberately taken of perspective to increase the dramatic qualities of a view."

"The instinct of formality considered the garden so much a part of the house, that in its simplest phase it was regarded as nothing more or less than an extra room, a salon flooded with unlimited light and air. But it had a difference. It belonged as much to the countryside as to the house, the mutual ground on which the two met and absorbed each other's views."

"The most natural bond is scale. ...In Tuscany, the rich valley of the Arno, smaller and more personal, is reflected in the greater intimacy of the Florentine gardens."

"In its turn, a difficult climate, precluding flowers and unprotected grass, and demanding unlimited cool suggestion, had reasoned with and modified, finally allowing the use of three elements only, evergreens, stonework, and water. These are the essence of Italian gardens."[552]
Maria Ponti, Translated by Edward G. Lawson

Ponti's book simplified the Renaissance garden language of old to the following: Architectural rooms, transitions from the house to countryside, abstraction, asymmetry, and the use of only three elements - evergreens, stonework, and water. Edward G. Lawson, an American landscape architect stranded in Italy during World War I, was drawn to Ponti's work. A conscientious objector then living with an Italian family, he volunteered for humanitarian work with the Red Cross in Rome. It was through this work that Lawson met many in the diplomatic community in Rome, and specifically both Scott and Ponti. During the four years of World War I, Lawson translated Ponti's book, *Il Giardino Italino,* into English. After the war, Lawson made numerous visits to the Gamberaia and produced the only accurate and correctly measured drawing of its gardens. He also identified all plantings, producing the only complete planting plan of any Italian villa. Additionally, he profiled all the architectural and landscape architectural built-elements, producing a reference book of details for other landscape architects. On his return to America, he provided to the Cornell and Harvard University libraries, the two leading professional programs in landscape architecture, Ponti's thesis in English and the measured plans of Villa Gamberaia, the body of his work. In addition, he furnished copies of these reference documents to many of the leading American landscape architectural firms, among them, Ferruccio Vitale, and Fletcher Steele, and also to architectural firms as well - McKim Mead, and White, for example. In Florence, his work reinforced the continued development of the second renaissance landscape architecture designed by Cecil Pinsent, Diego Suarez, and Pietro Porcinai.

Later Rome Prize Fellows included landscape architects Ralph Griswold, Michael Rapuano, Norman T. Newton and Richard Webel, all of whom made the pilgrimage to Villa Gamberaia and brought back to America its new design expression. Lawson's drawings were published in American professional journals, influencing still others. Lawson joined the design faculty at Cornell University's professional program influencing still more landscape architects. The influence of Princess Ghyka's gardens at Gamberaia could be felt on American and Italian landscape designers as early as 1920, when Ferruccio Vitale, Fletcher Steele and others began to develop similar, but differing, expressions of abstract classicism and Modernism. The influence of the second renaissance design philosophy, with its pronounced simplification, abstraction and asymmetry, provided a significant antecedent to America's Modernist landscape design movement.

While the owners were dealing in fake art, they were not, on the other hand, dealing in fake gardens. They may have had copied, as was the case, Cézannes, Renaissance masters and sculptors, but their gardens were original works. The premise of guilt by association that some critics would argue - that the gardens of the three villas discussed in this book were eclectic copies, Renaissance forgeries or derivatives - is plainly untrue. While Acton, Berenson, and Miss Blood were all engaged in the reproductions of art treasures, none ever proffered that their gardens were actual copies of anything. Even though Sir Kenneth Clark states in his memoirs that Cecil Pinsent "constructed an imitation Baroque garden,"[553] the truth remains that Pinsent and the other revival humanists were merely conceptualizing from the past in order to fashion their own present.

In the new Gamberaia, La Pietra and I Tatti gardens, one cannot find, as several scholars have tried to do, any direct design references from villas of the classical periods. Does the checkered arrangement of the parterre garden at I Tatti draw its inspiration from the Villa Medici at Castello? Or was Pinsent only utilizing standard humanist (*rationale*) principles of composition to guide his fresh and new parterre designs? Pinsent, in the only article written by any of the second renaissance designers, refers to the Gamberaia for his new idealized Moderne villa garden designs; there are no references to any of the classical Italian gardens. The second renaissance designers did not reference their works to any specific historic garden or period and, therefore, their new works cannot be considered as fakes or forgeries common to architecture, paintings and sculpture of this era.

Like the wealthy merchants of the Renaissance, the new humanist took advantage of building sites that were underused, or unused, and that were adjacent to the established villa houses, as was the case at La Pietra or I Tatti. Unlike the Renaissance merchants, the modern libertines put greater emphasis into the innovation and construction of their gardens than into their houses. With the exception of I Tatti, these buildings were modestly remodeled or refurbished and had few major / grand salas or reception spaces. In all three villas, the houses were not re-designed with architectural components that would integrate their interior spaces with those of the exterior development.

The second renaissance designers did not copy famous gardens, as did most architects and other landscape architects of this time. Henry Duchene, for instance, copied in their entirety the famous Le Notre parterres, fountains, etc. For the main gardens at Vanderbuilt's Biltmore in America, Olmsted Brothers likewise employed the "humanized formal mode" in the "grand manner," openly citing Le Notre's work at *Vaux-le-Vicomte*.[554] F. L. Olmsted, Jr., admittedly copied the parterres of the *lemonaia* of Villa Medici at Castello, Florence for the Walled Garden at Biltmore. George E. Burnap, a Washington, D. C. landscape architect, publically announced his copy of the water cascade of Villa Farnese, Caparola in his 1920 proposed design for Meridian Hill Park, Washington, D.C.

Princess Ghyka, Arthur Acton and Martino Porcinai in their lifetimes were each devoted to only one garden. Martino Porcinai raised his son, Pietro, in the gardens of the Gamberaia, instilling in him the new second renaissance philosophy. As an adult, Pietro Porcinai embarked on a career in landscape architecture greatly influenced by the second renaissance landscape vocabulary. Diego Suarez and Cecil Pinsent each continued their professional careers designing and establishing second renaissance landscapes. These designers of the new second renaissance gardens developed their art after their initial involvement in Villas Gamberaia, La Pietra and I Tatti:

Pietro Porcainai   Porcinai the younger, began his career in the late 1920s with gardens for Villa La Striscia at Arezzo, Villa I Collazzi, and the garden Scarselli at Sesto Fiorentino, all in the late 1920s to 1930s. Mostly, they were small enclosed garden spaces featuring a water pool or basin. He began to develop abstract and asymmetrical compositions just before the Second World War in the gardens of Villa des Vergers, San Lorenzo (1938), the Villa Reale in Lecce, and the viale de Re in Arezzo's public garden. But after the devastation of that war, Pietro Porcinai's landscapes changed dramatically. Following a plan he made for the rehabilitation of the war-damaged Gambaraia, which furthered the concept of green architecture, he worked exclusively in a severely limited palette of one or two materials, used in contemporary abstract compositions.

During the Second World War, the German troops occupied the villa for more than a year. On retreating, they destroyed most of the Villa Gambaraia:[555] Fire completely destroyed the house and bombs and tanks damaged the water parterres. The bombs of the Allied forces added to the damage. Luckily, the main elements of the garden survived, among them the *exedra* and western perimeter hedges. In 1957, the new owner, Marcello Marchi,[556] rebuilt the water garden using the plan of Princess Ghyka as drawn by Lawson. But Marchi made subtle changes, and it is his garden that we see today. He changed the form of the planting of the parterres, and throughout the garden, replanted evergreen hedges to line the walks and border the pools. The pool edge was now solely defined by wide hedges. Gone were the oleanders and flowering trees of Pinsent, or the irises of Princess Ghyka. Gone were the posted roses that gave the garden its rhythm. Now the rhythm was achieved by geometric topiary forms emerging from the broad hedge line - domes, cones, and vertical cylinders. They mark the cross axes that form entries to each parterre area. Without the flowering trees, the scale and intimacy is achieved with large-scale topiary, such as the huge globe at the terminus of the western path. Mannerist in scale and all evergreen, they comprise the "green architecture" of the garden. Now the changing seasons matter little to the palette of the garden as it remains constant, with the lone exception being the changes seen in the pools' "sky mirrors." The water parterre garden, as it stands, is now the ultimate expression of second renaissance unity.

Dr. Marchi did not create the new version of Villa Gamberaia alone; he was guided by Pietro Porcinai.[557] In 1955, before the reconstruction of the gardens began, Porcinai drew up a planting plan that created the final idealization of the entire garden in its evergreen form. How much else he contributed, and if anyone else took part in advising Marchi, is still unknown. But, if the very tools of attribution were to be applied to the garden, they would certainly reveal the fingerprint of a Pietro Porcinai garden.

In the late seventies, Pietro Porcinai designed some of the most austere minimalist landscapes known, building upon the total mono-green theme. Porcinai's Villa il Roseto, Florence (1962-65) uses only one type of evergreen, as is seen at the post-war Gamberaia parterres. These are low, flat, clipped topiary forms of one height, planted in circular segments with only well-manicured lawn as infill to the voids. Other compositions utilize only grass in step and terraces, formed with thin white stone risers as seen at the Villa Pucci at Granaiolo outside Florence (1970). Porcinai's work is the ultimate expression and refinement of the second renaissance philosophy.

"He (Porcinai) is remembered as among the most qualified of our time as both *architecto de jardino* and *architecto de passaigo*."[558]
Milena Matteini

Diego Suarez   In 1914, with the outbreak of World War I, all work on La Pietra stopped. Fearing conscription, Diego Suarez left for America and accepted the invitation of James Deering to visit Miami and his estate, Vizcaya, then under construction.[559] Accompanied by Lady Sibyl Cutting, owner of the Villa Medici, Fiesole and her daughter Iris Origo, the little group made their visit in the heat of the Miami summer. Suarez did not return to Florence after the Vizcaya visit, but instead went to New York, taking an apartment with a young architectural historian, James Mather while working in an architectural firm. Henry Hope Reed tells an interesting story that, some time later while Suarez was in one of the typically New York places he frequented - lunch at the Ritz, then at Madison and 42nd, in its stylish Japanese room - Suarez ran into Chalfin and Deering. Deering described the progress on the fabulous house that Chalfin had advanced at Vizcaya, and asked Suarez to design the estate's accompanying gardens. "After showing me [the architect, Hoffman's] plans and drawings, he [Chalfin] asked me if I felt capable of designing an Italian classical garden to complement the house," Suarez recalled later in an undated memo.[560] Suarez sat down and immediately sketched out a master plan from his memory of the site.[561] Reed recalls that it was "a Tuscan design."[562]

Returning to Florence in 1918, when Italy's conscription had ended, Suarez took up with Acton again. In May 1921, Acton and his garden designer, Diego Suarez, were Deering's guests at Vizcaya, ostensibly a reciprocal gesture in repayment for Acton's original hospitality.[563] Deering had ulterior motives though as his estate was still under construction and he had begun following Suarez's scheme for the site. He now wanted to persuade Suarez to stay at Vizcaya and execute the full design.[564] Deering was successful; Diego Suarez remained in Miami in 1921 to design and execute the extensive estate grounds. His composition is perhaps the most bold and daring for any of America's country place estates. Situated on one of the most dramatic sites in the Miami area, Suarez designed the entry forecourt as a surprise reached through a gladed Florida hummuck. From a circular space defined only by sculptural figurines, a surprise axis to the house leads though the shaded downhill slopes, lined on both sides by defining evergreen hedges and by two raised Baroque water chains, copies of Acton's Boboli garden originals. These, though, are correctly installed and abound with the sound of water. The arrival court is a sun filled wall-enclosed area, beautifully proportioned to the house's facade. It is a more refined version of Villa Acton's forecourt.[565]

The side formal gardens show the genius of Suarez for false perspective and complex, non-orthogonal geometries. The gardens are more Baroque inspired than Renaissance, as axes radiate diagonally from the house and from each of the axes's outer ends. From the house, the central axis contains first a still pool parterre inspired certainly by the Gamberaia, ending in a raised, oak-covered mountain for dining, recalling that of I Tatti's. Two diagonal axes are elaborate embroidery parterres, perhaps learned from his experience with Duchene, ending in enclosed formal garden spaces at their far end, the axis adjacent to the shoreline containing a *boschetto*-like garden development of *vascas* in series carved into the native mangroves. These *vascas* are startlingly similar to Villa Acton's in concept, use and treatment.

The south *vasca* contains a massive central fountain from which radiate water channels that form an Arabic pattern incised in the g rass plaza, and radiate out to irrigate the trees that define the space. The massive fountain was procured in Rome, probably through the agis of Arthur Acton.[566]

It is the Suarez bay front terraces that are the most original and daring. Diego stripped away the native mangroves, opening the house's front to Biscayne Bay. He carved into the native coral stone rock ledge a formal half-ellipse and built an enormous mannerist Venetian *barca* with the excavated coral stone. The noted Philadelphia sculptor Sterling Calder, father of Alexander, was engaged to provide appropriate figure on the ship. The 100 feet long by 75 feet wide *barca* sitting out in the water like a Wagnerian ghost ship, was the site of elaborate sunrise parties. With the 1929 crash of the stock market, the parties ended and Deering filed for bankruptcy.

The whole Vizcaya landscape composition, like Suarez/Acton villa, was another example of queer architecture as defined by Aaron Betsky. With its closeted spaces, fantasy theme and appointments, and its eclectic cluttered pastiche, it reflected the taste of its designer as well as its wealthy patron.

After Vizcaya, Diego Suarez moved to New York and devoted himself to his greatest passion - his family's genealogy and history. He pursued that interest for the rest of his life, discovering and documenting the accomplishments of his great, great grandfather, the South American leader, San Martine.

In 1931 he married the much older Mrs. Evelyn Field, the former wife of the Chicago department store heir, Marshall Field, III; it was suspected to be a marriage of convenience. She was able to offer Suarez the life style to which he had become accustomed, but could never afford. She had a major estate at Syosset, L.I., designed by David Adler, the house architect to the Chicago's elite. The landscape architecture for the estate was designed by Innocenti and Webel in 1936, both protégées of the Florentine native, Ferruccio Vitale. Mrs. Diego Fields was listed as the client, not Suarez himself.

Diego Suarez died after the Second World War, without any further landscape architectural projects to his credit.

Geoffrey Scott   Geoffrey Scott never really took part or interest in his profession architecture. His partnership with Cecil Pinsent was a reality on paper only. Too much a thinker, theorist and philosopher, Scott continued his budding writing career. After his book, *The Architecture of Humanism*, he tried his hand at writing a novel, receiving mildly kind reviews. The war, an unfulfilled and mostly fantasized love affair, and a failed marriage left him distracted and up-rooted from any literary production.

Mary Berenson had commented to Scott much earlier, in his formative years, that his unresolved homosexuality would be his undoing. She harshly noted Florence's old, single men who, in her mind, led a pathetic existence. Without mates, they were continuously on the prowl for sexual partners. They were ravished with age, and broken in physical appearance. She warned Scott that a similar fate awaited him, hoping that he would choose the straight or covered lifestyle that would suit her desire. Scott's marriage to Lady Sybil Cutting in 1918 was his attempt at resolving the issue. After its failure, and a following unsuccessful attempt at a relationship with the lesbian garden designer Vita Sackville-West, Scott was severely depressed and dysfunctional. His close homosexual partner, Cecil Pinsent, though, helped him through this difficult period, and with Pinsent's support, Scott was able to find a worthy literary commission in 1927 in the United States; he was to archive and publish the papers of Samuel Boswell, the noted eighteenth-century, American biographer and to write Boswell's biography. Pinsent accompanied Scott to America and aided his settling into a productive regimen. With fiendish dedication and workaholic zeal, in one years's time Scott had accomplished the archiving of the Boswell Papers and had returned to England. Again with Pinsent's aid, he returned to America to begin Boswell's biography.[567] Two days after his arrival, he was stricken with pneumonia and died in1927 with Pinsent at his side.

Cecil Pinsent Cecil Pinsent began other landscape architectural commissions even while I Tatti was under development. He aimed to establish himself in Florence in professional practice, even entering into partnership with Geoffrey Scott at one time. Pinsent's first project was undertaken independently, and was a guest lodge at the Villa Gattaia, outside Florence (1908), for Berenson's Harvard classmate, Charles Loeser. Its major accomplishment was to furnish Pinsent with a letter of recommendation for his artistic accomplishments. With Scott as his partner after 1912, Pinsent designed Le Balze, a new house and gardens for Charles Augustus Strong, another classmate of BB's. It was considered "a splendidly well-engineered interpretation of the Tuscan vernacular style, and a demonstration of exceptional talent for garden design in the 'Moderne Italian Style'."[568] The villa, small but prestigious, was located across the road from the famous Villa Medici. The work, although under the firm name of Pinsent and Scott, was all Cecil's. The first project that could be considered a collaboration involving the two partners was the gardens at the Villa Medici in 1915. The villa was owned by the widowed Lady Sybil Cuffe Cutting. (Geoffrey Scott would later marry her in a fit of spite at a lost lover, only to divorce within a year.) The Pinsent designs for both these early commissions were slight variations on the sketches he had produced for the Villa Gamberaia.

After World War I, Pinsent continued with commissions at Villa Palmerino for the English writer, Vernon Lee who famously said, "[gardens] have little or nothing to do with nature;" at Montegulfoni for an English essayist, Sir Osbert Sitwell, at Villa Palmieri in Fiesole; for Balcarres, an Englishman who was interested in "Tuscanizing" the gardens; and at Villa Gattaia (also known as the Torre Gattaia), Florence, for Charles Loeser, another art historian.[569] (Bernard Berenson would not speak with Pinsent during this work, for he disdained the "despicable" Loeser.) In all, Pinsent designed more than twenty gardens in and around Florence.

Perhaps the best of Pinsent's work is the Villa La Foce at Chianciano Terme near Siena done for the Marquis Antonio Origo and Marchesa Iris Cutting Origo, daughter of Lady Sybil of the Villa Medici. Pinsent had known Iris since childhood, first from the redesign of her childhood residence, Villa Medici, and then through the difficult time of Scott's marriage to her mother, and afterwards, through continued contacts of friendship. Iris was an avid garden enthusiast and visited many gardens on her extensive travels.

In 1924, Iris married Antonio Origo, a scientific farmer. His consuming interest was to reconstitute the depleted agricultural base of the Sienese hillside. Erosion and semi-arid conditions had made farming marginal and often fallow lands were ravished further by wind and water. The Origos had bought La Foce, an old casa farmhouse on 3500 hectares of treeless and shrubless bear clay hill ridges. It would be the ultimate test to reconstitute any worthwhile agriculture. They immediately began to reforest its steep lands that had been wasted by erosion. They planted all stream embankments in order to conserve water and promote sedimentation for soil development in the flood planes. Hilltops were made arable through contour farming, innovative then for Italy, crop rotation and other advanced farming practices. Antonio Origo had exceptional success and his novel practices were expanded by the commune to rehabilitate thousands of hectares throughout the Siena region.

How much if anything, Pinsent contributed to this new rational agriculture is not known, but he became involved in several aspects of this ideal farm. He developed the *podere*'s infrastructure with roads and support components for the *mezzadrina*, and he aided Iris in the development of an exceptional and extensive garden for the main villa. The gardens stepped away from the house in a series of topiary and mixed flower gardens typical of his work at I Tatti. One of the most exceptional elements of the garden design is the marriage of Antonio's farming interests with Iris's garden interest. Pinsent tied the central axis of the garden to the distant hillside farm by an unusual vertical cypress alee and used the farm road from the valley floor to the hilltop to create a series of switchbacks, or "S"curves, in a vertical alignment. Along the roadsides, he planted a low hedge of wild country roses and widely-spaced Italian cypresses for vertical accent. This wide band of planting stands out against the wheat production on the sloping hillside. To the casual traveler, it is startlingly beautiful to discover this obviously carefully structured landscape element amidst the Italian farmlands, but from within the Villa La Foce's garden, it is also the perfect terminus to the axis. So powerful and simple is this landscape statement that one finds photographs of it in guidebooks and promotional brochures.

Cecil Pinsent, after the death of his second closest male friend, Edmund Houghton, retired from professional work in 1953, moved to Hilterfinger Thunersee, Switzerand and lived a solitary life. He began a hobby of geometric measurements, measuring the heights and positions of the mountains of Austria, Switzerland and America, a practice that seems very similar to the studies done by Violet le Duc in his recording of the French Alps. Pinsent died in 1963.

R. Terry Schnadelbach

Fate has been kind to the three first Modernist villas of Florence. All three have survived ravishes of war and the uncertainties of new ownership. While their plantings have matured and in some cases died of old age, they have been replanted and maintained in a pampered and near pristine state. Only one of the gardens, La Pietra, has suffered greatly from aging and plans are underway to fully restore it.

Villa Gamberaia   Currently the Villa Gamberaia is beautifully preserved in the pristine state left by its post-war restorer Marchi. Its current owner, Luigi Zolon, has prided himself in the Gamberaia's conservation, especially its Modernist garden, and has held workshops and seminars on its history and design. There are no plans to restore the water parterre garden of the Ghyka era. The garden, although privately held, is open to the public for visits.

Villa La Pietra The Villa La Pietra complex, including Villa Acton, was inherited by Arthur Acton's son, Harold, after his father's death. Harold found the extensive gardens difficult to maintain, both financially and practically. He retained the post-war *capo giardinere,* who would have kept Arthur's last topiary scheme intact, except that the expansive topiary required more than one gardener. A compromise solution was found which kept the space forming topiary but removed many of the decorative forms within the parterres. The remaining forms were simplified further, all to reduce the trimming maintenance. Much of this simplification was ill-conceived as Harold, although he studied and wrote on the history of Italian gardens, did not have any architectural training. His choice of shapes and proportions was ungraceful. This, coupled with a natural tendency of the plants to grow coarse with aging, left the gardens at Harold's death, in 1991, in poor form.

At his death, Harold Acton donated the villa complex to New York University (NYU). The University now uses the villa as a center for a study-abroad program for its students and faculty. NYU has undertaken a study of the gardens, under the directions of a noted English landscape architect / historian and has begun an extensive program to completely rebuild the Villa Acton's gardens as they were in 1928. The restoration landscape architects have made extensive use of historic photographs. When complete, the gardens of La Pietra will be a beautiful example of second renaissance landscape garden design when it was in its prime.

Villa I Tatti is held by Harvard University since Bernard Berenson's death. Berenson, with the lingering dream of Altamura, donated the site with its art collection, library and gardens to the university as an institute for the scholarly research on art of the Renaissance. Since the bequest, Harvard has maintained the gardens exactly as designed. It has also retaining its post-war *capo giardinere,* who had worked with Cecil Pinsent to reshape the grounds after the war. While much of the topiary and vegetation has thickened and matured, the proportions and spaces have changed little and the original second renaissance garden is retained. Unfortunately, the gardens are unavailable for viewing, except for one morning a week, and then only to visiting scholars.

The American landscape architectural historian, Norman T. Newton, would always end his Harvard lectures on Italian Villas by showing a lantern slide of the water parterre gardens at the Villa Gamberaia taken in the 1920s. The view was taken at sunset when the sky was a particularly vivid composition of small puffy clouds reflecting the brilliant golden and rose-colored rays of the setting sun as it played against the dark azure blue of the open sky. With all paths and topiary turned a dark green / black, a perfect reflection of them could be seen in the pools of the water parterre. It was at this point that Newton describes the perfect stillness of the air, the absence of village and agrarian noises from the villa's surrounds, and of the garden's only sound, that of the evening nightingale. Newton would say that if you were there, you might see the ghostly image of a lady and her two white hunting dogs afoot on the lawn of the cypress allee. Ethereal, his words and picture could as easily bring to mind the garden's hunting goddess, Diana, or the ghost of the mere mortal, Giovanna Ghyka.

Appendix

Photograph Credits:

Author
p19, p30, p95, p107, p200, p201, p202, p204, p205, p207, p209, p210

American Academy in Rome, Library:
p10, p26, p31, p32, p35, p64

Cornell University, Rare Books Library
p21

Decordoba Museum, California
p110, p112, p113, p115, p121, p131, p133

Harvard University, Loeb Library
p206

Kim and Associates, London:
p81, p92, p96, p97, p99, p114, p116, p117, p118, p127, p128, p156

Georgina Masson Archives:
p29, p33, p34, p39, p40, p41,

Mattrasco, grand niece of Jeanne Ghyka
p16, p17, p55

Villa I Tatti, Archives:
p65, p159, p161, p162, p163, p165, p188, p191, p196, p203, p208, p222, p226, p227, p233, p240, p242

No Copyright:
Cover, p0, p2, p3, p12, p22, p36, p37, p42, p57, p67, p80, p113, p164, p169, p170, p175, p180, p182, p229, p243

Chronology

Date	European Events	Gamberaia Events
1877	Natalie and Alexander (Sasha) reside in Wiesbaden	
1880	Ghyka studies art in Paris France.	
1881	The nation of Romania is established	
1882	Queen Natalie becomes the Queen consort of Serbia (1882-1889)	
	Enactment of the Criminal Law Amendment Act in England, codifying the act of sodomy	
1884		
1885	Art patron of Cezanne, Egisto Paolo Fabbri (Fabry) moves to Florence, ; buys Villa.Bagaano near the Gambaraia	20 April Luigi Zalum and Anna Marchi acquire all the shares of villa Gamberaia.
1887	May, Queen Natalie separates from King Milan I and with son, Alexander, settles in Russia.	
1888	July, Queen and son return to Belgrade	30 April. Acquisition of Gamberaia is done by Paolo and Tito di Ferdinado Fazzini.
1889	Plan of Biltmore Mansion, Ashville N.C. Designed by FLW Olmsted Queen Natalie and King Milan divorce. March 6, Alexander I crown King of Serbia. His prime minister ruled until his maturity.	

La Pietra Events	I Tati Events	Date
		1877
One of four villino was rented to the Queen Natalie of Serbia		1880
Vialle viaduct and tunnel for perimeter road built		
Villa house remodeled - cortile volume fill-in and exterior form becomes a box		1881
		1882
	Berenson entered Harvard College	1884
	Mary Smith of Philadelphia married the Irish barrister Benjamin Conn "Frank" Costelloe,	1885
	Bernard Berenson graduated from Harvard College and left for a Grand Tour of Europe, Italy his first stop.	1887
	Berenson moves to Florence renting and apartment in the historic center	
	Berenson, on a lark, visits Mary Smith Costello's family house, Friday's Hill, in Fernhurst, Sussex, and romance builds.	1888
		1889

Date	European Events	Gamberaia Events
1891	Natalie had separated from Milan I, build an enormous chateau at Bidart.,	
1892		1 July. Ugo Pazzini succeeds the father Paolo of the property of Gamberaia.
1893	April, King Alexander I declares his maturity and acting King	14 December because of the division of the family the property of Gamberaia passes onto Ugo Paolo Fazzini.
1894	Charles A. Platt; *Italian Gardens* published	
1895	Natalie returns to Belgrade	
	Diego Suarez goes to America and takes up with Deering and Chalfont in the design and development of Viscaia, Miami Florida	
	The Oscar Wilde trial in England+B142+B142	
1896	Istituto Geografico Militare map, Planta della Citta di Firenze	7 March Giovanna Jeanne Keshko married to the prince Eugene Ghika- Comanesti buys the complex.. Ghyka immediately moves-in with her life companion, Miss Florence Blood.
		summer; Ghyka, through Carlo Placci, meets and befriends Bernard and Mary Berenson
		Princess Ghyka hosts parties for Florence expatriate nobility. to 1914
1897		One of Princess Ghyka's artist soirees at which Carlo Placci and Serge Wolkonski performed.
		Countess Stanislas de Montebello (Marie-Stani Cambaceres), from Paris, was in residence at the Gamberaia for a period
1899	dilitant, Isabell Garner starts constructing, Boslong the Fenwaruction on her new house a	
	Bloomsberry Group forms at Trinity College, England. All were frequent visitors to I Tatti	

La Pietra Events	I Tati Events	Date
	Mary Smith Costello arrives in Florence	1891
One of four villino was rented to the Queen Natalie of Serbia		1892
		1893
Guy Mitchel and Arthur Action move to Florence	Berson publishes his first book on art, *The Venetian Painters of the Renaissance"*	1894
		1895
Tunnel via dei Bruni under viele completed.		
	Mary Smith of Philadelphia married the Irish barrister Benjamin Conn "Frank" Costelloe,	1885
Main villa, was renter after years of abandon	Mary has an affair with the German artist, Wilfrid T. Blaydes, who was in a relationship with the known homosexual Oscar Wield	1896
Pomarior re-designed shown on at Pianta della Citta di Florence, Instituto Geografico Militare		
		1897
	Mary's husband Frank Costello died	1889
	Bernard rents a villino called I Tatti in Settignano. He and Mary move in together.	

Date	European Events	Gamberaia Events
1900	Scavando, Through one of the foundations of an independent of the villa a fragment of the coat of arms of Lapi have been found.	At the beginning of the 1900's the cypresses remain that were planted by Andrea Lapi and the rest of the reservoir and its conduits.
1901		Princess Ghyka begins restoring the gardens focusing on the southern parterre.
		Earliest photographs of the Ghyka's water parterre garden taken by
1902	Queen Natalie, then at her summer residence at Bidart, converted to Catholicism. Jeanne Ghyka designs a sculptural baptismal font for the occasion..	American novelist and garden aficionado, Edith Wharton visits the villa and issues negative comments on Ghyka's design.
1903	Considered the beginning of Modernism with the works of Wassily Kandinsky	
1904-5	Edith Wharton, Italian Villas and their Gardens published	Completion of Ghyka's water parterre garden
		Stanford White, American Architect visits Princess Ghyka and Villa Gamberaia.
1905	Russian Revolution breaks out	
	Standford White's wherehouse in Brooklyn burns	Princess Ghyka hosts Vita Sackville-West, then sixteen, and her passionate lover Violet Trefusis for a extended residency.

La Pietra Events	I Tati Events	Date
	Mary and brother Logan Smith found intellectual journal, The Golden Urn. Bernard outlines his utopian community Altamura	
	December 27; Bernard and Mary marry. Mary begins to make repairs to house	1900
	Mary Berenson has affair with young visiting painter Arthur Jeremy Monteney Jepson	
		1901
		1902
15 August; Arthur Acton marries Hortense Mitchell in Chicago		1903
Arthur takes up with Diego Suarez and worked together on the plans and design of the gardens.	Berenson returns to America for research and business connection to New York art dealers.	1904-5
Harold Acton born at Villa Acton.		
Architects of Villa I Tatti, Cecil Pincent and Geofrey Scott sketch a new plan for the gardens. It was never accepted or executed.	Cecil Pinsent, architect on his Grand Tour, visits Florence and picks up with Berenson's chaufeur	1905

Date	European Events	Gamberaia Events
1906	Standford White murdered at a Garden performance	
1908		
		Gertrude Stein and brother Leo visits with Ghyka and Miss Blood
1910	First Italian Exhibition of Impressionism, Lyceum of Florence featured Cezannes. Visited the foreign art colony.	Cecil Pinsent makes design changes to the water parrterre garden
1911	British painter Duncan Grant, a Cezanne copiest visits Miss Blood	
1912		Princess Ghyka is recorded to have hosted a private party for the lesbian community.
1914		
	June 28, Assassination of Archduke Ferdinand, Austria/Hungary declare war on Serbia, July 28, start of First World War	
	Edward G. Lawson wins the first biennial Rome Prize, American Academy in Rome	
1915-17	May 27, 1915, Italy declares war on Austria/Hungary	Villa closed and boarded due to the Great War in Europe. Ghyka assists in war effort for France by traveling to Bidart and nursing wounded troops.

La Pietra Events	I Tati Events	Date
William Acton born at La Pietra	Easter; Mary invites her daughters to visit Florence and arranges male escorts to accompany their travels. The two young men, Geoffrey Scott and Maynard Keyes were gay lovers.	1906
Viale planted with cypresses		
Acton commissioned survey by Francesco Fava of Villa Acton property, ovelaid in pencil layout of the garden	Bernard Berenson buys the villino I Tatti.	1908
Development of the garden begun	Berenson meets Belle Greene and take up an affair lasting 5 years	
	Gertrude Stein and brother Leovisits with Bernard Berenson	
Competition of the Vialle, the garden's long north south axis designed by Acton and Suarez.	Duncan Grant, a British Painter copiest of Cezanne visits Bernard for the Exhibition	1910
Architect Corsi-Home works on Palazzo's Primo muratore	Cecil Pinsent and Geoffrey Scott secretely commissioned by Mary to design their renaissance II garden	1911
Pinsent's Alterations to Contadino House with art-deco façade rejected	Pinsent hires capo giardinere Raffaelo Capecchi	
		1912
	Scott published *Architecture of Humanism*	1914
	Scott takes up with Nicky Marino who jealous Mary extricates from I Tatti.	
Diego Suarez goes to America to escape the war and end design and relationship at la Pietra	Mary and Bernard flee to London for the duration of the war	1915-17

Date	European Events	Gamberaia Events
	Diego Suarez goes to America and takes up with Deering and Chalfont in the design and development of Viscaia, Miami Florida	
1918		
1919	June 30., Versailles Treaty, End of war	
	1919-1933, Gropius established the Bauhaus in Germany	Lawson measures and draws-up plans, elevations and details of Gamberaia garden
	Cezanne visits Florence while exhibiting at the Venice Biennale. Fabbri owned 20 works.	Cezanne visits with Miss Blood and Princess Ghyka at their villa.
1925	Istituto Geografico Militare map, Planta della Citta di Firenze	
1926		Florence Blood dies in Florence.
	Expositions des Arts Decrative et Industrial in Paris begin Art Deco and Cubis movement	May Matilda Ledyard Cass de Enrico, widowed Ketteler, buys the property of Gamberaia from the princess Ghika.
1928		
1929		
		Book: Andre Le Blond; *The Gardens of Italy : and how to visit them*. First guide book to include Gamberaia.
1930s		November 13; Ghyka sell her jewelry at auction in London.
	24 October: US: 'Black Thursday' – the beginning of the Great Wall Street Crash.	

La Pietra Events	I Tati Events	Date
	Geoffrey Scott maries Lady Syble Cutting	
	Berenson takes up with Marino in a long lasting relationship	1918
		1919
	Cezanne visits with the Berensons at their villa	1920
Main structure and rooms are completed	Sir Geoffrey Jellicoe visits Cecil Pinsent and inspects the new landscape composition admiring its design	1923
		1924
		1925
Villas Sassetti, Natalie, Ulivi and Colletta gardens designed and built along with swimming pool at the valley bottom.		
Teatrino built		1926
		1928
Queen Natalie terminates her renting of the Villa Natalie and leaves Florence.		1929
Arthur Acton changed parts of the garden to the English Arts and Crafts style.		1930s

277

End Notes

1. F. W. Kent. "Gardens, Villas and Social Life in Renaissance Florence". http://www.arts.monash.edu

2. Nymphaea were originally associated in Roman times with baths and /or marriage halls, hence its connotation in bathing and lovemaking.

3. Uffici Collection, Palazzo Riccardi, Florence

4. For the purposes of this book, the phrase "turn of the century" will mean from nineteenth to twentieth century.

5. Le Corbusier. *Modulor: Essao sur une Mesure Harmonique a l'Echelle Humaine Applicable Universellement a l'Architecture et a La Mechanique*, (Paris, L'Architecture d'Aujourd'Hui, 1950)

6. They also ring true in the description of another cross-over between a performing art, music, and another visual art, painting. Painting is commonly thought of a directly related to architecture but not commonly recognized for its relationships to music. But the American composer Richard Trythall (1939-) has composed many of his early pieces based on the rational compositional elements of the painter Paul Klee in his book, *The Pedological Sketchbook*. To hear Trythall's score we would not be so surprised as its tonality is similar to famailiar pieces by Stravinski, but to see Trythall's score for his piece, ... is to look at a contemporary painting of Klee, Kandinski and Miro all wrapped into one. One would not easily think that it contains the norms of musical annotation which it clearly does.

7. Webster's *New International Dictionary*, Second Edition

8. The American composer, Chris Theofanidis, while in residence at the American Academy in Rome, in 1999.

9. Webster's *New Collegiate Dictionary* ; (Springfield, Massachusetts, Merriam Co. 1973).

10. Webster's *New Collegiate Dictionary*.

11. The term nymphaea was not used in the Roman nor Renaissance times and has been applied to rusticated grotto spaces containing statuary of nymphs during the eighteenth century. The author will continue with its modern use.

12. Geoffrey Scott. *The Architecture of Humanism*; (London, W. W. Norton, 1914), pp. 25-39

13. Patricia Osmond de Martino, Professor and Director of the Rome Program, Iowa State University

14. J. C. Shephard and G. A. Jellicoe; *Italian Gardens of the Renaissance*; (London, Earnest Benn Limited, 1927).

15. Edith Wharton, *Italian Villas and Their Gardens*, 1904.

16. Mrs. Aubrey. *The Old Gardens of Italy: How to Visit Them*; (New York, New York, Dodd, Mead and Company, 1912).

17. "(Gamberaia,) One of the most characteristic seventeenth-century gardens in the neighborhood of Florence, with grottoes inlaid with shells of different kinds and various colored marbles, statues, vases, fountains and jeux d'eaux of every description." Janet Ross, *Florentine Villas*, (London, J. M. Dent, 1901) "The plan of Gamberaia... combines in an astonishingly small space, yet without the least sense of overcrowding, almost every typical excellence of the old Italian garden: free circulation of sunlight and air about the house; abundance of water; easy access to dense shade; sheltered walks with different points of view; variety of effect produced by the skillful us of different levels; and finally, breath and simplicity of composition " Edith Wharton. *Italian Villas and Their Gardens*; (New York, New York, Scribners and Sons, 1904). "From the moment that you pass the gate, with its sentinal cypresses, the impression is one of such perfect loveliness that .... (one) is bathed in the perfection of the Tuscan villa." Charles Latham, *The Gardens of Italy*, Vol.2; (London, Phillips, 1905), p. 113 "You will come in sight of the great Gamberaia villa with its marvelous cypresses and hedges of pink roses, those 'twice-blooming roses of Palestrium' of which Virgil speaks." Edward Hutton. *Country Walks About Florence*; (London, Methuen and Company, 1908). The book was dedicated "To my dear friend Janet Ross." "The gardens have a breath and airiness and variety that could be equal by no ground laid out in the landscape style." Aubrey Le Blond, *The Old Gardens of Italy: How to Visit Them*, p.x "More Italian than the Italians themselves....the most thoughtful the western world has known." J.C and G.A. Jellicoe, *The Italian Gardens of the Renaissance*, 1925 "One of the finest villas in Italy." Richard K. Webel, FAAR (Fellow of the American Academy in Rome), *Guide to the Villas of Italy*, (Rome, American Academy in Rome, 1929). "Its beauty..is..great enough to absorb one almost completely, the terraces, ponds, the great apse of cut cypresses, the bowling green as you look at it from the

grotto toward the south like a great boat sailing through space, the view over the great landscape of the Chianti hills and further over domes and towers to the snow-capped Apennines and the Arno glimmering in the plain... For years Gamberaia remains of..the haunts of my life." Barnard Berenson, Sunset and Twilight, Dairies of 1947-58, March 4-5, 1948 "In Florence, whenever you wanted to give an example of an enchanting, unforgettable garden, you mentioned the Gamberaia." Ginori Lisci, 1953 "Today, the garden is at once the loveliest and the most typically Tuscan I have seen." Georgina Masson, *Italian Gardens*, (New York, New York, Harry Abrams, 1961). "Were I asked which garden near Florence is the most poetical, I would answer without hesitation that of the Villa Gamberaia...triumph where the gardener and the architect have felicitously solved the problem they have set themselves that the critic can conceive of no happier solution" Sir Harold Acton, *Great Houses of Italy*, 1971 "Villa Gamberaia is a rare jewel. Its smooth and harmonious facade blends perfectly with the beautiful ensemble of gardens, the most perfect of which is without doubt the south water parterre.... This garden enchants the eye with its rigorous geometric pattern and multiple perspectives which make it seem bigger than it really is" Sophie Bajard and Raffaello Bencini, *Villas and Gardens of Tuscany*, (Paris, Terrail, 1993). "This formal garden seems as richly patterned as a Persian carpet." Ethne Clark. "Villa Gamberaia: a Classic, Italian Garden in the hills of Tuscany," *Horticulture*, Vol. 71, January 1993, p 52.

18. As a stated premise throughout this book, the author will be using two words, Modern (Capitalized) and renaissance (un-capitalized) with very specific purpose. Moderne, used herein refers to the stylistic period called "Moderne," which correlates with the era from 1900 to 1925 roughly and should not be confused with the word "modern" which when also used, will generally refer to the phrase, "of its time." The word Renaissance, when capitalized, will retain its normal meaning defining the period of art during the fifteenth century. But the word "renaissance," un-capitalized, shall be used to refer to a rebirth in classical garden design begun in several Florentine garden of the Modern period, the Villas Gamberaia, La Pietra and I Tatti being the first of many of these new Modernist gardens. It is the author's contention that this shift in paradigms of garden design at this time concurs with and grows out of similar shifts in art, religion, architecture. When viewed together and in the context with numerous other convergent global, cultural forces, it produce what this author term as a second renaissance or rebirth of the humanist and classical structured garden design.

19. The Princes's full name had many variations in both composition and spelling. His married surname is found as Eugene Ghyka, Ghica or Ghika; the first being the most commonly used. The princess's maiden name was Keshko, spelled sometimes Kechko, was assumed to be Russian but may have actually been either Montenegro or Macedonian in origin. Her full married name in Italian is utilized here. Her Italian legal name was "Caterina Giovanna Keshko, maritata di Principe Eugenio

Ghika." [C.G.T.S 16 di Fiesole - c4390 Janet Ross, "Documenti d'Archivo," *Florentine Villas*; (1901).] Most commonly, the full name is shortened to simply Giovanna Ghyka, although her maiden name was French equilivants, Catherine Jeanne. Prince Euginio's sur-name was officially Ghika-Comenistri. To the thoroughly confused English community Caterina Giovanna Keshko, maritata di Principe Eugenio Ghika-Comenistri was known simply as Jeanne.

20. C.G.T.S 16 di Fiesole - c4390 Janet Ross, "Documenti d'Archivo," *Florentine Villas*; (1901).

21. The book, *Settignano*, 1865-1919 contains no reference of Princess Ghyka or the Villa Gamberaia even though the book presents a section or chapter on the foreign nobility in residence. The book includes a detailed section on Bernard Berenson and Villa I Tatti. The absence of any mention of Villa Gamberaia in village's historic documents is striking. Colle Armonioso. *Settignano*, 1865-1919; (Settignano, 1998). The book, *Settignano*, 1865-1919 contains no reference of Princess Ghyka or the Villa Gamberaia even though the book presents a section or chapter on the foreign nobility in residence. The book includes a detailed section on Bernard Berenson and Villa I Tatti. The absence of any mention of Villa Gamberaia in village's historic documents is striking. Colle Armonioso. *Settignano*, 1865-1919; (Settignano, 1998).

22. Letter, Bernard Berenson to Mrs. Gardner, November 14, 1897. Rollin Van N. Hadley. *The Letters of Bernard Berenson and Isabella Stewart Gardner, 1887-1924*; (Boston, Massachusetts, Northeastern University Press, 1987).

23. Giovanna was born in 1864 to a Colonel in the Russian Imperial Guard, Keshko and to the Romanian Princess Pulcherie Sturdza from the area known as Bessarabia, an area annexed by Russia in the War of 1812. The family were Russian Orthodox Catholics. Gian Luca Simonini. "Il Gardino la Gamberaia e l'Addizione di Catherine Jeanne Ghyka". *Storia Urbana* No. 85, 1998, p 151. Professa Trgovevic, the biographer of Giovanna's sister Natalie, My Memories; Personal Records of Queen Natalija Obrenovic, has conflicting information on her place of birth citing Florence, Italy. Letter to author: Ljubinka Trgovevic, January 10, 2000. From these sources the author believes Giovanna was born in Nice and in her early years, moved to Florence where she spent her youth

24. John Ghika-Comanesti, great-great nephew. Letter to Author; Hampshire, England, December 2, 1999.

25. John Ghika-Comanesti, Letter to Author, December 2, 1999.

26. Eugene was Prince of Moldavia and represented a long Ghyka family line of royalty from both Wallachia and Moldavia. Both territories were part of the weak Romanian Kingdom established

in 1881 by the Secret Convention with Austro-Hungary led by Eugene's older brother, Carlos I de Hohenzollern.

27. Natalija Keshko was born in Florence on May 14, 1859, her father an Russian ambassador to Florence. She died on May 5, 1941 in the convent of Notre Dame de Sion, Paris, France.

28. Milan I signed the Berlin treaty of 1878 and the Secrest Convention of 1881 establishing the independent country and Kingdom of Serbia. "The Centuries Under Turkish Rule and the Revival" of Statehood; http://www.suc.org/history/Hist_Serb_Culture/chb_Rados_Ljusic.html and Thierry Etchelecou. *Bidart: Le Passe du Village*; (Bidart, 2001 The wedding was a sinister, but unsuccessful, attempt by King Milan I to form a new Serbia from the central Balkans east to the Black Sea.

29. The term lesbian has many meanings and definition since its first use in the late nineteenth century. Initially it was a term meant to describe women who opposed sex with males and who showed physical attraction to other women. "Abhorrent" lesbian behavior is hard to pin down in the early writings of 1890s; it could be exhibited by women kissing - lips to lips, (whereas lips to cheek, forehead or other parts of the face was considered innocent) or it could be women walking holding hands (whereas it was accepted behavior for two women to be walking arm in arm or with one women holding the arm of the other). Cross dressing was observed but did not become part of the definition of lesbian until after 1910s. At no time were the actual act of lesbian love defined as it has been today - muff diving/oral sex, joint masturbation genital fondling, etc. Freud called lesbianism, a woman's love for other women exclusively. [This too misses contemporary definitions, ie. there are "fag hags / gayhounds," for example, women who do not necessarily love other women exclusively but who associate almost exclusively with gay males, rarely for sex, usually for gay self-identity. When sex is involved in this case, it usually consist of voyeurism, mutually masturbation or in group homo-sex.] As this book's subject covers the period from 1890s to 1930s roughly, the author chooses the latter definitions of lesbianism which includes all its forms. It is not known what form of lesbian interest Giovanna Ghyka practiced, but it is entirely clear that she hated men and was attracted to women exclusively.

30. In England in 1885, a Tory MP, Frederick Macquister, proposed and passed in the House of Commons, a new law as part of England's Criminal Law Amendment Act. It deplored the decline of female morality, condemned lesbianism as "neurasthenia and insanity," stating it threatened the nation's birth rate and was caused by an abnormality of the brain. Dianna Souhami. *Mrs. Keppel and Her Daughter*; (New York, New York, St. Martin's Press, 1990) p. xi.

31. It was during this period that the pejorative terms, Sappiest and bugger was first used to denote homosexual women and men. Lesbians were named after Sappho, the famous Roman poet living on the island of Lesbos, who wrote on the love between two women. Sappho's writings were

love lyrics recalling various amors including many with her younger pupils. The term became widespread as a result of the performances of Sappho's verses by the expatriate American Natalie Barney in her Paris gardens where she had erected a copy of the Greek temple found on Lesbos. Attendees, clad in white togas, became known as sisters of Lesbos or Sappist. James M. Saslow. *Pictures and Passions: A History of Homosexuality in the Visual Arts*; (New York, New York, Viking Press, 1999) pp. 1-21, 209.

32. Dianna Souhami. *Mrs. Keppel and Her Daughter*; p. 147.

33. Violet Trefusis wrote in a letter to the noted English gardener and her lover, Vita Sackville-West. Dianna Souhami. *Mrs. Keppel and Her Daughter*.

34. Emmanuel Cooper. The Sexual Perspective: Homosexuality and Art in the Last 100 Years in the West; (London, Routledge, 1994) pp. 45-46; and James M. Saslow. *Pictures and Passions: A History of Homosexuality in the Visual Arts*, pp. 209-211.

35. As a physician in Vienna, Sigmund Freud (1856-1939) studied the human psychosis. Two relevant areas for this book were suicide and hypnosis but moved on to develop psychoanalysis and the theory that many neuroses were caused by suppressed sexual desires. His works include: *The Interpretation of Dreams* (1899) and *Totem and Taboo* (1913).

36. Ester Newton in her chapter, "The Mystic Mannish Lesbian," cites four generations of New Women lesbians. The first were those born between 1850s and the 1860s, educated in the 1870s and 1880s and emerged in one of the lesbian communities in the 1890s. "They sought personal and economic independence rejecting their mother's domestic roles." Martin Dauberman, Martha Vicinus and George Chauney, Jr., Editors. *Hidden From History: Reclaiming Gay and Lesbian Past*; (London, Meridian, 1990) pp.283-284.

37. Attributed to Princess Marthe Bibesco of Serbia, niece. Peter Coates . *Great Gardens of the Western World*, (New York, New York, Putnam's Sons, 1963), p 25.

38. Judith Chatfield, *A Tour of Italian Gardens*; and C.G.T.S 16 di Fiesole - c4390 Janet Ross, "Documenti d'Archivo," Florentine Villas; (1901).

39. Serbia invaded Romania in 1896 and was defeated. King Milan I of Serbia, resigned in disgrace appointing his son Alexander I to succeed to the throne. Alexander brought added disgrace to Serbia by marring his mother's maid Draga Maschin who was pregnant by another man.

40. "...openly lesbian circles of Paris, Capri (imitating Sappho's community on Lesbos) and Florence..." (Author's note). Emmanuel Cooper. *The Sexual Perspective: Homosexuality and Art in the Last 100 Years in the West*; p. 90.

41. Spoken in 1902, by the noted lesbian Violet Keppel, the daughter of La Favorita or "Little Mrs. George" Keppel, the long term mistress of King Gerorge of England the successor of Edward VII. Numerous European royals vacationed here. Dianna Souhami. *Mrs. Keppel and Her Daughter.*

42. "The End of the Obrenovic Dynasty"; http://www.lib.msu.edu/sowards/balkan/lect13.htm

43. Thierry Etchelecou. *Bidart: Le Passe du Village.*

44. La Pietra was the former Austro-Hungarian embassy in Florence.

45. Henry James, *Portait of Places*, 1883

46. On 8 October 1869, a lesbian couple, Maria Luisa Rosa Adele (Italian) and Luisa Alessandrina d"Outreleau (French) utilized an unrelated male, Luigi Mario Emanuele di Armando Baudesson to buy the Villa Gamberia. C.G.T.S 16 di Fiesole - c4390 Janet Ross, "Documenti d'Archivo," Florentine Villas.

47. Sue Bennet, Five Centuries of Women and Gardens; (London, National Portrait Gallery, 2001) as reported in Jennifer Potter. "Escape to Eden: the Horticultural Emancipation of Women Gardeners." *The Literary Supplement* December 8, 2000, p 18

48. Carlo Placci was an Italian playwright, an essayist in residence and a prominent Florentine socialite. He was the only social connection between the many and varied expatriate community communities living in the hillsides surrounding Florence. He moved between the strict closed German circle and the three or four promenant American/ British circle, The Acton and Berenson circles in particular. Ernest Samuels, *Bernard Berenson: The Making of a Connoisseur*, (Cambridge, Massachusetts, Belknap Press, Harvard University, 1979) p.264.

49. Ghyka made known her limited financial conditions and in bargaining with Placci, she states that the price was very high and that it was more money than she had and that it will take every cent she could gather to buy the villa. She utilized her legacy monies then in Russian banks, obviously the Keshko family inheritance as her father was the former Romanian ambassador during the Russian controlled era (pre 1878). Attributed to Patricia Osmond, Historian of the Villa Gamberaia, from her readings of letters, in French and Paris dated, from Princess Ghyka to Placci in the privately held Archives of Carlo Placci, Florence.

50. "We shall be able to grow our own fruit, wine, oil - even champagne." Sir George Sitwell, Villa Montegufoni.

51. Conversations with Amanda Lilly, British art historian and historian of Villa La Pietra.

52. Edward Hutton. *Country Walks About Florence.*

53. Janet Ross was quoted as saying in 1908

54. In the definition, the "dancers in couples, the partners going through a series of steps which cause them to whirl around and at the same time advance round the room" (or a garden room in this case), the "partners" here can be considered either Princess Ghyka and Miss Blood, or the Princess and her narcissistic self.

55. J. C. Shepherd and G. A. Jellicoe. *Gardens and Design*, p. 121.

56. Pre-1770s and the Lappi era, the entrance must have been from the east in what is now the Grotto. There are indisputable signs that the walls of the Grotto are additive and are newer than the preexisting retaining walls of the Lemonaia and the boundary walls along the roadway, the current route of Via Lorelina. This explains the question raised by Judith Kinnard as to the reason that the house's main entrance was designed on the east. Judith A. Kinnard. "The Villa Gamberaia in Settignano: The Street in the Garden," *Journal of Garden History*, London, (Winter 1986).

57. The Renaissance garden walks and allees were typically constructed in *terra battuta*, the exceptions were major walks in rocaille /pebble mosaics. With the exception of the rear allee to the casino at Villa Caparola, grass was not used, and even here we do not have any documentation that grass was originally employed.

58. Patricia J. Osmond. "L'Amina della Villa Toscana"

59. Indigo Triggs. *The Art of Garden Design in Italy*; (London, Longmans, 1906) pp.83-84.

60. It would seem logical that the allee was changed at this time, from terra battuta to grass as the Ghyka pallet was a simplified and unified space - green architecture. The illustration done on-site by Maxfield Parrish, executed in 1897, the only visual record prior to the Ghyka construction, is inconclusive. It shows a brief section of the allee to be tan and stippled as indicative of the traditional dirt paving. But as this area is currently paved in stone, it could quite possibly indicate only the stone paving of the midpoint of the allee. Furthermore, also not definitive, readings from Gabreile d'Annunzio, according to Particia Osmond, give the impression that the allee was grassed.

61. Aubrey Le Bonde, *The Old Gardens of Italy: How to Visit Them*.

62. Based on the 1919 measured drawing by Edward G. Lawson. The Villa Gamberaia is one of the few Italian villas to have been accurately measured and drawn to scale so that its proportions and geometric relationships could be analyzed and studied.

63. L. Einstein. "The Tuscan Garden," *Architectural Review*, February, 1927, p. 4.

64. D'Annunzio resided in the Villa La Capponicina, in Settignano, just downhill from the Villa Gamberaia. His Notebooks contain observations of the Villa Gamberaia at the time of its purchase by Ghyka. Patricia J. Osmond. "L'Amina della Villa Toscana," Villa Gamberaia: Incontri e Prosoecttive Symposium; (Settignano, Villa Gamberaia, 5 July, 1999). D'Annunzio was well known as a homosexual who married for social acceptance, fulfilling the marriage with several children but lived apart from his wife, in Settignano "where he could write and concentrate better." Because of D'Annunzio, Settignano had a libertine reputation which attracted Ghyka and Blood. D'Annunzio's lover of the time was Francesco Paolo Marchettio. They were photographed together on the beaches of Villafranca. D'Annunzio (1863-1938), Exhibition; Musee D'Orsay, Paris, April-July 2001.

65. Patricia J. Osmond. "L'Amina della Villa Toscana."

66. Edith Wharton, *Italian Villas and Their Gardens*.

67. Maria Wellington Gahtan. "Standing on a Garden Wall or Assembling in a 'Rustic Closet:' Seasonal Statuary at the Villa Gamberaia," Villa Gamberaia: Incontri e Prosoecttive Symposium; (Settignano, Villa Gamberaia, 5 July, 1999).

68. Harold Acton. *The Tuscan Villas*; (London, Thames and Hudson, 1973)

69. Patricia J. Osmond. "L'Amina della Villa Toscana

70. Edith Wharton, *Italian Villas and Their Gardens*.

71. Ethne Clark. "Villa Gamberaia," p 52.

72. Janet Ross, *The Florentine Garden*.

73. See historic maps

74. It would appear contradictory that Ghyka would totally enclose the garden with high hedges thereby cutting off the fresh breezes and zephers , a trademark of the Frortine hillside, but the privacy of queer space was her goal.

75. "These, the hedges and pools, are later but entirely satisfactory additions to the garden." Peter Coats, *Great Gardens of the Western World*.

76. "The liquid and the solid: carved stonework, evergreen foliage, huge mirrors to reflect the sky - nowhere have these been composed with such refinement of taste on so human a scale." Sir Harold Acton, "Preface," *Gamberaia: A Photo Essay by Balthazar Korab*; (Florence, Centro Di, 1971).

77. Sir Harold Acton, *Great Houses of Italy*.

78. Daniela Cinti. "I Gardini Degli Antiquari," *Gardini Parchi Paesaggi*, 1998; and Patricia Schultz,"An Italian Idyll," *Garden Design*, Spring 1987, Vol. 6, No 1, pp 46-55.

79. "Their head gardener and ours became close friends: they belong to a vanishing species whose passion for horticulture was religion and all-embracing." Sir Harold Acton, "Preface," *Gamberaia*.

80. Richard K. Webel, *Guide to the Villas of Italy*.

81. Sir Harold Acton, *Great Houses of Italy*.

82. F. W. Kent. "Gardens, Villas and Social Life in Renaissance Florence."

83. F. W. Kent. "Gardens, Villas and Social Life in Renaissance Florence."

84. Gian Luca Simonini. "Il Gardino la Gamberaia e l'Addizione di Catherine Jeanne Ghyka." p 151.

85. In the late 1930s when Princess Ghyka was in dire need of money to live and had to sell her house and furniture, as a last resort. She sold, at auction in London's Sotheby on November 12 and 13, 1928, her entire remaining collection of jewelry. Of note, the collection included her princess tiara comprised of six lotus flowers and rosettes formed in ribbons of gold.

86. From Gabriele D'Annunzio's Notebooks; entries from the period of 1896-1898.

87. Letter to Isabella S. Gardner, from Bernard Berenson, November 14, 1897, Hadley, Rollin Van N. The Letters of Bernard Berenson and Isabella Stewart Gardner, 1887-1924, p. 99

88. Ernest Samuels, *Bernard Berenson: The Making of a Connoisseur*, p.264. The information of Placci's hosting many of the social affairs is attributed to Patricia Osmond and her reading of Placci letters to Princess Ghyka found in his archive, Florence.

89. Secrest, Meryle, *Being Bernard Berenson: A Biography*.

90. Samuels, Ernest, *Bernard Berenson: The Making of a Connoisseur*.

91. The chapel is a small structure inserted between the ocean fronted hotel and the doctor's residence across a garden space. The chapel itself was originally entered through a garden space from the west side. The rectangular hedge entry garden could have been a Ghyka contribution, a replica of the Gamberaia style. Information obtained from conversations with the current Mother Superior. Thierry Etchelecou. *Bidart: Le Passe du Village*; (Bidart, 2001).

92. The church is a large structure adjacent to the main square and is built in typical Basque architecture. It is a masonry structure white-washed with a large central nave, which is distinguished inside by side walls of the nave lined with two-story women's balconies. These expressed the days when women were separated form participating in the service. The interior, except for these wooden balconies is completely unadorned except for an altear - no saints, way of the cross or other Catholic icons. Ghyka provided a space in the rear under the side balcony for a new baptistry which would be designated only by new polished marble paving and a new stone baptistry font. The font itself is a statement of classical simplicity reflective of her Thomist philosophy. Thierry Etchelecou. *Bidart: Le Passe du Village.*

93. At that time, the institute was of major international importance for its innovative treatments for tuberculosis. The many artists recovering there, contributed art to the walls of the institute. The institute was run by the noted French Doctor Peyret, with nursing assistance from Dominican nuns headed by Mother Jacques-Marie. Mother Jacques-Marie was passionate for art and in her youth had been the model seen in Henri Matisse's paintings. She was probably the dominant influence behind the institute's, and the chapel's, art program. Though Ghyka was not sick, nor in-residence, her baptistry work was probably known to the Mother Superior and she was asked to adorn the chapel's interiors.

94. Jennifer Laurie Shaw. *Nation and Desire in the Paintings of Pierre Puvis de Cahrvanne* from 1879-1895: a dissertation; (Berkeley, CA, University of California, 1999).

95. Gian Luca Simonini. "Il Gardino la Gamberaia e l'Addizione di Catherine Jeanne Ghyka," *Storia Urbana* No. 85, 1998, p 160.

96. Secrest, Meryle, *Being Bernard Berenson: A Biography*, p. 75

97. Ernest Samuels,, *Bernard Berenson: The Making of a Connoisseur*, p 324.

98. Ernest Samuels, *Bernard Berenson: The Making of a Connoisseur*.

99. Samuels, Ernest, *Bernard Berenson: The Making of a Connoisseur*.

100. Prince Mikhailorites of Wolkonski. Ernest Samuels. *Bernard Berenson: The Making of a Connoisseur.*

101. Letter, Bernard Berenson to Mrs. Gardner, The Letters of Bernard Berenson and Isabella Stewart Gardner, 1887-1924, November 14, 1897.

102. Nicky Mariano, *Forty Years with Bernard Berenson*, (New York, New York, Alfred Knopf, 1966) p 5.

103. Simonetta Angeli Festin. *Settignano Colle Armonioso*, 1865-1910; (Firenze SP44 Editore, 1994) p. 212

104. Mary Berenson told the story of Blood's seduction of Hutchins Hapgood, a frequent I Tatti visitor. While Hapgood was giving Miss Blood a Greek lesson, she jumped up and tore off all her clothing. *Nicky Mariano, Forty Years with Bernard Berenson.*

105. Examples are Violet Paget whose nom de plum was Vernon Lee.

106. Ernest Samuels. *Bernard Berenson: The Making of a Connoisseur*

107. Ernest Samuels. *Bernard Berenson: The Making of a Connoisseur.*

108. Radclyffe Hall was a member of the famous women rights group incongruously called, the Knitting Circle, at the beginning of the century in England. Though often seen attending parties and literary affairs in Florence where her sexuality was not an issue, she later became known as a writer and wrote the first openly lesbian novel in 1928. Lesbian and Gay History, South Bank University: http://www.southbank-university.ac.uk

109. The Pink Lily: Gay and Lesbian Guide to Florence and Tuscany ; http://www.gay.it/pink-_lily.htm

110. Nicky Marino. *Forty Years with Berenson;* Alfred Knopf, New York, 1966

111. Christopher Hibbert. *Florence: A Biography of a City;* (New York, New York, Viking, 1993), p

112. 112. Michael Fields, a man's name, was a nom de plum used jointly by a lesbian literary couple living in Fiesole.

113. Hibbert, Christopher, Florence: A Biography of a City, p 270.

114. Ernest Samuels, *Bernard Berenson: The Making of a Connoisseur*, p.153.

115. Ernest Samuels, *Bernard Berenson: The Making of a Connoisseur*, p. 153.

116. Ernest Samuels, *Bernard Berenson: The Making of a Connoisseur*, p.177.

117. Hibbert, Christopher, *Florence: A Biography of a City*, p.277.

118. Ernest Samuels, *Bernard Berenson: The Making of a Connoisseur*, p.354.

119. Aaron Betsky. *Queer Space: Architecture and Same-Sex Desire;* (New York, NY William Morrow and Company, 1997)

120. "Various terms were used to describe the subject of homosexuality which was emerging as a

new topic and as a scientific study at the end of the nineteenth century. Studies were made in America and England, beginning from 1889, as to the phenomena of homosexuality and its "causes." "By the century's end, the medical studies on the subject was large and growing fast with dozens of American contributions and considerably more in Europe." The term used for describing homosexuals were: "sexual inversion, contrary sexual instinct or sexual perversion." Bert Hansen. "American Physicians' Earliest Writings About Homosexuality, 1880-1900." *The Milbank Quarterly*, Vol. 67, p.92. The first book in English on the subject of homosexuality was called *Sexual Inversion*, by Havelock Ellis and John Addington Symonds published in 1897.

121. Ibid, p 97.

122. Vita Sackville-West was already a passionate gardener. At Knole, the estate of her youth, she had developed a wondrous display garden of year-round delphiniums (cut from tin cans and hand painted) amidst the herbaceous border. Dianna Souhami. *Mrs. Keppel and Her Daughter* p. 84. Vita became later the creator of famous gardens at Sisinghurst, England. Her visit/stay at the Gamberaia is remarked by many historians as a minimum being influential and contributing to her love of gardening, and at its fullest, the inspiration of many parts of her Sisinghurst landscape.

123. Dianna Souhami. *Mrs. Keppel and Her Daughter*, p. 91; and Gian Luca Simonini. "Il Gardino la Gamberaia e l'Addizione di Catherine Jeanne Ghyka," p 154.

124. Dianna Souhami. *Mrs. Keppel and Her Daughter*, p. 97.

125. Ernest Samuels, *Bernard Berenson: The Making of a Connoisseur*, p.264.

126. "Placci who, as Mary (Berenson) noted, had the only permesso to enter the magnificent gardens." Letter, Bernard Berenson to Mrs. Gardner, The Letters of Bernard Berenson and Isabella Stewart Gardner, 1887-1924, November 14, 1897.

127. "Under no circumstances is it possible to see the garden while the family is in residence, but when absent permission may be applied for from the Princess's agent in Florence, (Bernard Berenson.) Aubrey Le Bonde, *The Old Gardens of Italy: How to Visit Them*.

128. "This morning I finally succeeded in getting the finest Maremma she-dog I have ever seen. I have sent it off to you for Mr. Whitney. I will find a worthy mate for her and send on another steamer. Not full grown, about nine months cost 200 L. She has the disposition of a lamb. To make her a good watch dog, chain her up all day and let her loose at night. Feed her on bread and broth and bones. She has a tail like an angora cat (strange reference to Miss Blood's pets) but she will need a bath and a purge on arriving." Letter of Arthur Acton to Stanford White, Florence October 7, 1905, Stanford White Archives, Columbia University, New York

129. Attributed to Iris Origo, who grew up in the Villa Medici in Fiesole and whose mother was married to Cecil Pinsent's partner, Geoffrey Scott.

130. Aaron Betsky. *Queer Space: Architecture and Same-Sex Desire*

131. Aaron Betsky. *Queer Space: Architecture and Same-Sex Desire*.

132. Articles by Bevilacqua and Marcello Fagiolo, "The Garden of Gamberaia in the Seicento: Waters, the Elements, Earthquakes and their Mysteries." describe the many of the structural changes during the Lapis period of the seventeenth century.

133. Weather or not it is designated as a Renaissance, Renaissance-like, or a restored Renaissance garden or from other periods, as a Mannerist, Baroque or Mannerist or Mannerist/Baroque garden, is not pertinent to a wholly or partly Modern interpretation

134. This is a perfect example for the need of garden photography collections. The historian can reconstruct and match garden styles and techniques attributed to successive owners

135. Judith A. Kinnard, "The Villa Gamberaia in Settignano: The Street in the Garden."

136. "The linear element which dominates the composition, the garden avenue, does not focus on the villa, but bypasses it, running adjacent to the building's east facade. ...An examination of site planning used in other Florentine villas reveals the originality of this compositional device.... In each of the seven villas (the Utens lunettes) which include gardens, the garden is organized about an axis that is generated by the villa 'front' and centers on the facade's entry. ...The entry avenue has the expected, direct relationship to the villa's 'front' door. "It is this garden avenue that provides the basis for an urban interpretation of the villa's composition. The continuous definition of its edges results from a combination of built and natural elements. The east facade of the villa is extended on both sides by the attachment of curious thin walled two bay arcades which seem to exist only to connect the facade with this space...to make gateways onto the garden thoroughfare. Opposite the house, this space is defined by a long wall with pilasters and rectangular panels that are etched and painted onto its surface. This articulation suggests that the wall was intended to be read as a building facade rather than simply a retaining wall.... The perspective view of the villa's facade with its attached facades together with the opposite wall with the grotto entrance, present an urban street scene." Judith A. Kinnard, "The Villa Gamberaia in Settignano: the Street in the Garden."

137. Patricia Osmond in *L'Anima della Villa Toscana: Gabrielle D'Annunzio at the Gamberaia, 1896-1898*, cites the account of the Italian poet and visitor to the Gamberaia, (1896) who, in contrast with the description given by Edith Wharton (1904) describes what appears to be the generally

good conditions of the gardens. In contrast, Edith Wharton, who had earlier (than 1904) visited the "boarding house," described the gardens as "in ruinous condition." Edith Wharton. *Italian Villas and Their Gardens;* (New York, Scribners and Sons, 1904).

138. "the house was let out to summer lodgers." Georgina Masson, *Italian Gardens*, (New York, Harry N. Abrams, 1961).

139. "Superbest villa for its grandiose / splendid construction and superb annexes." (*Guido Cardocci*. Florence, 1881), p.32. Wilfredo Pareto dal Carteggio, Carlo Placci and Miss Paget attended an affair at the Gamberaia on May 28, 1894, two years before Ghyka bought the villa. It would seem that the place was in good order then or it would have been noted. Tommaso Giacalone. *Monaco Guida;* (Padova, CEDAM, 1957) p. 51 "The villa was still a 'lodging house' when Beatrix Ferrand visited it on her grand tour 1895. Roses and vegetables filled the plots around the fishpond. The structure of the garden was fine - "a mysterious and intriguing masterpiece with wonderful spaces. The fishpond garden, the grotto, the secret ilex boschi, eight garden rooms held together by a unifying green allee." Jane Brown. *The Gardening Life of Beatrix Jones Ferrand, 1872-1959,* p 50. "A fish pond with a rabbit hutch in its center." Caputo, Margherita, "From the Knowledge of the Past, the Future of the Garden," Proceedings of the 33rd IFLA World Congress; 1996. "A degringolade - simple guest-house. The parterres were used to grow cabbages and corn rather than profitless flowers, and there was no money to spare for nineteenth-century improvements." Peter Coates. *Great Gardens of the Western World*, p.23. "When Mrs. Wharton saw the garden about 1900, this fish pond, as she described it, was still in existence, but the parterres were planted with roses and vegetables and the house was let out to summer lodgers." Georgina Masson, *Italian Gardens*, 1961. This is an important quote as Princess Ghyka had been in residence at this date. It confirms that the changes to the water parterre garden did not begin before 1900. "The Florentine architect Filarete, speaking of a 1470 description of a Florentine villa, Villa Badia, that resembles the 1717 Lappi parterre garden at the Gamberaia, describes a fish pond, fed by crystal clear waters from a nearby pond, filled with fish of all types, and surrounded by fruit trees whose ripe or spoiled fruit conveniently fall to feed the fish." F. W. Kent. *Gardens, Villas and Social Life in Renaissance Florence*. Add to this the nutrients from runoff of the rabbit island, and the scene is a description of a perfectly balanced, self-sustaining ecological garden. It is obvious that Ghyka's remake of the parterre garden was for artistic considerations and not for any utilitarian concerns.

140. "Broderie," Encyclopedia Britanica; http:/eb.com "A type of French parterre garden that featured integrated swirling patterns of low boxwood, flowers, and colored soil/stone chips." This type of garden went out of fashion in the Eighteenth Century in Italy and was replaced by the English naturalesque style. The Gamberaia probably was spared such fate as its south garden was

elevated high above adjacent areas so as not to easily incorporate surrounding landscape and was too small for any naturalesque passage within its walls.

141. "- the long sweep of mown grass which runs the length of the formal garden; a lawn anywhere in Italy is unusual, and this one is all the more so by reason of size....Expanses of turf were never taken for granted as they are in cooler, damper climates." Peter Coats, *Great Gardens of the Western World*; (New York, G. P. Putnam's Sons, 1963).

142. John Dixon Hunt. *Garden and Grove*;

143. Patricia Osmond in *L'Anima della Villa Toscana: Gabrielle D'Annunzio at the Gamberaia, 1896-1898*, [pp..]. D'Annunzio described the allee as "a long viale (avenue) carpeted in grass, lined with flowers," from his Notebook entry of April 1898.

144. Zangheri cites the fact that on 15 February 1896, "Princess Catherine Giovanna (Jeanne) Kesko Ghyka estranged wife of Prince Eugene Ghyka of Serbia, buys Villa Gamberaia. She lives there with her American companion, Miss Florence Blood. I. Zangheri. "Pietro Porcinai e le Gamberaia *I Gardini del XX Secolo: l'Opera di Pietro Porcinai*, (Milano, Alinea, 1993). "(Princess Ghyka) is restoring the old-fashion garden to its pristine splendor with infinite patience and taste" Janet Ross. *The Florentine Villas*. "Water Garden designed by Princess Ghyka, 1902." Richard Webel. *Guide to Villas of Italy*, (Garden Club of America, 1930). Ross personally knew the Princess while Webel, from his time at the American Academy, examined documents at the Villa.

145. Charles Latham, *The Gardens of Italy, Volume II*; (London, Office of Country Life, 1905).

146. Mariachiara Pozzana, "I Primi Restauri," in *Gardini Parchi Paesaggi*; (Milan, Electra, 1998).

147. From conversations of June 5, 1999, with Nicholas Damin-King-Elliot, horticulturist of Villa La Pietra who has examined sections of the Sir Harold Acton Archives.

148. These two parts, the spiral columned dining area and the raised bench, were placed in the section that had contained one half of the oval fish pond. Since their character and detailing is so different from that of the original parterre garden, it gives further evidence that the area of major changes by Princess Ghyka, was from the southern edge of the former parterre garden to the mid-line of the fish pond.

149. "The liquid and the solid: carved stonework, evergreen foliage, huge mirrors to reflect the sky - nowhere have these been composed with such refinement of taste on so human a scale." Sir Harold Acton. "Preface," *Gamberaia: Photo Essay* by Balthazar Korab; (Roma, Centro Di, 1971).

150. The elliptical pool with its rabbit hutch island as generally indicated on the Cabreo, was ringed

in low fruit trees allowing views through to the fascinating animal life on the island. The Florentine architect Filarete, speaking of a 1470 description of a Florentine villa, Villa Badia, that resembles in plan the 1717 Lappi parterre garden at the Gamberaia, describes a fish pond, fed by crystal clear waters from a nearby pond, filled with fish of all types, and surrounded by fruit trees whose fruit convenient fall to feed the fish. F. W. Kent. "Gardens, Villas and Social Life in Renaissance Florence;" http://www.arts.monash.edu.au/visarts/diva/kent.html Add to this the nutrients from runoff of the rabbit island, and the scene is a description of a perfectly balanced, self-sustaining, ecological garden. It is therefore obvious that Ghyka's removal of these elements of a sustainable relationship and the complete remake of the parterre garden was accomplished for artistic considerations and not for any utilitarian concerns.

151. Patricia Schultz states that Arthur Mario Acton constructed the gardens at Villa la Pietra, from 1904 to 1924. Stanford White is the architect and Diego Suarez is the landscape architect. Daniela Cinti. "I Giardini Degli Antiquari," *Gardini Parchi Paesaggi*, (1998); and from published interviews, Patricia Schultz, "An Italian Idyll," (Washington, D.C., *Garden Design*, Spring 1987).

152. From unpublished conversations between Professor Amanda Lillie and Sir Harold Acton told to the author by Prof. Lillie.

153. An examination of the Acton, Villa La Pietra peristyle defining the exedra reveals that all the stone elements, columns and stone lintels, were from another installation where they were used in an orthogonal structure. Their ends and joints are designed for right-angle connection. At La Pietra, they are mortared to fit and visually appear to be connected smoothly in their curved form.

154. "...the Princess Ghika and Miss Blood, who had restored the parterres which had lapsed into plots of vegetables, fed me with cakes and fresh lemonade and allowed me to play with their snowy 'maremmani,' while my father discussed his plans for improving our garden." Sir Harold Acton. "Preface," *Gamberaia: Photo Essay* by Balthazar Korab.

155. From conversations with Osmond,

156. Between 1905-06, Indigo Triggs visited the garden and drew the first plan. The plan has major inaccuracies - the lemonaia, the wrap-around terrace and the southern end of the allee. Indigo Triggs. The Art of the Garden, (London, Longmans, 1906).

157. Ovidio Guaita. "Giardino della Gamberaia," pp 179-180.

158. Between 1905 and 1913, Martino Porcinai was landscape architect and head gardener to Princess Ghyka. Arthur Acton and Suarez along with Princess Ghyka and Porcinai had many meetings on the design of their gardens. Their landscape architects were the best of friends. "Their

head gardener and ours became close friends: they belong to a vanishing species whose passion for horticulture was religion and all-embracing." Sir Harold Acton, "Preface," *Gamberaia: Photo essay by Balthazar Korab.*

159. Photographic plate collection, Loeb Library, Visual Resource Archives, Harvard University. There are no historic credits to this collection and the origins of each photograph are unclear.

160. Loeb Library, Visual Resource Archives, Harvard University.

161. Cecil Pinsent draws a sketch plan of Villa Gamberaia in 1910.Ethne Clarke, *A Biography: Cecil Pinsent and His Gardens in Tuscany.*

162. In 1909, Cecil Pinsent, (1884-1963) architect / landscape architect, is said to have arrived in Florence and began to practice villa restoration. Between 1909 - 1914, Cecil Pinsent and Geoffrey Scott begin construction on the Villa I Tatti Mariachiara Pozzana. "I Giardini Degli Antiquari,"

163. Loeb Library, Visual Resource Archives, Harvard University.

164. Edith Wharton visited Gamberaia only once. She wrote in her book that the new parterre gardens were in keeping with the rest of the classical garden. This offended Princess Ghyka and Miss Blood and Wharton was never allowed to visit the garden again.

165. Berenson was seen often at the Villa and helped the recluse Princess Ghyka control guest visitations. The Zach guide *Seeing the Italian Villa* cites the requirement of obtaining a "card" from Bernard Berenson at I Tatti before visiting. Harold Acton cites Bernard as the only person with a key to the gardens.

166. "Today these gardens (Florentine) exist in forms which it is easy and tempting to see as authentic survivals of Renaissance garden art....When I came across similar characteristics of this 'new' Renaissance style again and again in other gardens and was told that they too had been designed by Pinsent, ..." Erika Neubauer. "The Garden Architecture of Cecil Pinsent, 1884-1964," *Journal of Garden History.*

167. In 1913-15, Luigi Messeri takes over as head gardener. http//english.firenze.net/passeggiate

168. " and I wondered about hoping that I might catch a glimpse of the place's owner, Princess Ghyka, a famous beauty who, from the day that she had lost her looks, had shut herself up in complete retirement with her English companion, refusing to let anyone see her unveiled face again. Sometimes, I was told, she would come out of the house at dawn to bathe in the pools of the water-garden, or would pace the long cypress avenue at night - but all I ever saw...was a glimpse of a veiled figure at an upper window." Lady Sybil Cutting Scott

169. In the period from 1919 to 1920, Edward Lawson, a Rome Prize winner, measured the garden and produced a series of drawings and notes now part of the Landscape Archives of the American Academy in Rome.

170. "(The) cypress hedge was trimmed to form arches, (such) that one cypress forms the pier and is trimmed to form one half of each arch. Cypress are set in holes about one foot deep and three foot square. Holes are covered with wire netting over which is spread a thin layer of soil, dead cypFress needles and moss form mulch...(the hidden) frame of iron pipes which carry jasmine and roses. This densities the cypress arches." Edward Lawson, Planting Plan, 1919.

171. Between 1923-25, Susan and Geoffrey Jellicoe visited the gardens and produced measured plans and sections. These Jellicoe drawings were beautiful sepia ink renderings with accurately cast shadows. They illustrated the parti of the garden but did not reflect the geometric irregularities of the garden. The lemonaia, though, was accurately drawn.

172. "write ahead ...so as not to disturb Miss Blood - an invalid." Leon H. Zach, "Seeing The Italian Villa," *Landscape Architecture*, (October 1921).

173. In May 1925, Princess Ghyka sold the Villa to the widowed Baroness Matilda Cass Ledyard Broekhalst who later sold it to Mrs. Enrico von Ketteler. I. Zangheri, "Pietro Porcainai e le Gamberaia."

174. "The Villa was mined and burned by the Germans during the war. It is now a combination of charred or blown out walls and rubble. In the garden, the plumbing is ruined and the pools and fountains are dry. The remainder of the gardens are well maintained and the skillful plan of the Villa Gamberaia is apparent everywhere". Laurence Roberts, typewritten notes of July 1953 in *A Guide to Villas and Gardens in Italy*. The annotated book is in the library of the American Academy in Rome.

175. In 1954, Doctore Marcello Marchi bought the Villa Gamberaia from the Vatican. From 1957 to 1961, Dr. Marchi reconstructed the water parterres. Marella Agnelli, *Gardens of the Italian Villas*, Rizzoli, 1987

176. In 1955, Pietro Porcinai produces a Planting Plan (Schema di Piantaggione) for the Villa Gamberaia. Milena Matteini. "Pietro Porcinai: Architectto del Giardino e del Paesaggio," *I Gardini del XX Secolo: l'Opera di Pietro Porcinai*, (Milano, Alinea, 1993).

177. Pinsent and Scott originally designed and constructed the modernist version of Villa Medici in the 1920s for Lady Sybil Cutting. It was heavily damaged in the World War. Sybil's daughter, Iris

Origo, commissioned Pinsent to restore the garden to pre-war conditions. Marcello Fantoni, Heidi Flores, and Pfordresher, *Cecil Pinsent and His Gardens in Tuscany*, (Turino, EDIFIR, 1996).

178. Ethne Clark, "Cecil Pinsent: A Biography:" Marcello Fantoni, Heidi Flores and John Pfordresher. *Cecil Pinsent and His Gardens in Tuscany*; (Florence, EDIFIR, 1996). 179

179. Mariachiara Pozzana. *Gardini Degli Antiquari*.

180. Indigo Triggs. *The Art of Garden Design in Italy*, pp.83-84.

181. Photographic Collections and Archives, American Academy in Rome, Rome, Italy.

182. *Memoirs of The American Academy in Rome*, Vol II ; (Bergamo, American Academy in Rome, 1917-18).

183. Patricia Osmond, "Notes for an Anthology of Writings on the Gamberaia".

184. Acton Letter to BB.

185. Sybil Cutting Scott

186. The disease affects only a small percentage of persons inheriting the trait and has been inconsistent as to those effected. A recent study, cited by the ....Canadian... links one rare cause to the occurrence of syphilis and its initial phase of skin lesions. As the lesbian couple were young and presumably sexually active at that time, and as the other partner became terminally ill, the presence of syphilis is both possible and plausible.

187. In its first stages of syphilis, a disfiguring rash is normally clearly visible on the skin. Men who have contracted it were known, at this period, by their wearing in public black hand gloves and being totally suited in black from head to toe.

188. C.G.T.S 101 di Fiesole - c29076, Janet Ross, "Documenti d'Archivo," Florentine Villas.

189. Sotherby's, London. "Prehistoric implements; Egyptian, Greek and Roman antiquies: Princess Ghyka, et alia". November 13-13, 1928 Sale code: SEKHET.

190. Indigo Triggs. The Art of Garden Design in Italy, pp.83-84.

191. "Editorial," *Apollo*; 1984.

192. The first published case study which used the term homosexuality was by Karoly Maria Kertbeny on May 6, 1868. "Timetable of Lesbian and Gay History" South Bank University London, http://www.southbank-university.ac.uk.

193. Bert Hansen. "American Physicians Earliest Writings about Homosexuality; 1880-1900." *The Milbank Quarterly*, Spring 1989, vol 67, p.92

194. Peter M. Nardi. "The Globalization of Gay and Lesbian Socio-political Movement: Some Observations about Europe with a Focus on Italy." *Social Perspectives*, Fall 1998, v41, p 585

195. Eugene F. Rice, Jr. "Forbidden Friendships: Homosexuality and Male Culture in Renaissance Florence" *Renaissance Quarterly*, Spring 1999, v52 p373.

196. Two German researchers emerge as important within this period. Karl Heinrich Ulrichs was the most prominent spokesman lobbying the repeal of criminality to homosexuality as early as 1867. His effort was partially successful in that the mediaeval law on homosexual acts as punishable by death was replaced in 1971 with a new penal code, Paragraph 175, stating that "an unnatural sex act committed between persons of male sex or by humans with animals is punishable by imprisonment: the loss of civil rights may also be imposed." Magnus Hirshfeld founded the Scientific-Humanitarian Committee dedicated to ending legal and social intolerance of homosexuality on May 14, 1897. South Bank University London, http://www.southbank-university.ac.uk. These early case-studies also noted several interesting aspects of sexual inverts: One, that such behavior was found in "marriages" where the same sex attraction could be practiced by either sex "for years and even decades without detection." Two, that inverts had a need and ability to recognize and be recognized by each other mainly for their own self-identification and confirmation. And Three, that inverts were very self-aware and highly self-educated in their phenomena. Dr. William Lee Howard wrote in 1904, "they are well read in literature appertaining to their condition; they search for everything written relating to sexual inversion; and many of them have devoted a life of silent study and struggle to overcome their terrible affliction." Bert Hansen. "American Physicians Earliest Writings about Homosexuality; 1880-1900.p.95

197. In the infamous Oscar Wilde trial of 1895, science, social moree, and law all were brought to the fore of the public mind. Bert Hansen. "American Physicians Earliest Writings about Homosexuality; 1880-1900." p.95

198. Peter M. Nardi. "The Globalization of Gay and Lesbian Socio-political Movement: Some Observations about Europe with a Focus on Italy." *Social Perspectives*, Fall 1998, v41, p 576.

199. "article on Florentine gay history"

200. The Romans distinguished the nuances of oral male sex by the verbs fellare (to suck a penis) and irrumare (to penetrate a mouth with a penis). The two uses can be seen in their corresponding nouns. The irrumatore was the active inserter and usually an older male, the fellatore the passive receiver generally a youth. The irrumatore received no social disesteem, again assuming the

normal heterosexual role, while the fellatore was socially unaccepted and was considered sexually inferior. In 1900s Florence the social acceptance was reversed with the older male fellating the younger male. If the act continued to sodomy, the Florentine practice had the older male become both the poppatore and buggerone or agens. Eugene F. Rice, Jr. "Forbidden Friendships: Homosexuality and Male Culture in Renaissance Florence" p372.

201. Harold Acton. "Villa la Pietra: Sir Harold Acton's Florentine Aesthetic." *Architectural Digest,*

202. Oscar Wield, the flamboyant and openly gay English playwrite of such homoerotic acclaimed works as Dorian Gray, was criminally tried for his public announcement of sodomy with the young Lord Alfred Douglas. Oscar was married to Constance and had a family (two sons) as was typical for social cover, openly stated that he was homosexual and dressed accordingly in dandy clothes posing in effeminate stands. These were reported with outrage in the British press and his practice of sodomy, was suspected but unproven until his self confession. The trial required Lord Douglas, from one of most prominent London families and a son to a member of British parliament to take the stand describing in the most intimate details his relations with Wield. For nearly one year, the press and the English public was immersed in the Wilde affair.

203. Natalie was the Italian spelling of Natalija, in Serbia.

204. Conversations by Amanda Lille with Sir Harold Acton, Arthur's son and heir, reveals that his father, on several earlier occasions discussed the possibility of buying a villa in Florence and in that eventuality, the garden design envisioned.

205. The 1896 date for renting the Villa conflicts with the date in the NYU / Wilkie report which states a far later date of 1903 and corresponded to Acton's wedding of Hortense. The 1896 date comes from correspondence between Stanford White and Acton - "I want you to come and see my new villa" - found in the Stanford White Archives, Avery Library, Columbia University.

206. New York University has denied the author direct access to the Acton archives because of a current legal case involving a paternity claim against Arthur Acton. It is impossible to verify many of the rumors that abound about Arthur Acton and the beginning years of Villa La Pietra. The author has interviewed many persons having/had partial access to the Acton archives and assess this information as fairly reliable to very probable.

207. There is much conflicting dates for the purchase of the villa. The termination of the 1896 lease would produce a date of 1901 for either renewal or purchase. Arthur was in no financial position to purchase the villa and there is no records of a new or extended lease. Harold Acton, in his interviews published in the Spring 1987 issue of Garden Design stated that his father bought the villa in 1902. In an article he authored for Architectural Digest , he states that the villa was

bought in 1903. It was bought in Hortense's name and with William Mitchell monies that the villa was purchased. Arthur and Hortense were married in 1903 and this would mark the first possible date for the villa's purchase. In the correspondence between Arthur Acton and Stanford White, part of the Stanford White collection, Avery Architectural Library, Columbia University, Acton states that he ownes the villa in his letters of 1903. The New York University/ Kim report is the only document that states it's purchase in 1907 which would place its purchase after Author had begun significant renovations utilizing monies from his father-in-law Mitchell - an improbable scenario if Hortense had not owned the villa.

208. Located on the via del Pian de Guillarri just south of Villa Caponi in Arcetri. Giulio Lensi and Orlando Cardini. *Le Villa Di Firenze*; (Florence, Vallecchi, 1954) It is very unclear who Don Giovanni Guiso was and why he placed this plack on the villa's walls. Don Giovanni Guiso was a Sardinian photographer, and son of Guise senior who was a collector of models of Italian opera stage sets. As the Actons produced opera along with drama and music in their teatri boscherecci, it is a possible common interest friendships. Their name was chosen as tribute to Verdi's great opera by the same name.

209. The plaque is organized in three columns, the center one reads as follows: "ARCHITETTI - Consulenti:" and lists "Stanford White, Charles Platt, Giuseppi Castellucci, Edwin Dodge and H.O. Watson." There is evidence that the first two were only buyers of Acton's objet d'art as was H. O. Watson, and did not produce any sketches or drawings for the villa. No information is available for the names Giuseppe Castellucci or Edwin Dodge.

210. The author has not found any notation of drawings or sketches on the Villa La Pietra in the archives of the firm McKim Meade and White, (M,M,&W) Avery Architectural Library, Columbia University. The only M,M,&W commission in Europe is the American Academy in Rome which was designed in New York and supervised by a lower staff member in Rome. Similarly, there is no evidence of any travel to Florence to assist at La Pietra. The academy's main building was designed and built in the years 1913 to 1915, long after the death of Stanford White. Similarly, research by the author has discovered no connection by Charles A. Platt for the design of La Pietra. La Pietra as well as Gamberaia were not part of Platt's 1893 Italian trip. A review of his photograph collection bound in over 24 bound volumes plus his professional library are now archived at the Century Association, New York, New York. This collection does not include any photographs of either villa. Platt took many of these photographs on his travels or bought finished prints from commercial studios at each location. There is no evidence to the claim by Harold Acton with design credits as published in his interview in the Spring 1987 issue of Garden Design that Stanford White and his father collaborated.

211. R. Terry Schnadelbach. *Ferruccio Vitale: The Landscape Architect of the Country Place Era*; (New York, Princeton Architectural Press, 2001).

212. The house was finished and officially open in 1895, two years after the Chicago World Columbian Exhibition. Its fame immediately spread.

213. *Biltmore House and Gardens: Biltmore Estate - Ashville, North Carolina* ; (Ashville, Tennessee, The Biltmore Company, 1965).

214. Norman T. Newton. *Design on the Land: The Development of Landscape Architecture*; (Cambridge, Massachusetts, The Belknap Press of Harvard University,1971), pp. 346-351.

215. Norman T. Newton. *Design on the Land: The Development of Landscape Architecture*.

216. "...nor is it one of Olmsted's best designs." Norman T. Newton. *Design on the Land: The Development of Landscape Architecture*, pp.328 and 428.

217. The native Florentine, now a leading American landscape architect, Ferruccio Vitale made a career designing the landscape architecture of many of the most impressive of these estates. R, Terry Schnadelbach. *Ferruccio Vitale: Landscape Architect of the Country Place Era*.

218. Correspondence from December 22,1890, Stanford White's purchases include the following contacts and acquisitions: Henri O. Watson, New York - a client, a vase, a screen, and others. Duveen Brothers, London - for the Whitneys, bought the Reynolds and two Etts E. Lowengard, Paris Godfrey Kopp, Rome -bought Orrok pictures. Galerie Sangiorge, Pallais Borghese, Rome - bought columns and vases Stefano Bardini, Piazza Mozzi 1, Florence - tables and the Taromina painting. F. Schutz, 18 rue Boneparte, Paris - bought tapestries. Arthur J. Sully, 15 Bond Street London - bought paintings Stanford White Archives, Avery Architectural Library, Columbia University, New York.

219. 219. Moore, Charles, *The Life and Times of Charles Follen McKim*, (New York, New York, Houghton Miffl in, 1929)

220. Acton is an old and prominent name in England. Arthur's father was a Lord and served in several British governments. His grandfather and great grandfather similarly held political posts in the Burbon government of Naples, appointed by Napoleon. Arthur, like his father and his grandfathers, attended Eton, the prestigious English prep school. Eton boasts of its array of Prime Ministers among its alumni. With such family credentials it is surprising that Arthur broke tradition and chose art as his field, later attending the Ecole des Beaux-Arts, Paris.

221. Stanford White, Letter to Arthur Acton of April 29, 1902, Stanford White Archives, Avery Architectural Library, Columbia University, New York

222. Arthur, an art student at the Ecole des Beaux-Arts in painting had actually met Stanford White previously through Guy Mitchell. Both White and Mitchell were students in architecture at the Ecole at the same time. Kim Wilkie. *Villa La Pietra: Landscape Master Plan*; (New York, New York University, May 1999).p. 12 It is strange that White would write Acton a formal letter of introduction when the two had met earlier as students of the Ecole Beaux-Arts. Perhaps in his following reply (missing from the archives), Acton reminded White of this fact. Correspondence between the two are friendly but formal especially on business matters. White though often request personal services and personal travel notes unusual to a straight business relationship. Arthur is far more solicitous and accommodating to White's requests, again offering personal invitations for joint travel and vacations at European spas again not typical to straight forward business relationships.

223. Stanford White Letter to Arthur Acton of Sept 4, 1903, Stanford White Archives, Avery Architectural Library, Columbia University, New York

224. Stanford White Letter to Arthur Acton of April 21, 1903, Stanford White Archives, Avery Architectural Library, Columbia University, New York

225. Stanford White Letter to Arthur Acton of December 16, 1897, Stanford White Archives, Avery Architectural Library, Columbia University, New York

226. From White's partner Charles Follen McKim's letters, it is improbable, that on this trip White provided Arthur any advise on the restoration of La Pietra which Acton was just beginning. His time was brief; he and McKim were again accompanied by clients, Mr. and Mrs Payne Whitney. Nor did they stay at the villa. No formal plans exist authenticating White's direct involvement at La Pietra. Stanford White Archive, Avery Architectural Library, Columbia University, New York.

227. Roth, Leland M., *McKim, Mead and White, Architects*; (New York, New York, Harper and Row, 1983)

228. The firm's only building in Italy for the American Academy in Rome was planned and constructed from 1910 to 1915, as record show, without any communication with Acton.

229. Stanford White Letter to Arthur Acton of November 27, 1897, Stanford White Archives, Avery Architectural Library, Columbia University, New York

230. The Charles A. Platt Library and archives at the Century Association of New York.

231. Kim Wilkie. *Villa La Pietra: Landscape Master Plan*, Appendix, p. 4.

232. Sir Harold Acton, "Villa La Pietra: Sir Harold Acton's Florentine Aesthetic," *Architectural Digest*; January 1990, pp 75-78.

233. Letter of Bernard Berenson to Isabelle Gardner, July 16, 1921

234. It is not clear whether Berenson was referring to Arthur's sexual conduct when using this phrase and we do not know for certain any specific or rumored homosexual liaisons after his marriage to Hortense, but it is quite possible for his relationship with Diego Suarez, an unmarried attractive young male was constant from 1904 to1921. Acton also made immediate bonds with James Deering, an unmarried single male who traveled, lived and is reported to have had an intense homosexual relationship with his designer, Paul Calfin, from 1912 until 1929, ending only when Deering died.

235. Stanford White in letter to Arthur Acton, New York, NY April 29, 1902. Stanford White Collection, Avery Architectural Library, Columbia University,

236. Giulio Lensi and Orlando Cardini. *Le Villa Di Firenze*; (Florence, Vallecchi, 1954)

237. The pen type is thin with squarish letters; his "I's" start top, stroke moves right then down and across bottom to curl up at end; "T's" are tortured with crooked cross strokes.

238. Maryellen Lawrence, *The Villa La Pietra: New Findings, History and Myth*; an unpublished thesis cited by Kim Wilkie, *Villa La Pietra: Landscape Master Plan*.

239. Harold Acton, "Villa La Pietra" , *Architectural Digest*

240. Kim Wilkie. *Villa La Pietra: Landscape Master Plan*, p.5

241. Kim Wilkie. *Villa La Pietra: Landscape Master Plan*, p.5

242. Kim Wilkie. *Villa La Pietra: Landscape Master Plan*, p.5

243. "Villa la Pietra" http://en.wikipedia.org

244. Patricia Schultz, "An Italian Idyll."

245. Eberlein's book contains the first published photographs of the completed La Pietra gardens. Harold Donaldson Eberlein, *Villas of Florence and Tuscany*; (Philadelphia, Pennsylvania, Lippincott, 1922), pp 330.

246. None of these murals have ever been published.

247. From Author's visit and inspection

248. Lionella Scazzosi, "Da monumento a Documento: Restauri in Lombardia tra Fino Ottocento e Inizi Novecento" Vincenzo Cazzato, Editor. *La Memoria, Il Tempo, La Storia nel Giardino Italaiano* Fra 1800 e 1900;(Roma, Instituto Poligrafico e Zecca Dello Stato, 1998], p64.

249. This is probably attributable to Georgio Galletti. who is associated in the book's writings. Penelope Hobhouse, *The Garden Lover's Guide to Italy*; (New York, New York, Princeton Architectural Press, 1998).

250. While the majority of Henri Duchene's work was in historic French garden restorations, he did produce a number of landscapes in France, Italy and America. He sketched in plan and perspective, highly decorative, enclosed formal spaces. Few were executed.

251. The plan, by date, occurs well after the redevelopment of the gardens began, after his "consultations with the Duchenes. And after Diego Suarez joined Acton as his landscape architect. The authorship of the plan therefore is not entirely clear.

252. Landscape Architect Diego Suarez. Kim Wilkie. *Villa La Pietra: Landscape Master Plan.* p.13

253. Patricia Schultz, "An Italian Idyll ." The two in collaboration is perhaps similar to a pair of music composers such as Gilbert and Sullivan. While they worked together, predominantly, Arthur wrote the script and Suarez provided the music.

254. He was the only man that the classical architectural historian Henry Hope Reed had ever known that had shook the hand of Proust. Conversations by the author with Henry Hope Reed, New York, NY December 20 1999.

255. Conversations by the author with Henry Hope Reed, New York, NY December 20 1999.

256. Rebecca Warre Davidson. "Past as Present: Villa Viscaya and the 'Italian Garden" in the United States." *Journal of Garden History*, vol 12, p1-28.

257. Conversations by the author with Henry Hope Reed, New York, NY December 20 1999.

258. There is attribution that ths villas was designed by Cecil Pinsent as well. Its attribution is unclear. It is possible that Suarez first worked on the villa pre 1903 and the Pinsent later work on it in the 1920s.

259. Only a few of these are known and are in the Florence region. Rebecca Warre Davidson. "Past as Present: Villa Viscaya and the 'Italian Garden" in the United States." *Journal of Garden History*, vol 12, p1-28 Others are reported to have been accomplished in the Veneto. After a thorough search

of histories of Italian gardens, these restorations remain unknown. Henry Hope Reed, who knew Suarez and considered him America's greatest living landscape architect in the 1960s, makes reference to their location in Florence but others cite his knowledge of the Brenta region where other concurrent garden restoration were occurring. Conversations by the author with Henry Hope Reed, New York, NY December 20 1999.

260. The slide collection in the archives of the Fine Arts Library University of Pennsylvania, Philadelphia contains several historic slides of the villa attributed to Diego Suarez. Notes state that they were supplied by Suarez.

261. Landscape Architect, Diego Suarez. Kim Wilkie. *Villa La Pietra: Landscape Master Plan*, p.13.

262. Charles Platt, in a New York Times story, has been reported to have consulted and possibly have designed the garden restoration at La Pietra. There is little evidence to support this claim. Platt's visit to Florence was in 1892 prior to Acton's arrival. His book, Italian Villas do not mention visiting any of the various names synonymous with La Pietra's historical past. Searches in the photographic albums, part of the Platt library archives that Platt amassed during his career and currently housed at the Century Association in New York, contain no photographs of La Pietra. Similarly, no evidence support contributions made by Edwin Dodge or H.O.Watson as cited by Mariachara Pozzana, "Restauri in Stile e Progetto del Nuovo a Firenze" (1900-1940), La Memoria, *Il Tempo, La Storia nel Giardino Italaiano Fra* 1800 e 1900; Cura di Vincenzo Cazzato; Instituto Poligrafico e Zecca Dello Stato, Roma, 1998, p311 263

263. Harold Acton. "Preface," *Gamberaia*.

264. Richard Dunn, "An Architectural Partnership: C. Pinsent and G. Scott;" Marcello Fantoni, et al, Editor, Cecil Pinsent and His Gardens in Tuscany: Papers from the Symposium, Georgetown University, Villa Le Balze, Fiesole, 22 June 1995; (Firenze, EDFIFIR, 1996).

265. "It is suspected that the Baroque pen itself seeing the winds of the region in the discussion of the garden and its theater - two provinces that permitted the major liberty of design." Geoffrey Scott quoated in: Kim Wilkie. *Villa La Pietra: Landscape Master Plan*, p.39. Translation by the author.

266. Georgina Masson. *Italian Gardens*

267. Arthur Acton probably developed an interest in garden design to augment his sculpture collection as these pieces were all exterior works placed in gardens. He had a acquired an historic print / engraving collection that possible included the painting known to be part of Harold Acton's collection. Two prints from Arthur's collection, Villa D'Este, Tivoli and Villa Mattei, Rome were

published in an article; Lewis Einstein. The Tuscan Garden" *Architectural Review*, London, February 1929.

268. Florentine expatriate who wrote: *On the Making of Gardens, London* 1909.

269. Kim Wilkie. *Villa La Pietra: Landscape Master Plan*

270. Harold Donaldson Eberkein. *Villas of Florence and Tuscany*; (Philadelphia and London, Lippincott, 1922)

271. Chalfin was curator of Chinese and Japanese art at the Boston Museum of Fine Arts, 1902-1905, and studied mural painting in Italy after his leaving the Museum. Latter from Issabella Gardner to Bernard Berenson, December 19, 1904. Hadley, Rollin Van N., Editor,*The Letters of Bernard Berenson and Isabella Stewart Gardner*, 1887-1924, Northeastern University Press, Boston, 1987, p.236.

272. Suarez also took the Florida pair to see other villa gardens in the vicinity. They tour Villa Medici and met Lady Sybil Cutting who later would be invited to visit Viscaya in reciprosity. It is probable that they also visited the Villa I Tatti meeting Pinsent and Scott as they were engaged as the designers of the Medici's new second renaissance gardens. With these two visits, it is also therfore probable that Calfin / Deering also visited the Gamberaia. Therefor, the Vizcaya's design can be definitively associated with the Renaissance rebirth of this period. William Howard Adams. *Grounds for Change: Major Gardens of the Twentieth Century*; (Boston, Little, Brown, 1993).

273. Deering was known to have purchased on this trip a set of wrought-iron gates from the Palazzo Pisani in Venice which established the heights of the ceiling of Viscaya's south loggia. Rebecca Warre Davidson. "Past as Present: Villa Viscaya and the 'Italian Garden" in the United States." *Journal of Garden History*, vol 12, footnote 20

274. Henry Hope Reed, Foreword, *The Architecture of Humanism*, 1914.

275. J.C.Jellicoe and G.A.Jellicoe,, *Italian Gardens of the Renaissance*.

276. A symphonic poem is a piece usually written in one movement but with many parts. It is a symphonic orchestral work created for narrative - either literary or poetic - created to give passion and emote emossions to romantic works. The term tone poem and symphonic poem are interchangeable as the word "tone" comes from the German "Tonekunst" or tone work where tone denotes the full spectra of a symphonic work. Symphonic poems that are written for or employ choreography - which Arthur Acton's garden tours require - would are called choreographic poems. Oxford Dictionary of Music

277. Modest Mussorgsky, *Pictures at an Exhibition* (1874)

278. The hedge-lined road is clearly visible in the engraving by Giuseppe Zocchi, Roccolta della pia celebri ville della Toscana, 1760.

279. At this point, Diego Suarez had left Italy to work with Paul Chalfin and John Deering at Vizcaya in Miami, Florida, Princess Ghyka had sold the Gamberaia and moved out the area, and the gardens at I Tatti were complete and the Scott / Pincent firm dissolved.

280. Kim Wilkie. *Villa La Pietra: Landscape Master Plan*, p.21.

281. The research of classicist............ American Academy in Rome Fellow, 1999 into the source and origin of grottos has shown that all the traditional elements of rocaille work were both rocks from garden excavations and remains from domestic seafood consumption.

282. Quote of Kim Wilkie. Kim Wilkie. *Villa La Pietra: Landscape Master Plan*, p.67.

283. Kim Wilkie. *Villa La Pietra: Landscape Master Plan*, p.67.

284. Kim Wilkie. *Villa La Pietra: Landscape Master Plan*, p.67.

285. F. W. Kent. "Gardens, Villas and Social Life in Renaissance Florence;" http://www.arts.monash.edu.au/visarts/diva/kent.html

286. "Cabreo" di Villa Gamberaia: "Pianta della Villa dell'Ill.mo Signre Marchese Vincenzio Capponi detta Gamberaia." Anonymous drawing, first half of the seventeenth century (from photographs of the archives of the Villa Gamberaia

287. Kim Wilkie. *Villa La Pietra: Landscape Master Plan*, p.67.

288. Kim Wilkie. *Villa La Pietra: Landscape Master Plan*, p.67.

289. The American composer, Chris Theofanidis, while in residence at the American Academy in Rome, 1999, noted that largo also referred to a broad musical structure that builds and expands off common and often repeated themes and with multiple variations. The cross axis structure of the garden expands into numerous sub-axis often repeating the themes of the main axis. The overall garden's repetition and sameness produces a rather lethargic movement or pace.

290. Kim Wilkie. *Villa La Pietra: Landscape Master Plan*, p.13.

291. Patricia Schultz, "An Italian Idyll."

292. Neither Kim nor this author have not seen such a plan. There is also a problem with dates. The survey cited in the Wilkie report is stated as 1906, well after the work began on the gardens. The

work therefore could have been begun without such an historic base, or the date of the survey, like many other parts of the Wilkie report is inaccurate, or the survey was used only after 1906 and used only for the boschetto section.

293. Sir Harold Acton, *The Villas of Tuscany*.

294. Harold Acton, "Villa La Pietra," *Architectural Digest*

295. Georgina Masson, *Italian Gardens*

296. The current statuary are described in Sophie Bajard, Villas and Gardens of Tuscany; Terrail, Paris, 1993, Pp 129. They were placed by Acton after Suarez departed, but before 1928, first appearing in Nichol's book, Italian Pleasure Gardens, p. 120. The terrace in 1922 show only two graceful maidens framing the staircase: Harold Donaldson Eberlein, *Villas of Florence and Tuscany*, Lippincott, Philadelphia, 1922, pp 330.

297. Harold Acton. "Villa La Pietra: Sir Harold Acton's Florentine Aesthetic" *Architectural Digest*. p7578

298. Harold Acton, An Anglo - Florentine Collection

299. Harold Acton, An Anglo - Florentine Collection

300. Harold Donaldson Eberlein, *Villas of Florence and Tuscany*, Lippincott, Philadelphia, 1922, pp

301. 301. Harold Acton. "Villa La Pietra: Sir Harold Acton's Florentine Aesthetic" *Architectural Digest*. p7578

302. Harold Acton, The Tuscan Villas

303. Harold Acton, An Anglo - Florentine Collection, p. 275

304. Kim Wilkie. *Villa La Pietra: Landscape Master Plan*, p.48.

305. Guy Mitchell bought the Villa il Giullarino which was described as in poor condition. He made many improvements that are noted in Florentine books as being revolutionary in its day. He for example installed modern telephone system that could connect Florence to New York directly. The house was a rambling castelated farmhouse with an off-center tower. Guy modernized it and added art works including a noted Renaissance crucifix (bought throug Arthur perhaps). The site concept resembles Acton's Villa La Pietra in general composition. The site plan was completely reorganized with a new entry road, an allee of cypresses and extensive garden on the opposite and south side continuing the axis. To the west side, there is a formal garden with poor quality sculptures from Vicenza, probably copies of ones in Arthur's collection. For the south garden

Guy Mitchell built a garden that Italians called "anglofied" but was really an upscale American back yard. It was all grass with a few shade trees and a patio/terrace adjacent to the house. The facade was liberally covered with vines. Around 1918 the house was sold to a French Baron De Favot (and erroneously credited with Guy Mitchell's improvements) who rented it for twenty years to an American Miss Daws. Giulio Lensi and Orlando Cardini. *Le Villa Di Firenze;* (Florence, Vallecchi, 1954)

306. Kim Wilkie. *Villa La Pietra: Landscape Master Plan*, p.59.

307. Harold Acton, from Patricia Schultz. "An Italian Idyll".

308. Kim Wilkie. *Villa La Pietra: Landscape Master Plan*, p.4.

309. Aaron Betsky. *Queer Space: Architecture and Same-Sex Desire;* (New York, NY William Morrow and Company, 1997.)

310. Kim Wilkie. *Villa La Pietra: Landscape Master Plan*, p.13.

311. "All Italian" is a name used by the Florentine villa historian Luigi Zangheri to describe Acton's style. Luigi Zangheri. *Ville Della Provincia di Firenze, La Citta;* (Milano Rusconi, 1989) pp. 13244, 287-88

312. This meeting between White and Acton was their first face to face contact and must have been of major importance to both parties. Acton, on his honeymoon staying with his uncle Watson in New York, waited an extra week for Stanford White to finish his private vacation in Canada and return to New York. Expenses for this stay were to be paid by White. Letter of Stanford White to Arthur Acton, New York, June 11, 1903. Stanford White Collection, Avery Architectural Library, Columbia University.

313. Ernest Samuels, *Bernard Berenson: The Making of a Connoisseur*

314. Letter of Stanford White to Arthur Acton, New York, June 11, 1903. Stanford White Collection, Avery Architectural Library, Columbia University.

315. Harold Acton. "Villa La Pietra:" *Architectural Digest.* p75-78

316. Christopher Hibbert, *Florence: A Biography of a City;* (New York, New York, Viking, 1993), p284.

317. Kim Wilkie. *Villa La Pietra: Landscape Master Plan*, p.13.

318. Nodern science has shown that homosexuality is a human gene and is passed to other generation from the father.

319. Harold Acton. "Villa La Pietra:" *Architectural Digest*. p75-78

320. Nicky Mariano, *Forty Years With Berenson*

321. Ernest Samuels, *Bernard Berenson: The Making of a Connoisseur*, p.93.

322. Meryle Secrest, *Being Berenson: A Biography*, p. 143.

323. "'IT' is every experience that is ultimate, valued for its own sake. 'IT' accepts what is as if what is were a "Work of Art" in which the qualities so outweighed the faults that these could be ignored. 'IT' is incapable of analysis, requires no explanations and no apology, is self-evident and right." Bernard Berenson, Sketch for a Self-Portrait. It also stands for the initials of I Tatti and accounts for the deliberate error in capitalization. Additionally, there is a very well known Frescotti wine in Italy called, Est! Est! Est! Or It, It, It. The Renaissance story often told is of the personal secretary of Cardinal d'Este who, when the Cardinal traveled, would race ahead, before meals and sample a number of local inn's food and particularly their wine. He would write on the outside wall next to the entrance, "Est!" to let the Cardinal know that this inn was worth the stop. Est! became a most desired recommendation which owners would never erase and probably was Berenson's humorous double entendre.

324. Meryle Secrest, *Being Berenson: A Biography*, p.2

325. A villa of the Zatti family would be called gli Zatti in Italian. Gli could easily have been simplified to I. The "t" and "z" sounds easily switched in Italian.

326. Ernest Samuels, *Bernard Berenson: The Making of a Connoisseur*.

327. John Temple Leader also installed a romantic side grotto/lake garden, il laghetto della Colonne. Built into an overgrown, bear-face rock escarpment is a miniature Dante scene - Villa Dante, (villa le falle or follie) accompanied with stairs, lakeside docks and landscape elements all in miniaturization. It was featured on the cover of The *Illustrated London News* in 1893 and became a tourist attraction, and a small but needed source of Leader's income. Gianni Pettena. "Introduzione al Moderno: John Temple Leader,"*Giardini Parchi, Paesaggi*, (Florence, Le Lettre, 1998) pp. 67-68.

328. Meryle Secrest, *Being Berenson: A Biography*

329. Ernest Samuels, *Bernard Berenson: The Making of a Connoisseur*, p.342.

330. Meryle Secrest, *Being Berenson: A Biography*

331. Meryle Secrest, *Being Bernard Berenson: A Biography*.

332. Ellery Sedgwick, *The Happy Profession*

333. Ernest Samuels,, *Bernard Berenson: The Making of a Connoisseur*, p.35.

334. Ernest Samuels, *Bernard Berenson: The Making of a Connoisseur*, p. 39.

335. Meryle Secrest, *Being Berenson: A Biography*

336. Ditto

337. Bernard Berenson, from Ernest Samuels. *Bernard Berenson: The Making of a Connoisseur*, p.

338. Ernest Samuels, *Bernard Berenson: The Making of a Connoisseur,*, p. 50.

339. Ernest Samuels, *Bernard Berenson: The Making of a Connoisseur*, pp.90-1

340. Ernest Samuels, *Bernard Berenson: The Making of a Connoisseur*, p.187-188

341. Although attracted in his youth to Mrs. Gardner, Sargent was attracted to no other women and never married. As an mature adult, he was attracted to males and his numerous charcoal sketches of male nudes show his "hidden sexuality." He, like other prominent Americans, - Walt Whitman and Henry James - had public acceptance of their inverted sexuality in their work, " as long as they led 'proper' public lives." Trevor Fairbrother curator of *John Singer Sargent: The Sensualist*, Seattle Art Museum March 2001.

342. Ernest Samuels, *Bernard Berenson: The Making of a Connoisseur*,

343. Ernest Samuels, *Bernard Berenson: The Making of a Connoisseur*, p.148.

344. Ernest Samuels, *Bernard Berenson: The Making of a Connoisseur*, p.133.

345. Ernest Samuels, *Bernard Berenson: The Making of a Connoisseur*, p.134

346. Ernest Samuels, *Bernard Berenson: The Making of a Connoisseur*, p.110.

347. Ernest Samuels, *Bernard Berenson: The Making of a Connoisseur*, p.106

348. Mary Costelloe, from Sylvia Sprigge, *Berenson*

349. Sylvia Sprigge, *Berenson*.

350. Ernest Samuels, *Bernard Berenson: The Making of a Connoisseur*, p.120-122.

351. Sylvia Sprigge, *Berenson*

352. Ernest Samuels, *Bernard Berenson: The Making of a Connoisseur*, p. 143.

353. Frank Costelloe, as a devout Irish Catholic, worked incessantly for a free Ireland, promoting Gladstone's Home Rule, which Mary politically subscribed to. Frank also lived within the restrictive strictures of his Catholic faith. Mary being raised a Quaker, could not and this caused deep-seated conflicts between the couple. Mary refused to believe in Hell; Frank insisted that a Catholic must. Frank imposed a father-as-superior control over their household. With Mary's rebellious innerself, married life for her was unbearable. As a release, Mary had involved herself in women's rights and temperance issues, becoming one of England's noted advocates. Infirmed Mary, desperate with her life, was delighted to hear the doctor's prescription. Ernest Samuels, *Bernard Berenson: The Making of a Connoisseur*, pp.114-117

354. Meryle Secrest, *Being Berenson: A Biography*.

355. Ernest Samuels, *Bernard Berenson: The Making of a Connoisseur*.

356. "a perfectly recognized fact" one traveler reported in London. Ernest Samuels, *Bernard Berenson: The Making of a Connoisseur*, p.271.

357. Ernest Samuels, *Bernard Berenson: The Making of a Connoisseur*, p.162.

358. Ernest Samuels, *Bernard Berenson: The Making of a Connoisseur*, p.336

359. Meryle Secrest, *Being Bernard Berenson: A Biography*

360. Bernard Berenson from Ernest Samuels; *Bernard Berenson: The Making of a Connoisseur*

361. "Tactile values", http://www.xrefer.com

362. "Style," http://www.refer.com

363. "attribution" http://www.refer.com

364. Letter from Arthur Acton to Stanford White. Florence, Feb 2, 1898. Stanford White Collection, Avery Architecture Library, Columbia University, New York, NY.

365. It was erroneously reported that Bernard Berenson practically assembled the whole collection, but in fact, the statement may only be made of the paintings, drawings and prints, and even here the collection was equally strong in works of the Orient, assembled by others.

366. Ernest Samuels, *Bernard Berenson: The Making of a Connoisseur*, p.311.

367. Ernest Samuels, *Bernard Berenson: The Making of a Connoisseur*, p.205.

368. Such as at Lynnewood Hall, Elkins Park outside Philadelphia, Pennsylvania.

369. Auction Announcement. Much of Berenson's early consulting and art dealings are unrecorded. http://www.netrax.net/~rarebook/s960605b

370. In 1906, BB garnered his first retainer fee as advisor for the Agnew Galleries.

371. Richard Offner became the primary challenging authority to Berenson and in the later part of Berenson's life, his nemesis. His Corpus of Florentine Painting, scholarly contradicted many Berenson attribution. Professor Gabriel Laderman, University of California, Berkley to Professor Maria Bustillos, May 17, 1999

372. Richard M. Dunn, "An Architectural Partnership: C. Pinsent and G. Scott;" p 38.

373. Hadley, Rollin Van N., Editor, *The Letters of Bernard Berenson and Isabella Stewart Gardner*, 18871924, Northeastern University Press, Boston, 1987, p.287

374. Letter from Bernard Berenson to Isabella S. Gardner, February 23, 1908. Hadley, Rollin Van N., Editor, *The Letters of Bernard Berenson and Isabella Stewart Gardner*, 1887-1924, Northeastern University Press, Boston, 1987, p.419

375. Richard Dunn. *Geoffrey Scott and the Berenson Circle: Literary and Aesthetic Life in the Early 20th Century*, p.29

376. Meryle Secrest, *Being Berenson: A Biography*, pp. 179-180.

377. David Ottewill, "Outdoor Rooms: Houses into Gardens in Britain at the Turn of the Century," Cecil Pinsent and His Gardens in Tuscany, Symposium Papers Edited by Marcello Fantoni, Heidi Flores and John Pfordresher, (Firenze, EDIFIR, 1996) p. 10.

378. "The very first winter, just a month after moving in, the pipes froze and burst, the well gave out and the heating system broke down." Meryle Secrest, *Being Berenson: A Biography*, p. 179.

379. Meryle Secrest, *Being Berenson: A Biography*, p. 275.

380. Only once, Mary made the mistake of telling Bernard of her sexual conquest, that with a young visitor named Blyades. Thinking that it was only fair to keep Bernard informed as part of their open and honest life style, she recounted the tryst. But it was too much for Bernard, and he became furious. Even though it was only one of many of Mary's flings that went no where and was quickly over, it had broken Bernard's trust in her. He felt betrayed, and was consumed with jealousy. Mary regretted her openness, but not her transgressions. She vowed never to tell him again.

381. References were compiled from: Meryle Secrest, *Being Bernard Berenson: A Biography*, p.108-109, and Ernest Samuels, *Bernard Berenson: The Making of a Connoisseur*, p.200.

382. Ernest Samuels, *Bernard Berenson: The Making of a Connoisseur*, p.198.

383. Mary Berenson, Letter to Rachel Berenson. Meryle Secrest, *Being Bernard Berenson, : A Biography.*

384. Ernest Samuels, *Bernard Berenson: The Making of a Connoisseur*, pp280-1

385. Ernest Samuels, *Bernard Berenson: The Making of a Connoisseur*, p.292.

386. Ernest Samuels, *Bernard Berenson: The Making of a Connoisseur*,

387. Ernest Samuels, *Bernard Berenson: The Making of a Connoisseur*, p.280.

388. Meryle Secrest, *Being Bernard Berenson: A Biography*, p. 320.

389. Ernest Samuels, Bernard Berenson: The Making of a Connoisseur,

390. Descriptions of the boys role by Mary Berenson in her various correspondences on the occasion.

391. Meryle Secrest, *Being Bernard Berenson: A Biography*, pp.285-287.

392. Meryle Secrest, *Being Bernard Berenson: A Biography*, p.285.

393. Before such events, it was Mary's practice to consult her friends for a list of eligible young men for her daughters to meet and for her to invite for future holidays in Tuscany. She would then meet each candidate while on trips back to England with Bernard. Those she personally liked would be the top-of-the-list of invitee. For this Easter holiday, Mary had received suggestions from her sister, Alys, now the wife of Bertrand Russell. Alys gave her the names of two suitable young men, a budding economist, Maynard Keynes and the young architect and literary writer, Geoffrey Scott. Meryle Secrest, *Being Bernard Berenson: A Biography*, p.285.

394. Karin's description of Menard Keynes. Richard Dunn. *Geoffrey Scott and the Berenson Circle: Literary and Aesthetic Life in the Early 20th Century*, p.26.

395. Karin's description of Geoffrey Scott. Richard Dunn. *Geoffrey Scott and the Berenson Circle: Literary and Aesthetic Life in the Early 20th Century*, p.34.

396. Meryle Secrest. *Being Berenson: A Biography*. p. 286

397. Ditto.

398. Ernest Samuels, *Bernard Berenson: The Making of a Connoisseur*.

399. Ernest Samuels, *Bernard Berenson: The Making of a Connoisseur*.

400. Meryle Secrest, *Being Bernard Berenson: A Biography*, p.286.

401. Meryle Secrest, *Being Bernard Berenson: A Biography*

402. Keynes describing to Lytton of his affair with Scott; in a letter April 2, 1906 written in Sienna while on an excursion with Mary and her daughters: "Even in his (Scott's) sodomy, which he takes more solidly than anything else, he seems to want to worship an idealized vision in which he has clothed some good-looking absurdity rather than to come close quarters." Richard Dunn. *Geoffrey Scott and the Berenson Circle: Literary and Aesthetic Life in the Early 20th Century*, p.33 Similar to the discussion on lesbianism and Princess Ghyka, the term homosexual has had an ever changing definition since the word's first use in the 1890s' German case studies. In these, homosexuality was defined by sodomy and specifically applied to the recipient. The male penetrator was not considered homosexual as it was common (although unsavory) heterosexual behavior for the male species to penetrate, weather it's a vagina, an anus, a sheep or as was the case in Portnoy's Complaint, liver. Later in the 1910s, both penetrator and recipient of sodomy became considered as homosexuals. The Labouchere Amendment in England which criminalized homosexuality, used sodomy as its definition but did not specify both partners. By practice, prosecutors charged the recipients as sodomites while the penetrators were freed. Such was the notorious case of Oscar Weile Frued defined homosexuality as same sex attraction weather acted on or not. Unlike women, the amendmant does not cite exclusivity. Therefor homosexuality may be exclusive or bisexual; the current term gay is closer to this meaning. Oral sex was not considered homosexual behavior initially. Fellatio was considered homosexual behavior only in the 1930s and then only the giver of oral sex was the fellatio; the male receiver was not considered gay or homosexual. Even today that understanding is common as heterosexual guys consider "blow-jobs" not abhorrent. Furthermore, even today in many circles, oral sex is still not considered as having sex; ie., the Clinton/Lewinski affair. So it becomes difficult to arrive at common ground in understanding the terms homosexual. The author uses homosexual to mean a man's sexual attraction and response toward other men, gay as men to men attraction exclusively; and bisexuality as man to man sexual attraction as well as man to women sexual attraction. The author includes all forms of sexual behavior and gratification inclusive to these terms.

403. Meryle Secrest, *Being Bernard Berenson: A Biography*

404. Richard Dunn. *Geoffrey Scott and the Berenson Circle: Literary and Aesthetic Life in the Early 20th Century*, p.33.

405. Richard Dunn. *Geoffrey Scott and the Berenson Circle: Literary and Aesthetic Life in the Early 20th Century*, p.26.

406. Meryle Secrest, *Being Bernard Berenson: A Biography*

407. Keynes was not to be heard of again at I Tatti until he returned, years later, as a noted economist and a romantic companion of the Bloomsbury Group painter, Duncan Grant.

408. Sylvi Sprigge, *Berenson: Biography*, p. 200.

409. Meryle Secrest, *Being Bernard Berenson: A Biography*

410. William Rothenstein; *Men and Memories*

411. Meryle Secrest, Being Bernard Berenson: A Biography

412. There are many accounts of Cecil Pinsent's meeting and relationship with the Houghton, as well as how he first met Geoffrey Scott. A similar common theme runs throughout, but the accounts differ and most conflict The author has had to make a judgement of the real events and has constructed the narrative based not on personal accounts but on dates and known events. One of the key points is the date of August 1906, when Cecil graduated from the Royal Academy and won the Bannister Fletcher Bursary sponsoring Cecil's first trip to Italy.

413. Ethne Clark, "Cecil Pinsent: A Biography:" Marcello Fantoni, Heidi Flores and John Pfordresher. *Cecil Pinsent and His Gardens in Tuscany*, p. 19.

414. Ethne Clark, "Cecil Pinsent: A Biography:" Marcello Fantoni, Heidi Flores and John Pfordresher. *Cecil Pinsent and His Gardens in Tuscany*

415. Pinsent's Mother had died at his age of 16.

416. Richard Dunn cites the seduction of Cecil, but notes it was "in vain." Nicky Mariano cites the "Houghtons were intimate friends of Cecil." The intimacies is apparent also by the body language of the threesome picnicking over Christmas 1906 in each others's arms.

417. Ethne Clark, "Cecil Pinsent: A Biography:" Marcello Fantoni, Heidi Flores and John Pfordresher. *Cecil Pinsent and His Gardens in Tuscany*, p. 20.

418. Coincidentally, around the corner from two known centers of Florentine international gay-life, the alley, Chiasso del Buco and the Pensione Berticelli. Ethne Clark, *"Cecil Pinsent: A Biography:"* Marcello Fantoni, Heidi Flores and John Pfordresher. *Cecil Pinsent and His Gardens in Tuscany*, p. 21.

419. Berenson saw other problems: Loeser was a Jew, the faith that had been rejected by Berenson, and he, Berenson, had cast the secret ballot at Harvard that was the cause of Loeser's rejection into an honors club.

420. Richard Dunn. "An Architectural Partnership: Cecil Pinsent and Geoffrey Scott in Florence"

421. Richard Dunn. "An Architectural Partnership: Cecil Pinsent and Geoffrey Scott in Florence"

422. Richard Dunn. "An Architectural Partnership: Cecil Pinsent and Geoffrey Scott in Florence" p. 37.

423. Richard Dunn. *Geoffrey Scott and the Berenson Circle: Literary and Aesthetic Life in the Early 20th Century*, p.37.

424. Marino, Nicky, *Forty Years with Berenson*, p137.

425. Letters from Mary Berenson to Geoffrey Scott, June 23, 1906. Richard Dunn. *Geoffrey Scott and the Berenson Circle: Literary and Aesthetic Life in the Early 20th Century*, p.41.

426. At times unaware, Scott displayed his true desires. In the autumn of 1907, he had toured Florence with his former Oxford classmate, the handsome, respected young painter, William Rothenstein. Rothenstein had just returned to his Munich studio after painting Berenson's portrait at I Tatti. Scott wrote passionately of his longing for Will's company while describing a painting with strong homoerotic and sadomasochistic subject matter. "It is too tantalizing when one is a lonely exile to lose any chance of seeing one's friend... and whom I want to see quite particularly.... ....at the Munich Mussulman (Islamic) exhibition, I have only yet indulged in looking at one - the late Titian Flagellation: so completely absorbing and mysterious." Letter, Geoffrey Scott to William Rothenstein; *Men and Memories*; September 6, 1910

427. Richard Dunn. *Geoffrey Scott and the Berenson Circle: Literary and Aesthetic Life in the Early 20th Century*, p.39.

428. Nicky Marino, *Forty Years with Berenson*, p.10

429. Mary Berenson, Letter to Family, April 13, 1909. Richard M. Dunn, "An Architectural Partnership: C. Pinsent and G. Scott," p 39.

430. Nicky Marino, Forty Years with Berenson

431. Geoffrey Scott, *The Architecture of Humanism*.

432. Meryle Secrest, *Being Bernard Berenson: A Biography*.

433. Mary, and her brother Logan, were enraptured their whole life by Bottecelli's two famous paintings, Primavera and The Birth of Venus. In their college days in Cambridge, Massachusetts, they bought prints of both of these paintings, then a rarity, and hung them on their dormroom walls in a state of "near ecstacy." Through out his life, Berenson held Botticelli in the highest esteem. "The greatest

artist of linear design that Europe has ever had," Meryle Secrest, *Being Berenson: A Biography*, p. 192. Berenson was successful in buying the famous Botticelli for Isabella Gardner, making her Boston Museum a desitinions overnight. The painting in its subject matter hints at secularism and was debated at the time as work on the "Death Of God"

434. Deism is generally define as a belief in a god or supreme being/spirit. Many new religions were formed around the concept that spirituality resided in oneself without the need to be tied to a form of deism. The Ethical Culture Society of New York and Philadelphia, and the Unitarian church in America's major urban centers are examples of non-diest or individual choice faiths. The aesthetic movement at the time was centered around "the Deat of God" theory and amost all self claimed aesthetes were or became asthetes. Although Bernard Berenson was a converted Catholic, he did nto practice the faith. And took the anti diest side in dinner debates.

435. Meryle Secrest, *Being Berenson: A Biography*, pp. 176-178.

436. "There is no greater pleasure than to have quite sanctuary well stocked with learned instruction." Meryle Secrest, *Being Bernard Berenson: A Biography*; p. 2.

437. Meryle Secrest, *Being Bernard Berenson: A Biography*

438. A monastery here, can be generally defined as spiritual center permitting a retreat from disdained or forbidden life styles or values. Altamura was conceived as a retreat from non-elevating forms of daily life. Berenson was the head high priest of taste and people purposely accepted the regimen imposed at I Tatti to be in his company and to hear his discourses. Excluded from such discussions were world politics, and current event topics. Prized were discourse on topics within the humanities, the arts and letters, and the fine arts. Even here any topics not derived from a Grecco-Roman basis were quickly brushed aside or the proponent was never invited back.

439. Meryle Secrest, *Being Bernard Berenson: A Biography*

440. Meryle Secrest, *Being Bernard Berenson: A Biography*

441. Richard M. Dunn, "An Architectural Partnership: C. Pinsent and G. Scott", p 40.

442. Meryle Secrest, *Being Bernard Berenson: A Biography*

443. Ethne Clarke, *The Gardens of Tuscany*

444. Bernard Berenson, Letter Isabelle Gardner, May 16, 1909: The Letters of Bernard Berenson and Isabella Stewart Gardner, 1887-1924.

445. Bernard Berenson, Letter to Isabelle Gardner, May 17, 1909

446. As already mentioned, Acton also had engaged the boys, as Mary called them, when she was affectionately inclined toward them, to design new buildings for the garden.

447. John Maynard Keynes from Geoffrey Scott, *The Architecture of Humanism*

448. Nicky Marino, *Forty Years with Berenson*, p.32.

449. Adding to Berenson's keen interest in the use of a car was a competitive motive: Arthur Acton had a Fiat and was scouring the Veneto for treasures. Berenson saw his primacy lost if he did not also have the use of the new invention, the automobile.

450. It is often mistaken that the partnership designed the garden, i.e: "Two English architects, Cecil Pinsent and Geoffrey Scott, collaborated in the revival of Tuscan gardens." Sir Harold Acton, Forward, The Gardens of Tuscany. The corrected reference is from Mary Berenson's letter to the family, Collection of Letters given by Barbara Halpern, I Tatti Archives. Scott is never mentioned as part of the conception of the garden nor its construction. It becomes apparent that Mary Berenson, publicly included Scott for propaganda reasons. The Pinsent/Scott architectural partnership never function on I Tatti projects, instead, it functioned only on projects other than I Tatti. The Artichokes received commissions for work on other English speaking foreign expatriates on the Mugello hillside. At this time, The Pinsent / Scott Partnership was commissioned to design several villas in the Fiesole area. One was a new Villa Balze for Charles A. Strong, a Harvard classmate of Bernard and a fierce BB intellectual competitor; and the famous Renaissance Villa Medici for Mrs. Cutting and Professor Kiessling's villa. Evidence supports the fact that the partnership was engaged and that the two partners worked on the projects together, but Cecil's hand dominated, especially on Villa La Balze.

451. Aubrey fell madly in love with Mrs. Ross's niece Linda Guff Gordon, married her against Janet's wishes and had a child. Janet talked poorly of Aubrey even though the couple lived with her. Meryle Secrest. *Being Berenson: A Biography*, p. 222.

452. An un-dated and un-addressed letter by Mary Berenson, circa 1909-1911. Collection of Letters given by Barbara Halpern, I Tatti Archives.

453. Barbara Halpern states in a letter conveying to the I Tatti Archives, Mary Berenson's letters to the Family, that: "Clearly, Aubrey Waterfield had one set of ideas and Cecil Pinsent another with constant quarrels. Mary preferred Cecil's ideas but made a number of modifications."

454. Mary Berenson: Letter to the Family, Jan 20 1911; Collection of Letters given by Barbara Halpern, I Tatti Archives.

455. Although Mary refers to Aubrey approving Cecil's ideas, no known drawings existed at this

point, just a conceptual model. Mary, in her letter to a family, twice included her own freehand sketch interpretation of a "Cecil plan." Mary Berenson, Letter to the Family, Jan 20 1911. Barbara Halpern states in a letter conveying to the I Tatti Archives, Mary Berenson's letters to the Family, that her mother, Mrs. Halpern had received sketches that referred to the planning of the garden that Mary Berenson had made in her letters.

456. Bernard Berenson, Letter to Isabelle Gardner, Dec 11, 1910, The Letters of Bernard Berenson and Isabella Stewart Gardner, 1887-1924.

457. Mary Berenson, Letter to the Family, Novemebr 24, 1910.

458. Mary Berenson, Letter to Family, March 30, 1911

459. Mary Berenson, Letter to Alyn and Logan, October 21, 1911

460. Ethne Clarke, *The Gardens of Tuscany*

461. The metaphor of Sylvia Sprigge in Berenson: A Biography, Ruskin House, London, 1960. The voices in the fugue here is that of Mary Berenson and Cecil Pinsent where the full array of landscape elements are employed (polyphonic) to develop the repeated theme of an axial garden emanating from the house and its main terrace. The axial themes are first presented in one full length space, them halved and then divided into thirds with a further internal division into fourths. The architectural elements, in contrast to the vegetative elements form the primary basis of counterpoint. There is even a counterpoint voice, in the form of Bernard Berenson, himself, ragging against "yhis folie" and answering the two primary design voices, Mary and Cecil.

462. Meryle Secrest , *Being Bernard Berenson: A Biography*

463. Mary was the only person that really knew of the working arrangements and the personal contributions that Cecil was still making for the resolution of the gardens at I Tatti. The period proved to be purposeful and productive for Cecil Pinsent in finalizing the design drawings. The time away from the construction site allowed him unpressured time to resolve his design concepts of a Green Garden axis. It is obvious that Cecil had studied and admired the water garden's composition at the Villa Gamberaia as its topiary and parterres became the Green Garden's main theme. It is also reflective of their commission for Arthur Acton's proposed farmer's vallino for La Pietra. Cecil had had the opportunity to study the garden when in progress as well as finished and to have been part of discussions on its design rational from Arthur and his landscape architect, Diego Suarez. From these contacts, "Il processo di Toscanizzare,"or the process of Tuscanized design and the unity of landscape materials became a dominate element of the new I Tatti's garden, especially employed throughout the plan of the Green Garden axis. Within three

months, Cecil presented the final designs of the entire Villa gardens. Mary writes with excitement that "The 'artichokes' are coming up for Sunday, and Cecil will do me all his designs, he swears he will." While Mary refers to the Pinsent / Scott Partnership with the nickname "artichokes" it is clear that the work is that of Cecil Pinsent. Scott's contribution is unrecorded if at all. The fact is that Cecil and Mary Berenson were the only voices in the creation of this garden and Cecil's was primary. Mary, like Berenson, grew disillusioned, from time to time, with the professionalism of Cecil Pinsent. On one hand, she wanted his design talent and his involvement at I Tatti, and on the other hand she wanted what would really have been, not an architect, but a landscape architect - a professional with knowledge in landscape construction, horticulture and the employment of plant material. His on-the-job training in that profession was a real hindrance.

464. Mary Berenson. "Errori di Giardinaggio" Il Giardio Fiorito, (Florence, No. 3 April1931) pp. 42-3

465. The following December, a disastrous stormed uprooted and killed most of the newly planted cypresses and Mary unfairly charged Cecil with planting on an "exposed site, the cause for their loss." Luckily BB was out of the country at the time and failed to note replacements when he returned. Richard Dunn. *Geoffrey Scott and the Berenson Circle: Literary and Aesthetic Life in the Early 20th Century.* Once replanted a second and more comprehensive disaster occurred. Mary, in an attempt to accelerate root development, insisted on fertilizing the young plants with raw horse manure, "high in iron sulfate. applied in March." In an article in a Florentine garden magazine in 1931, Mary stated this to be "a severe error of Gardenage destroying the entire allee" of plants. Mary Berenson. "Errori di Giardinaggio" *Il Giardio Fiorito*, pp. 42-3

466. Nicky Mariano, *Forty Years With Berenson.*

467. Silvia Sprigge, *Berenson: A Biography*

468. Silvia Sprigge, *Berenson: A Biography*

469. Meryle Secrest , *Being Bernard Berenson: A Biography*

470. It might be noted that Nicky Mariano did not like Cecil Pinsent evident in her remarks. Nicky Mariano, *Forty Years With Berenson.*

471. Richard Dunn. *Geoffrey Scott and the Berenson Circle: Literary and Aesthetic Life in the Early 20th Century*, p.89

472. Ethne Clarke, *The Gardens of Tuscany.*

473. Sprigge, Sylvia, *Berenson: A Biography*, Ruskin House, London, 1960

474. Ernest Samuels, *Bernard Berenson: The Making of a Connoisseur*, p.353.

475. Mary during the construction was having real doubts that perhaps the plans for the entire garden were too extensive. Evidently, the entire podere was consumed by the garden development. While Pinsent's designs extended from the facade to the property line, it would have eradicated any remaining production areas of the podere. But it was Aubrey Whitside who is charged with the denuding of the hillsides of its olive and fruit orchards in Arbrey's attempt to convert the whole site into an English picturesque garden. After Mary's re-considerations, Cecil saved what remained of the orchards on the west and integrated them through paths and axis into the composition as an argro-geometric landscape composition, quite unique to any Italian garden.

476. Silvia Sprigge, *Berenson: A Biography*

477. Silvia Sprigge, *Berenson: A Biography*

478. Silvia Sprigge, *Berenson: A Biography*

479. "Gioto, Bernardo Daddi, Simone Martini, Giovanni Bellini, etc" Sophie Bajard and Raffaello Bencini, Villas and Gardens of Tuscany; " St. Francis altarpiece by Sasetti hung in the sitting-room," Sylvia Sprigge, *Berenson: A Biography*, Boston, Houghton, Mifflin, 1960; "Madonna and Child by Domenico Veneziano" Meryle Secrest, *Being Berenson: A Biography*.

480. Ernest Samuels, *Bernard Berenson: The Making of a Connoisseur*, p.266.

481. Bernard Berenson, *Sketch of a Self Portrait*

482. Post World War II. Meryle Secrest, *Being Berenson: A Biography*, pp.14-15.

483. Ernest Samuels, *Bernard Berenson: The Making of a Connoisseur*, p.222

484. Ernest Samuels, *Bernard Berenson: The Making of a Connoisseur*, p.253

485. "Samuel H. Kress" http:/www.xrefer.com

486. Meryle Secrest, *Being Bernard Berenson: A Biography*

487. Meryle Secrest, *Being Bernard Berenson: A Biography*, p.172

488. Sylvia Sprigge, *Berenson*

489. Ernest Samuels, *Bernard Berenson: The Making of a Connoisseur*, p281.

490. Bernard Berenson, *Sketch for a Self-Portrait*.

491. Bernard Berenson, *Sketch for a Self-Portrait*

492. Letter, Bernard Berenson to Isabella Gardner, April 10, 1909.pp441-442

493. Meryle Secrest, *Being Bernard Berenson: A Biography.*

494. Bernard Berenson from Meryle Secrest, *Being Bernard Berenson: A Biography*

495. A Mary Berenson quotation. Meryle Secrest, *Being Bernard Berenson: A Biography*

496. Meryle Secrest, *Being Bernard Berenson: A Biography*

497. Meryle Secrest, *Being Bernard Berenson: A Biography*

498. Meryle Secrest , *Being Bernard Berenson: A Biography*

499. Nicky Mariano, *Fourty Years with Berenson.*

500. Although there are numerous references to the suddenness of the Scott / Cutting marriage, there are no descriptions of Geoffrey's or Lady Sybil pre-marriage romance nor convincing reasons for their speedy union.

501. Meryle Secrest , *Being Bernard Berenson: A Biography*

502. Harold Acton from Christopher Hibbert, *Florence*

503. Lady Kepple and Violet were frequent visitors to the royal compound at Biaritz at the same times that Ghyka vacationed in adjacent Bidart. Lady Kepple and Violet eventually bought a villa near La Pietra in Florence and installed a new Tuscanized landscape.

504. Letter from Bernard Berenson to Iasbella S. Gardner, December 3, 1900. Hadley, Rollin Van N., Editor,The Letters of Bernard Berenson and Isabella Stewart Gardner, 1887-1924, p.236.

505. Letter from Bernard Berenson to Isabella S. Gardner, April 21, 1901. Hadley, Rollin Van N., Editor,The Letters of Bernard Berenson and Isabella Stewart Gardner, 1887-1924, pp.254-255.

506. "Alas, it is not talent which he lacks. All in all, he is the cleverest Anglo-Saxon man of letters now alive." Letter from Bernard Berenson to Iasbella S. Gardner, March 27, 1898; Hadley, Rollin Van N., Editor,The Letters of Bernard Berenson and Isabella Stewart Gardner, 1887-1924, p.2131

507. Meryle Secrest, *Being Bernard Berenson: A Biography.*

508. Mary Berenson , from Samuels, Ernest, *Bernard Berenson: The Making of a Connoisseur*, p.218

509. Ernest Samuels, *Bernard Berenson: The Making of a Connoisseur*, p.191.

510. Ernest. Samuels, *Bernard Berenson: The Making of a Connoisseur*, p.218.

511. Richard Dunn. *Geoffrey Scott and the Berenson Circle: Literary and Aesthetic Life in the Early 20th Century* p.39.

512. Ernest Samuels, *Bernard Berenson: The Making of a Connoisseur*, p.218

513. Bernard Berenson, from Ernest Samuels; *Bernard Berenson: The Making of a Connoisseur*.

514. Meryle Secrest, *Being Berenson: A Biography*, p. 220.

515. Charles Ricket, 1903, Self Portrait from the Journals of Charles Rickets. Charles Ricketts was a noted English painter and illustrator who stayed for a period at I Tatti. Sylvia Sprigge, *Berenson: A Biography*, p. 164.

516. A composite list from all sources.

517. Meryle Secrest , *Being Bernard Berenson: A Biography*

518. Meryle Secrest, *Being Bernard Berenson: A Biography*

519. Sylvia Sprigge, *Berenson: A Biography*, Boston, Houghton, Mifflin, 1960, p. 168.

520. The daily regimen was constructed from three sources: Marino, Nicky, *Forty Years with Berenson*; Alfred Knopf, New York, 1966 pp. 95-118; Meryle Secrest, *Being Berenson: A Biography*, pp. 12-13; and Sylvia Sprigge, *Berenson: A Biography*.

521. Meryle Secrest, *Being Berenson: A Biography*, p. 12.

522. Meryle Secrest, *Being Bernard Berenson: A Biography*

523. Kenneth Clark, former director of the National Gallery in London. Meryle Secrest, *Being Berenson: A Biography*, p. 8

524. Meryle Secrest, *Being Berenson: A Biography*, p. 7.

525. Ernest Samuels, *Bernard Berenson: The Making of a Connoisseur*, p. 275

526. Christopher Hibbert. *Florence: A Biography of a City*; Viking, New York, 1993, p. 368.

527. Altamura, like its monastic lifestyle was so out of contact with its world or even reality, that in November of 1914, the day that the Archduke Ferdinand of Serbia was assassinated and the European nations were in the process of declaring war, a household staff member bursted into the lunch affair with the news. To the horror struck guest attendees, the news was chlamydeous; to Berenson it was merely a disturbance to his discussions which he promptly continued. Meryle Secrest, *Being Berenson: A Biography*.

528. With the exception of Carlo Placci, there were almost no Italians invited or attending any of the I Tatti functions. The Berenson circle was overwhelmingly Anglo-American expatriates and visitors.

529. "The Knitting Circle: History." http://www.southbank-university.ac.uk

530. Edith Wharton, Letter to Bernard Berenson, 1933. Vivian Russell, Edith Wharton's Italian Gardens, Boston, Little, Brown and Company, 1997.

531. Ernest Samuels, *Bernard Berenson: The Making of a Connoisseur*, p.270.

532. Ernest Samuels, *Bernard Berenson: The Making of a Connoisseur*, p.266.

533. Nicky Marino, *Forty Years with Berenson*, pp.30-31.

534. Meryle Secrest, *Being Bernard Berenson*: A Biography

535. Ernest Samuels, *Bernard Berenson: The Making of a Connoisseur*, p.343

536. Bernard Berenson, Letter to Harold Acton, 8 July 1946. McComb; Selected Letters of Bernard Berenson

537. Meryle Secrest , *Being Bernard Berenson: A Biography*

538. Interview of Henry Hope Reed, December 20, 1999.

539. Ethne Clarke, *The Gardens of Tuscany*

540. Bernard Berenson, *Sketch for a Self-Portrait*

541. Ernest Samuels, *Bernard Berenson: The Making of a Connoisseur*, p.216.

542. Bernard Berenson, *Sketch for a Self-Portrait*

543. The author has chosen this name for the collection of Second Renaissance designers. The group of Florentine expatriates were called "circles." Also of this same period was the "Bloomsbury Circle, who were prominent and habitue of the Villa I Tatti.

544. Article on Porcinai.

545. 545. John Stubbs, Chief Architect, World Monument Fund, New York, 1999. Spoken on site on June 2, 1999.

546. The water parterres of Gamberaia have been adopted into the designs of numerous other

gardens: the Cummer Museum, Jacksonville, Florida and Longwood Gardens, Kenneth Square, Pennsylvania.

547. The style called Beaux-Arts is defined as "a theory ...(in which) the Greek and Roman structural systems are synthesized." It usually results in "the planning and massing of buildings that are strictly and sometimes elaborately symmetrical, with ...a clear articulation of functions and a hierarchy of major and minor axes and cross-axes, and with clear articulated (architectural masses) parts resulting in a five-part composition - a climatic central mass dominating wings and their terminal features.... (The facades have) coupled classical columns, monumental flights of stairs, arched or lintel openings between columns or pilasters, figure sculpture in relief or in the round." Marcus Whiffen. *American Architecture Since 1780: A Guide to the Styles*; M.I.T. Press, Cambridge, Massachusetts, 1969. Pp.149-152. Whiffen's definition is the first of many additional styles defined as part of the Chapter, "Styles That Reached Their Zenith in 1890-1915." It is applicable in its definition of architectural planning and design among the others styles which are described as: Georgian Revival, Gothic Revival, Jacobean Revival. It does not include others also of this period such as French Provincial and Italian villa or country domicile. A more general definition of the term beaux-arts, which is inclusive of all "historic" and classical styles, has evolved through common usage. It thus means the literal and eclectic coping of prior European architectural styles.

548. R. Terry Schnadelbach. *Ferruccio Vitale: Landscape Architect of the Country Place Era*; (New York, New York, *Princeton Architectural Press*, 2001).

549. Michael Greenhalgh. *What is Classicism?*; (London, Academy Editions, St. Martin's Press, 1990).

550. Meryle Secrest, *Being Bernard Berenson: A Biography*

551. Geoffrey Scott. *The Architecture of Humanism*; (London, Norton, 1914), pp. 25-39

552. Meryle Secrest, *Being Bernard Berenson: A Biography*

553. Meryle Secrest, *Being Bernard Berenson: A Biography*

554. "Rick" Olmsted, in his writings on the fine art of landscape design, mentions its major styles as the "Humanized Mode," (formal design), for landscape architecture: "Moorish, Italian Renaissance, French 'grand manner,' and the 'Landscape Style' (English naturalistic)." Frederick Law Olmsted, Jr. "Landscape Design," American Institute of Architects, Committee on Education, The Significance of the Fine Arts; (Boston, Massachusetts, Marshall Jones Company, 1923), pp. 334-335.

555. "The Villa was mined and burned by the Germans during the war. It became post-war a combination of charred or blown out walls and rubble. In the garden, the plumbing is ruined

and the pools and fountains are dry. The remainder of the gardens are well maintained and the skillful plan of the Villa Gamberaia is apparent everywhere". Laurence Roberts, typewritten notes of July 1953 in *A Guide to Villas and Gardens in Italy*. The annotated book is in the library of the American Academy in Rome.

556. In 1954, Doctore Marcello Marchi bought the Villa Gamberaia from the Vatican. From 1957 to 1961, Dr. Marchi reconstructed the water parterres. Marella Agnelli, *Gardens of the Italian Villas*, (New York, New York, Rizzoli,1987).

557. In 1955, Pietro Porcinai produces a Planting Plan (Schema di Piantaggione) for the Villa Gamberaia. Milena Matteini. "Pietro Porcinai: Architectto del Giardino e del Paesaggio," *I Gardini del XX Secolo: l'Opera di Pietro Porcinai*, (Milano, Alinea, 1993).

558. Milena Matteini. "Pietro Porcinai: Architectto del Giardino e del Paesaggio," *I Gardini del XX Secolo: l'Opera di Pietro Porcinai*, (Milano, Alinea, 1993).

559. Davidson erroneously states that in 1914, Chalfin ran into Suarez in New York "quite by chance," inviting him to work on the project.

560. Undated, but written from memories after a 1960 re-visit to Viscaya. Rebecca Warre Davidson. "Past as Present: Villa Viscaya and the 'Italian Garden' in the United States." *Journal of Garden History*, vol 12, pp.1-28.

561. Davidson erroneously stated that Suarez produced any plan without ever seeing the site.

562. Conversations by the author with Henry Hope Reed, New York, NY December 20 1999.

563. The Viscaya trip was preceded by an early March visit to Italy by Derring and Chalfin. They visited Acton at La Pietra presumedly to acquire art and to reciprocate by inviting Acton and Suarez to visit Florida. Chalfin (with possibly Deering) visited the American Academy in Rome and delivered an evening lecture on art history, while researching Fellows' recent measured drawings of Italian villas. Archives of the American Academy in Rome.

564. It did not take much persuasion for Suarez after seeing the landscape development, he immediately knew he had made a grave error in design. "I made a terrible mistake, and I knew it as soon as I stepped from one of the main rooms out onto the south terrace overlooking the garden site. It was exactly noon and I looked straight ahead where the garden would be, and I couldn't see a thing. I was blinded by light, for out there at the far end was a lake. It was like a mirror. I told Chalfin immediately that I had made a mistake and would have to start over." Pride of ownership or possibly the challenge contributed to Suarez's decision and to revise the landscpe composition.

565. Rebecca Warre Davidson. "Past as Present: Villa Viscaya and the 'Italian Garden" in the United States." *Journal of Garden History*, vol 12, pp.1-28

566. William Howard Adams. *Grounds for Change*, p92.

567. There is a wonderful photograph of Geoffrey Scott on the deck of a steamer sailing to New York City with Pinsent to begin his new life by his side.

568. Vincent Shacklock and David Mason, "Villa Le Balze, Florence: a Broad Assessment of 'a Modern Garden in the Italian Style'," *Journal of Garden History* (London, Taylor and Francis, Vol 15, Autumn 1995) pp. 179 -187.

569. The main sala housed all Cezannes which upon his death were given to the White House and are now part of the National Gallery of Art's collections.

Index

Abstract classicism garden; P63, 71-72, 247, 254
Acton, Mario Arthur; Px, 4, 50, 60, 66, 69-70, 77, 81-83, 85-86, 89-94, 99-103, 105-106, 135-136, 138, 142, 146, 149-151, 153-158, 174-175, 178-179, 218, 239, 245, 247, 249-250, 255, 258, 262
Acton, Harold; P46, 49-51, 62, 69-73, 75, 95, 102, 104, 137-138, 143, 146, 151, 153, 156-158, 229, 249, 262
Acton, Hortense Mitchell; 85-87, 91-93, 104, 135, 155-156, 222
Acton, William, P57, 91, 92, 157
Les Ailes, P19
Alexander, Francis, P91, 143
Altamura, P162, 180, 189-191, 212, 220-221, 234-235, 239, 246, 262
Ambroziewicz, Mariano; P105, 140-141, 149
American Academy in Rome; Pix, 9-10, 72-73, 105, 239
d=Annunzio, Gabriele; P43, 45, 66, 69, 84, 153, 236
Anstruther-Thomson, Kit; P58, 236

BB, mom de plum, see Bernard Berenson
Beacci, Ersilla; P92
Bennet, Sue; P21
Berenson, Bernard; Pix, 4, 6, 16, 52, 54-57, 59, 70, 77-78, 92, 105, 155-156, 161-173, 176-182, 184-, 188-196, 199, 221-230, 233-235, 237-239, 241-243, 250-255, 260, 262
Berenson, Mary Costello; P, 23, 46, 52, 54-55, 58, 156, 161-163, 165, 168-236, 202, 205, 216, 218-220, 223, 226-233, 235-239, 241-243, 250-251, 259
Berenson, Rachel; P180

Betsky, Arron; P58, 61, 152, 258
Biltmore; P87-88, 255
Blaydes, Wilfrid T.; P181-182
Bood, Florence; Px, 17-18, 51, 54-56, 58-59, 63, 73-74, 76-78, 141, 148, 156, 224-225, 194, 238-240, 254, 271
Brotherhood of Sodomites;

Capecchi; P198
Capponi, Cardinal Luigi; P3, 94, 97, 99, 141
Capponi, Francesco; P3, 94, 97, 134-136,141
Capponi, Marchesi; P 3, 21, 23, 94, 97, 141
Capponi, Piero di Nicolo; P3, 94, 97, 141
Capponi, Scipioni; P3, 94, 97, 99, 108, 141
Chalfin, Paul; P105, 257
Clarke, Ethne; P47, 199, 212, 217, 241
Costello, Benjamin Francis Conn AFrank@; P163, 168-172, 180
Costello, Mary Smith, see also Mary Berenson;
Costello, Rachel "Ray"; P180, 182
Comanesti, Princess Catarina Giovanna, See Princess Jeanne Ghyka
Comanesti, Eugene Ghyka; P16-17, 19-20
Cult of Florence; P188, 232
Cutting-Scott, Lady Sybil; P 78, 228-229, 239, 257, 259-260
Cuttwell, Miss Maud; P56

Deering, John; Px, 104-105, 257-258
Display gardens; P63, 72-73, 84
Duchene, Archille; P101
Duchene, Henri; P101, 245, 255, 258
Duveen, Lord Joseph; P88,176, 222-223

Ecole des Beaux-Arts; P4,14,18, 81-89, 101

Festin, Simonetta Angeli; P56
Field, Mrs. Evelyn "Diego"; P259
Fields, Micheal; P57
Fontana, Carlo; P78, 99
Freud, Sigmund; P18

Gardino inglese; P99, 101
Gardner, Isabella; P92, 105, 156, 162, 164-168, 170, 172, 174-175, 180, 230-231
Gardner, John "Jack"; P164, 168
Ghyka, Prince Eugene; See Comanesti, Eugene Ghyka;
Ghyka, Giovanna, see Princess Jeanne Ghyka,
Ghyka, Princess Jeanne; Px, 4, 10, 16-22, 24, 26, 43-44, 46-66, 69-70, 73-78, 81, 84-85, 95, 100, 102, 135, 141, 153, 155-156, 162, 217, 230, 239, 245, 248, 250, 254-256, 262-263
Green, Belle da Costa; P225-227

Horn, Herbert; P155, 175, 179, 194, 239
Houghton, Edmund; P185-188, 236, 239, 261
Houghton, Mary; 185, 187, 236, 239
Hutton, Edward; P24, 155

Incontri, Marchesi; P3, 94, 98, 100, 108-109, 135, 139, 151
Isabella Club, see Isabella Stewart Gardner
ITness, see also Villa I Tatti; P15, 64, 162, 164, 178, 193-236, 212, 221, 234-194, 238

James, Henry; P20, 57
Jekyll, Gertrude; P72, 104, 179
Jellicoe, Geoffrey A.; P13, 23, 26, 72-73, 105-106, 199
Jephson, Arthur Jeremy Monteney; P230-231

Keshko, Jeanne, see Princess Jeanne Ghyka
Ketteler, Baron Enrico von; 74
Ketteler, Baroness Matilda "Maud" Ledyard Cass; P74, 78
Keynes, Maynard; P182-184, 236, 240

Lappis., Zanobi; P23
Latham, Charles; P65-66, 69, 71

Lawson, Edward G.; Pix-x, 9-10, 21, 24, 72-74, 76, 106, 253-254, 256
Leader, John Temple; P163, 176
Le Corbusier; P4
Lee, Vernon; nome de plum, Miss Violet Paget; P21, 55-57, 60, 194, 239, 245, 260
Loeser, Charles; P4, 102, 155, 178, 185-186, 160

Marchi, Marcello; P63, 66, 74-75, 256-257, 262
Marino, Nicky; P57, 228-229, 277
Masson, Georgina; Px,105, 138
Medici; P3, 94, 97-81
Messeri, Luigi; P73
Metaphysical gardens; P247
Milan Obrenovic ,Queen Natalie Keshko; Px, 17-18, 51, 54-56, 63, 73-74, 76-78, 141, 148,156, 224-225,194, 239-240, 254, 271
Miss Blood, nome de plum, Florence Blood
Miss Violet Paget; see Vernon Lee
Mitchell, Guy Hamilton; Px, 81-86, 93, 109, 149,273
Mitchell, Hortense; see Hortense Acton
Mitchell, William; P81, 85, 104, 136, 155, 157

Norton, Charles Eliot; P164-166

Obrist, Hermann; P180-181
Olmsted, Sr., Frederick Law; P87, 174, 255
Ottewill, David; P179

Placci, Carlo; P22, 51, 54-55, 59-60, 78, 156, 236
Palazzo Pogo; P3
Palazzo Riccardi; P3
Pharrish, Maxfeld; P12
Pinsent, Cecil Ross; P6, 36, 64, 72-75, 77, 103, 159, 177, 183-189, 191-197,199, 212-213, 219-221, 228, 133-246, 248, 254-256, 250-261
Platt, Charles A.; P86, 90-91
Poggio Gherardo; P3, 72, 162-164, 193, 219
Ponti, Maria; P251, 253-254
Porcaini, Martino; P71, 75, 102, 245, 255
Porcaini, Pietro; P39, 75, 77, 245, 254-257
Puvis de Chavanne, Pierre; P53-54

Reed, Henry Hope; Px, 105, 241, 257
Second Renaissance Circle and renaissance II garden; P4-5, 8,11,15, 66, 69, 70, 72-73, 75-76, 78, 94, 105, 110, 136, 139, 149, 152, 154, 237, 245-251, 254-257, 262-263
Ross, Janet; P21, 56, 58, 60, 65, 72, 104, 140, 155-156, 162-164, 193, 195, 219, 194, 239, 245, 251, 282
Russell, Bertrand; P180

Sackville-West, Vita; P 230, 241
Samuels, Ernest; P57, 171
Santayana, George; P4
Sassetti, Francesco di Tommaso; P11, 94-97, 109, 153, 174
Schultz, Patricia; P138
Scott , Geoffrey; P8, 36, 72, 75, 77, 103-104, 155, 181-184, 187-189, 226-231, 241, 245-246, 249, 251-253, 258-260, 275
Scott, Lady Sybil Cutting, See Lady Sybil Cutting
Secrest, Meryle; P165, 172, 190, 224-225
Second renaissance garden, See renaissance II garden
Second Renaissance Circle; See renaissance II garden
Sitwell, Sir George; P 104, 155, 251, 269
Smith, Logan Pearsall; P162, 169, 189-190, 199, 215
Smith. Mary Whitall, See Mary Berenson; P6, 52, 54-55, 58, 156-172, 175, 178-189, 191-
199, 212, 215, 218-219, 224, 225-232, 235-239, 241-243, 250-251, 259
The Souls; P186
Stein, Gertrude; P18, 58-59, 169, 241
Stein, Leo; P56, 241
Strong, Charles Augustus; P4, 72, 239, 260
Suarez, Diego; P8, 71, 77, 101-103, 105, 110, 136, 138-141, 144-147, 151-153, 245-
246, 248-249, 254-255, 257-259

Toklas, Alice B.; P18, 59, 185
Topiary gardens; P43-45, 61, 65, 69-71, 74-76,103, 105-106,110, 136-140,142-145, 150-152, 156, 215-217, 220, 237-240, 242-243, 247-250, 256-257, 261-263
Trefusis, Violet; P18, 59, 72, 104, 230
Triggs, Indigo; P18, 69-70, 78

Uten lunette; P2-3, 8, 110

Vanderbilt, George W.; P87-88
Villa Acton, see also Villa La Pietra; P91, 96-97, 99, 103-106, 109, 137-138, 152, 154, 156-157, 178, 247, 252, 258, 262
Villa Caparola; P1
Villa Capponi; P75
Villa Gamberaia; Pix-x, 2, 4-5, 7-9, 12, see Chapter 1(P13-80),85, 94, 06, 100, 102, 104, 106, 108, 110, 135, 138, 141, 146-147, 152, 162, 176, 236-185, 200, 121, 216-217, 194, 245-250, 252-258, 260, 262-263
Villa Lante; P1, 5, 9, 48-49, 69, 142
Villa La Pietra; Pix-x, 2, 4-6, 8, 20, 50, 66, 69-72, 75, see Chapter 2,(P81-160), 184, 200, 212, 218-220, 245-246, 248-249, 254-257, 262
Villa il Giullarino; P85-86, 93, 109, 149
Villa Montughi; P95, 97, 99
Villa Il Palmerino; P57, 72, 260
Villa I Tatti; Pix-x, 4-6, 8, 11, 16, 55, 71-72, 75, 96, 103, 105, see Chapter 3 (P161-244), 245-248, 250-251, 254-255, 258, 260-262
Villa Medici, Fiesole; P3, 9, 75, 78, 228-229, 257-260
Vitale, Ferruccio; P72, 87, 91,142, 254, 259

Wolkonski, Serge; P55, 271
Waterfield, Aubrey; P195-197
Watson, H. (Henry) O.; P86, 89, 93
Webel, Richard K.; P51, 72, 254, 259
Wellesley, A. Dorothy; P17
Wharton, Edith; P13, 15, 45, 65, 72, 76,104, 224, 240, 251
White, Stanford; P60, 86, 88-93,104,155
Wilde, Oscar; P84, 92, 181, 231
Wilkie, Kim; P135-136, 150
Woolf, Virginia; P17

Zocchi, Giuseppe; P22-23, 63